Conter

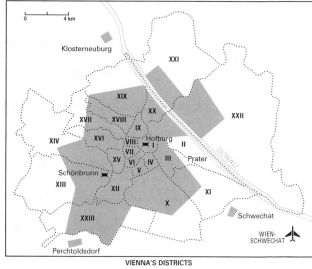

VIENNA'S DISTRICTS

I.	Innere Stadt	VII.	Neubau	XIII.	Hietzing	XVIII.	Währing
II.	Leopoldstadt	VIII.	Josefstadt	XIV.	Penzing	XIX.	Döbling
III.	Landstraße	IX.	Alsergrund	XV.	Rudolfsheim-	XX.	Brigittenau
IV.	Wieden	X.	Favoriten		Fünfhaus	XXI.	Floridsdorf
V.	Margareten	XI.	Simmering	XVI.	Ottakring	XXII.	Donaustadt
VI.	Mariahilf	XII.	Meidling	XVII.	Hernals	XXIII.	Liesing

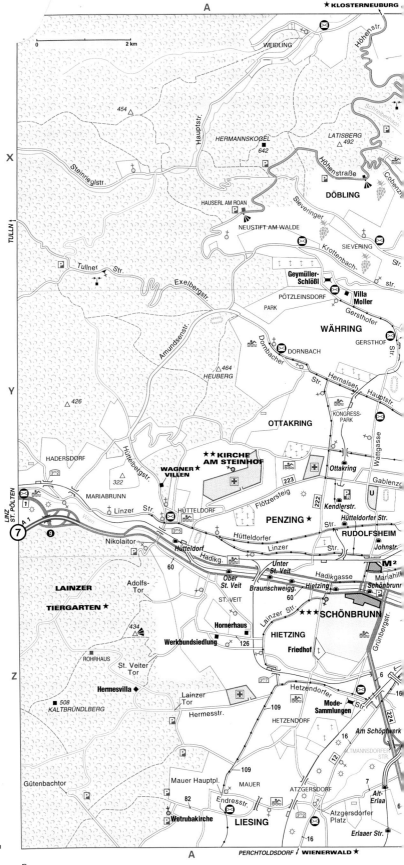

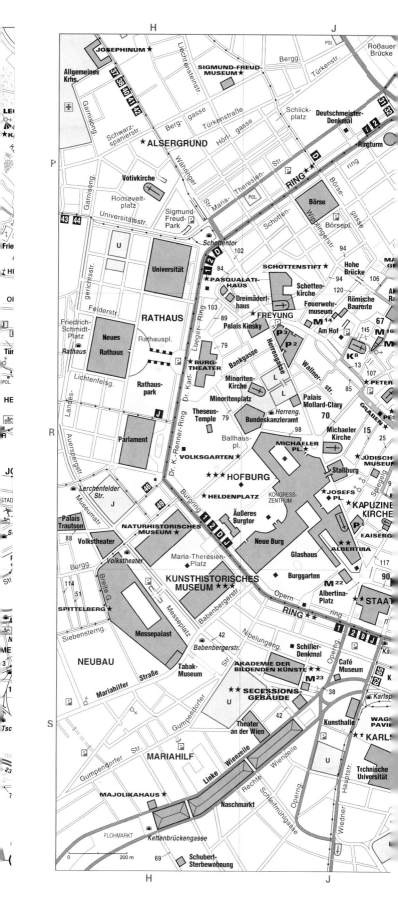

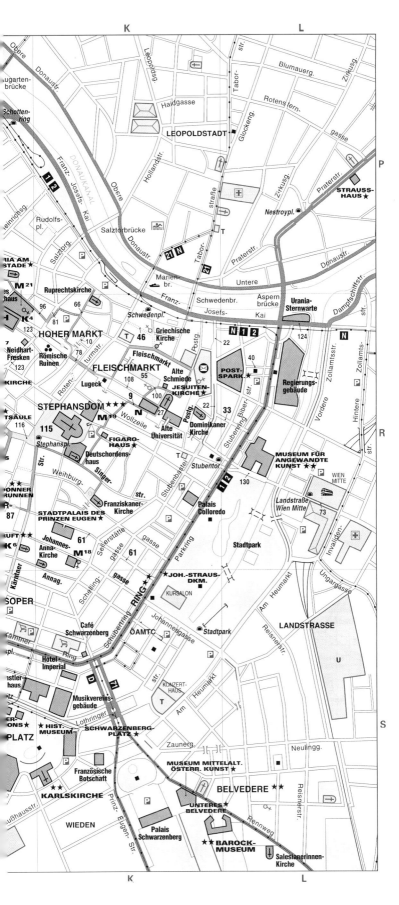

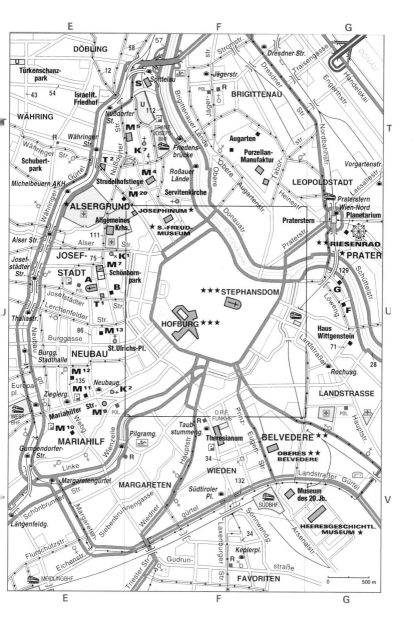

VIENNA!

Situated at the very heart of Europe, between Prague and Budapest, on the amber route linking the Baltic to Italy, Vienna is the last western city before the Balkans. With the Alps to the west and the Carpathian mountains to the east, this city on the Danube is indeed a gateway to the Orient; it stands at the intersection of several nations of which it was once the Imperial capital.

The Austrian capital straddles a cultural and geographical divide; it was both a bridgehead for Germanic culture and a cradle of the Biedermeier school. In the reign of Franz-Josef who was husband to the celebrated Sissi, Vienna was home to nearly a dozen nationalities.

Vienna with its elegant architecture has a visual style veering from the playful to the melancholic, the baroque to the modern. The city has always been dedicated to music and its name is synonymous with the waltz. It both fascinates and disturbs, as it seems to hesitate between the past and the future.

Any tourist would fall under the spell of this city which cultivates its own special art of living, Gemütlichkeit, a smiling welcome everywhere, from the comfortable ambiance of the cafés in the city centre to the lively bustle in the local taverns, the Heurigen, where the new wine is sipped.

The traditional view of Vienna as essentially a living museum does not do justice to this great city. Visitors will discover its true character with the help of this guide.

Peterskirche and Stephansdom jutting up above the rooftops of the city centre

Introduction

Vienna and
the surrounding region

BETWEEN THE ALPS AND THE CARPATHIANS

Vienna lies at the base of the most easterly foothills of the Alps, in a plain opening onto the Hungarian steppes and the Little Carpathians. A Danubian city, it stands with its back to this river, which links Bavaria to the Black Sea. Initially a maze of streams and marshes, the Danube became navigable after the construction of a canal.

Situation – Vienna stands at a distance of about 60km/37 miles from Hungary, the Czech Republic and Slovakia. The city is 53km/32 miles from Bratislava (Slovakia), 193km/119 miles from Graz (Styria), 251km/155 miles from Budapest (Hungary), 300km/186 miles from Salzburg (Salzburg) and Prague (Czech Republic), 440km/272 miles from Munich (Germany), 475km/294 miles from Innsbruck (Tyrol) and 1,295km/802 miles from Paris.

The Vienna basin – The *Wiener Becken* lies sunken amid the Weinviertel valleys to the north, the Marchfeld plain to the east, the first undulations of the Alpine Leithagebirge chain to the south and the wooded reliefs of the Wienerwald to the west. This 40km/24 mile wide basin heralds the Pannonian plain of the Hungarian *puzta*, which begins with Burgenland.

Vienna is at the heart of a fertile agricultural region, which, for several decades has had to contain the development of industry and the migration of urban population. Vienna has buildings rising to heights of between 170m/557ft (Stephansdom) and 150m/492ft (Arsenal). The site is remarkable in that Vienna is the only European capital to produce wine, at least in such large quantities. On the slopes rising from the right bank of the Danube, 720ha/1,779 acres support 250 small winegrowing estates, giving a rural ambiance to the city outskirts. Vienna and its surroundings display vineyards and wooded hills to the north and west, and green meadows and industrial developments to the east and south.

The Danube – The second longest river in Europe after the Volga, it is the longest in Central Europe, about 2 800km/1 736 miles (its precise length has not been established). The Danube forms a natural link between Germany and southeast Europe. It crosses or borders nine countries and four capitals are built on its banks, evidence of its strategic importance as an international route.

Between Ulm and Vienna, it flows through a vast and fertile alluvial plain, then takes on an alpine character, flowing fully in summer. At the level of Leopoldsberg, north of Vienna, the last alpine foothill overlooking the Austrian capital, the river winds

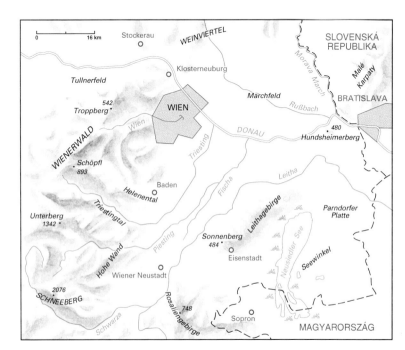

Cruising on the Danube in Vienna

through the first of the alluvial plains between the Alps and the Carpathians. After Bratislava, as it flows more slowly down the gentle slope, it spreads over an exceedingly flat plain and divides into numerous arms, which silt up with sand.

The Danube is vital to the country's economy (360km/223 miles in Austria, 20km/12 miles in Vienna). When it reaches Vienna, it does not display, particularly when in spate, the colour immortalised in Johann Strauss' *Blue Danube.*

Moreover, strictly speaking, the Danube lies more than 2km/1 mile from the historic centre of the city. First-time visitors to Vienna may be amazed at being able to cross the Danube four times. The eastern section of the city is crossed by the small Danube canal, the wide rectilinear Danube canal (300m/327 yds), the additional New Danube canal (200m/218 yds) and the meander of the Old Danube (a dead channel with many bathers along its banks). After the 1501 floods there was a project for flood control of the river by building a canal; this was not completed until 1972, by which time several canals were in use.

Finally, the Danube has a small tributary, 34km/21 miles long, the Wien. This small river of weak and irregular flow gave its name to Vienna.

Climate – Vienna is exposed to every wind and experiences the strong depressions of the climactic continental regions. For some, it has an ideal climate with definite seasons: hot summers, cold, snowy winters, few precipitations over the year (715mm/28 in annually west of the city, 561mm/22 in along the course of the Danube).

Average temperatures are 0° C in winter (although extreme temperatures down to − 15° C are not unusual), and about 25° C in summer (with extreme temperatures rarely above 30° C, since the wind blowing across the Pannonian Plain reduces the heat).

THE "LAND"

A federal capital since 1920, Vienna and its immediate surroundings constitute one of the provinces of the Austrian Republic. A federal state, the country consists of 9 independent *Länder*: Burgenland, Carinthia, Lower Austria, Upper Austria, Salzburg, Styria, Tyrol, Vienna and Vorarlberg. These provinces are vastly differing ethnic, economic and cultural entities; the differences are evident as much in the hills and dialects as in the customs of all these regions.

An enclave in the vast expanse of Lower Austria, the Vienna *Land* covers an area of 414km² – 157 sq miles and has a periphery of 133km/82 miles.

Every five years, the population of the *Land* elects the members of the **Provincial Diet.** Their number varies between 36 and 56, in proportion to the numbers of inhabitants in the province. The Vienna Diet is the only one to have 100 members. Using proportional representation, the Diet elects the members of the **provincial Government** which, as the administrative arm of the Diet, enjoys the confidence of the Diet and makes decisions by majority voting.

The territory of the Vienna *Land* overlaps that of the city and is the centre of the country's economic activities (the Vienna *Land* accounts for 30% of the country's GDP). It includes the departments and ministries of the federal government and the *Land.*

Klosterneuburg and its vineyards

THE CITY

Vienna is the political, intellectual and cultural centre of Austria. Owing to the permanent neutrality of the country, it has become the headquarters of various international organisations such as IAEA (International Atomic Energy Agency), UNO (United Nations Organisation) and OPEC (Organisation of Petroleum Exporting Countries). In 1988, the Austrian capital was home to the offices of 115 international organisations, which placed it in 9th position worldwide. The Austrian capital enjoys a strategic position between northern Europe and the Mediterranean, between central Eastern Europe and the area which before the fall of the Berlin Wall went under the name of Western Europe; since the 1815 Congress of Vienna, it has been a major international congress centre (225 international conferences in 1989). It is also a centre for trade fairs and a prestigious tourist centre: 6,000,000 visitors in 1986, which, in Europe, places it just behind London, Paris and Rome; it is a figure which will certainly have been exceeded after the festivities in 1996 to celebrate one thousand years of the city's existence.

Both an urban district and a Land, Vienna's administration has a twofold purpose. The city council corresponds to the provincial Diet (100 members elected for 5 years). Elected from the members of the Council, the mayor acts as federal governor (*Landeshauptmann*). The city comprises 23 districts *(see map of the districts)*, around the historic centre which the Viennese call the "inner city" *(innere Stadt)*.

Population – Over the passage of time, men and women came from all parts of the vast Habsburg empire to the city which in 1991 numbered 1,539,848 inhabitants, including about 200,000 not of Austrian nationality: Yugoslavs (91,000), Turks (47,000), Poles (16,000), Iranians (8,000), Rumanians (5,000), Czechs and Slovaks (5,000), Egyptians (4,000), not counting members of diplomatic corps.

It is a surprising fact that, about 1800, what is today an average-sized metropolis was the 4th largest city in Europe, after London, Paris and Naples.

Demography – Vienna's population has declined constantly since the end of the First World War, namely since the fall of the Austro-Hungarian empire. The two main causes are a higher death rate than birth rate and a higher annual number of people migrating from the city compared to the number of people moving into it.

In 1900, the city numbered 2,030,000 inhabitants, twenty years later it numbered 1,841,326 people; it was the start of a decrease in population. The Danube, which for a long time served as a "pipeline» during the Empire, has since ceased to supply the capital with immigrants. Since the fall of the Berlin Wall and Austria's membership of the EU in 1994, which boosted the city's economic role, this process is gradually going into reverse. Moreover, Vienna has a policy of welcoming political refugees and for several decades has absorbed many people from nations which were once part of its Empire, as well as from Asian and African countries. The languages of Eastern Europe are heard increasingly in the streets of the Austrian capital.

Religion – 75% of the Viennese are Roman Catholic, in a country where 84% of Austrians are of that religion. The remaining 25% consist of Protestants (7.5%), Greek, Russian or Bulgarian Orthodox, as well as Methodists, Muslims (50,000 practising Muslims), members of the Armenian Church and practising Jews. However, for several years, many Jews have been returning to live in Vienna (many come from countries which were part of the USSR). The city used to be a stopover for Jews leaving the Soviet Union for Israel.

Industry – Because of its geographical situation, Vienna was during the Cold War a major centre of commercial exchange between the Eastern and Western blocs, an "interface". The disappearance of the Iron Curtain strengthened its position as a commercial staging post, which is probably why over 700 European, American and Japanese companies have subsidiaries in Vienna. The Austrian capital has become a focus of commerce.

Vienna, the industrial hub of the country, is particularly well represented in sectors such as food, electricity (no nuclear energy in Austria), electronics, metallurgy (engineering), chemistry (especially the Vienna-Schwechat refinery which processes Austrian or imported crude oil), pharmaceuticals, precision engineering, steel construction, car manufacture (large General Motors factory in Aspern), crafts and the fashion industry. Its fluvial port is increasing in importance, as is the Vienna-Schwechat airport which compensates for the deficiencies of Prague, Bratislava and Budapest airports. Vienna is also home to the head offices of the country's main banks, savings banks, insurance companies and major firms.

Vienna, Birthplace of Sionism

Theodor Herzl (1860-1904) was born in Budapest but brought up in the capital of the Austro-Hungarian Empire which he considered his homeland. From 1891 to 1895, he worked as a correspondant for the largest Viennese daily paper, the *Neue Freie Presse*, in Paris. At that time, the French capital was swamped by waves of anti-Semitism as a result of the trial of Captain Dreyfus. Herzl was the author of *The Jewish State* (1896) and the founder of Sionism, a movement which aimed to find a collective solution to the Jewish question *(Judenfrage)*. Although it was the Viennese journalist Nathan Birnbaum who created the word "Sionism" in 1890, the movement would not have become an ideology nor led to the setting up of a Jewish State in Palestine if it had not been for Herzl. The "new Moses" died in Lower Austria before being able to see the "Promised Land".

Historical table and notes

Origins, at the crossroads

800-400 BC	Between the Baltic and the Adriatic, between the Alps and Hungary, foundation of Vienna on the Danube by the Celts of Noricum.
1C-2C	At *Vindobona*, "the white city", the Romans build a military camp facing the Germans, near *Carnuntum*, headquarters of the governor of Pannonia.
180	Death of the Emperor Marcus Aurelius at *Vindobona*, following a campaign against the Marcomanni.
213	*Vindobona*, with a population of 20,000, is raised to the status of *municipium*, a Roman city.
Towards 400	After crossing the Rhine in 376, the Goths overrun the boundaries of the Roman Empire near the Danube and destroy the city.
6C-8C	Fall of the Western Roman Empire in 476 followed by domination by the Avars, a nation of horsemen from central Asia.
End of 8C	Defeat of the Avars by Charlemagne who creates the eastern March of Bavaria (Ostmark), germanises it and establishes Christianity there. *Vindobona* is reborn under the name of *Vindomina*.
881	*Wenia*, a fortress and trading centre on an eastward-flowing Danube, is mentioned in the Salzburg annals.
955	Emperor Otto I puts an end to the barbarian invasions with the victory of Lechfeld, in Bavaria, over the Magyars from south of the Urals.
962	Emperor Otto I receives the new crown of the Holy Roman German Empire from Pope John XII.

S. Chirol

Marcus Aurelius

Vienna under the Babenbergs, a strategic centre of Christianity

976	Bishop Leopold, ancestor of the Babenbergs, becomes first Margrave of the Marche, where he consolidates Christianity (Österreich-Klösterreich).
1030	The city appears under the name of *Wienne*.
1137	The city is granted borough status *(civitas)* and acquires fortifications.
1156	Emperor Frederick Barbarossa grants the Marche the status of hereditary duchy under **Margrave Henry II Jasomirgott**. Vienna is adopted as ducal capital.
1193	On his return from the Holy Land, Richard the Lionheart is captured in what is now the Erdberg district by Leopold V. Imprisoned at Dürnstein in the Wachau, the King of England is freed for an enormous ransom, which is used to build a castle on the square now known as Am Hof.
Towards 1200	The first coins are minted.
12-13C	A stopping place for the Crusaders on their way to Jerusalem, Vienna grows and becomes the second largest city in Germany after Cologne. It already acts as a link between East and West.
1246	Friedrich II, "the Warlike", last member of the House of Babenberg, is killed in battle against the Magyars, leaving Vienna a prosperous Christian city with municipal privileges.
1250	Death of Emperor Frederick II bringing an end to the Hohenstaufen dynasty. Ottokar II Przemysl, King of Bohemia and Duke of Moravia, wishes to create a great Slav state in central Europe.
1251	**Ottokar II Przemysl** enters Vienna and marries the heiress of the Babenbergs. He receives the investiture of Richard of Cornwall, puppet Emperor of Germany.

The power of the
Habsburgs and the rise
of Vienna

1278	Supported by the Pope and the German princes, Rudolf of Habsburg defeats Ottokar II Przemysl at the Battle of Dürnkrut. With this victory, the Habsburgs acquire what is now Austria and Rudolf moves to Vienna which he elevates to the rank of Reichsstadt, a free city.
1326	Great fire of Vienna.
1348	Massive outbreak of the plague throughout Europe. Jews accused of causing it escape persecution only in Ratisbon and Vienna (40,000 victims), thanks mainly to the intervention of Konrad von Megenberg.
1365	**Rudolf IV**, first archduke, founds the University of Vienna, the oldest German-language university after Prague. Vienna is an economic forum on the great trade route linking Nürnberg to Byzantium.
1396	Dukes Wilhelm, Leopold IV and Albert IV grant the "Wiener Ratswahlprivileg" to tradesmen and craftsmen who may now be elected mayor or members of the town council.
1420	The Hussite heresy in Bohemia threatens to spread into the north of Lower Austria; Viennese Jews do not escape repression and are driven from the city.

Rudolf I

Fotostudio Otto/Museen der Stadt Wien

1438	Albert V (of the Albert branch) is elevated to the throne of the Holy Roman Germanic Empire under the title of Albert II. Vienna, where the University abandons scholasticism for humanism, becomes an imperial residence.
1462	Rebellion of the Viennese against the reduction of their privileges. For two months Emperor Frederick III (of the Styrian branch) is held hostage in the Hofburg.
1485	**Matthias I Corvinus**, King of Hungary, occupies Vienna for five years, abolishing privileges and concessions which are restored by the Habsburgs after the death of this king, nicknamed the "Crow".
1493	Emperor Maximilian I resides in Innsbruck in the Tyrol, to the detriment of the wealthy Danube city. In the east, the Ottoman expansion, which led to the defeat of Byzantium in 1453, progresses towards the Danube, gradually depriving Vienna of its market in the Balkans.

The Cross versus the Scimitar

1515	**Maximilian I** summons to Vienna a large assembly to decide on ways of resisting the Turkish peril, the first requirement being solidarity between Christian princes.
1521	Vienna adopts the ideas of the Reformation launched in 1517 by Martin Luther who proclaims "better a Turk than a Papist!". The Turks have in fact seized Belgrade.
1526	After having eliminated opponents of imperial authority, Archduke Ferdinand signs a decree limiting the administrative autonomy of the city to honorary functions. Turkish victory at **Mohács**, in Hungary.

1529	Suleyman the Magnificent, one of the world's most powerful rulers, camps outside the city gates for three months with an army of 120,000 men. Resistance from Count Salm and the Viennese winter prompt the Turks to raise the siege.
1530-1560	Erection of a massive circle of fortified ramparts, which survive until 1857.
1533	Ferdinand installs the central administration of the States in Vienna. A free city, it gradually becomes the capital of a heterogeneous and multi-ethnic empire.
1550	The city's population grows to 50,000. Vienna's economic position is weak, since it no longer benefits from the spice trade, which has deserted the Danubian valley.

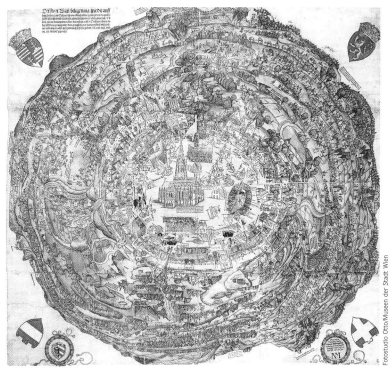

Circular map of Vienna

Fotostudio Otto/Museen der Stadt Wien

The imperial capital of the Austrian nation

1556	The Jesuit Petrus Canisius is summoned to Vienna by Emperor Ferdinand I. Launch of the Counter-Reformation. Vienna recovers some of the splendour lost after the Turkish siege and becomes the permanent seat of the imperial court.
1577-1618	Protestant services are banned in Vienna (80% of the population are Protestant in 1571, including the burgomaster). The city becomes a Catholic city once again.
1618-1648	From the Defenestration of Prague to the Treaty of Westphalia, the armies of the rebelling Bohemians and the Swedes threaten the capital, during the Thirty Years' War. The Treaty of Westphalia confirms the unity of Austria at the heart of the Holy Roman Empire.
1620	Triumph of the Counter-Reformation after the battle of the White Hill. With the encouragement of Cardinal Melchior Khlesl, numerous religious orders are established in Vienna.
1629	The plague kills 30,000 people.
1679	A further 30,000 deaths caused by the plague.
1683	Grand Vizier Kara Mustafa with over 200,000 men lays siege to the city, which is defended by less than 20,000 Viennese, commanded by Count Starhemberg. Vienna is delivered with the help of King John III of Poland, John Sobieski. Although the west has triumphed over the east, Vienna has been devastated.
1699	Peace of Carlowitz, under which Hungary is ceded to the Habsburgs. Vienna, which has gradually been rebuilt and embellished despite Leopold I's indifference, is now the leader of a genuine hegemonic Austrian Empire.

Vienna, a city that nearly became Turkish

14 July 1683. The grand vizier Kara Mustafa, representative of Mehmet IV, lays siege to Vienna with over 200,000 spahis and janissaries together with contingents from Bosnia, Serbia, Moldavia and Walachia. The sultan's energetic deputy deploys his troops in a crescent moon, with the tips touching the banks of the Danube. Faced with Mustafa's overwhelming army, about 16,500 Viennese, many without military training, decide to put up resistance with 312 cannon under the command of Count Ernst Ruediger von Starhemberg. As the situation becomes critical, Charles of Lorraine arrives on 10 September. The Christian princes have proved their solidarity. With him are the Prince-Elector Max-Emmanuel, George Frederick of Waldeck, Ernest Augustus of Braunschweig-Luneburg and his son the future King George I of England, under the command of John Sobieski, King John III of Poland. France has promised the Pope not to attack Austria but French military engineers are advisers to the Turks. On 12 September, Mustafa retreats (the skull of Mustapha, executed on 25 December, is now in the Vienna museum). Emperor Leopold I, who had taken refuge at Passau, does not reach Vienna until 14 September.

"Vienna gloriosa"

1700	Vienna's population rises to 80,000.
1700-1740	The Baroque style, originating in Rome and Prague, flourishes in Vienna. The city thrives, enthralled by the victories of a French nobleman disdained by the Sun King; Prince Eugène of Savoy, the "Saviour of Christendom", finally vanquishes the Ottoman menace. Vienna is a focus for intellectual and artistic activity.
1706	Founding of the Wiener Stadtbank with the support of Count Gundaker Starhemberg.
1714	Last plague epidemic.
1722	A bishopric since 1469, Vienna becomes an archbishopric.
1740-1748	**War of the Austrian Succession:** France and Prussia dispute the validity of Maria-Theresa's claims to the imperial crown. Vienna prospers thanks to new commercial outlets: access to the new Austrian Low Countries; relatively close proximity to Belgrade, now a centre for trade between Austria and Turkey; construction of a road suitable for vehicles linking the capital to Trieste.
1754	First population census. Vienna has 175,000 inhabitants (including suburbs) and is an important industrial centre with a rapidly growing textile industry.
1756-1763	**Seven Years' War:** Switch of alliances: Austria allied to France, Russia, Saxony and Sweden, fights Prussia and Britain to recapture Silesia.
1776	The Hofburgtheater founded by Maria-Theresa in 1741 becomes a German-speaking national theatre, to break the cultural monopoly of the Italian language in the capital.
1780	Death of Empress Maria-Theresa.
1782	Pope Pius VI visits Vienna. He asks Emperor Josef II, eager to reform the Church and strengthen the monarchy, to be more sympathetic. Spread of Freemasonry throughout high society.
1784	Adoption of German as the official "national" language. This seals Vienna's dominance over the Empire, despite the statutory exception for Hungary.
End of 18C	Vienna is an international capital of music and the arts in general have shaken off the hold of transalpine influences. The city, with almost 200,000 inhabitants, has become a European metropolis owing chiefly to its cosmopolitan aristocracy and luxury goods industry.

From the Congress of Vienna to the revolution

1805	Following Beethoven's composition of his *Farewell Song to the Burghers of Vienna*, first occupation of Vienna by the French (12 November 1805 to 13 January 1806) who guarantee respect for religious observances and the safety of the inhabitants.
1809	Second occupation by the French (12 May to 19 November), which leads to the financial collapse of the State. The chancellor, Count Stadion, is replaced by Prince Metternich.
1814-1815	Three years after a devaluation of 80% mainly due to the Continental Blockade, the Congress of Vienna, which at times resembles a Whitehall farce, summons the European monarchies to redraw the map of Europe after the fall of Napoleon.

1815-1848	This period of Metternich's regime is known as **Vormärz** (i.e. before the revolution of March 1848), a climate of political conservatism to the strains of the waltz. Signs of decadence may be discerned beneath the apparent renaissance.
1820-1830	From the heart of the Holy Alliance, Metternich creates Austria's industrial power along a line extending from Vienna to Prague. The city numbers 318,000 inhabitants. Appearance of the Biedermeier style, symbol of the 19C Viennese bourgeoisie.
1837	First railway line between Vienna (Floridsdorf) and Deutsch-Wagram.

Prince von Metternich

March 1848	Following the uprising led by Kossuth in Hungary, a coalition of students and workers with the support of the lower middle classes is formed in Vienna. As barricades spread throughout the city, the army opens fire. The number of dead leads to a revolution, prompting the government to dismiss Metternich, who is forced into exile at the age of 74.
May 1848	New revolutionary movements drive the Court from Vienna to Innsbruck. A committee of public safety is formed in the capital under the leadership of Adolf Fischlo. The city has a population of 400,000.
October 1848	A popular republican uprising in which Count Baillet de la Tour, Minister of War, is hung from a lamp-post by the mob, forces the government and parliament to join the Court at Olmütz in Moravia. The Viennese middle classes and aristocracy support the policy of repression carried out by Field Marshal Prince of Windischgrätz.

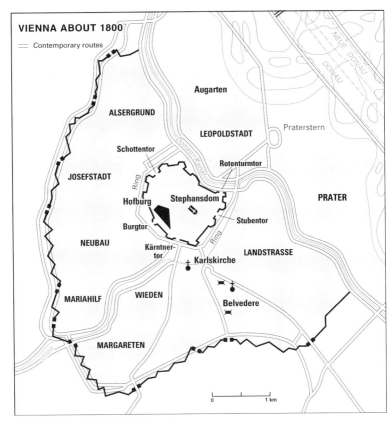

Splendours and miseries of Emperor Franz-Josef

1854 | Despite the advice of the Archduchess Sophy, the "irrepressible" Sissi becomes Empress of Austria. Vienna is entranced by her charm and beauty.

1857 | Vienna, with its population of 500,000, yearns for grandeur. The razing of the fortifications dating from the Turkish sieges marks the start of what is known as the "Ringstrasse era", where industrialisation combines a modern economy with a traditional society.

1867 | With the creation of the dual monarchy, Vienna becomes the capital of Cisleithania (Austria), a new state at the heart of the Austro-Hungarian Empire. Arrival of numerous Jews, following their emancipation by Franz-Josef.

1870-1875 | Building of the Danube Canal after the 1862 floods.

1873 | Opening of the World Fair at the Prater (a failure despite 7 million visitors), against the background of a Stock Exchange crash bringing defeat for Viennese liberalism and heralding the rise of the Christian Socialist party.

1889 | 36km/22 miles southwest of Vienna, in Mayerling, Archduke Rudolf commits suicide at his hunting lodge.

1890 | 43 suburbs are incorporated in the city to form districts. The capital has 800,000 inhabitants, of whom 55% are immigrants.

1897 | Karl Lueger, founder in 1889 of the Christian Socialist party, becomes Burgomaster of the city. His talents as an administrator bring unexpected prosperity to the city. He is, however, a Pan-Germanist and an anti-Semite, of ill portent, despised by the emperor.

1910 | *Gross-Wien* numbers just over 2,000,000 inhabitants. Vienna is the fourth largest city in Europe after London, Paris and Berlin.

1910-1914 | Vienna, in appearance the most delightful city in the world, is in reality a mass of insalubrious lodgings and declining industries. Without being aware of it, Vienna is harbouring social conflict.

1914 | After the assassination at Sarajevo, Franz-Josef, sure of Germany's support, declares war on Serbia on 28 July. Start of the First World War.

1916 | Emperor Franz-Josef dies on 22 November at the age of 88, after a reign lasting 68 years.

1918 | Charles I's abdication. From being the head of a state with a population of 52 million, Vienna becomes overnight the capital of a country with just 6 million inhabitants.

Scarlet and Black

1919 | Republican Vienna, in the midst of chronic unemployment, elects the Social Democratic party to power. Jacob Reumann is the new mayor.

1920 | The capital has a population of 1,841,326 – a decrease compared to the massive urbanisation of the 19C.

1921	The city is granted the status of *Land*.
1920-1934	"Vienna the Red" launches a programme of council housing and develops a communal policy for the building of workers' housing, which revives the local tradition of housing estates around a central courtyard *(Hof)*.
July 1927	Militia from each party confront each other in the capital. There are 89 dead and 1,057 wounded during days of fierce fighting caused by tensions between socialist Vienna and the rest of Austria.
February 1934	During three days of civil war in the capital, militants belonging to the Republikanischer Schutzbund take cover in the blocks of council flats. The official death toll from the fighting is 314.
July 1934	Assassination of the Chancellor **Engelbert Dollfuss** by a local branch of the S.S. during an attempted putsch in the chancellery. **Dollfuss**, a patriot and a Christian, was totally opposed to Marxist ideology and had also banned the Nazi party.
1938	Despite the hopes and efforts of Chancellor Kurt von Schuschnigg, Austria is annexed by **Hitler**. On 14 March Hitler enters Vienna which becomes an administrative region of the German Reich. Von Schuschnigg is imprisoned and the city witnesses a rehearsal of Nazi methods of ethnic cleansing of the Jewish population.
1939-1944	After the "Heil Hitler" salute by Archbishop Innitzer and the economic pillaging by the Germans, Vienna pays a heavy human price – in addition to deportations there are nearly 6,000 executions in the Landesgericht prison. The Jews pay dearly for their economic and cultural role in Austrian society.
1945	Owing to the Resistance, Vienna is not destroyed despite 52 air raids. It is liberated by the Soviet army on 13 April. Division of Vienna in September into four zones administered by the USSR, the United States, Great Britain and France.

Chancellor Dollfuss

Fotostudio Otto/Museen der Stadt Wien

Contemporary Vienna

1951	The mayor of Vienna, the socialist Theodor Körner, is the first president of the Republic to be elected by universal suffrage.
1955	The occupation forces leave Vienna following the Austrian State Treaty undertaking permanent neutrality. Austria joins the UN.
1956	The Austrian capital becomes the seat of the Atomic Energy Authority (AEA).
1961	John F. Kennedy and Nikita Kruschev meet here for the first time for a "summit meeting" at Hietzing.
1967	Vienna becomes the seat of the United Nations Industrial Development Organization (UNIDO).
1970-1996	Vienna is the setting for various international meetings: the SALT talks (until 1979), OPEC discussions between Arab countries and Israel, and talks between communities from the former Yugoslavia.
1978	Opening of the first Underground railway (U1) between Reumannplatz and Karlsplatz.
1979	Opening of United Nations City. Vienna becomes the third most important site of United Nations activities after New York and Geneva.
1981	The population continued to decline after the Second World War with the Allied military occupation and the development of residential areas on the outskirts of the city – the capital now has a population of only 1,500,000. A positive consequence is that Vienna does not suffer from the excessive urbanization of other cities.

1989 The "Velvet Revolution" in Czechoslovakia underlines the dominant economic role played by Vienna in central Europe. Burial of the former Empress Zita of Habsburg in the Capuchin vault.

1992 The Hofburg is damaged by fire.

1995 Austria is admitted to the EU.

1996 Celebrations for the one thousandth anniversary of Austria.

The meeting between John F. Kennedy and Nikita S. Khrushchev in June 1961

Dalmas/SIPA PRESS

The Habsburg Empire

EVOLUTION OF THE HOUSE OF AUSTRIA

Rudolf I and the sceptre of Ottokar – After the death of Friedrich II the Warrior, the last of the Babenbergs, in 1250, the duchy of Austria passed to Ottokar II Przemysl, King of Bohemia and Duke of Moravia, who was not in the line of succession. He wished to create a great Slavonic kingdom in central Europe, but died fighting at the battle of Dürnkrut in 1278 against Rudolf of Habsburg. This family came from Aargau in Switzerland and traced its descent probably from ancestors in Lower Alsace. Habichtsburg ("vultures' castle", 1020) still stands in Switzerland. This newcomer to the Austrian scene was Rudolf I of Germany, elected King of the Romans in 1273, to establish a strong northern Christian power. He was of a calculating nature with far greater political acumen than the German princes had imagined. He was suspicious of Ottokar's recent ascendancy, and of his refusal to return the imperial fiefs. Rudolf needed no further motive to attack him with the assistance of his Alsatian and Swabian knights. His victory at the battle of Marchfeld changed the destiny of his House, and also affected the destiny of Austria itself. In 1282, this

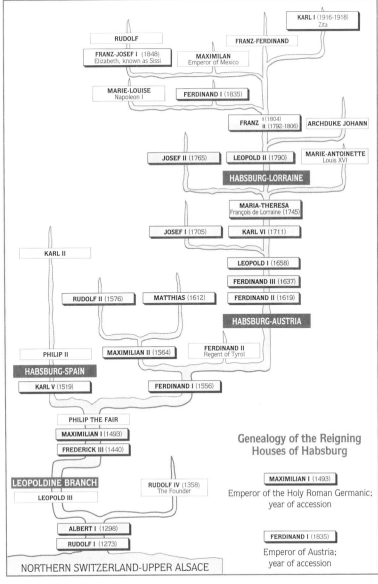

Genealogy of the Reigning Houses of Habsburg

great statesman obtained from the prince electors the right for his sons Albrecht and Rudolf to share the possessions of the Babenbergs. Thanks to Rudolf I, the Habsburgs and Austria became synonymous.

Entrenchment – History records that Albrecht of Austria was grasping. At any rate, he brought about the Habsburgs' loss of power in Alemannic Switzerland. Furthermore, the Electors preferred Adolf of Nassau to him, for the imperial crown was not hereditary, and would not become the prerogative of the Habsburgs again for another 130 years. However, this loss had one favourable consequence, in that it encouraged the Habsburgs to concentrate on their Austrian heritage. Through a policy of judicious marriages and diplomatic compromise, Friedrich the Fair, Albrecht II the Wise and Otto the Merry enlarged their domains, which now extended from the Vosges to the Carpathians.

Rudolf IV, the "Founder" – This domain secured the southern frontier of the empire and thus controlled access to Italy. Albrecht II's son founded Vienna University in 1365, hence his nickname. He also responded intelligently to the menace to Trieste from the Venetian Republic. After having annexed the Tyrol to Austria, Rudolf granted his protection to the Adriatic port in 1382, thus giving *domus austriae* its famous outlet to the sea, which the nation was to retain until 1918. To consolidate his claims to independence, Rudolf acquired the title of archduke, which greatly displeased his father-in-law, Emperor Karl IV. Vienna was now an economic centre on the great trade route linking Nürnberg to Byzantium.

Rudolf IV

THE IMPERIAL CROWN

A.E.I.O.U. – After a period during which there was a division of the House of Austria between its Albrecht and Leopold branches, Albrecht V, a member of the first branch, acceded to the throne of the Holy Roman Germanic Empire in 1438 under the title of Albrecht II. His was a brief reign, as he died the following year. This was immediately followed in 1440 by the coronation of Frederick V of Habsburg, of the Styrian branch (part of the Leopold branch) as King of the Romans, since the seven electors did not want a strong king, and thought Frederick was feeble-minded. However, the emperor persuaded the Pope to crown him as Frederick III (Karl V would not succeed in this). The German princes now had to face a man convinced of the supremacy of his House *(see inset A.E.I.O.U., Schatzkammer, Hofburg)*, a man who then showed immense political flair by marrying his son to the daughter of Charles the Bold, Louis XI's great rival.

Territorial expansion – Charles the Bold dreamed of becoming king or emperor. He longed for a rich and powerful Lotharingia, between Germany and France. Frederick III requested for his son the hand of the heiress of the western archduke. Charles the Bold considered as a necessity the marriage which took place in 1477, the year of his death. By his marriage, Maximilian inherited most of the Burgundian estates (Low Countries and Franche-Comté). Unfortunately Marie died from a fall from a horse, thus surviving her father by only five years. However, she had given her husband an heir, which a decidedly less feeble-minded Frederick III had crowned as King of the Romans. Matthias I Corvinus, King of Hungary, briefly posed a threat to the emperor, when he occupied Vienna in 1485. However, after his death without an heir in 1490, the emperor could take a legitimate satisfaction in his achievement. A near-destitute widower, Maximilian I worried about the European situation and the future of his inheritance.

He pursued an anti-Valois policy, gaining the support of the Flemish nobility, and married his son Philip the Fair to Joan the Mad, daughter of the King of Spain. Thus, Castille, Aragon, Sardinia and Naples became Habsburg territory. He then remarried, taking as his wife Bianca Maria Sforza, from a recently ennobled family, who brought a dowry of 300,000 gold ducats and countless jewels to "penniless Maximilian", as the Italians nicknamed him. This marriage provoked further antagonism from the King of France, Charles VIII, who had designs on Milan. Unlike his son, Maximilian did not object to this, preferring to concentrate on the administration of his estates. He also thought of becoming pope; his second wife had died and he "never wanted to sleep with a naked woman again". Upon the death of this great Renaissance prince, his grandson, Karl V, was elected as Holy Emperor and was to reign over an empire "on which the sun never set".

Maximilian I

Kunsthistorisches Museum

TOO VAST A DOMAIN

Within just a few decades, Austria had acquired an immense west European domain, enlarged by Italian possessions from the marriage of Leopold II to a Visconti. Such rapid increases generally bring about harmful consequences: the domain proved ungovernable.

Karl V – His father, Philip the Fair, died in 1506 at Burgos, at the age of twenty-eight, from drinking icy water on a hot day. Karl was born at the start of the century and inherited the Americas on his maternal grandfather's death. He was elected emperor in preference to François I, King of France. By his own admission, he "risked all to win all". At the age of nineteen, he was of a serious, cold temperament, in comparison to the brilliant, lighthearted François I. Their rivalry was legendary. After his defeat at Marignan, Karl achieved a crushing victory over François at Pavia where he took the French monarch prisoner. In 1525, he was at the peak of his power. However, two events dampened his enthusiasm: Martin Luther launched the Reformation in 1517, while in 1521, the Turks conquered Belgrade and threatened Vienna. Administration of the Empire, under attack on several fronts, became impossible. It was hard for this prince to take action, particularly since he preferred living in Brussels to Vienna.

Partition of the Empire – In the 1522 Treaty of Brussels, Karl V entrusted the destiny of Austria to his brother, Ferdinand. The situation was worrying. On the one hand, Lutheranism was gaining ground, on the other hand, François I allied himself to the Turks, although, as King of France, he was the oldest supporter of the Roman Catholic Church. In 1526, Ferdinand of Habsburg became King of Hungary and Bohemia. This did not impede in any way the progress of the Ottoman Empire, which was so impressive that in 1529 Suleyman the Magnificent and his troops camped outside Vienna. Count Salm's resistance and the rigours of winter forced the Turks to raise their siege, but Ferdinand ensured their absence by paying the sultan an annual tribute. The price of security was heavy, swallowing up the remainder of the American gold, which Karl V used in payment of his debts. In his contest with France for supremacy in Europe, the loss of Metz in 1552 affected him deeply. Four years later, he abdicated, leaving to his son Philip II the Low Countries, Franche-Comté, Spain, Portugal, Italy and America; he renounced the hereditary Habsburg possessions and the imperial crown in favour of his brother, Ferdinand I.

THE TWO-HEADED EAGLE: ONE HEAD FACING WEST, THE OTHER FACING EAST

The heirs – While Spain and the Low Countries suffered under the yoke of Philip II, Ferdinand I's rule was exemplary. He endowed his kingdom with institutions that lasted until the 1848 revolution. He died in 1564. Maximilian II succeeded him and granted his subjects peace in a war-torn Europe, until his death in 1576. Morose and vindictive, his son Rudolf II was passionately fond of astronomy and totally uninterested in politics. He chose Prague as his capital. While he had to contend with the Hungarian insurrection of Stephen Bocskay, his brother Matthias became leader of a rebellion in 1612, had himself crowned emperor, then died disillusioned in 1619. Ferdinand II took up the challenge. An uncompromising Catholic, he crushed the Czechs at the battle of the White Hill, the following year. The ensuing repression was devastating. Austria seemed to have forgotten the meaning of monarchy, and the arrival of Ferdinand III on the throne in 1637 did nothing to change the situation.

The defeat of the Turkish menace – Thus in 1658, Leopold I reluctantly became emperor. This shy man, who had wanted to enter the priesthood, was to surprise his contemporaries. Turkey revived: exploiting a rebellion of the Hungarian nobility against the Habsburgs, the Grand Vizir Kara Mustapha besieged the city in 1683 *(see Historical table and notes, inset Vienna, a city that nearly became Turkish)*. The Austrian victory over the Ottoman peril had major symbolic repercussions which Leopold exploited by engaging in a war for the reconquest of eastern Europe. It was a stroke of genius which set Austria back up among the major powers. The author of Leopold's triumph was Eugène of Savoy, a French nobleman eager for glory. The emperor could now bequeath a prestigious imperial crown to his sons.

The Pragmatic Sanction – In 1711, Josef I died without an heir. His brother, Karl VI, succeeded him just before renouncing all rights to Spain, following the Treaty of Utrecht in 1713. He was an astute, ambitious man who had retained sovereignty over the Low Countries and aimed to unite the various kingdoms in his empire. In Austria, he initiated the era of the enlightened despot. There was, however, a serious obstacle to his policy: he lacked a male heir. In Hungary, for example, the Diet recognised the succession of the House of Habsburg only through the male line. Karl VI, therefore, concentrated all his energy on persuading the European powers to recognise the Pragmatic Sanction, adopted in 1713, which declared his possessions indivisible, while at the same time appointing as his heir his daughter Maria-Theresa. On his death in 1740, the coffers were empty, since there was a heavy price to pay for the Pragmatic Sanction (future loss of Lorraine, suppression of the Ostend Company, etc.). The army was weak and Silesia fell into the hands of the King of Prussia, Frederick II, Voltaire's admirer.

THE GLORY OF A PRESTIGIOUS QUEEN

Maria-Theresa, a model – Even before her accession to the throne, this courageous woman proved her independence by marrying François-Étienne of Lorraine, in 1736. It was a love match with a somewhat unpopular prince, to whom she gave sixteen children. Maria-Theresa had to face attacks from Bavaria and Saxony (claims to the Habsburg heritage), Spain (designs on Italy), France (anti-Austrian by conviction) and Prussia whose ascension she always feared. At her coronation as Queen of Hungary at Pressburg, she guaranteed the independence of that country. Immediately, the Hungarians recognised François Étienne as co-regent and raised an army of 30,000 men. Thus, the queen succeeded in repelling her enemies' attacks and, in having her husband crowned as Emperor Franz I in Frankfurt, in 1745. Three years later, the Treaty of Aix-la-Chapelle brought the conflict to an end. Maria-Theresa had saved the Empire be-

ROGER-VIOLLET

Maria-Theresa

queathed to her by her father in its entirety. She left the imprint of her personality on her long reign. She did a colossal amount of work, gave a hearing to the myriad communities in her Empire, and gained popularity by useful financial and administrative reforms, without offending Hungarian, Italian or Dutch susceptibilities. Her success stemmed from this mixture of willpower and cheerfulness, which vanished upon the death of François Étienne in 1765.

To preserve and reno-vate – After his father's death, Josef II was given a share of royal authority and continued the reor-ganisation of the Empire, a conservative reformism begun by his mother. However, the head of State did not possess the clear-sighted approach of his mother's forty-year-long reign. Impatient, au-thoritarian and brusque (he refused a coronation in Hungary), Josef II be-gan by abolishing what he called the "feminine re-public" and encouraging reactionary policies in a Europe in the throes of change. His policies her-alded a new Austria, with one national language, German, one capital, Vi-enna, and one supreme authority, the emperor's. On the other hand, he abolished serfdom despite opposition from the nobil-ity and introduced equality

Josef II

in law and taxes. He died in 1790, after asking for the following inscription on his tomb: "Here lies a prince who was well intentioned, but failed in everything he wanted to achieve."

THE END OF THE AGE OF ENLIGHTENMENT

A land of contradictions – The Enlightenment *(Aufklärung)* ended not just with the death of Josef II the "philosopher", who contributed much to his Empire's cultural's development, but also with the Austro-Hungarian agreement of 1790. The monarchy was centralised, but did not know how to cope with the specificities of the nation as a whole; pre-industrialisation occurred in an empire with a sparse population; the inhabitants were German-speaking, but an increasingly competitive Prussia drove them to the east and south. Moreover, Leopold II died too soon, in 1792. For Austria, it was a tragedy, since in a mere two years, this emperor had displayed exceptional political flair. His eldest son came to the throne with the reputation of being mediocre, and then had the misfortune to cross the path of an extraordinary man, Napoleon.

The occupation of the capital – Napoleon's visionary aims overthrew the Italian prin-cipalities; this left open the road to Vienna, particularly as hatred of the Habsburgs dated from the time of Maximilian I. Napoleon twice occupied Vienna, in 1805 and 1809. Between these two dates, on 6 August 1806, Franz II relinquished the impe-rial crown of the Holy Roman Germanic Empire, as he knew it to be doomed to extinction – in 1804, he proclaimed himself hereditary Emperor of Austria as Franz I. This event was to have enormous repercussions on the latent aspirations of minori-ties in Bohemia, Hungary and Italy. Now, in the shadow of these monarchs, two men of brilliantly acute intelligence played a leading role in Europe, moulding it in the light of their ambitions: a Frenchman, Charles Maurice de Talleyrand-Périgord and an Austrian, Klemens Wenzel Nepomuk Lothar von Metternich.

The Congress of Vienna – With the fall of Napoleon's empire in March 1814, Vienna replaced Paris as Europe's capital. It became the seat of an international congress determining the fate of winners and losers. For a year, all the crowned heads of Europe attended the congress: the Emperor of Austria, Czar Alexander I of Russia, King Friedrich-Wilhelm of Prussia, the Kings of Wurtemberg, Bavaria and Denmark, as well as numerous princes and archdukes. Among the diplomats were Lord Castlereagh representing Britain, Nesselrode for Russia, Wilhelm von Humboldt for Prussia, Talleyrand for France and Metternich for Austria. Alexander I attracted atten-tion by his dissipation and sumptuous receptions. Talleyrand, on the other hand, was astute enough to secure a privileged position at the heart of the countries partici-pating by making himself the champion of the minorities. However, it was Prince Metternich, Austrian Minister of Foreign Affairs, who played the principal role in the congress. He imposed his view of a balanced conservative Europe by developing three main themes: restoration – of the 1789 political situation; legitimacy – which entailed the return of the Bourbons to the throne of France; and solidarity – in the face of revolutionary movements.

Metternich, a true master – Thanks to the remarkable diplomatic ability of this lucid and worldly aristocrat, Austria regained a major position in central Europe by chairing the Germanic Confederation (coalition of 39 states). 1815 saw the founding of the Holy Alliance, comprising Orthodox Russia, Protestant Prussia and Catholic Austria. These three powers undertook to govern in a "Christian" way and had the authority to "intervene against all national uprisings". Besides his native language, Metternich spoke fluent English, Italian, Latin and the Slavonic languages. An admirer of Josef II, he established from 1815 to 1848 a "system", which was of immediate benefit to Austria, which it transformed into a bastion of the *ancien régime*, whereas in Europe the forces of liberalism were active. Meanwhile, Franz I died in 1835 and his successor Ferdinand I was totally incompetent, even feeble-minded. Metternich pursued his authoritarian regime governed by a "secret State conference" consisting of Archduke Ludwig, Count Kolowrat and Metternich. *Vormärz* denotes the period before March 1848, a curious mixture of Biedermeier ambiance and police repression.

THE IMPERIAL MYTH

The 1848 revolution – In Austria, there occurred at the same time a social rebellion against the government and a nationalist uprising in Bohemia (which belonged to the Confederation), Hungary and the Lombard-Venetian kingdom (which did not belong to it). In Vienna, there were three insurrections (also in Berlin and Munich) which forced the government to ask for Metternich's "resignation" (exile) and prompted the Court to seek refuge in Olmütz in Moravia. After the recapture of the capital by force, the army crushed the national uprisings – Radetzky in Italy, Windischgrätz in Prague, Hungarian surrender under pressure from Russia who came to the aid of Austria: 13 Hungarian generals were executed. Ferdinand abdicated in favour of his nephew Franz, aged 18, who added Josef to his Christian name, in memory of Josef II. By this, he wished to indicate that he wanted a centralised state open to modernisation. The age of **Franz-Josef** had begun.

The reign of the status quo – Franz-Josef embodied the concepts of uprightness and integrity. Despite innumerable family misfortunes and political upheavals throughout his reign of sixty-eight years, he remained a sovereign who commanded the love and respect of his subjects. His mother, Archduchess Sophia, shaped the young emperor's development. It was to her that he owed his unfailing courtesy, sense of duty and talent for bureaucracy, but also his reactionary outlook. However, neo-absolutism was not a suitable formula for governing a monarchy whose subjects had just rebelled and demanded closer involvement with public affairs. In this potentially explosive context, a solution came in the form of Elizabeth of Bavaria, known as Sissi. She and Franz-Josef were an unusually romantic couple, not because they projected a sickly sweet, stereotyped image, but because destiny separated these two beings who loved each other.

Austria-Hungary – When in 1848 the Hungarians declared their independence, they immediately suffered a crushing defeat. This merely reinforced the desire for independence in this country, which by that time was the only Habsburg state to be a separate monarchy. It led to the famous 1867 compromise which created the dual

Kaiser Franz-Josef

monarchy of Austria-Hungary. Franz-Josef became emperor *(Kaiser)* in Austria and king *(König)* in Hungary. In practical terms, this meant that the constitution, administration and legislation were separate, and that the army, finance and foreign policy were common to both. It was also an admission of powerlessness. "Dualism" was the name of this new regime which lasted for the duration of Habsburg rule. Its inception provoked dissension among the Serbs, Croats and Czechs. Further weakening of the Empire occurred as a result of Napoleon III's support of the Italian cause, Prussian hegemony and the Balkan crisis. Franz-Josef was not a statesman. Defeats succeeded one another. The emperor compromised, often without acting. Unfortunately, catastrophes became too numerous and began to overshadow the internal economic prosperity which fostered artistic life.

"I have been spared nothing" – An impressive succession of setbacks and tragedies marked Franz-Josef's long reign to such an extent that he declared "I have been spared nothing". It is impossible to list all these events here, but the main ones give some idea of the extraordinary life of a man who remains the symbol of his dynasty. In 1853, a Hungarian tailor Libényi stabbed the sovereign in the back of his neck. In 1857, the emperor lost his first child, Princess Sophy, aged 26 months. In 1859, the Peace of Zürich deprived the Empire of Lombardy, following the defeats of Magenta and Solferino. In 1866, the Treaty of Vienna deprived the Empire of Venetia. In 1867, Juarez' republican revolutionaries shot Maximilian, brother of Franz-Josef, in Mexico. In 1868, Croatia obtained independence. In 1878, death of Franz-Karl, brother of Franz-Josef. In 1882, proclamation of the kingdom of Serbia. In 1889, suicide of his son, Archduke Rudolf, at Mayerling. In 1889, Johann, Franz-Josef's cousin, relinquished the title of archduke and assumed the name of Johann Orth, before disappearing in mysterious circumstances. In 1897, his sister-in-law, the Duchess of Alençon, perished in a terrible fire at the Bazar de la Charité, in Paris. In 1898, his wife Elizabeth died, stabbed by the Italian anarchist Luccheni, in Geneva. In 1914, the heir to the Empire, Archduke Franz-Ferdinand, was assassinated in Sarajevo with his wife.

"Es ist passiert" – In Europe, it was a period of systematic alliances, armed peace among the great powers, insoluble problems within the Austro-Hungarian Empire, and Russia's Balkan policy. The atmosphere was explosive, and finally it was the assassination in Sarajevo which detonated the time bomb on 28 June 1914. World War One had begun.

In Austria, when people wish to evoke the ephemeral and futile quality of time, they say *es ist passiert* (it is over). Franz-Josef died on 22 November 1916; he had clung to the idea of a supranational Empire. Karl I succeeded him under apocalyptic conditions. He began a tentative attempt at a separate peace with France, which seemed to favour the survival of the Austro-Hungarian Empire. However, in February 1918, Clémenceau promised Czechoslovakia and Yugoslavia to the Czechs and the Serbo-Croats. This signaled the death of the Empire, particularly as the allies of the Entente supported the separatists. On 11 November 1918, at Schloss Schönbrunn, Karl I signed the act of abdication which ended Habsburg rule.

DID YOU KNOW?

1. Who was the last member of the imperial family to be buried in the Capuchin crypt (*Kapuzinergruft*)?

2. Where is the world's finest collection of paintings by Brueghel the Elder?

3. What nationality was the engineer who designed the Giant Ferris Wheel in the Prater? French, British or German?

4. What was the inaugural performance of the Vienna State Opera? *Fidelio* by Beethoven? *Don Giovanni* by Mozart? Or *Tristan and Isolde* by Wagner?

5. Where and when did Sigmund Freud have the sudden inspiration that dreams were of great significance in the study of neurosis?

6. Prince Eugène of Savoy played a major role in Austrian history. Does he lie buried in the Capuchin vault with the Habsburgs, in Stephansdom or in the Belvedere?

7. What is the origin of the word *Biedermeier*? A fictitious character, a furniture designer, or a composer of waltzes?

8. *"Oh you men, who consider me hostile or inflexible, even a misanthrope, you deeply misjudge me! You do not know the hidden cause of all these symptoms..."* This sentence describing Beethoven's deafness is an extract from a famous document. Which document and where is it?

8. Beethoven's "Heiligenstadt Testament". A facsimile is on view at Beethovenhaus, Heiligenstadt.

7. A fictitious character, the invention of two writers in the early 19C.

6. In the Chapel of the Holy Cross in Stephansdom.

5. During an excursion into the Kahlenberg heights, north of Vienna, 24 July 1895.

4. *Don Giovanni* by Mozart, 25 May 1869.

3. It was an Englishman, Walter B. Bassett.

2. At the Kunsthistorisches Museum.

1. Empress Zita of Bourbon-Parma, wife of Karl I, emperor from 1916 to 1918.

Art

ABC OF ARCHITECTURE

Religious architecture

Apsidal or **axial chapel**. In churches not dedicated to the Virgin Mary, this is often the Lady Chapel. It lies along the east-west line of the building.

Ambulatory: An extension of the side aisles around the chancel. The ambulatory enabled people to file past relics in churches that were places of pilgrimage.

Chancel: Almost always east-facing.

Crossing or **transept arm:** They may or may not be projecting.

Span: Transversal division of the nave. The area between two pillars.

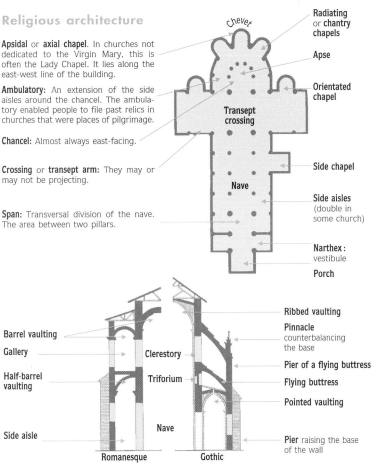

Chevet

Radiating or **chantry chapels**

Apse

Orientated chapel

Transept crossing

Side chapel

Nave

Side aisles (double in some church)

Narthex: vestibule

Porch

Barrel vaulting

Gallery

Half-barrel vaulting

Side aisle

Cleerstory

Triforium

Nave

Romanesque

Gothic

Ribbed vaulting

Pinnacle counterbalancing the base

Pier of a flying buttress

Flying buttress

Pointed vaulting

Pier raising the base of the wall

Giants' Portal, Stephansdom (1230-1240)

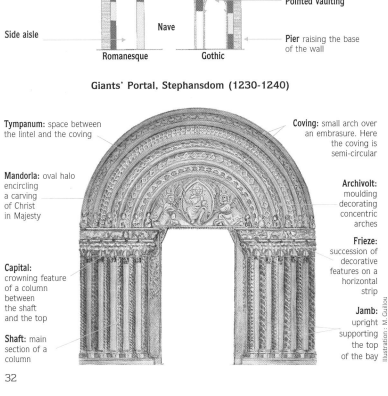

Tympanum: space between the lintel and the coving

Mandorla: oval halo encircling a carving of Christ in Majesty

Capital: crowning feature of a column between the shaft and the top

Shaft: main section of a column

Coving: small arch over an embrasure. Here the coving is semi-circular

Archivolt: moulding decorating concentric arches

Frieze: succession of decorative features on a horizontal strip

Jamb: upright supporting the top of the bay

Illustration : M. Guillou

Church of the Dominicans (1631-1634)

Spandrel: area of a wall between two arches.

Reredos: back of the altar, usually containing a painting. Also refers to the painting itself.

Sounding board: canopy over the pulpit.

Pulpit: raised platform for preaching.

Tabernacle: small cupboard in the centre of the altar, containing the ciborium.

Cherub: winged child's head symbolising an order of angels.

Culot: French term for a stucco ornament, consisting here of foliage with stems emerging from it.

Foliage: plaster ornament consisting of a stylised stem with regular undulations.

Predella: lower part of the reredos, usually divided into three panels. panneaux

High altar: main altar, on the centre line of the nave.

Church of St Charles Borromeo (1716-1737)

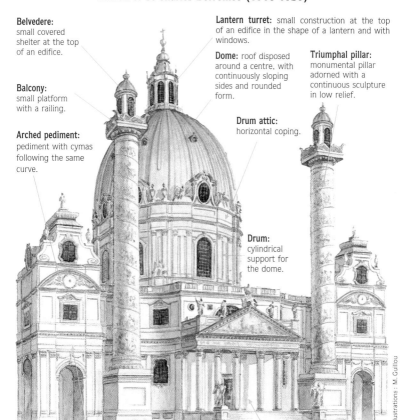

Belvedere: small covered shelter at the top of an edifice.

Balcony: small platform with a railing.

Arched pediment: pediment with cymas following the same curve.

Lantern turret: small construction at the top of an edifice in the shape of a lantern and with windows.

Dome: roof disposed around a centre, with continuously sloping sides and rounded form.

Triumphal pillar: monumental pillar adorned with a continuous sculpture in low relief.

Drum attic: horizontal coping.

Drum: cylindrical support for the dome.

Pavilion: wing, square in plan; in this case, included in the overall dimensions because linked to the main section.

Pronaos: in a classical temple, porch at the entrance to the sanctuary; in a church, this porch is called a galilee.

Illustrations : M. Guillou

33

Schönbrunn: Gloriette (1775)

Amortizement: decorative element at the top of an edifice.

Piece of entablature: raising of the support, like a classical entablature in outline.

Arcade: open bay covered by an arch.

Pediment: triangular gable above an entablature.

Tuscan capital: differs from a Doric capital in its lack of ornamentation.

Niche: recess for a decorative object.

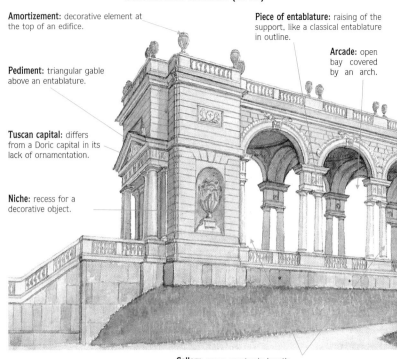

Gallery: space greater in length than width, serving as a passageway.

Upper Belvedere (1722)

Mansard roof: roof having two slopes on the same side.

Pier: the part of a wall between two adjacent openings.

Piano nobile: storey where the ceiling height is loftier than that of the other floors.

Attic storey: half storey forming the crowning feature of the façade.

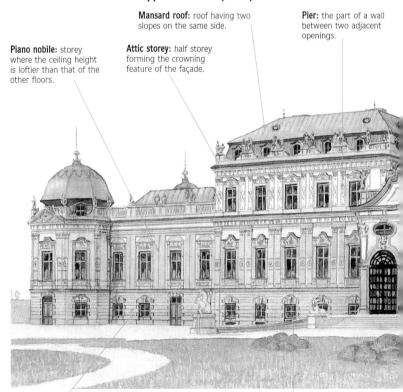

Foundation floor: floor designed to compensate for a slope.

Trave: series of openings on the same vertical line.

Decorative table: clad surface limited by a projection.

Trophies: decorative motifs consisting of emblems and arms, usually around a armour or a helmet.

Perron: external flight of steps leading to an entrance.

Balustrade: railing consisting of a row of balusters.

Twinned columns: columns grouped in twos.

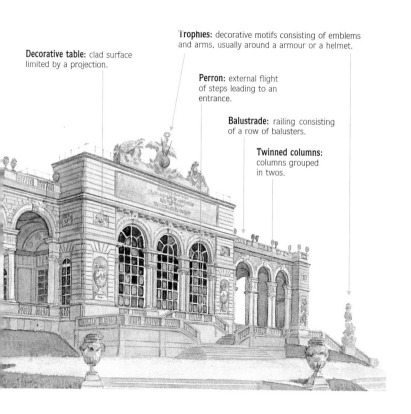

Skylight: window placed in a roof to admit daylight.

Cowl: end of a ventilation shaft.

Acroter: a plinth bearing a statue or ornaments at the apex of a pediment.

Modillion: small bracket under a cornice.

Entablature: a construction having an architrave, a frieze and a cornice.

Portico: gallery forming an entrance to a building.

Mascaron: carved mask decorating the crown of an arch.

Pilaster: fake engaged column projecting slightly from the wall.

Illustrations · M. Guillou

The Romanesque Style (12C-13C) – There are few remaining examples of this. Apart from those in Ruprechtskirche and Virgilkapelle, the finest Romanesque work still in existence is the west façade of Stephansdom and its superb Giants' Doorway, Riesentor.

The Gothic Style (14C-1515) – Gothic architecture originated in Vienna with the construction of the new Stephansdom, which is of the German hall-church *(Hallenkirchen)* type. Built in late Gothic style, St Stephen's cathedral is the best illustration of Austrian Gothic; its master builders were in touch with those in Ratisbon and Strasbourg. Despite certain alterations, Annakirche, Augustinerkirche, Deutschordenkirche, Minoritenkirche and Maria am Gestade belong to the Gothic era, of which Michaelerkirche has retained some traces. Another example of this style is Spinnerin am Kreuz outside the centre.

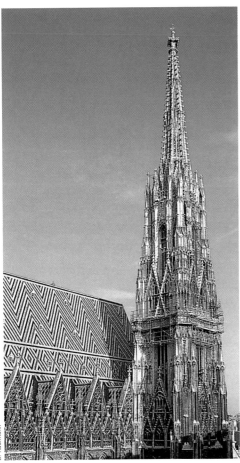

South spire of the cathedral

B. Kaufmann

The Renaissance (1515-1627) – Vienna is not the best place in which to study Renaissance architecture. Rudolf II resided mainly in Prague; this led to the emigration of some of the nobility and hence to a certain hiatus in Vienna's artistic history during the 16C. Moreover, nothing now remains of the Neugebäude in Simmering which Maximilian II commissioned in 1587 from Pietro Ferrabosco. Buildings still in existence are therefore few in number. Among them are Amalien Trakt (Hofburg, In der Burg), the pediment of Franziskanerkirche, the Salvatorkapelle entrance, Schweizertor (Hofburg, In der Burg) and the inner courtyard of Stallburg.

The Baroque Style (1627-1753) – An offshoot of Italian Baroque, Austrian Baroque is a combination of French and German elements. Initially a religious art in essence, it was in total harmony with the mood of mystic joyfulness following the Council of Trent. It enjoyed the favour of the Habsburgs, ardent supporters of the Counter-Reformation. There are two forms of this style, known as Early Baroque and High Baroque. Early Baroque, which covers the 17C, is a style of foreign origin. It is an extension of Italy's monopoly in the arts, which began in Austria during the Renaissance. Of a slightly later date than Borromini's or Bernini's monuments in Rome, Early Baroque is contemporaneous with the establishment of a series of religious orders and is responsible for churches based on the famous model of the Gesù: single nave with side chapels, tripartite façade with pilasters beneath a voluted pediment (Dominikanerkirche, Jesuitenkirche, Kirche "Zu den neuen Chören der Engel"). Palaces were also the work of Italian architects, such as Lodovico Burnacini, Pietro Tencala and Domenico Martinelli, who built the Liechtenstein palace. High Baroque could be termed Austrian Baroque, since its great practitioners were of local origin, and covers a period from 1690 to 1753. It gave Austria its most brilliant artistic triumphs. Architects working in this second style were Johann Bernhard Fischer von Erlach and Johann Lukas von Hildebrandt *(see below)*. One must also include Isidore Canevale (Allgemeines Krankenhaus), Josef Emmanuel Fischer von Erlach

Josefsplatz

B. Kaufmann

(Michaelertrakt and Winterreitschule in the Hofburg), Gabriele Montani (Peterskirche), Nikolaus Pacassi (completion of Schönbrunn, Josefsplatz), Andrea Pozzo (interior of Jesuitenkirche).

Johann Bernard Fischer von Erlach (1656-1723) – A native of Graz, he became Court Architect and Building Superintendent in 1687. He was a prolific architect: 7 churches, 3 castles, about 10 palaces, high altars, mausoleums and fountains, in Vienna, Salzburg, Prague, Brünn, Breslau and Mariazell. In the capital, he built Karlskirche, a masterpiece still capable of amazing the most enlightened of art lovers, the Trautson palace, the world-famous Schönbrunn Palace, Prince Eugène's Winterpalais and the Hofburg library. He also contributed to the building of the Liechtenstein and Lobkowitz palaces and Dreifaltigkeitssäule (Trinity pillar) in the Graben. Prince Schwarzenberg once described him in a letter in the following terms: "the imperial architect has no equal in Austria, yet he must have one beam too many in his head". A cutting remark, to say the least, illustrating how often geniuses seem nothing more than fanciful eccentrics to their entourage. He died in Vienna on 5 April 1723. One of the four children from his first marriage, Josef Emmanuel, continued his work.

Johann Lukas von Hildebrandt (1668-1745) – Born in Genoa of German parents, he was the second genius of Austrian Baroque. From an historical point of view, a whole generation separates him from his renowned colleague. This is partly because he reached Vienna in 1696, ten years later, but mainly because he brought back fom his studies in Italy and his stay with Carlo Fontana a less monumental architecture,

Schloss Schönbrunn

3BIS/MICHELIN

which already was a precursor of neo-Classicism. He collaborated with Fischer von Erlach on Prince Eugène's Stadtpalais and the Schwarzenberg palace. A man of great energy, he built the Kinsky, Starhemberg and Schönborn palaces, Peterskirche (which he completed), Bundeskanzleramt and his two masterpieces designed for Prince Eugène of Savoy: Unteres and Oberes Belvedere (Lower and Upper Belvedere). Ennobled in 1720, he worked mainly for Prince Eugène, but also found time to enter the service of the elector of Mainz (Würzburg Episcopal Palace).

Unteres Belvedere

Classicism and Biedermeier (1753-1848) – The two principal architects belonging to the Classical tradition were the Frenchman Jean-Nicolas Jadot de Ville-Issey (Akademie der Wissenschaften, Maria-Theresa crypt in the Kaisergruft) and Ferdinand Hetzendorf von Hohenberg (Pallavicini Palace and Gloriette). The chief representative of the Biedermeier style *(see Decorative arts)* was Josef Kornhäusel (refurbishment of Schottenstift).

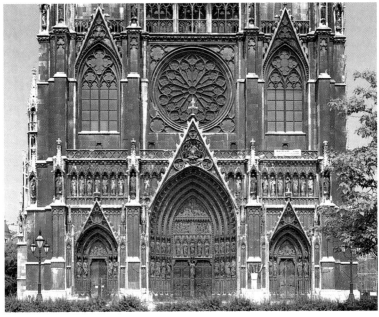

Votivkirche

Historicism (1849-1896) – This highly eclectic style is best illustrated by a walk along the Ring. The romantic objective of this architectural movement was to create "a work of total art". This totality, however, encompasses a great variety of past styles, recreations of historical models, such as Heinrich von Ferstel's neo-Gothic Votivkirche. The style fell from grace at the end of the century with the founding of the Secession *(see below)*.

Jugendstil and Secession (1896-1914) – A German version of Art Nouveau, Jugendstil acquired its name from the Munich periodical *Jugend*, founded in 1896. It was a neo-Baroque movement in evidence about 1900 but was never part of Historicism, because of its characteristic sinuous lines and lack of symmetry, in short its anti-academic attitude.

Otto Wagner *(see below)*, originally an exponent of the eclectic Ring style became one of its most illustrious representatives (Linke Wienzeile buildings). The Secession's exact title was *Vereinigung Bildender Künstler Österreich* or Association of Austrian Artists, founded in 1897. It was a movement in opposition to official art. Unlike Jugendstil, with which it is often confused, it has a geometrical, rectilinear conception of ornament, which differs from the organic conception of the great master of Art Nouveau, Victor Horta, and his European counterparts. The purest expression of this movement is Josef Maria Olbrich's Secessiongebäude.

Otto Wagner (1841-1918) – Born in the Biedermeier era and a product of the Classical tradition, he rose to become Imperial Architectural Advisor for Vienna and Professor at the Academy of Fine Arts. At the age of 50, he made a new start in his artistic career.

His most interesting achievements were still to come, namely the Karlsplatz Metro stations, Kirche am Steinhof and Postsparkasse. He went from Historicism to the sinuousness of Jugendstil, then to the smooth, geometric ornamentation of the Secession. He had a decisive influence on European architecture.

Adolf Loos (1870-1933) – A native of Brünn, this architect who qualified in Dresden settled in Vienna on his return from a trip to the United States. His essay *Ornament and Crime* condemns the excessive decoration of Jugendstil then at its peak.

In Vienna, he built the Steiner house and Looshaus. He then left for Paris, where he built the Tzara house before returning to Vienna. A rationalist, he was a strong opponent of the *Wiener Werkstätte*, since, according to him, any link between art and craftsmanship was not feasible: "a work of art is eternal; the creation of a craftsman is ephemeral".

From 1921 to the 1990s – The Austro-Marxist municipality under Karl Seitz, Mayor of Vienna, administered the city after the fall of the empire. They were responsible for much public housing *(Höfe)* built to solve the housing shortage. The whole city became a showcase for experimental architecture in socialist functionalist style, displaying a huge program of large housing estates which attracted the attention of the whole world.

Coop Himmelblau building

Their most spectacular achievements were Karl-Marx-Hof by Karl Ehn, Reumannhof by Gessner, and Liebknechthof by Karl Krist. In 1932, Josef Frank headed the Werkbundsiedlung experimental project for minimalist housing in Hietzing. Among contemporary architects working in Vienna are Hermann Czech, the "deconstructivist" duo Coop Himmelblau (W. Prix and H. Swiczinsky), Friedensreich Hundertwasser (who is a sculptor), Robert Krier from Luxemburg, Hans Hollein and Johann Staber.

PAINTING AND SCULPTURE

Baroque architecture is unimaginable without its natural complements of painting and sculpture. Together with the brilliantly realistic work of artists in stucco, these breathe life into the space of the buildings. A profusion of altarpieces appear in churches, myriads of angels and saints people the ceilings, and armies of statues put to flight remarkable Gothic works, now considered "barbaric". Great artists contributed to the sumptuous interior decoration of palaces and churches: **Johann Michael Rottmayr** (1654-1730), Fischer von Erlach's favourite assistant and the precursor of a specifically Austrian Baroque pictorial style; **Paul Sturdel** (1648-1708), founder of the Academy of Fine Art and Court sculptor; **Balthasar Permoser** (1651-1732) whose famous marble Apotheosis of Prince Eugène adorns the Österreichisches Barockmuseum; **Paul Troger** (1698-1762) was one of the first to become aware of the originality of Austrian painting and devoted his life to painting religious subjects; **Johann Martin Schmidt** ("Kremser Schmidt") whose altarpieces are visible in numerous churches; **Martino Altomonte** (1657-1745), a Neapolitan painter who entered the service of the Court in 1703 and died in Vienna; **Lorenzo Mattielli** (about 1680-1748), a great sculptor from Vicenza working in Vienna from 1714; **Balthasar Ferdinand Moll**, the creator of the famous double sarcophagus in Kapuzinergruft; and **Georg Raphael Donner** (1693-1741), who enjoyed the flattering nickname of the "Austrian Michelangelo", best known for his fine fountain in Neuer Markt. However, it is with the highly creative **Franz Anton Maulbertsch** (1724-1796) and the German **Franz Xaver Messerschmidt** (1736-1783), whose amazing grimacing heads are visible in the Österreichisches Barockmuseum, that Austrian painting and sculpture of that period reached their peak.

In the 19C, Biedermeier *(see Decorative arts)* and Eclecticism (second half of the century) produced a new generation of first rate artists. It was the age of realist painting, with an abundance of landscape painters producing small works. The great master of this genre was **Ferdinand Georg Waldmüller** (1793-1865), a master of light and colour. One must also include **Friedrich Gauermann** (1807-1862), who faithfully reproduced the atmosphere of his time, and **Leopold Kupelwieser** (1796-1862) who devoted himself to religious painting after executing portraits of people in Schubert's circle. An important development in the world of sculpture occurred as a result of the large number of public commissions. **Anton Dominik Fernkorn** (1813-1878) created martial statues, while there were still some talented artists in the domain of religious art, such as **Karl Georg Merville** with his remarkable *Fall of the Angels* (1782) for the high altar in Michaelerkirche.

The end of the century was a time of transition for Austrian painting. The highly successful artist **Hans Makart** (1840-1884) gave his name *(Makartism)* to monumental and refined paint-

ing, while the extremely original talent of **Anton Romako** (1832-1889) emerged, marking a break with the serene painting of past centuries *(see also Galerie des 19. und 20. Jahrhunderts)*. A profound artistic revival swept through German-speaking countries, bearing the name Jugendstil. In Vienna, the most brilliant exponent of this movement was Gustav Klimt.

Gustav Klimt (1862-1918) – *See also Galerie des 19. und 20. Jahrhunderts.* A native of Vienna and the son of a modest goldsmith, he began painting in an academic style before becoming a co-founder and head of the Secession in 1897. Supremely a painter of the 1900s, he was one of its most famous artists and his work is constantly reproduced. His Beethoven frieze in the Secessiongebäude established his close connection with the great European Symbolist School. Despite his reputation for mawkishness, he is nevertheless a painter of unusual profundity.

The high altar in Michaelerkirche

Self-portrait with Splayed Fingers by Egon Schiele

Egon Schiele (1890-1918) – *See also Galerie des 19. und 20. Jahrhunderts.* Although Klimt is the most highly-acclaimed painter, Schiele deserves similar appreciation. His turbulent creations convey with rare lucidity a picture of Man and his neuroses. The expressionism of this outstanding artist drew inspiration from the body and led to a prison sentence in 1912, as his paintings were considered pornographic.

Oskar Kokoschka (1886-1980) – Born in Pöchlarn (Bohemia), he soon joined the Viennese and Berlin avant-garde. After working as a teacher in Dresden, he settled in Vienna in 1931, before moving to Prague and London. An admirer of Munch, his painting reveals a lyrical, tortured expressionism with violent colouring.

DECORATIVE ARTS

Porcelain – 1718 was the date of the founding of the second European factory producing hard paste porcelain. The founder was Claudius Innocentius du Paquier, a potter from Trier of Dutch Huguenot origin. Under the directorship of S. Stölzel, the **Vienna factory** with its "beehive" monogram produced decorative statuettes and tableware drawing inspiration from the Meissen factories in Saxony. Late Baroque in style, the decoration was varied, displaying zoomorphical handles and spouts, scrolls, foliage and Chinese motifs. It became a state factory in 1744 in Maria-Theresa's reign and produced Rococo services adorned with landscapes and animals, then from 1770 with themes from French painting (the influence of Marie Antoinette's marriage with the Dauphin of France). The "Old Vienna" pattern of simple flowers on a white ground was a great success throughout Europe, but Augarten also continued manufacturing in great numbers the porcelain statuettes, which constitute its corporate image today. The factory's golden age occurred between 1784 and 1805, under the leader-

Late 18C Viennese porcelain

ship of K. Sorgenthal, who encouraged the production of Neoclassical forms and decoration. In 1805, Napoleon occupied Vienna. Count Daru, manager of the Sèvres porcelain works, became head of the imperial factory. The style of the French Empire was dominant (many items from this period are on view at the Hofsilber– und Tafelkammer), but after the 1815 Congress of Vienna it soon gave way to Biedermeier decorative styles. Among these was the "Idyll" pattern, the creation of Daffinger, a miniaturist. In

Writing desk (1825)

1864, the factory closed its doors, to reopen in 1923 as the **Porzellanmanufaktur Augarten** *(see Augarten)*. Since that date, it has been under the administration of the municipal authorities.

Herr Biedermeier – In Germany and Austria, the Biedermeier style applies mainly to decorative arts, but it also refers to architecture, painting and sculpture, of the 1815-1848 period, namely from the Congress of Vienna to the 1848 Revolution. Most non-German speakers believe that Biedermeier was a cabinetmaker who gave his name to this style. In fact, Wieland Gottlieb Biedermeier never existed!

The character made his first appearance in the early 19C in the work of the German authors Adolf Kaussmaul and Ludwig Eichrodt, as a worthy bourgeois full of fine feelings; *"bieder"* means "worthy, upright"; *"Meier"* is a very common name. Herr Biedermeier emerged from a literary satire to become a symbol of an age and the personification of a certain style. This style reflects the way of life and convictions of a rising social class, and introduced a new artistic terminology. It was not surprising that it replaced the French Empire style, since Herr Biedermeier was a nationalist; Biedermeier did not favour bronze ornamentation or dark wood from distant regions. In furniture, for example, the characteristic features of this style are: massive proportions with sober but varied lines and smooth surfaces; light wood (cherry, ash); and veneers inlaid with darker woods (mahogany or ebony). The most common pieces of furniture are writing desks, sofas, chairs, smaller items and a kind of small sideboard. This furniture would not be wholly Biedermeier if it were not comfortable, in an opulent setting with plants, thick curtains and ornaments on the mantelpiece. Finally, the backs and legs of the chairs are of varied, extravagant designs. In Vienna, the outstanding Biedermeier cabinetmaker was **Josef Danhauser** (1805-1845); his work surpasses that of Nepomuk Geyer (Innsbruck), Voigt (Berlin), Wanschaff (Berlin) and Knussmann (Mainz). When the Bundessammlung Alter Stilmöbel reopens its doors, there will be an opportunity of appreciating numerous examples of furniture from this period and noticing how some anticipate the 1925 style.

The term Biedermeier also designates a type of glassware, very precise and with three characteristics: massive form, engraved glass and coloured subjects.

Thonet chair

Thonet – Thonet chairs are world famous. This name belongs to a dynasty of furniture designers, starting with **Michael Thonet** (1796-1871), the creator in 1859 of the famous bentwood "chair No 14". In 1841, a year before moving to Vienna, he patented the mechanical and chemical process for bending beechwood, an invention which enabled the Thonet brothers to break new ground in the domain of quality mass production. The firm displayed great business acumen, exporting its products from Austria by distributing sales catalogues. Both commercially and aesthetically, all the groundwork for the Wiener Werkstätte *(see below)* was complete, the forms determined by the structure and the sales addressed to all. Therefore, it was not surprising when during the first quarter of the 20C, avant-garde personalities like Le Corbusier, Breuer and Mies van der Rohe were the first to test curved metallic tube furniture from the Thonet factory, which proved its capacity for innovation.

At the end of the 19C and the beginning of the 20C, the great Viennese furniture designers, Adolf Loos and Josef Hoffmann, designed furniture for the **J. & J. Kohn** factory.

Wiener Werkstätte – 19 May 1903 was the date of the founding of the **Vienna Workshops** by the architect Josef Hoffmann, Koloman Moser and the banker Fritz Waerndorfer, who knew the Scottish designer Charles Rennie Mackintosh. The Vienna Workshops set out to make objects of artistic worth accessible to all and to put both artist and craftsman on a firm professional footing. Their full title is interesting: "Wiener Werkstätte. Association of artists and craftsmen. Unlimited company, registered in Vienna". To fulfill their mission, the founders created workshops which they equipped with modern machinery for the training of craftsmen, and decided to publicise their products by taking part in exhibitions. The Wiener Werkstätte artists and craftsmen exercised their talent in a variety of spheres: jewellery, fabrics, wallpaper, bookbinding, utilitarian

objects, glass, stained glass, posters, mosaic, fashion garments, tableware, and also architecture and interior decoration in an attempt at producing total art. Through the Workshops, they attained a vast public and great popularity. Their first clients were, of course, personal friends or patrons of the arts, like the Belgian Adolphe Stoclet who commissioned in Brussels between 1905 and 1911 a mansion entirely equipped by the *Wiener Werkstätte*. Though expensive, the products soon appealed to a wealthy clientèle. The novelty of these utilitarian objects lay in their beauty and purity of form, resulting both from their functionalism and the use of high-quality materials. After 1907, the early geometric style gave way to more sinuous lines. With the arrival of Dagobert Peche in 1915, this tendency became more marked and the products increasingly decorative. The *Wiener Werkstätte* closed in 1932, in the face of insurmountable financial difficulties due to the economic situation but also to declining standards in quality. In 1937, the Österreichisches Museum für Angewandte Kunst bought the archives and now displays numerous fine items.

The main artists of the Wiener Werkstätte were J. Hoffmann and K. Moser, and also A. Böhm, C. O. Czeschka, G. Klimt, B. Löffler, R. Luksch, D. Peche and M. Powolny.

Josef Hoffmann (1870-1956) – Born in Pirnitz in Moravia, died in Vienna. He was a brilliant pupil of Otto Wagner, from whom he received his diploma in 1895, and won the Prix de Rome the same year. From 1899 to 1937, he taught at the School of Applied Arts. A versatile artist, architect and designer, he was responsible for the interior decoration of the houses he created and he also designed the furniture and tableware. As co-founder of the Secession, he played a decisive role in the *Wiener Werkstätte*, with whose cooperation he executed a major architectural project at the turn of the century, the **Hôtel Stoclet** in Brussels, his most spectacular and famous achievement. He worked extensively for private clients, particularly the Primavesi. He also received many commissions from Vienna city council, particularly in the field of low-income housing in the years 1923/25. He had a considerable influence on many modern architects and designers.

Cutlery by Josef Hoffmann

Koloman Moser (1868-1918), known as Kolo Moser – Born and died in Vienna. One of the most gifted and prolific artists of the Secession movement, of which he was one of the founders, Moser was undeniably one of the most important figures of the turn of the century in the domain of applied arts. Through the activities of the *Wiener Werkstätte*, of which he was a co-founder, he displayed his versatility. He worked as goldsmith, designer of wallpaper or geometrical furniture. One of his principal achievements in Vienna was his contribution to Otto Wagner's Am Steinhof church, for which he made magnificent stained-glass windows. Finally, a lesser known but significant aspect of his career is his series of posters.

Stained-glass window by Koloman Moser in Am Steinhof

Vienna, capital of music

An ancient tradition – By the 12C, Vienna under the Babenbergs had become an important centre of secular music. Many German-speaking troubadours, the **Minnesänger**, came to Vienna where by the end of the 13C they had become members of guilds. At the end of the Middle Ages, Maximilian I moved his dazzling court choir from Innsbruck to Vienna, confirming the city's status as a musical capital. The choir, now a venerable institution, was the subject of public acclaim in the 15C and still arouses the enthusiasm of today's audiences under the name of "**Hofkapelle**".

Music-loving emperors – The Baroque era (17C-18C) saw the arrival of opera which originated in Italy around 1600 and was immensely popular with the Viennese court. Generous patrons of music, some emperors were themselves distinguished composers. The most prolific of them, **Leopold I**, left a number of religious works which still form part of today's repertoire. The Court and the royal family sang and performed his operettas. Maria-Theresa's father, Karl VI, was a talented violinist. All received a solid musical education: Maria-Theresa played the double bass, Josef II the harpsichord and cello.

Gluck and the reforming of the opera – Born in Bohemia, **Christoph Willibald von Gluck** (1714-1787) was one of the most important composers of the pre-Classical era. He considered opera as an indivisible work of art, that was both musical and dramatic in character; he sought above all natural effects, simplicity and a faithful portrayal of feelings. In 1754, he became Kapellmeister at the Imperial Court. It was in Paris that he achieved his musical aims. His most characteristic operas are *Orpheus and Eurydice* (1762) and *Alcestis* (1767).

The great Viennese Classics – These include great composers, Viennese by birth or adoption, such as Haydn, Mozart, Beethoven and Schubert. Their primarily instrumental work ensured for over a century the dominance of Germanic music in Europe and made Vienna its musical capital. Italian music also played a leading role until the early 19C. An artist like **Antonio Salieri** (1750-1825), director of the imperial chapel in 1778, was arbiter of the city's musical taste. Finally, it is surprising to learn that the young **Gioacchino Rossini** (1792-1868) came to Vienna in 1820 to meet Beethoven and achieved greater success than the latter.

Josef Haydn (1732-1809) – Born in Rohrau (Lower Austria), he was a choirboy in Stephansdom in Vienna. In 1760, he entered the service of the Esterházy family for thirty years, composing works which became famous throughout Europe. He laid down the laws of the string quartet, classical symphony and piano sonata. In 1790, he went to London then returned to Vienna where he wrote his two celebrated oratorios, *The Creation* (1798) and *The Seasons* (1801). He died in the imperial capital three weeks after Napoleon's occupation of Vienna.

Wolfgang Amadeus Mozart (1756-1791) – Born in Salzburg, he moved to Vienna in 1781 after a dispute with the archbishop of his native city where he was director of chapel music. In the capital, his relations with Josef II then Leopold II were not particularly good and his works did not often find a sympathetic audience. He brought every form of musical expression to perfection, owing to his exceptional fluency and ever-renewed inspiration. His dramatic genius developed in the school of the German *Singspiel* and the Italian *opera buffa* and flowered in masterpieces such as *The Marriage of Figaro*, *Don Giovanni*, *Cosi fan Tutte* or *The Magic Flute*. Despite his outstanding musical genius, he experienced severe poverty and died in relative obscurity, leaving his *Requiem* unfinished.

Ludwig van Beethoven (1770-1827) – Born in Bonn (Germany), he first visited Vienna in 1786 to become Mozart's pupil. Irresistibly attracted by the capital of music, he returned at the age of 20 and found a patron in Baron Gottfried van Swieten, curator of the Court Library, who invited him to perform before the Esterházys, Kinskys, Liechtensteins, Lobkowitzes and Schwarzenbergs. They all provided the young musician with their patronage. He wrote about Vienna that "nobody can love this country as I do". His

Wolfgang Amadeus Mozart

colleagues included Hummel, Cramer, Seyfried, Wranitzky and Eybler. Beethoven outstripped them all. He had a romantic conception of music which enabled him to compose works revolutionising musical expression. On the point of death, the composer of *Fidelio* and the *9th Symphony* said to his friend Hummel "Applaud, my friends, the comedy is over."

Franz Schubert (1797-1828) – The great composer was born and died in Vienna, a city which he seldom ever left. His contemporaries did not understand his work. He sang at the Hofkapelle (Royal Chapel), studied under Salieri then rediscovered and made famous the *lieder*. Even more than his symphonies, Masses, impromptus and chamber music, his *lieder* established him as the leading lyrical composer of the 19C. 1825 saw the appearance of Schubert evenings, when Schubert would sing *Lieder* to a small circle of friends and

Ludwig van Beethoven

Franz Schubert

religious music. His great symphonies reflect the influence of Beethoven and reach a high level of dramatic intensity. He died in Vienna and is buried at the foot of the great organ in St Florian Abbey in Upper Austria.

Johannes Brahms (1833-1897) – Born in Hamburg (Germany), he moved to Vienna in 1862 and lived there for the rest of his life. A director of the Singakademie then of the concerts of the Gesellschaft der Musikfreunde, he attained international fame. He composed a large body of work of a lyrical nature, striking a balance between Classicism and Romanticism: *Lieder*, piano quartets, symphonies and concertos. The first performance of his *Deutsches Requiem (German Requiem)* was given in the capital where he composed his four symphonies.

Hugo Wolf (1860-1903) – Born in Windischgrätz (Styria), he came to study at the Vienna Conservatory at the

which ended with a dance. Of a solitary, somewhat pessimistic temperament, the prince of *lieder* was happy and Bohemian in spirit, utterly lacking in Byronic melancholy. He died from an incurable venereal disease and did not have time to conquer the Viennese who favoured light music *(see also A prolific composer, Schubert-Museum)*.

Symphonic revival – The great Viennese composers defined the symphony as the greatest of all forms of music. However, it acquired new musical instruments and modified its syntax, without any loss of identity.

Anton Bruckner (1824-1896) – Born in Ansfleden (Upper Austria), this pious and modest man became director of music in Vienna in 1861 and organist of the imperial chapel in 1868. Compared to Johann Sebastian Bach for his talents of improvisation, he has the reputation of being the greatest 19C composer of

Anton Bruckner

age of 15. Apart from a few journeys, he never left the city. A tormented spirit, he had two creative phases. During the first (1878-1887), he tried his hand at every form of composition. During the second (1887-1897), he produced and published some magnificent *Lieder* based on poems by Goethe, Mörike and Eichendorff.

Gustav Mahler (1860-1911) – Born of a German-speaking Jewish family in Kalischt (Bohemia), this follower of Bruckner embarked in 1880 on a twofold career as conductor and composer after three years at the Vienna Conservatory. From 1897 to 1907, he conducted the orchestra of the Staatsoper. He died in Vienna from incurable heart disease. At a turning point between the Romantic and the modern era, he composed ten symphonies and five song cycles, his music being a mixture of idealism and realism. The "Adagietto" of his *5th Symphony* (1902) became famous after being used in Luchino Visconti's film *Death in Venice* (1971).

Gustav Mahler by Emil Orliek

Museum der Stadt: Wien

The "New School of Vienna" – Schönberg was at the centre of this movement which arose in 1903 and had a crucial influence on the development of 20C music; it affected many contemporary musicians, such as the Austrian Ernst Krenek and the Frenchman Pierre Boulez.

Born in Vienna, **Arnold Schönberg** (1874-1951) revolutionised traditional music by rejecting the tonal system of the past three centuries, which he assessed in his *Treatise on Harmony* dedicated to Mahler. In 1912, he gained some recognition with *Pierrot Lunaire*, a melodrama consisting of a 21-part cycle for narrator and five instruments. With his most important followers, **Anton von Webern** (1883-1945), born in Vienna, and **Alban Berg** (1885-1935), he developed a new method of atonal composition, founded on serialism. It was the theory of dodecaphonism or, in its more elaborate form, of serial music. Also born in Vienna, Alban Berg has been called a "mathematician-poet"; his opera *Wozzeck*, composed between 1917 and 1921, played a vital role in the history of 20C dramatic music.

LIPNITZKI-VIOLLET

Arnold Schönberg

THE WALTZ

Invitation to the waltz – The word waltz comes from the German *Walzer* derived from the High German *wellan* meaning "to turn". Of uncertain origin, it probably developed out of 16C and 17C country dances from South Germany. The oldest triple-time waltz is the slow waltz, or *Ländler,* which villagers danced at inns in the open air. This country dance underwent a change which was slight but sufficient to revolutionise it: in a 1782 treatise on choreography, the Viennese waltz first appeared in its modern form with gliding swinging steps. Now a more sprightly and intoxicating dance, it found admirers everywhere.

Its appeal to the greatest composers – The waltz played a vital role in Viennese history. The greatest composers wrote waltzes: Beethoven composed eleven. Other composers included Brahms, Chopin, Ravel, Schubert and Sibelius to name only a few. They wrote concert waltzes. Kings of the genre, the masters of the ballroom waltz were the Strauss family and Lanner *(see below)*. The success of this type of waltz was so great that it found acceptance at the Austrian Imperial Court.

Illustration : Michel Guillou

A Biedermeier lifestyle – To understand fully the phenomenon of the waltz In Vienna, one must bear in mind the political situation in the city at the beginning of the 19C (see *The Habsburg Empire, The End of Enlightenment*). Metternich's system was one of repression which depended for its enforcement on the constant supervision of the police under the command of his underling, Seldnitzky. Vienna was a city living in the shadow of implacable censorship both on the printed word and religious activity. A consequence of this was a physical and intellectual need amongst the inhabitants to live a life of pleasure. The moralists of the time, mostly foreigners, were quick to point out the unacceptable "intimacy" of couples performing this indecent dance which seemed to attract every age group. The Viennese found their comments amusing, since women enjoyed whirling in their partners' arms. Moreover, because the authorities had grasped its political advantages, the waltz reigned supreme.

The first balls – Very soon, the waltz lost its skipping steps and other characteristics of an 18C folk dance. The waltz of the *Vormärz* (period of Metternich's government) replaced it. This was a simpler, but more audacious dance: individual couples were free to lose themselves in the anonymity of a crowd. This development might have been due to an unconscious desire for a brief encounter. It certainly accounted for the success of the new dance halls. They were so popular and so crowded that it is impossible to envisage any formation dancing.

Balls were in vogue. Attracted by anything to do with pleasure, the French arrived in Vienna with an aura of Parisian prestige and luxury, to open dance halls where dancing became mass entertainment. In their thousands, Viennese danced at the *Clair de Lune, Nouveau Monde* or *L'Apollon*, dance halls sparkling with chandeliers lit even in daytime and, most importantly, laid with parquet floors on which couples could glide into ever more intimate swirling movements.

Josef Lanner (1801-1843) – He was born and died in Vienna. On the one hand, he was responsible for defining the acceleration and cadence of the Viennese waltz; on the other hand, he was the first to give titles to individual pieces of this music. At an early age, in 1819, he formed a trio with friends and played potpourris of fashionable tunes. It was a success. The trio became a quartet with the arrival of a young first violin aged 15, Johann Strauss, with whom Lanner soon quarrelled. Now a composer and conductor of his orchestra of 12 musicians, the latter could no longer meet the demands of the dance halls; this helped to launch his rival's newly created orchestra. In 1829, he became Court Musical Director.

He died of typhus while still young and left about 230 works, including *The Romantics*, waltz opus 141.

The Strauss family – Only the Habsburgs stamped their name so indelibly on the history of the capital of the Austro-Hungarian Empire. The name of the Strauss dynasty evokes the enchantment of the waltz, the lighter side of 19C Vienna.

Johann Strauss the Elder (1804-1849) was born and died in Vienna. There he started out as a member of Lanner's orchestra (see above), sharing with him the privilege of raising the waltz to a music form in a class of its own. Very rapidly, he created his own orchesta, playing in various dance halls. Without ever learning the rules of composition – a feature he shared with Lanner – he composed and used rhythmic variations to lend new lustre to his orchestra of 28 musicians. Vienna fell under his spell, as did Berlin, London and Paris where people admired this brilliant violinist who drew inspiration from gypsy music. In 1830, he managed 200 musicians, whom he divided up into various orchestras to meet demand. He played at the *Sperl*, Lanner at the *Redoute*. When the latter died, Strauss had not yet written his famous *Radetzky March* (1848), and felt himself to be the one and only "Waltz King".

This sentiment was short-lived, since **Johann Strauss the Younger** (1825-1899) soon demonstrated that this title belonged to him (see *The Stormy Early Career of Johann Strauss the Younger, Hietzing*). After his father died from scarlet fever, leaving some 250 waltzes, he amalgamated the two orchestras and went on a series of tours as far as the United States. Under his direction, the waltz acquired more contrasting themes. From 1863, when he became Director of Court balls, he wrote some of his immortal works, such as *The Blue Danube* (1867), *Tales of the Vienna Woods* (1868), the operetta *Die Fledermaus* (1874) and the *Emperor Waltz* (1888).

He appointed his brother **Josef Strauss** (1827-1870) as head of the orchestra. An engineer by training, he was a shy man who was surprised by his own popularity and composed over 300 waltzes, including *Austrian Swallow*.

AKG Paris

Johann Strauss the Elder

ROGER-VIOLLET

Johann Strauss the Younger

SELECTED DISCOGRAPHY

This selection includes most of the works featuring in this guide.

Ludwig van Beethoven – *Fidelio*, Otto Klemperer, Philharmonia Orchestra and Chorus, EMI. *Symphony No 3 "Eroica"*, Herbert von Karajan, Berlin Philharmonic Orchestra, Deutsche Grammophon. *Symphony No. 6* or *"Pastoral Symphony"*, Bruno Walter, Columbia Symphony Orchestra, Sony. *Symphony No 9 "with choir"*, Karl Böhm, Vienna Philharmonic Orchestra, Deutsche Grammophon.

Alban Berg – *Wozzeck*, Pierre Boulez, Paris National Opera Choir and Orchestra, Sony.

Johannes Brahms – *Quartet for Piano and Strings Opus 26*, Sviatoslav Richter, Borodin Quartet, Philips. *A German Requiem (Ein Deutsches Requiem)*, Herbert von Karajan, Berlin Philharmonic Orchestra, Deutsche Grammophon.

Anton Bruckner – *Mass in E Minor*, Philippe Herreweghe, The Royal Chapel, Harmonia Mundi. *Symphony No 5*, Wilhelm Furtwängler, Vienna Philharmonic Orchestra, EMI.

Christoph Willibald von Gluck – *Orpheus and Eurydice*, Georg Solti, Covent Garden Royal Opera Choir and Orchestra, Decca.

Joseph Haydn – *The Creation*, Igor Markevitch, Berlin Philharmonic Orchestra, Deutsche Grammophon. *The Seasons*, Walter Goehr, Norddeutsche Rundfunk Choir and Orchestra, Via Classique.

Gustav Mahler – *Das Lied von der Erde*, Bruno Walter, Kathleen Ferrier, Julius Patzak, Vienna Philharmonic Orchestra, Decca. *Symphony No 5*, Neeme Järvi, Scottish National Orchestra, Chandos.

Wolfgang Amadeus Mozart – *The Abduction from the Seraglio (Die Entführung aus dem Seraglio)*, Sir Thomas Beecham, Royal Philharmonic Orchestra, EMI. *The Magic Flute (Die Zauberflöte)*, Arnold Östman, Orchestra of the Drottningholm Court Theatre, L'Oiseau Lyre. *The Marriage of Figaro (Nozze di Figaro)*, Herbert von Karajan, Vienna Philharmonic Orchestra, Deutsche Grammophon.

Arnold Schönberg – *Pierrot Lunaire*, Pierre Boulez, "Domaine Musical" Orchestra, Adès.

Franz Schubert – *Lieder*, Gundula Janowitz, Irwin Gage, Ulf Rodenhäuser, Deutsche Grammophon. *Lieder on Poems by Goethe*, Christoph Pregardien, Andreas Staier, Deutsche Harmonia Mundi. *"Unfinished" Symphony No 8*, Josef Krips, Vienna Symphonic Orchestra, Orféo.

Johann Strauss the Elder and Johann Strauss the Younger – *The Strauss Family in Vienna*, Willi Boskovsky, Vienna Johann Strauss Orchestra, EMI. *The Blue Danube, The Emperor Waltz, Waltzes*, Lorin Maazel, Vienna Philharmonic Orchestra, Deutsche Grammophon. *Die Fledermaus*, Herbert von Karajan, Vienna Philharmonic Orchestra, Decca.

Hugo Wolf – *Lieder*, Elisabeth Schwarzkopf, Wilhelm Furtwängler, Fonit Cetra.

Miscellaneous – *Boxed set for the 150th anniversary of the Vienna Philharmonic*, various conductors, Deutsche Grammophon. *New Year's Concert 97*, Riccardo Muti, Vienna Philharmonic Orchestra, EMI. *Viennese Waltzes* (Lehar, Kalman, Dohnanyi, etc.), Antal Dorati, Minneapolis Symphony Orchestra, Philharmonia Hungarica, Mercury Living Presence.

Information in this Guide is based on data provided at the time of going to press; improved facilities and changes in the cost of living make subsequent alterations inevitable.

Viennese literature

Authors in this section are those who have a connection with Vienna either through birth or by living there. This is why writers such as Leopold von Sacher-Masoch, Rainer Maria Rilke or Leo Perutz do not feature here.

The 19C – In the early 19C, the German Romantic movement heralded the dawn of Austrian literature.

A poet, **Franz Grillparzer** (1791-1872) is probably Austria's greatest playwright. Withdrawing into himself in response to the sordid Metternich censorship, he produced works showing the influence of Goethe and Schiller. He is the author of several Neoclassical dramas, such as *The Golden Fleece (Das Goldenes Vlies*, 1828), *The Waves of the Sea and of Love (Des Meeres und der Liebe Wellen*, 1831), and his masterpiece *Sappho (Sapho*, 1818). Among his tragedies, *King Ottokar's Prosperity and Demise (König Ottokars Glück und Ende*, 1823) is the only one to have been staged. Born in Hungary but brought up in Vienna, **Nikolaus Lenau** (1802-1850) depicted tortured characters, as in his lyrical poem *Don Juan*. His most profound work is *The Albigensians (Die Albigenser*, 1842). A native of Bohemia, **Adalbert Stifter** (1805-1868) came to study at Vienna University. Nietzsche and Hoffmannsthal considered him a master of German prose. He wrote novellas and novels reflecting his distress at the political difficulties of the *Vormärz*. A great admirer of Grillparzer, he became a writer relatively late in life and published, amongst others, *Multicoloured Stones (Bunte Steine*, 1852), *Indian Summer (Der Nachsommer*, 1857), and *My Great-Grandfather's Notebooks (Die Mappe meines Urgrossvaters)*. He was found dead, his throat slashed by a razor.

Although he was neither a dramatist nor a novelist, one cannot overlook **Sigmund Freud** (1856-1939), the founder of psychoanalysis, which grew out of his experiences in treating perversions, analysing neuroses and studying the subconscious. He explained the theory underlying this science in his fundamental work, *The Interpretation of Dreams, (Die Traumdeutung*, 1900) which appeared in English in 1909. Other works include *Totem and Taboo* and *The Man Moses and the Monotheistic Religion*.

The turn of the century – Because he gently portrayed the decadence of Viennese society, **Arthur Schnitzler** (1862-1931) has the reputation of being superficial. This is not the case. Revealing the influence of psychoanalysis, the works of this doctor delve into the subconscious of his protagonists who are often wrestling with erotic scepticism as in *Anatol* (1893), *Flirtation (Liebelei*, 1895), *Merry Go Round (Reigen*, 1900) and *Miss Else (Fräulein Else*, 1924). **Hugo von Hofmannsthal** (1874-1929) belongs to an entirely different category. His talent, evident from an early age, displays both pathos and irony. He excelled in lyric poetry, then in metaphysical drama very different from the folk theatre of 19C Austria. A friend of Richard Strauss, he wrote the libretto for many of his operas, such as *Der Rosenkavalier* (1911). His major works include *Death and The Fool (Der Tor und der Tod*, 1893), *Jederman* (1911) and *The Salzburg Great Theatre of the World (Das Salzburger grosse Welttheater*, 1922).

Hugo von Hofmannsthal

ROGER-VIOLLET

The 20C – In his first novel *The Confusions of Young Törless (Die Verwirrungen des Zöglings Törless*, 1906), **Robert Musil** (1880-1942) depicted the martyrdom of a young boy at a military academy. This won him great renown and heralded the start of a literary career which he had embarked upon out of boredom with his profession as an engineer. Born in Klagenfurt (Carinthia), he moved to Vienna in 1910 and lived there from his meagre earnings until his death in Geneva after going into exile in 1938. An unfinished novel which remained totally unknown in his lifetime, *The Man without Qualities (Der Mann ohne Eigenschaften*, 1930) epitomises the essence of his work. A man of acute psychological insight, **Stefan Zweig** (1881-1942) was a doctor of philosophy and a great traveller. He tried his hand at every genre, using the language of the 19C. He first became famous with his novellas, depicting mainly the irruption of violent passion into middle class lives, such as *Confusion of Feelings (Verwirrung der Gefühle*, 1927). A novelist, he wrote brilliant literary monographs, where under Freud's influence he analysed the inner motivation of human beings: *Fouché, Erasmus, Marie Antoinette*, etc. **Hermann Broch** (1886-1951) is a writer difficult to get to grips with who described the end of the Empire as a "joyous apocalypse", observed the deterioration of traditional values, as in his trilogy *The Sleepwalkers (Die Schlafwandler*, 1932), but believed in a new system. He is undeniably one of the 20C's greatest German-language novelists. His masterpiece is *The Death of Virgil (Der Tod des Virgil*, 1945). Born at Prague of Jewish parents, **Franz Werfel** (1890-1945) was attracted to Christianity and belonged to the Expressionist movement. Liberal pacifism permeates his poetry, such as *Friend of the World (Der Weltfreund*, 1911), his plays and novels, like *The Victim Not the Assassin is Guilty (Nicht der Mörder, der Ermordete ist Schuldig, 1920)*. Born in Brody (Galicia), **Josef Roth** (1894-1939) studied philosophy in Vienna before becoming a journalist and emigrating to Paris in 1933. His thirteen novels include the *Radetzky March (Radetzkymarsch*, 1932), which describes the defunct Austrian empire in the days of Franz-Josef, and the *Capuchin Crypt (Die Kapuzinergruft*,

Stefan Zweig

1938) depicting characters who are the victims of their fate. **Heimito von Doderer** (1896-1966) is the most Viennese writer of them all and perhaps the most brilliant. As soon as Hitler proclaimed the *Anschluss*, he created works opposed to any ideology; his most famous novel *Die Strudlhofstiege oder Melzer und die Tiefe der Jahre* (1951) has not yet been translated into English. Of Hungarian, Croat, Czech and German descent, **Ödön von Horváth** (1901-1938) is the only one of these writers to avoid constantly questioning man's role and society's values. This citizen of the Austro-Hungarian Empire without a country lived in Vienna before settling in Berlin. He was killed accidentally in Paris at the age of 37 and left work of astonishing lucidity, such as *The Italian Night (Italienische Nacht*, 1931) and *Tales of the Vienna Woods (Geschichten aus des Wiener Wald)*. A novelist and dramatist of Bulgarian origin, **Elias Canetti** (1905-1994) lived for a long time in Vienna before emigrating to England. A symbolist work, his *Comedy of Vanity (Komödie der Eitelkeiten*, 1934) is a precise description of mass hysteria; the author became world-famous when he received the Nobel prize in 1981. Born in Vienna, but living in Germany, **Ilse Aichinger** (1921) produced work expressing human anguish and solitude, first with *Greater Hope (Die grössere Hoffnung*, 1948) then with *The Chained Man (Der Gefesselte*, 1953), published one year earlier in Austria under the title of *Speech Beneath the Gallows (Rede unter dem Galgen)*. Born in Klagenfurt, **Ingeborg Bachmann** (1926-1973) studied in Vienna and left two collections of lyrical poems close in style to Hoffmansthal: *Time in Remission* (1953) and *Invocation to the Great Bear* (1956); she shares the despair of Handke and Bernhard. Born in the Netherlands in conditions which left him with problems of identity, **Thomas Bernhard** (1931-1989) first gained recognition as a lyrical poet, but he became famous for his novels and plays which were full of realism and pessimism about human nature. From *Frost* (1963) to *Extinction* (1986), the novels of this great writer pushed German syntax to its furthest limits, in a way reminding some of serial music. A filmmaker, **Peter Handke** (1942) ranks as one of the most outstanding Austrian writers. His avant-garde work conveys the anguish of solitude and lack of communication through novels such as *The Goalkeeper's Fear of the Penalty* and plays like *Ride across Lake Constance*. There is also **Elfriede Jelinek** (1946) whose novel *The Pianist* (1983) created a considerable stir.

The cinema

Austria, and Vienna in particular, is the homeland of great film directors. However, few of them worked for their native country. Born in Vienna, **Erich von Stroheim** (1885-1957) deserted from the army, left for the United States in 1914 and became an American citizen. The creator of a masterpiece, *Greed* (1923), he was also a brilliant actor, with a career both in France and Hollywood. Born in Bohemia, **Georg Wilhelm Pabst** (1890-1976) directed in Vienna, in 1920, the Neue Wiener Bühne theatre company before making his first film, *Der Schatz* (1923). He then left for Germany where he made 19 films, including *Lulu* (1928) with Louise Brooks. Born in Vienna, **Fritz Lang** (1890-1976) started his career as a director in 1919 before leaving in 1933 for the United States, where he acquired US citizenship. He made about 50 films, including *Doctor Mabuse* (1922), *Metropolis* (1926), *M the Accursed* (1931) and *House by the River* (1949). Born in Vienna, **Josef von Sternberg** (1894-1969), who discovered Marlene Dietrich, was the creator of *The Blue Angel* (1930), *Shanghai Express* (1932) and *The Devil is a Woman* (1935). He died in Hollywood at the end of a versatile career. **Peter Handke** was joint scriptwriter in Wim Wender's German films and adapted for the screen his novel *The Left-handed Woman*. Other contemporary filmmakers include **Niki List** *(Müllers Büro)*, **Michael Synek** *(Dead Fish)* who has recently moved to Paris, **Wolfram Paulus** *(Holes in the Moors)* and **Xaver Schwarzenberger**.

Only a few Austrian productions have achieved renown outside their own country, such as the *Sissi* film series (1955-1957) directed by **Ernst Marischka** (1893-1963) which launched the international career of Romy Schneider (born in Vienna). The Vienna trilogy directed by **Axel Corti** (1933-1994), consists of *God No Longer Believes in Us* (1981), *Santa Fe* (1985) and *Welcome in Vienna* (1986).

FILMS ABOUT VIENNA

The Third Man (1949), Carol Reed.
Der Kongress Tänzt (*The Congress is Dancing*, 1931), Jean Boyer.
The Radetzky March (1996), Axel Corti.
Rollercoaster (1977), J. Goldstone.
Purgatory (1988), Wilhelm Hengstler.
Sissi film series (1955/57), Ernst Marischka
Welcome in Vienna (1986), Axel Corti.

Orson Welles in *The Third Man*

Bibliography

GENERAL

Bérenger, Jean *History of the Habsburg Empire, 1273-1918*, London, 1994.

Brion, Marcel *La Vie quotidienne à Vienne à l'époque de Mozart et de Schubert*, Paris, 1965 (English translation not available).

Cars, Jean des *Élisabeth d'Autriche ou la fatalité*, Paris, 1983 (English translation not available).

Clair, Jean *Vienne 1880-1938, L'Apocalypse joyeuse*, Paris, 1986 (English translation not available).

Coster, Léon de et Nizet, François *16 Promenades dans Vienne*, Tournai, 1992 (English translation not available).

Johnston, W.H. *Vienne The Golden Age, 1815-1914*, New York, 1981.

La Grange, Henry-Louis de *Vienne, histoire musicale, 1800-1848*, Paris, 1990 (English translation not available).

Lander, X.Y. *Vienne* Paris, 1989 (English translation not available).

Mallinus, Daniel, *Vienne* Brussels, 1985 (English translation not available).

Schorske, C.E. *Fin-de-Siècle Vienna, Politics and Culture*, London, 1980.

Schweiger, Werner J. *Wiener Werkstätte: Design in Vienna*, London, 1990.

Tasnadi-Marik, Klara *Vienna Porcelain*, Budapest, 1971 (English translation not available).

Waissenberger, Robert *Vienna Secession*, London, 1977.

SELECTED LITERATURE

Bernhard, Thomas *Old Masters*, London, 1989.

Broch, Hermann *The Sleepwalkers*, London, 1996.

Canetti, Elias *The Tongue Set Free, Remembrance of a European Childhood*, London, 1988.

Doderer, Heimito von *The Demons*, London, 1989.

Handke, Peter *Plays*, London, 1997.

Hofmannsthal, Hugo von *Selected Plays and Libretti*, Princeton University Press, 1997.

Horvárth, Ödön von *Jugend ohne Gott*, London, 1997.

Kokoschka, Oskar *My Life*, New York, 1974.

Lernet-Holenia, Alexander *Le Régiment des Deux-Siciles*, Paris, 1953 (English translation not available).

Musil, Robert *The Man without Qualities*, London, 1996.

Perutz, Leo *Le Tour du Cadran*, Paris, 1988 (English translation not available).

Rostand, Edmond *L'Aiglon*, Paris, 1900 (English translation not available).

Roth, Josef *The Radetzky March*, London, 1996.

Schnitzler, Arthur *My Youth in Vienna*, London, 1970.

Stifter, Adalbert *L'Homme sans Posterité*, Paris, 1978 (English translation not available).

Werfel, Franz *Cella ou les Vainqueurs*, Paris, 1987 (English translation not available).

Zweig, Stefan *The World of Yesterday*, London, 1943.

Exploring Vienna

SUBDIVISION OF THE CITY

The city centre covers the 1st district, namely Innere Stadt, around which lie the Ring and Franz-Josefs-Kai which is part of it. To simplify the use of this guide during visits, the city centre has been divided into areas bearing the names of the best-known or most important sights, names already familiar to visitors or famous in the city's history. Often, they are the same. This subdivision of the city is artificial, but it has the advantage of concentrating sightseeing tours in one zone and making it easy to move from one area to another.

Sights beyond the Ring form part of Greater Vienna; they lie in the 22 districts around the Ring and Gürtel. To assist the reader, the boundaries of these districts have been retained and, with a few exceptions, their actual names serve as landmarks. These exceptions are the Belvedere, Grinzing, Karlsplatz, Prater and Schönbrunn, since the names of these sites are more famous than those of the districts in which they lie. The outskirts of Vienna extend as far as Mayerling and Wiener Neustadt, via the roads in the Vienna Woods; they reach as far as the Slovak and Hungarian frontiers and beyond into Bratislava and Sopron. The coverage of this guide stretches further east for two reasons: on the one hand, because until the Treaty of St-Germain-en-Laye, Viennese history did not take account of the present eastern frontiers of Austria, and on the other hand, because geographically, Vienna belongs to the Danube plain.

SIGHTSEEING PROGRAMMES

There is much to see in Vienna. For a first visit, it is preferable to decide on a touring programme based on the time available and one's field of interests. It is also possible to follow some of the (comprehensive) suggestions below. It is a good idea to end the tour with a visit to one of the capital's cafés for some excellent coffee, local white wine or one of the numerous Viennese cakes and pastries.

A few hours in Vienna

Stephansdom★★★ (St Stephen' Cathedral) – **Graben★** – Kohlmarkt – **Hofburg★★★** (Palace): exterior – Heldenplatz – **Ring★★**: from Rathaus (Town Hall) to Staatsoper (State Opera House) – **Kunsthistorisches Museum★★★ (Art Gallery)**.

A day in Vienna

Stephansdom★★★ – **Graben★** – Kohlmarkt – **Hofburg★★★**: exterior and **Schatzkammer★★★ (Treasury)** – Heldenplatz – **Ring★★**: from Rathaus to Staatsoper – **Kunsthistorisches Museum★★★** – **Karlskirche★★ (St Charles' Borromeo Church)** – **Secessiongebäude★★ (Secession Building)** – **Schönbrunn★★★ (Palace)**.

Three days in Vienna

Day One – **Stephansdom★★★** – **Around Stephansdom★★** – **Staatsoper★★** – **Secessiongebäude★★** – **Karlskirche★★** – **Oberes Belvedere★★ (Upper Belvedere)** – and its museum – the **Riesenrad★★ (Giant Ferris Wheel)** on the Prater at night.

Day Two – **Hofburg★★★**: exterior and **Schatzkammer★★★** and (if possible) **Spanische Reitschule★★ (Spanish Riding School)** or **Sammlung alter Musikinstrumente★★ (Collection of Old Musical Instruments)** – **Kunsthistorisches Museum★★★** – walk along the **Ring★★** in the evening.

Day Three – **Kaisergruft★★ (Imperial Crypt)** – **Schönbrunn★★★** and its park – walk in **Grinzing** with an excursion up to **Leopoldsberg★★** (weather permitting) – return to the centre for a stroll along Freyung, Michaelerplatz, **Graben★**, Kärntnerstrasse and another view of the cathedral by night.

On the town

57

Quick transport links in Vienna

WIENER LINIEN

U1 — Underground line
S1 — City and suburban railway line
⚡ — Local railway, Vienna - Baden
🚌 — Bus station
P&R — Park and Ride
— Wiener Linien - Customer Service Centre
— Wiener Linien Information Office

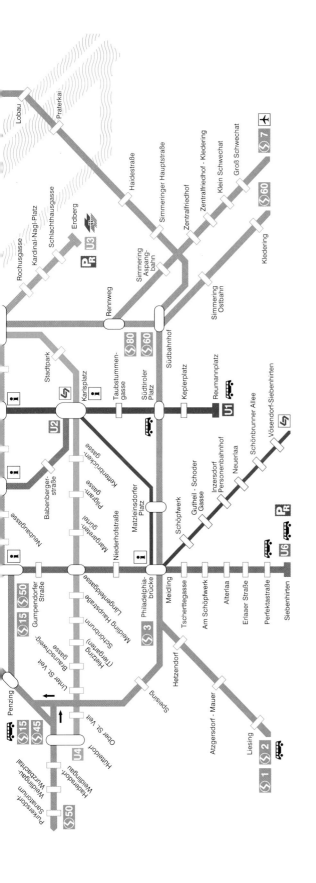

Vienna is famous as a city of culture with monumental architecture, which it is. Yet it also has the reputation of being an elitist city, somewhat cold and disdainful, harking back to its past as capital of a vanished empire, lacking close involvement with the modern world. There is some truth in this, but appearances are deceptive.

There is much more to Vienna than this collecion of clichés. It has a hidden charm, which it does not disclose at first sight. Beyond the barrier of traditions enfolding the Austrian capital lies a generous city, carefree at times and always seductive. There is no exact translation for *Gemütlichkeit*, a quality of which the Austrians are so proud that they often feel irritation at a foreigner's image of it. Indeed, this art of living is probably untranslatable, because to understand it, one must be Viennese not by adoption but by birth. However, it is pleasant to explore this city, which defies curiosity and stirs the emotions. Of it Stefan Zweig wrote: "It would be hard to find another European city where the desire for culture was more passionate than in Vienna." Passion is the right word to apply to this ageless city set between two worlds.

GETTING AROUND IN VIENNA

By car

It is inadvisable to drive in Vienna, not because there are more traffic jams there than in any other European city, but because public transport is excellent. For those who prefer going by car, there is a speed limit of 50km/30 miles per hour in built-up areas. One must pay for parking in Vienna, either at parking meters or by buying parking coupons from petrol stations or banks (these coupons must be placed in a conspicuous position behind the windscreen). In the city centre, there are several car parks, which are usually full.

Taxis – These are available by telephoning or from taxi ranks. Taxis rarely stop to pick up passengers in the street. Numbers for radio-taxis are 31300, 40100, 60160 or 81140; the operator will state the length of waiting time. Whereas trips in town are relatively inexpensive, jouneys between the city and the airport are very costly (about 450 ATS); it is customary to round up the sum in multiples of 5 or 10 ATS or more. In the taxi, the meter shows the price of the ride on the left and, on the right, any extra charge (week-end or night-time).

However, a car is the best way of making the excursions around Vienna described in this guide, partlcularly Wlenerwald (Vienna Woods) or Neusiedler Lake. *Radio Blue Danube* (102.5 Mhz) broadcasts bulletins on traffic conditions, and all information is available from the Austrian Automobile Club: **Österreichischer Automobil-Motorrad- und Touringclub** (O.A.M.T.C.), Schubertring 1 and 3, 1st district; ☏ 72 990.

Car Hire – The major car-hire firms have offices on the Ring or at airports. **Avis**: Opernring 3-5, 1st district. ☏ 587 62 41. **Europcar:** Kärntnerring 14, 1st district, ☏ 799 61 76. **Hertz**: Kärntnerring 17, 1st district, ☏ 711 10 26 61.

By underground, tram, bus or train

Vienna has an excellent public transport system. Travelling is quick and easy, either from the city centre to the outskirts or from one district to another. The underground, trams and buses operate from 5.30am to midnight.

Tickets – A **single ticket** costs 17 ATS. Once it has been stamped in a machine, it is valid for all types of public transport in Vienna (zone 100) and also for all changes, provided that one does not break one's journey. There are several types of passes. Flat rate **"24-hour"** and **"72-hour"** passes are valid from the time they are stamped and cost 50 ATS and 130 ATS respectively. They cover zone 100 but are not valid for night-time services. The **"8-day"** pass costing 265 ATS is excellent value for visitors staying a fairly long time in Vienna, because it is valid for eight 24-hour days; several people may use it, not necessarily on successive days (stamp one strip per person per day in the ticket machine); it is valid on all public transport (zone 100), except for night buses. For longer stays in Vienna, it is possible to buy a season ticket. **"Wien-Karte"** is a fixed price 72-hour pass costing 180 ATS offering entry at a reduced tariff to many museums as well as other benefits *(see Practical information)*; it should be stamped in the machine the first time of use. With the exception of the latter, tickets are available from the machines at all underground stations. Ticket offices are open Monday to Friday, from 6.30am to 6.30pm, at the following stations: Hietzing, Kagran, Karlsplatz, Landstrasse, Reumannplatz, Schottentor, Schwedenplatz, Stephansplatz, Westbahnhof.

Public transport is **free** for children under six. People under 15 may travel free on Sundays and public holidays, and when the schools are closed in the Vienna educational district.

Travelling without a ticket incurs a fine of 520 ATS.

The underground – The underground symbol is a capital U, white on a blue ground. The *U-Bahn* system consists of 5 lines covering the whole of the city *(see plan of the underground system)*. The 5 lines are colour coded: U1, red; U2, mauve; U3, orange; U4, green; U6, brown (the U5 line is still in the planning stage). There are electronic display panels on the platforms, with the name of the terminus. Locate it on the underground map in order to avoid travelling in the wrong direction. A loudspeaker system in the train calls out the stations. The underground is the best means of transport and it offers rapid train connections.

The tramway – The *Strassenbahn* (Viennese trams) are red and white, the city's colours. The carriages look somewhat old-fashioned and they have wooden seats, but the system works with an efficiency which many cities with ultramodern trams might envy. In the street, the stops have oval white

Two ways of getting around

panels outlined in red, bearing the words "Strassenbahn-Haltestelle". Inside, a loudspeaker system calls out the names of the stops. To enter or alight from the tram, press the button near the doors.

Bus – Also red and white, buses cover the city in a transverse direction, compared to tram routes. The stops have white semicircular panels outlined in black, bearing the words "Autobus – Haltestelle". Inside the bus, loudspeakers call out the names of the stops. To enter or alight from the bus, press the button near the doors. Buses are particularly convenient for travelling to outlying districts.

Train – There is a Schnellbahn and Bundesbahn service to and from several stations in Vienna and the surrounding region. A visitor to Vienna would mainly use the Schnellbahn (blue logo) from which there are numerous connections to the underground, tram or bus. Tickets for these means of transport are also are valid for the Schnellbahn, but only in zone 100.

Night-Line – 22 night lines operate from 0.30am to 4am. It is a bus system, running every 30 minutes and displaying an N for Nachtbus or Nachtline. Lists of these lines and their routes are available at the stations mentioned above with regard to tickets. A single ticket is slightly more expensive, at 25 ATS.

On foot, by bicycle or by horse-drawn carriage

In the town centre, walking is the best means of getting around. It is the only way to appreciate Vienna's historical centre fully. Many streets in the Innere Stadt are pedestrian precincts or relatively free of cars. However, beyond the 1st district, one must take extra care, for two reasons. On the one hand, there is a tram line on the Ring running in the opposite direction to the cars, which could cause problems if you are not careful when alighting from the tram; on the other hand, Austrian drivers do not pay the same attention to pedestrian crossings as Swiss drivers. However, it would be a major undertaking to explore on foot all the sights of this vast city.

Cycling is therefore an excellent mode of transport in this city which has plenty of cycle tracks, particularly all along the Ring (7km/4 miles of cycle track). Keen cyclists would do well to acquire the publication *Radwege* which describes every itinerary and is available from bookshops. Major stations have bicycle hire offices (you will be asked for means of identity).

A horse-drawn carriage is a delightful way of exploring the 1st district. The fee for this excursion may be as high as 1,000 ATS, so it is more advantageous to travel as a group. In any case, one should agree on a price before the ride. Coachmen are easily identifiable, since they wear a bowler hat. Stops for horse-drawn carriages are fairly mobile, but there are always some in Albertinaplatz, Heldenplatz, Petersplatz and Stephansplatz.

THE VIENNESE SKYLINE

Except for the first slopes of the Wienerwald (Vienna Woods) west of the city, Vienna's topography is scarcely hilly. No skyscraper dominates the Habsburg capital; there are no high-rise flats either. However, there are fine views of the whole city.

The cathedral towers *(see Stephansdom)* lie strategically at the heart of historic Vienna. One of the towers rises 137m/449ft above the cobblestones of Stephansplatz, with a room accessible at 73m/239ft; the other tower has a platform at a height of 60m/196ft.

The Giant Wheel in the Prater *(see Riesenrad)* raises its cabins to a height of about 65m/213ft above the merry-go-rounds and trees in this huge amusement park. There is a view of the east side of the city.

The Danube tower *(see Donauturm)* rises 252m/826ft in the centre of the Danube park, with a panoramic terrace at a height of 165m/541ft. It affords a sensational view.

Kahlenberg and Leopoldsberg *(see under these headings)* are elevated sites north of the city, on the northern edge of the Vienna Woods. The first rises to an altitude of 483m/1,584ft, and the second to 423m/1,387ft. Pollution or mist sometimes impede the view but this is an interesting angle from which to see the city, weather permitting.

Donauturm and UNO-City

The square in front of the church of the Steinhof psychiatric hospital *(see Kirche am Steinhof)* is an unusual site which offers views of the whole of the west side of Vienna and in particular Schloss Schönbrunn.

View from Lainzer Tiergarten *(see under this heading)* provides an unusual view of this church, and the Kahlenberg and Leopoldsberg heights.

PARKS AND GARDENS

The Austrian capital possesses many parks: there are 25 m²/29 sq yds of green spaces open to the public per inhabitant, compared to 1 m²/1 sq yd in Paris and 13 m²/15 sq yds in Berlin. They are all easily accessible from the city centre. Most of those mentioned below feature in the list of sights. This selection aims to satisfy any desire for a stroll.

1st district (Innere Stadt) – There is a succession of public parks along the Ring: **Rathauspark, Volksgarten, Burggarten, Stadtpark.** All are havens of peace between museum visits. Museum enthusiasts may enjoy studying their fine statues.

2nd district (Leopoldstadt) – The **Prater** and **Augarten** park are now major tourist attractions, for very different reasons.

3rd district (Landstrasse) – The **Belvedere** gardens suggest another age. The site is truly superb.

4th district (Wieden) – Resselpark on Karlplatz is tiny, but it enjoys an ideal situation between Karlskirche and Otto Wagner's underground stations.

13th district (Hietzing) – **Schönbrunn Park** is magnificent, undeniably Vienna's finest park. Full of historical associations, it offers a variety of sights. Keen walkers and nature lovers will enjoy visiting **Lainzer Tiergarten**, Maria-Theresa's former hunting ground in the Vienna Woods.

18th district (Währing) – **Schubertpark** and in particular **Türkenschanzpark** attract walkers in an old district which is now very residential. Northwest of the city on the edge of the Wienerwald, **Pötzleinsdorferpark** will be a children's paradise, because it has several play areas.

22nd district (Donaustadt) – **Donaupark** is huge and is identifiable by the Danube tower. It is very busy in summer because it lies on the edge of the Danube, as is **Donauinsel** which teems with joggers and cyclists in fine weather. Further east, **Lobau** is a vast stretch of relatively unspoilt land where many Viennese come to swim and cycle.

The "Wiener Heurige"

A secular tradition which Emperor Josef II popularised but dating from the 13C, the Viennese *Heuriger* is a strange institution, typically Viennese like the Stephansdom tower, the Giant Wheel of the Prater or the Vienna Boys' Choir *(Wiener Sängerknaben)*. The *Heuriger* is a kind of tavern-restaurant, old-fashioned and rustic, supplying new wine, namely this year's young wine. A true *Heuriger* offers only its own wine from its own vineyards which often lie behind the building. It is, in any case, subject to regulations covering even the time of opening.

As well as red or white wine, there is also newly pressed grape or apple juice, mineral water and lemonade. One should not ask for Coca-Cola, beer, coffee or any other drink. The waitress would almost certainly point out somewhat mockingly that this was a real *Heuriger*... One should order *"ein Viertel Weiss"* (a quarter litre of white wine), *"ein Gespritztes"* (a jug of wine with sparkling mineral water) or even *"ein Apfelsaft"* (an apple juice). The waitress in traditional dress will bring the order with a smile. It is usual to leave a tip (about 15%), as in all other restaurants in Austria. In a *Heuriger*, it is possible to eat. However, the meal is not served at table, but at a buffet where customers help themselves to cold or hot dishes. Each *Heuriger* has its own specialities, which always include various salads with lettuce, sweet corn, tomatoes and other vegetables such as cabbage; there will be cheese, *Brotaufstrich* (a slice of bread spread with spicy fromage frais), sausages and several kinds of cold and cooked meats (poultry, pork, veal). For dessert, there is a choice between *Apfelstrudel* (apple pastry slice) and *Topfenstrudel* (a cheesecake), always in generous portions. Eating and drinking in a *Heuriger* is pleasant, but one should not overlook the comfortable, friendly ambiance. The happiness on people's faces is not as naïve as a tourist might suppose; the typical *Schrammelmusik* of the *Heuriger* serves to remind everyone of the ephemeral side of life. A typical *Schrammel* ensemble consists of two violins, an accordeon – or a clarinet – and a guitar, but a violin and an accordeon alone are sufficient to create a purely Viennese atmosphere.

Where to go?

There are many *Heuriger* in the whole of Vienna, but not all are authentic. Urbanisation and tourism have somewhat distorted the name despite the rigourous selection, since not all establishments claiming to be *Heurigers* have cultivated the traditions associated with Viennese local wine.

A "false" *Heuriger* is easily recognized while a true one is less blatant. In any case, regulations state strictly that a leafy bough must hang over the entrance, and that the inscription "Ausg'steckt" appear on the façade.

Grinzing (19th district) – *Tram: Grinzing (38) from Schottentor station on the Ring. The last tram for Schottentor is at 11.48pm (as far as the Ring) and at 0.33am (as far as Gürtel). Nightline Bus N3 (Fridays, Saturdays, Sundays and holidays) connects Grinzing to Schottenring and Schwedenplatz, from 0.58am to 4.28am.* Grinzing is Vienna's most famous *Heuriger* district and attracts many tourists. Over twenty establishments lie along Cobenzlgasse and Sandgasse. Together with other restaurants, they

The terrace of a *Heuriger*

63

form almost a gastronomical centre. It is advisable to arrive in the district late in the afternoon, make a short exploratory tour then choose a table in one of these picturesque "houses", in the garden if it is fine.

– *Bach-Hengl*, Sandgasse 7-9, 1190 Wien. ☎ 32 30 84 or 32 24 39. Open daily from 4pm. Very spacious, large garden. There is a wide variety of wines and the buffet has a vast assortment of dishes. Live music.

– *Henl-Haselbrunner*, Iglaseegasse 10, 1190 Wien. ☎ 32 33 30 or 32 13 15. The same features as above, but without music.

– *Maly*, Sandgasse 8, 1190 Wien. ☎ 32 13 84. Open daily from March to the end of October, from 3.30pm to midnight. Bright and spacious, it offers a garden and musical entertainment. The atmosphere is very pleasant.

Other *Heurigers* in Grinzing open only during a set period. Names and addresses of establishments which are open are displayed on a board between Cobenzlgasse and Himmelstrasse, near the tram 38 terminus.

Nussdorf (19th district) – *Train: Südbahnhof-Nussdorf (S40) from Franz-Josefs-Bahnhof then tram (D) as far as Beethovengang. The last tram for Südbahnhof is at 11.46pm.*

– *Schübel-Auer*, Kahlenbergerstrasse 22, 1190 Wien. ☎ 37 22 22. Open from the end of January until Christmas, from 3.30pm. Closed on Sundays. Occupies a historic monument. Very large, it has a fine garden but no music. Several varieties of wine, even white wine for diabetics. Extensive buffet. On Sundays in June, there are *"Schrammel-Matineen"*, between 10am and 2pm, with actors from the Opera and members of the Vienna Philharmonic Orchestra playing traditional music.

Sievering (19th district) – *Underground: Heiligenstadt (U4) then bus (39A) to Sievering. The last bus to Heiligenstadt is at 11.10pm.*

– *Watz*, Krottenbachstrasse 148, 1190 Wien. ☎ 44 12 40. Open from March to December from 4pm. Closed on Sundays. Very welcoming, it has an attractive garden, the only one in Sievering where one may hear *Schrammelmusik*. In winter, it is noteworthy for its romantic ambiance and warm hearth.

"Stadt Heuriger"

The *Heuriger* mentioned above supply wine which is strictly Viennese. They lie on the outskirts because vines cover the first foothills of the Vienna Woods. The city centre does not have such open-air cafés, but it boasts some historical cellar establishments where the wine comes from vineyards outside Vienna, some of them famous.

– *Augustinerkeller*, Augustinerstrasse 1. ☎ 533 10 26. Open daily from 11am to midnight. Close to the Opera (Staatsoper). Musical ambiance.

– *Esterházykeller*, Haarhof 1. ☎ 533 34 82. Open from Monday to Friday from 11am to 10pm, and on Saturdays and Sundays from 4pm. Wines are from the estates of the celebrated Esterházy family.

– *Zwölf-Apostellkeller*, Sonnenfelsgasse 3. ☎ 512 67 77. Open daily from 4.30pm to midnight. Clients descend to the level of the medieval catacombs, but this *Heuriger* is suffering more and more from an influx of tourists.

"Kaffeehäuser"

Elegant, comfortable and traditional in character, a *Kaffeehaus* (coffee house) plays a major role in Viennese life. Even if Viennese cafés have changed over the years and are no longer a place where great authors discuss literature and politics, they have preserved some of their former glory. There, one may peacefully read a newspaper, write a love letter, skim through a favourite novel, muse on the state of the world or just watch time go by in congenial company in an elegant and tranquil setting. Almost as an afterthought, one might order something to eat or drink.

A Kaffeehaus will of course serve breakfast, lunch and dinner, but the best time to come is undeniably late afternoon or early evening, especially after a pleasurable yet tiring visit to one of the capital's great museums. It will probably not be time for a full meal, so a cake is the best choice, such as the famous *Sachertorte* or *Mozarttorte*.

– **Café Central**, Herrengasse 14, 1st district. ☎ 533 37 63/0. Open Monday to Saturday from 8am to 9pm. Closed on Sundays and holidays. This is one of Vienna's great literary cafés from the turn of the century, occupying the Palais Ferstel. The poet Peter Altenberg used to give this café as his address. Today, it has become a rendez-vous for business men and women, the smart younger set and retired people instead of artists. Its specialities are Mazagran and Pharisäer. A pianist plays at the end of the afternoon until 7pm and newspapers are available *(see also under this heading)*.

– **Café Griensteidl**, Michaelerplatz 2. 1st district. ☎ 535 26 92. Open daily from 8am to midnight. The menu includes seasonal dishes and there is a good wine list. Specialities are Maria-Theresia and Fiaker; they also stock six varieties of tea. Another café with a literary past, the Griensteidl has a smart and prosperous clientèle. Foreign papers and sometimes smoky atmosphere *(see also Michaelerplatz)*.

– **Café Landtmann**, Dr. Karl-Lueger-Ring 4. 1st district. ☎ 532 06 21. Open daily from 8am to midnight. Very pleasant terrace in summer, with a view of the City Hall and Burgtheater. Good menu. Specialities are Rüdesheimer (mocha and whipped cream) and Biedermeierkaffee (mocha, liqueur and whipped cream). International newspapers are available *(see also under this heading)*.

– **Café Schwarzenberg**, Kärtnerring 17. 1st district. ☎ 512 89 98. Open Sunday to Friday from 7am to midnight, on Saturday 9am to midnight. There is a pianist between 4pm and 7pm and from 8pm to 10pm. International newspapers available. The speciality is Kaisermelange and various varieties of foreign coffee. Popular with tourists *(see also under this heading)*.

– **Café Sacher**, Philharmonikerstrasse 4. 1st district. ☎ 512 14 87. Open daily 7am to midnight. More a teashop than a

Café Landtmann

café (in fact it is a hotel-café-restaurant), it is a veritable institution. In summer, there is a view of the back of the Opera from the terrace. International newspapers available to the rich clientèle and any tourists lucky enough to have found a table. The speciality is naturally Sachertorte *(see also Philharmonikerstrasse)*.

– **Café Mozart**, Albertinaplatz 2. 1st district. ☎ 513 08 81. Open daily from 9am to midnight. Terrace in summer and international press throughout the year. Specialities are Maria-Theresia, Kaisermelange and Türkischer Kaffee. The menu is in German, English, French and Italian. Many tourists frequent it, particularly the Japanese.

– **Café Frauenhuber**, Himmelpfortgasse 6. 1st district. ☎ 512 39 85. Open Monday to Friday from 8am to 11pm. Closed on public holidays. Less select than the preceding establishments, this is the oldest café in Vienna, as it opened in 1824. There is a wide choice of dishes and the clientèle includes people who long for the days of the old Empire.

– **Café Hartauer**, Riemergasse 9. 1st district. Open Monday to Friday from 8am to 2am. This has close connections with the Opera and on its walls are signed photographs of tenors, basses and sopranos.

– **Café Hawelka**, Dorotheergasse 6. 1st district. ☎ 512 82 30. Open daily except Sunday, 8am to 2am (4pm to 2am on Friday and Sunday). Another institution, this small café, always packed in the evenings, cultivates a Bohemian, relaxed atmosphere. In the 1950s it was a rendez-vous for intellectuals and the avant-garde. For lunch or dinner, there are only sausages on the menu.

– **Demel**, Kohlmarkt 14. 1st district. Open daily 10am to 6pm. It is not a Kaffeehaus, but a tea and pastry shop, the oldest and most aristocratic in Vienna. People come to sip coffee and admire the interior decoration. It offers numerous specialities and varieties of tea and coffee, such as *Melange mit Schlagobers* (coffee with cream), *Früchtetee* (fruit infusion) or *Schokolade* (hot chocolate) *(see also Kohlmarkt)*.

– **Café Museum**, Friedrichstrasse 6. 1st district. ☎ 586 52 02. Open daily 7am to 11pm. Adolf Loos designed it at the end of the 19C and it is particularly well-situated at the corner of Karlsplatz, near the Secession pavilion opposite. It was the writer Elias Canetti's favourite café. Light meals and an intellectual clientèle *(see also under this heading)*.

– **Café Sluka**, Rathausplatz 8. 1st district. ☎ 42 71 72. Open Monday to Friday from 8am to 7pm and Saturday 8am to 5.30pm. Delicious pastries.

– **Café Weingartner**, Goldschlagstrasse 6. 15th district. ☎ 982 43 99. Open daily 9am to midnight. This café has three billiard tables, popular with the city's best players.

– **Café Sperl**, Gumpendorferstrasse 11. 6th district. ☎ 586 41 58. Open from Monday to Saturday 7am to 11pm, and on Sundays and holidays from 3pm to 11pm. This old café opened in 1880 and was popular with Franz Lehár; apparently it has not changed much since then. People play cards and billiards there.

– **Dommayer**, Dommayergasse 1. 13th district. ☎ 877 54 65. Open daily from 7am to midnight. Close to Schloss Schönbrunn, this very Viennese café holds concerts on the first Saturday of the month from 2pm to 4pm (see also The Stormy Early Career of Johann Strauss the Younger, Hietzing).

Coffee Compendium

When the Turks retreated in 1683, they left huge quantities of coffee beans behind them, increasing the popularity of the already fashionable black beverage which gave its name to the establishments serving it.

As there are over thirty ways of making coffee, here is a small selection of the commonest versions of this delicious drink.

Grosser/kleiner Schwarzer large/small cup of black coffee.

Grosser/kleiner Brauner large/small cup of black coffee with a dash of milk.

Verlängerter Schwarzer black coffee with a little water.

Verlängerter Brauner black coffee with a dash of milk and a little water.

Mokka fairly strong black coffee.

Kurz strong black coffee.

Einspänner black coffee in a glass with whipped cream (Schlagobers).

Fiaker black coffee in a glass with rum.

Pharisäer rum in a cup with black coffee.

Franziskaner coffee with milk and grated chocolate.

Kaffee verkehrt more milk than coffee.

Kaisermelange coffee with a yolk of egg and brandy.

Mazagran cold coffee with ice cubes and rum.

Melange coffee with milk (or whipped cream)

Maria Theresia mocha with orange liqueur and whipped cream.

Türkischer Kaffee coffee brought to the boil in small copper vessels, served very hot in small cups.

Kaffeinfreier Kaffee decaffeinated coffee.

NB – one should not order a cup of coffee, but eine Schale Kaffee, which is a bowl of coffee. According to the amount of milk, one specifies a bowl of brown or golden coffee.

Bars open in the evening

Some offer meals.

– **Kolar-Beisl**, Kleeblattgasse 5. 1st district. ☎ 533 52 25. Open daily 5pm to 2am. Specialities: Tyrolean Fladen (warm rolls filled with cream, cheese and vegetables), Erdbeerwein (strawberry wine) and Ribiselwein (redcurrant wine). Very often full.

– **Relax**, Seitenstettengasse 5. 1st district. ☎ 533 85 06. Open daily 6.30pm to 2am. Quiet, pleasant, romantic ambiance.

– **Philosoph**, Judengasse 11. 1st district. ☎ 535 45 32. Open Sunday to Wednesday from 6pm to 2am, Thursday to Saturday until 4am. Young, relaxed clientèle. Offers beer, Erdbeerwein and Ribiselwein. Good music.

– **Casablanca**, Rabensteig 8. 1st district. ☎ 533 34 63. Open from 6pm to 2am, and on Fridays and Saturdays until 4am. This small bar in the "Bermuda Triangle" (see Fleischmarkt district) has small concerts on a small stage. It is a trendy venue with plenty of atmosphere. In winter, they have an excellent Glühwein; in summer, they offer a heady fruit wine.

– **Zum Bettelstudent**, Johannesgasse 12. 1st district. ☎ 513 20 44. Open from 10am to 2am, on Saturdays until 3am (meals served until 1am). A kind of grill-room which boasts many varieties of beer and Austrian dishes. Young ambiance and modest prices.

– **Kleines Café**, Franziskanerplatz 3. 1st district. Open daily from 10am to 2am. Wide choice of spirits. In summer, the terrace benefits from its location in an attractive square (see Franziskanerplatz).

– **Wunderbar**, Schönlaterngasse 8.1st district. ☎ 512 79 89. Open from 4pm to 2am. In fact, it does not display its name because it so well-known to everyone. Very comfortable and not conventional. Good music.

– **Zum Basilisken**, Schonlaterngasse 3-5. ☎ 513 31 23. Open daily noon to 2am, on Friday and Saturday until 4am, and on Sunday from 3pm. A kind of grill-room with good cuisine. A popular place, the setting for a filmed episode of the *Kommissar Rex* series. A suitable place for dinner or drinks.

– **Panigl**, Schönlaterngasse 11. 1st district. ☎ 513 17 16. Open from 4pm to 4am. The evocative words *Marienbad-Vienna-Trieste* appear below its sign. There is a wide selection of wine, mainly Austrian, Hungarian and Italian. It is packed with people on Friday and Saturday nights.

– **Reiss**, Marco-D'Avianogasse 1. 1st district. ☎ 512 06 38. Open from 11am to 3am. This bar specialises in sparkling wines from all over the world. Refined clientèle.

Viennese food

Viennese cuisine is varied, reflecting the numerous traditions of the nations of the old Empire. The *Schnitzel*, a pork or veal escalope, forms the basis of many menus in the capital. Everyone has heard of *Wiener Schnitzel*, the celebrated escalope which usually comes with sautéed potatoes; a good *Wiener Schnitzel* should be golden brown. *Knödel* are another Viennese speciality; these are dumplings, which accompany several dishes, including soups, such as *Leberknödelsuppe*, a beef broth with liver-flavoured dumplings. *Rindsgulasch* is a Hungarian dish, a paprika-flavoured beef stew, with Knödel. There are several kinds of *gulasch*, including *Erdäpfelgulasch*, a potato stew served with frankfurters. *Tafelspitz mit G'röste* is a classic dish which Franz-Josef apparently ate every day and consists of boiled beef with sautéed potatoes and horseradish sauce. *Gefüllte Kalbsbrust* is breast of veal stuffed with meat and vegetables. *Bauernschmaus* was originally a peasant dish and generally comprises frankfurters, roast or smoked pork, ham and Knödel. *Eierspeise* consists of scrambled eggs served in a casserole. This is not a comprehensive list; there are myriads of poultry, game and fish dishes. Every restaurant offers a wide range of dishes such as stuffed breast of goose, capon with anchovy sauce, roast woodcock, saddle of venison, jugged hare, and also carp eggs in butter or pikeperch with paprika. Viennese recipes reflect Bohemian, Jewish, Hungarian, Croatian, Slovak and even Italian influences. Viennese cuisine is therefore varied, but not light in texture; although rich in natural ingredients, it is high in calories.

The list of desserts is endless. The highlight of the *Mehlspeisen* is *Apfelstrudel*, a flaky pastry dessert filled with apple and sultanas. There is a huge selection of cakes including *Rehrücken*, with chocolate and almonds, *Esterházytorte*, sugar added to sugar, *Palatschinken*, thick wheat pancakes with fromage frais or jam filling, *Linzertorte*, with strawberry or redcurrant jam and enriched with almonds, *Mohr im Hemd*, a chocolate cake coated in chocolate sauce, *Kaiserschmarren*, puff pastry currant cakes browned in butter and sugar, *Topfenstrudel* with fromage frais, *MarillenKnödel*, apricot dumplings, etc.

ENTERTAINMENT

To reserve a seat, one may go directly to the ticket offices of the theatres, cinemas etc. or telephone beforehand. There are, however, other ways of booking described in the *Practical Information* section.

Cinemas

Apollo Center – Gumpendorferstrasse 63. 6th district. ☎ 587 96 51. The largest screen in Austria, except for the Imax.

Burg-Kino – Opernring 19. 1st district. ☎ 587 84 06. Generally major American productions, in the original language rather than dubbed in German. In summer, they show Carol Reed's *The Third Man* for the benefit of tourists and cinema buffs.

Cine Center – Fleischmarkt 6. 1st district. ☎ 533 24 11. 4 screens.

De France – Schottenring 5. 1st district. ☎ 34 52 36. 2 screens.

Erika-Kino – Kaiserstrasse 44 and 46. 7th district. ☎ 93 13 83. The city's oldest cinema, dating from 1900.

Filmhaus Stöbergasse – Stöbergasse 11 to 15. 5th district. ☎ 545 23 91. Specialises in avant-garde films.

Filmmuseum – Augustinerstrasse 1. 1st district. ☎ 533 70 54. Numerous festivals. Films are shown in their original language and not dubbed. A must for film buffs.

Imax Filmtheater beim Technischen Museum – Mariahilferstrasse 212. 14th district. ☎ 894 01 01; "Info Hotline": 1547. Films on show are productions suitable for this type of establishment, namely spectacular, fairly short films.

Star Kino – Burggasse 71. 7th district. ☎ 93 46 83. Numerous revivals and a festival.

Top Kino Center – Rahlgasse 1. 6th district. ☎ 93 46 83. Recent and international films in their original language and not dubbed.

Votiv-Kino – Währingerstrasse 12. 9th district. ☎ 34 35 71. 2 screens with a "breakfast" show on Sunday mornings.

Classical music

Vienna is a musical capital. Every night a variety of orchestras perform classical music concerts in the city's numerous auditoriums. It is impossible to list every event. Most churches are also used for recitals, in particular Hofburgkapelle where the **Wiener Sängerknaben** (Vienna Boys' Choir) sing at Sunday Mass. The easiest and most practical thing to do is to ask for the monthly programme available at the offices of the Tourist Information Centre (Airport, Kärntnerstrasse 38, Rathaus, Westbahnhof, Südbahnhof). In summer, there are many young men and women in the street dressed in 18C costumes, selling seats for summer concerts. Both summer and spring are seasons when numer-

New Year's Day Concert given by the Vienna Philarmonic Orchestra

ous street musicians emerge to play tunes from a previous age. Listed below are the main auditoriums for classical music, where renowned orchestras and soloists perform *(for festivals, consult the chapter on Principal Festivals, at the end of the guide)*.

Grosser Sendesaal des ORF – Argentinierstrasse 30a. 4th district. ☎ 501 01-0. A modern concert hall; headquarters of the Radio and Television Orchestra.

Konzerthaus – Lothringerstrasse 20. 3rd district. ☎ 72 12 11; information on programs: (222) 712 46 860. This non-profit society organises major musical events for lovers of classical music. There is an annual attendance of 250,000.

Street musicians

Musikverein – Dumbastrasse 3 and Bösendorferstrasse 12. 1st district. ☎ 505 86 81. Very well-known owing to the worldwide New Year television broadcast. Three orchestras, including the famous Vienna Philharmonic, perform here. According to music lovers, the accoustics of the Brahms auditorium is superb *(see also under this heading)*.

Opera, dance and ballet

Staatsoper – Opernring 2. 1st district. ☎ 514 44 29 59; information on programmes: 514 44 29 60. International renown and a colossal budget. Tickets are on sale a month before the day of performance: ticket office at No 40 Kärntenrstrasse, from 10am up to 1 hour before the performance *(see also under this heading)*.

Tanztheater – Burggasse 38. 7th district. ☎ 96 39 34.

Theatergruppe 80 – Gumperdorferstrasse 67. 6th district. ☎ 565 222.

Volksoper – Währingerstrasse 78. 9th district. ☎ 514 44 29 59. All the operas in its repertory are sung in German. A must for those keen on this type of music *(see also under this heading)*.

Wiener Kammeroper – Fleischmarkt 24. 1st district. ☎ 513 60 72. An opera for young singers who will attain fame in the city's two great opera houses. In summer, its performances take place at the Schlosstheater in Schönbrunn (☎ 811 13 12 38).

Operettas and musical comedies

Raimundtheater – Wallgasse 18. 6th district. ☎ 599 77 27. Spectacular shows and special programs during the *Wiener Festwochen* from mid May to mid June.

Theater an der Wien – Linke Wienzeile 6. 6th district. ☎ 588 30-265. A historic auditorium (*see also Linke Wienzeile*).

Volksoper – Währingerstrasse 78. 9th district. ☎ 514 44 29 59.

Theatres

Lovers of theatre should be German speakers, although there are two exceptions to this rule: the English Theatre and the Studio Molière *(see below)*. Vienna is particularly well-off for theatres and it is possible to attend great classical drama or avant-garde plays. Usually, performances start at 7pm or 7.30pm.

Akademietheater – Lisztstrasse 1. 3rd district. ☎ 51444/2959. The second largest auditorium of the National Theatre after the Burgtheater, it has a fairly eclectic repertory, focussing mainly on modern drama.

Burgtheater – Dr. Karl-Lueger-Ring 2. 1st district. ☎ 51444/2959. Undeniably the greatest of all Austrian theatres. Big productions for lavish plays with texts by Goethe, Hofmannsthal, Raimund, Schiller, Schnitzler, etc. *(see also under this heading)*.

English Theater – Josefsgasse 12. 8th district. ☎ 402 82 84 or 402 12 60. This English language theatre with plays by Shakespeare was founded in 1963 by Franz Schafranek and Ruth Brinkmann.

Jura-Soyfer-Theater – Neubaugasse 3. 7th district. ☎ 93 24 58. Performs only plays by Jura Soyfer, a Communist author who died in Buchenwald.

Kabarett Simpl – Wollzeile 36. 1st district. ☎ 512 47 42. A small theatre staging Viennese comic works.

Kammerspiele – Rotenturmstrasse 20. 1st district. ☎ 533 28 33. Satirical works and comedies. Frequent performers in this theatre are very popular in Vienna.

Odeon – Taborstrasse 10. 2nd district. ☎ 214 55 62. One show per year, specialising in the art of mime.

Ronacher – Seilerstätte. 1st district. ☎ 514 11 207. Often closed owing to financial difficulties, it always manages to re-open. It specialises in travelling theatre companies *(see also Himmelpfortgasse)*.

Studio Molière – Liechtensteinstrasse 37. 9th district. ☎ 319 65 03 05. There is no regular programme, because companies from French-speaking countries come to play in this theatre.

Theater in der Josefstadt – Josefstädterstrasse 26. 8th district. ☎ 402 51 27. It has a very fine auditorium. After having fallen out of favour with the public, this establishment has again become popular over the past few years. Its repertory includes classical drama, such as *The Threepenny Opera* by Bertolt Brecht, the Marxist dramatist, and also musical comedies *(see under this heading)*.

Burgtheater

Volkstheater – Neustiftgasse 1. 7th district. ☎ 93 27 76. Contemporary and avant-garde plays, although this theatre started out originally as a vehicle for light, popular comedies *(see under this heading)*.

Variety shows, discos and jazz

Atrium – Schwindgasse 1. 4th district. ☎ 505 35 94. A disco. At the same address is the **Papas Tapas** where Austrian jazz bands perform.

Diskothek – Schönbrunnerstrasse 222. 12th district. ☎ 85 83 07. The name of this establishment is self-explanatory. Very diverse clientèle.

Jazzland – Franz-Josefs-Kai 29. 1st district. ☎ 533 25 75. This jazz club is housed in a cellar beneath Ruprechtskirche and is a venue for international groups. Excellent ambiance. Music from 9pm.

Jazzspelunke – Dürergasse 3. 6th district. ☎ 57 01 26. A centre of musical eclecticism.

Splendid – Jasomirgottgasse 3. ist district. ☎ 535 26 21. This disco was recently very fashionable and is always very busy at weekends.

Stadthalle – Vogelweidplatz 14. 15th district. ☎ 98 10 00. This sports stadium is used for major concerts by world-renowned groups.

Take Five – Annagasse 3a. 1st district. ☎ 512 92 77.

U4 – Heumühlgasse 20. 4th district. ☎ 586 24 17. Very up-to-the-minute disco.

W.U.K. – Währingerstrasse 59. 9th district. A cultural centre that stages mainly rock concerts (*Verein zur Schaffung Offener Kultur– und Werkstättenhäuser*).

The ball season

In winter, there is an endless succession of balls. On New Year's Eve, the famous **Kaiserball** (Emperor's Ball) recreates the bygone imperial era beneath the chandeliers of the Hofburg. During the Carnival, the most diverse associations and professional groups hold about 300 balls, mostly in ceremonial halls (Rathaus, Hofburg, Musikverein). Among these are the gardeners' and florists' Flower Ball, the Rudolfina-Redoute Masked Ball, the Café Proprietors' Ball, the Philharmonic Orchestra's Ball, and the Technicians' Circle Ball. Doctors have their own ball, as do lawyers, messenger boys or firemen. Visitors are always welcome.

The most elegant ball is the **Opernball** or Opera Ball, which is held in February at the *Staatsoper (see under this heading)*. It attracts Austrian and foreign celebrities and is the year's most fashionable event. It opens with the Wiener Staatsoper ballet and a select group of young men and women with fans dancing the polonaise.

SHOPPING

Since the Viennese shop in their own districts, the city centre contains mainly luxury shops. They lie around the cathedral, on the Graben, Kärntnerstrasse, Kohlmarkt, Neuer Markt and Tuchlauben. In the 1st district, the sumptuous Ringstrassen Gallerien (Kärntnerring 7) are a major commercial centre. The main shopping street in Vienna is Mariahilferstrasse, which separates the 6th and 7th districts and links Westbahnhof to the Ring. It is a street featuring the large popular stores (C & A, Virgin, Billa, etc.). Another major commercial street is Meidlinger Hauptstrasse, in the 12th district. The city's main shopping arcade is SCS (Shopping City Sud), the largest in Austria, comprising numerous stores and restaurants.

Most shops open from Monday to Friday from 9/10am to noon/12.30pm and from 2/3pm to 6pm. Some supermarkets stay open until 7pm. On Thursday, many shops in the 1st district do not close until 8pm. On Saturday, shops close at 12.30/1pm, except for food shops which, on the first Saturday of the month, stay open until 5pm.

Specialist shops

Augarten GmbH – Stock-im-Eisen-Platz. 1st district. Retail outlet for the famous factory.

Backhausen – Kärntnerstrasse 33. 1st district. This textile factory stocks furniture fabrics and silk scarves with Jugendstil motifs.

Frimmel – Freisingergasse 1. 1st district. A paradise for buying buttons. The Imperial Court figured among its customers.

Gunkel – Tuchlauben 11. 1st district. Dating from 1796, this shop is famous for its household linens.

Herzmansky Kaufhaus – Mariahilferstrasse 26 to 30. 6th district. The toy department in this store is excellent.

Lobmeyr – Kärntnerstrasse 26. 1st district. This glass shop was supplier to the Court by appointment. It is renowned for its extremely fragile *Musselinglas*.

Maria Stransky – Hofburg, Burgpassage 2. 1st district. Stocks typically Viennese petit point embroidery.

Niederösterreichisches Heimatwerk – Herrengasse 6 and 8. 1st district. Numerous souvenirs from Lower Austria: literature, clothes and crafts.

Piatnik – Kandlgasse 33. 7th district. Dating from the end of the 19C, this firm sells splendid packs of cards, virtual works of art.

Rasper & Söhne – Graben 15. 1st district. Augarten porcelain, glass and silverware.

Schau Schau Brillen – Rotenturmstrasse 11. 1st district. This shop sells spectacles of amazing shape, although showing a classical influence, by Peter Kozich. Elton John is one of his clients.

Thonet – Kohlmarkt 6. 1st district. The world renown of this bistro chair is such that it needs no further introduction.

K. und K.

In Vienna, shop windows or shopfronts often display the letters "K. und K."

In 1867, the creation of the dual monarchy gave rise to Austro-Hungary. Franz-Josef then became Emperor (Kaiser) of Austria and King (König) of Hungary, after his coronation at Pest. Thus, "K. und K." signifies "imperial and royal", a title to which suppliers to the Court laid claim.

Clothes shops

Kettner Eduard – Seilergasse 12. 1st district. Clothes for all leisure activities, ranging from hunting to camping gear.

Lanz Trachten Moden – Kärnterstrasse. 1st district. This firm has branches in Salzburg and Innsbruck: traditional Austrian clothes.

Lodens Plankl – Michaelerplatz 6. 1st district. Austrian clothes including navy blue, grey or green overcoats. A widely known establishment.

Resi Hammerer – Kärntnerstrasse 29. 1st district.

Tostmann – Schottengasse 3a. 1st district. Traditional Austrian costumes, and fashion garments drawing inspiration from them. Wide selection of *Dirndl*, an embroidered costume (skirt, blouse and apron). Expensive, but of high quality.

Confectioners

Altmann und Kühne – Graben 30. 1st district. The packaging is magnificent.

Central – Herrengasse 11. 1st district. This establishment sells the *Sachertorte's* rival, the *Imperialtorte*, with a choice of 5 different packagings (it has a 4 week guarantee).

Demel – Kohlmarkt 14. 1st district. This celebrated café-teashop sells cakes and chocolates. Price and quality are equally high. Chocolate is on sale opposite at No 11.

Lehmann – Graben 12. 1st district. Less well-known, a very good firm.

Sacher – Philharmonikerstrasse. 1st district. It is possible to buy a *Sachertorte*, the star of Viennese cakes.

Delicatessen

Aida – This chain of shops stocks offers at a reasonable price: in the 1st district, Bognerstrasse 3 and Opernring 7.

Do & Co – Akademiestrasse 3. 1st district. This looks like a bistrot but specialises in typically Viennese gourmet products.

A shop window display at Demel

Julius Meinl – This shop has numerous branches in the city. The main shop is on the Graben (No 19), near Kohlmarkt. Its delicatessen products have 8% of the Austrian market.

Schoen-Bichler – Wollzeile 4. 1st district. Wide range of teas (good selection of blends, also on request) and wines.

Wild – Neuer Markt 10 and 11. 1st district. Sells the best brandies and first class wine.

Zum Schwarzen Kameel – Bognerstrasse 5. 1st district. An old established firm (Beethoven was one of their customers) which stocks fine food and good wine.

Flea markets

Donaukanal-Promenade – There are second-hand goods stalls on the banks of the Danube canal, between the underground stations Schwedenplatz and Schottenring, on Saturday from 2pm to 8pm, on Sunday 10am to 8pm.

Kunstmarkt im Heiligenkreuzerhof – 1st district. From April to September, on the first weekend of each month; from the end of November to 24 December, 10am to 7pm (Saturdays from 10am to 6pm). Halfway between second-hand goods stalls and a market selling works of art.

Kunstmarkt am Spittelberg – Spittelberggasse. 7th district. Saturday from 10am to 6pm.

Naschmarkt – Linke Wienzeile *(see under this heading)*. Astride the 4th and 6th districts. On Saturday, from 7am to 6pm, at the south end of the vegetable market is the Flohmarkt or flea market.

Christmas markets

In German-speaking countries, hence in Austria, and particularly in Vienna, Christmas is the most important festival of the year. It is not just a religious occasion, but a warm and festive time. The Advent period in the city is enchanting. However, tourists should be wary of the afternoon of 24th December: unlike the preceding weeks, streets will be utterly deserted.

During the Advent period, there are several Christmas markets throughout the city and its outskirts, both large and small, sometimes a mere stall as in Mödling. They are colourful, lively, noisy and friendly affairs, forming part of the Viennese heritage. Here are the main ones:

Christmas Market in front of the Rathaus (City Hall) – Rathauspark. 1st district. From 18 November to 24 December. Also goes by the name of Infant Jesus Market (Christkindlmarkt). Numerous vendors set up stall, selling cakes and confectionery, and mulled wine, an attractive feature of these markets.

Freyung Christmas Market – Freyung. 1st district. From the end of November until 24 December.

The Christmas market

Spittelberg Christmas Market – Spittelberggasse. 7th district. From 25 November until 23 December. The young frequent this market, which is also (almost) a craft market. There is an abundant supply of mulled wine when the temperature is low.

Christmas Market in front of Schloss Schönbrunn – 13th district. From 25 November until 26 December. A calmer ambiance than the preceding one, in a historic site with great tourist appeal. There are musical events at this market, known as Kultur– und Weihnachtsmarkt vor dem Schloss Schönbrunn.

Christmas Market in front of Karlskirche – Karlsplatz. 4th district. From 25 November until 23 December.

Markets

In general, they are open Monday to Friday 6am to 6.30pm, on Saturdays 6am to 1pm.

Augustinermarkt – Landstrasser Hauptstrasse/Erdbergerstrasse. 3rd district.

Blumengrossmarkt – Laxenburgerstrasse 365. 23rd district. A colourful flower market.

Brunnenmarkt – Brunnengasse. 16th district.

Hannovermarkt – Hannovergasse/Brigittaplatz. 20th district.

Naschmarkt – Linke Wienzeile *(see under this heading)*. Astride the 4th and 6th districts. Consists of the Naschmarkt (fruit and vegetables), Monday to Friday from 8am to 6.30pm, on Saturday from 6am to 2pm, and the Bauernmarkt (farm produce) Monday to Thursday from 6am to noon, on Friday from 6am to 1pm, on Saturday from 6.30 to 6pm.

Schwendermarkt – Schwendermarkt/Reichsapfelgasse. 15th district.

Fruit and vegetable market

J.-P. Garcin/DIAF

SPORTING ACTIVITIES

Badminton, Keep Fit, Golf, Squash, Tennis

The **Danube Club** is a chain of sports centres with excellent facilities.

Club Danube Erdberg – Franzosengraben: Parkhaus. 3rd district. ☎ 798 84 00.

Club Danube Lugner City – Geyschlägergasse 15. 15th district. ☎ 982 57 71.

Club Danube Alte Donau – Arbeiterstrandbadstrasse 85a. 21st district. ☎ 270 61 83. The facilities in this sports complex overlook the river.

Club Danube Golf Wien – Weingartenallee. 22nd district.

Football

Ernst-Happl Stadion – Meiereistrasse 7. 2nd district. ☎ 728 08 540. Home ground for the Vienna Rapid team *(see also Fussball-Museum)*.

Gerhard-Hanappl Stadion – Keisslergasse 6. 14th district. ☎ 94 55 19.

Swimming

Amalienbad – Reumannplatz 23. 10th district. Open from 9am to 6pm on Tuesday, from 9am to 9.30pm Wednesday to Friday, 7am to 8pm on Saturday, 7am to 6pm on Sunday; sauna open from 1pm to 9.30pm on Tuesday, 9am to 9.30pm Wednesday to Friday; 7am to 8pm on Saturday, 7am to 6pm on Sunday *(see also under this heading)*.

Dianabad – Lilienbrunngasse 7. 2nd district. ☎ 26 25 16. Open from 7am to 9pm on Monday, 6.30am to 9pm on Tuesday and Thursday, 9am to 9pm on Wednesday and Friday, 7am to 6pm on Saturday.

Bundesbad Schönbrunn – Schlosspark. 13th district. ☎ 83 01 32. In the park of Schönbrunn Palace, a spacious open-air swimming pool in a regal setting.

Bundesbad Alte Donau – Arbeiterstrandbadstrasse 93. 22nd district. ☎ 23 33 02. On the banks of the Danube, there are now several beaches where it is pleasant to bathe: Arbeiterstrandbad, Strandbad Alte Donau, Bundessportbad, etc.

Kongressbad – Julius-Meinlgasse 7 a. 13th district. ☎ 46 11 63. The pool has a slide and there is a children's section.

Schafbergbad – Josef-Redlgasse 2. 18th district. ☎ 47 15 93. The pool affords a fine view of the city.

Stadthalle – Vogelweidplatz 14. 15th district. ☎ 98 10 00. The pool is open 8am to 9.30pm on Monday, Wednesday and Friday, from 6.30am to 9.30pm on Tuesday and Thursday, from 7am to 6.30pm at weekends.

Thermalschwefelbad Oberlaa – Kurbadstrasse 14. 10th district. ☎ 68 16 11– 252/352. Open daily from 9am to 9pm (6pm on Sundays and holidays). In the large Oberlaa leisure centre, 20 minutes from the city centre, there are swimming pools (1 indoor and 3 open-air), thermal baths, saunas, massage parlours, etc.

Skating

Donauparkhalle – Wagramerstrasse 2. 2nd district. ☎ 23 61 23. Open from mid-September to the end of March, on Saturday from 1pm to 5pm, on Sunday from 8am to 10.30pm, other days from 11.45am to 5pm.

Eislaufanlage Engelmann – Syringgasse 6 and 8. 17th district. ☎ 421 42 50. Open from the end of October to the beginning of March, from 9am to 7pm from Saturday to Thursday, until 9.30pm on Friday.

Wiener Eislaufverein – Lothringerstrasse 22. 3rd district. ☎ 713 63 530. Open in theory from October to March (depending on the temperature), from 9am to 9pm, at weekends until 8pm, on Wednesday until 10pm. The Viennese Ice Skating Club has an open-air ice rink. Very near Stadtpark.

Walks in Vienna

Keen walkers will find plenty of footpaths in the Vienna Woods *(see Wienerwald)*, but it is also possible to appreciate nature in the city of Vienna. These woods encroach upon the west and north periphery of the capital. Throughout these woods forming part of the city, there are numerous waymarked footpaths.

Skater's Waltz

Some suggestions:

Beethovengang – This is the name of a walk which the composer of the *Eroica* favoured while living in Heiligenstadt. It extends along the Schreiberbach, west and south of Nussdorf.

Kahlenberg - Leopoldsberg *(see under these headings)* – From Grinzing, there are several footpaths through the northern part of the Vienna Woods. Some run along the hill-tops of Kahlenberg and Leopoldsberg to Josefsdorf, Kahlenbergerdorf and Nussdorf. The view of the city is superb in fine weather.

Lainzer Tiergarten *(see under this heading)* – By consulting the map at the entrance to this vast park, one may select an itinerary and preferred length of walk, also enjoying a fine view of the west of the city.

Sports Complex

Stadthalle – Vogelweidplatz 14. 15th district. ☎ 98 10 00.

Skiing

In Vienna, the first foothills of the Alps display some slopes mainly suitable for children, because of their low summits. Adults will have to travel further, into Lower Austria, to pursue the joys of skiing. In season, the Viennese's favourite ski resort is Semmering, near the Schneeberg.

Himmelhofwiese – Am Himmelhof. Access through Himmelhofgasse. 13th district. ☎ 97 11 57. Ski tow in operation from Monday to Friday, from noon till nightfall, at weekends and on public holidays from 10am.

Hohe-Wand-Wiese – Mauerbachstrasse 174. 14th district. ☎ 97 11 57. Open daily 10am to 10pm.

Michaelertrakt in the Hofburg

City Centre
and the Ring

City Centre and the Ring

FLEISCHMARKT District

Local map page 6, **KLR**
Underground: Schwedenplatz (U1, U4), Stubentor (U3)
Tram: Schwedenplatz (1, 2, 21, N), Stubentor (1, 2)
Bus: Riemergasse (1A), Rotenturmstrasse (2A)

The Meat Market occupies the centre of this area, the oldest in Vienna. It is the liveliest street in this district known as "the Bermuda triangle", where young Viennese and foreign tourists gather in the evenings. This imaginary triangle lies between the church Maria am Gestade *(see Hoher Markt District)*, Franziskanerplatz *(see tour around Stephansdom)* and the south end of Fleischmarkt. The tour starts with sights visible by daylight and continues towards Fleischmarkt, which some may enjoy more by night.

★ **Postsparkasse** – *Georg-Coch-Platz 2.* – To appreciate the new concepts which Otto Wagner's Post Office Savings Bank illustrated in 1906, it is best to view it from the Stubenring overlooked by the former War Ministry *(see Regierungsgebäude)* with its giant double-headed eagle. The contrast is striking. It is difficult to believe that this building is more recent than the smooth-surfaced Postsparkasse. The façade of this major work by Wagner displays a mottled appearance; plaques of Sterzing marble are in fact riveted to it, concealing a brick structure. Although set back from the Ring, Postsparkasse shares the same monumental grandeur. This is significant, because the architect, who had already constructed neo-Renaissance buildings on the Ring, built it in three years, thanks to this new method, whereas other monumental edifices on the Ring took ten years to complete. The novelty lay as much in the appearance as in the technique, one arising from the other. Indeed, his modernism consists of a functionalist approach. He left the aluminium bolt-heads visible, and did not wait for the plaques to bond with the mortar, which facilitated rapid construction

Postsparkasse: the counters room

3 BIS/MICHELIN

and produced a decorative effect. Wagner's Secession functionalism was not severe; at the top of the building are Othmar Schimkowitz's winged Victories. By their pomp these triumphant symbols create another link between Postsparkasse and the buildings of the Ring. In this, Wagner differed from Adolf Loos, who totally opposed any ornamentation.

The severe façade conceals a fine **counters hall** ⓘ. Its interior shows how much attention Wagner paid to detail. Light streams in, diffused through a vaulted glass roof and a glass tiled floor. Wagner turned columns for the heating system into graceful tubular sculptures and also designed the furniture, which is still in use today *(objects based on the designs of Wagner and Kolo Moser are for sale)*.

Proceed past Postsparkasse along Rosenbursenstrasse and turn left up the sloping Dominikanerbastei. Stop at the level of Falkestrasse on the left.

Falkestrasse – The architects of the Coop Himmelblau group redesigned the roof of the classical building at No 6 in 1988. This refurbishment is sufficiently obvious for anyone to guess that it is an avant-garde step. With a certain penchant for polemics, the company extols "deconstructionism", and also retains a remarkable feeling for the renewal of forms.

Turn right into Predigergasse then left into Postgasse

Dominikanerkirche – *Postgasse 4.* In 1226, Duke Leopold VI summoned the Dominicans to Vienna where eleven years later they consecrated their first church. In 1529, the Turks set fire to the edifice and devastated it. Antonio Canevale rebuilt it, from 1631 to 1634, while the west front and cupola date from the early 1670s. In 1927, the church acquired the higher status of minor basilica, hence its other name of Santa Maria Rotonda.

Its façade, without a tower, is an interesting example of Viennese Early Baroque, recalling the façade of the church of S.S. Domenico e Sisto built in Rome by Vicenzo della Greca in 1623. The interior contains several altars, some of which display delightful works of art: *The Coronation of Mary* by Karl Mayer (1840, first chapel on the left), *Christ Praising St Thomas* by Franz Leuyx (1638, 2nd chapel on the left), *St Vincent Raising a Man from the Dead* by François Roettiers (1726, 2nd chapel on the right), *Death of St Catherine* by K. Mayer (1836, 3rd chapel on the right). The frescoes in the nave are by Matthias Rauchmiller (17C), those in the cupola above the crossing by Franz Geyling (1836), and those in the chancel by Carpoforo Tencala (1676). The view from the nave ends with the high altar by Carl Rösner (1840); above it is a painting by Leopold Kupelwieser, *Institution of the Festival of the Rosary by Pope Gregory XIII* (1839). Much of the decorative appeal of this church lies in its **stucco** typical of Early Baroque *(see illustration: Introduction, Elements of architecture).*

Continue along Postgasse and turn right into Bäckerstrasse which connects with Dr. Ignaz-Seipel-Platz.

★**Jesuitenkirche** – *Dr. Ignaz-Seipel-Platz.* Together with Salzburg cathedral built from 1614 to 1655, this is one of the first Austrian churches inspired by the Gesù in Rome. It also bears the name of *Universitätskirche* (University church). It was designed by an anonymous architect between 1623 and 1627 in the Early Baroque style. The west front displays a feature typical of this style, a pediment with spiral scrolls set between two towers by Andrea Pozzo. He altered the west front and the lateral chapels. He also painted the ceiling frescoes.

The pulpit in Jesuitenkirche

3 BIS/MICHELIN

A. Pozzo is famous for decorating the ceilings of Sant'Ignazio in Rome (between 1685 and 1694). He worked on the interior of the Jesuitenkirche between 1703 and 1707. This Jesuit father, from southern Tyrol (Trente), achieved a sumptuous effect with a **trompe-l'œil cupola★** in the centre of the ceiling and a lavishly adorned **pulpit★** encrusted with mother-of-pearl; according to some, this luxurious decoration belied the principles of the Counter-Reformation, while to others it was the culminating point of the movement. The high altar is by A. Pozzo, also a talented painter. It displays a fine painting by him of the *Assumption*. One of the details is both picturesque and moving. The artist has painted himself as the apostle St Andrew, in the lower left-hand corner. Another interesting detail is that the altar pieces of the first chapels *(left entrance)* depict St Catherine embodying Philosophy on the left, and Theology on the right *(see inset).*

Alte Universität – *Dr. Ignaz-Seipel-Platz 1. Closed to the public.* Vienna University was founded by Rudolf IV, first archduke, in 1365 and was the first German-language university after Prague, founded in 1348. The first Faculty was that of Theology. The Dominicans nearby gave instruction in this subject until the Jesuits replaced them in 1623 *(see inset).* In 1803, the Court installed there "K. und K. Stadtkonvikt", a music school recruiting the 130 children who sang on Sundays in the chapel of the imperial palace. Franz Schubert was a pupil there from 1808 to 1813, from the ages of 11 to 16 *(see wall plaque).* After the building of the Ring, the University was moved there. Today, an art gallery occupies the ground floor.

Akademie der Wissenschaften (N) – *Dr. Ignaz-Seipel-Platz 3. Closed to the public.* Jean-Nicolas Jadot de Ville-Issey built the Academy of Sciences opposite the University from 1753 to 1755 at the request of Empress Maria-Theresa. This accounts for the note of French Classicism in this secluded quarter of old Vienna. Before housing in 1857 the ten-year-old Academy, this palace had been a huge ceremonial hall, with frescoes by Gregorio Guglielmi, who also painted the ones in the Grosse Galerie at Schloss Schönbrunn. Unfortunately, they were completely destroyed by fire in 1961. It was possible to restore the architecture, but new frescoes had to be painted, by Paul Reckendorfer. The sculptor Franz Joseph Lenzbauer created the two fountains adorning the façade (1755).

The Creation as a musical epitaph – The last concert which Joseph Haydn attended was a performance of his oratorio

> ### The reconquest of the Counter-Reformation
>
> In 1537, Ignatius of Loyola founded the Society of Jesus and Pope Paul III approved it in 1540. Its purpose lay more in action than meditation. The Society rapidly developed and became a kind of militia defending the Church against heresy. After the Council of Trent, which took place from 1545 to 1563, a movement arose, which the 19C termed the Counter-Reformation. Its aim was to repel the advance of Protestantism. The Jesuits were the most active participants in this Catholic reformation. They turned Austria and Bavaria into bastions of Catholicism. In 1623, Emperor Ferdinand II granted the order the monopoly for teaching philosophy and theology at Vienna University, which accounts for the proximity of Jesuitenkirche. The Jesuits continued with this mission until 1773.

The Creation played in his honour in the university's great hall. Aged 76 and very weak, Haydn, who scarcely left the house *(see Haydn-Museum)*, agreed to go to this gala evening. On 27 March 1808, Prince Nicholas Esterházy's *(see Eisenstadt)* carriage came to fetch him. As he reached the Jesuitenkirche, the princes of Lobkowitz and Trauttmansdorff, as well as Beethoven and Salieri, rushed to support the old man, who could hardly walk. At the same time, there was a drum roll and a blare of trumpets, a great fanfare, and the Viennese aristocracy rose to greet its national composer. Haydn advanced triumphantly in his wheelchair amid the cheering crowd. He was seated next to Princess Maria Josepha Esterházy (born Lichtenstein) and despite his protests was excused from taking off his hat. As he seemed somewhat cold, the princess gave him her shawl. A duo of poets sang in his honour. He drank some country wine, which seemed to revive him a little. Then came the opening bars of his masterpiece. He trembled. The emotion overwhelmed him. By the end of the first part of the oratorio, he felt obliged to return home. Beethoven, who was equally moved, kissed the hand of his former master, who waved to the audience as if blessing them. He left immediately, while the orchestra continued playing his music. Many of the men in the audience could not conceal their tears. This was Haydn's last public appearance. He died just over a year later, on 31 May 1809, three weeks after Napoleon's troops entered Vienna.

Return to Bäckerstrasse.

Bäckerstrasse – There is no lack of interesting façades in "Baker" Street. No 16 is a pleasant residential house built about 1712. On the right, Schwanenfeld House (No 7) is famous in Vienna for its Renaissance courtyard with Tuscan and Ionic columns; the arcades, now glassed-in, date from 1587. Opposite, at No 8, Count Seilern's palace dates from 1722, then, a little further to the left, No 2 and its tower were built in the 17C.

The street leads to the square known as Lugeck. Notice the narrow passage leading to Stephansplatz.

Lugeck – In its centre is the *Gutenbergdenkmal*, a sculpture cast in bronze in 1900 by Hans Bitterlich. The invention of printing (1440) was attributed to Johann Gutenberg, a goldsmith from Mainz. It heralded a new era in the history of ideas, since it was then possible to achieve the circulation of unlimited numbers of texts by means of moveable type. In fact, the Chinese had first perfected this technique in the 7C AD.

Turn right into Sonnenfelsgasse.

Sonnenfelsgasse – This street dates from the early 12C. Hildebrandthaus (No 3) is an elegant, impressive house built in several stages, but first constructed between the 14C and 15C. Its Baroque façade (1721) was designed by the architect after whom the house is named. It has fine window frames, separated at the 2nd and 3rd storeys by pilasters resting on consoles with scrolls. The *Virgin with Child* in a small Rococo pediment is noteworthy. At present the cellars of the building house a *Stadtheuriger* called *Zwölf-Apostelkeller*.

Turn left into Schönlaterngasse.

Schönlaterngasse – The winding street of the Lovely Lantern is undeniably the most charming street in the oldest quarter of the town centre. It derives its name from the wrought-iron lantern on the façade of the 1680 house at No 6 (a 1971 replica, the 18C original being in the Historisches Museum der Stadt Wien).

Opposite, at No 5, **Heiligenkreuzerhof** is a courtyard surrounded by buildings (17C and 18C), most of which belong to Heiligenkreuz Abbey *(see under this heading)* in Lower Austria. They include the residence of the abbot and St Bernard's chapel (where society weddings take place). Its delightful Baroque interior dates from 1662 and underwent refurbishment in 1730. It houses an altarpiece by the painter Martino Altomonte (1657-1745). This artist, some of whose works are visible in Peterskirche *(see under this heading)*, lived at the court of Heiligenkreuz.

At No 7 is **Wohnhaus "Zum Basilisken"** (basilisk house), mentioned as early as 1212 and therefore one of the oldest houses in the town. Its 1740 façade attracts notice, because it features a block of sandstone, a natural conglomerate, to which an unknown hand added an artificial beak and tail. There is no reason to doubt the popular Viennese legend related by Wolfgang Lazius in 1546 in his *Vienna Austriae*, according to which a basilisk – a mythical animal which came from an egg laid by a cock and incubated by a toad – poisoned with its breath the well in the house where it had its lair. The fresco on the façade describes how a fearless young masterbaker, Martin Garhiebl, destroyed the monster by showing it a mirror, making it die of fright at the sight of such ugliness.

Robert Schumann lived at No 7a from October 1838 to April 1839. His wife Clara was a pianist in the Habsburg capital. Being of too romantic a temperament to appreciate the frivolity of Viennese society, he did not stay long in Vienna. However, he spent some time there looking for an editor for his musical review *Neue Zeitschrift für Musik* and frequently met Franz Schubert's brother, Ferdinand.

Alte Schmiede (No 9) is the former smithy of Josef Schmirler, who made the street lantern. The workshop operated until 1974, after which it became a **museum** ☉ and cultural centre.

Schönlaterngasse leads into Postgasse.

Postgasse – The composer of *Deutsches Requiem*, **Johannes Brahms** (1833-1897) lived at No 6, in 1867.

At No 10 is the **Griechische Kirche Hl. Barbara**. The present façade of this church dates from 1854, but the edifice was built in the mid-17C. It belonged to the Jesuits until 1773, then was given to the Ukrainian Catholic community two years later.

Turn left into Fleischmarkt.

Fleischmarkt – The "meat market", or shambles, dates from 1220; the butchers' guild established their headquarters there, in the heart of medieval Vienna. Today, the street is famous for the bars and nightclubs that fill the area around it.

At No 15 is the Schwindhof (1718), birthplace of the painter Moritz von Schwind on 21 January 1804 (he died in Munich in 1871).

At No 13, the **Griechische Kirche Zur Hl. Dreifaltigkeit** ☉ displays a composite façade of bricks enhanced with gilding. Peter Mollner built the edifice, which also houses a school, between 1782 and 1787. In 1861, it underwent alterations, to a design by Theophil von Hansen, one of the creators of the Ring, and acquired its Byzantine appearance. A corridor with frescoes by Ludwig Thiersch leads to the Greek Orthodox church of the Holy Trinity, a sanctuary noteworthy for its oblong chancel; the iconostasis dates from the second half of the 18C.

At No 11 is the **Griechenbeisl**, a tavern frequented by celebrities such as Johannes Brahms, Franz Grillparzer, Franz Schubert, Johann Strauss and Richard Wagner. Mark Twain allegedly wrote *The Millionaires' Wager* in a room with walls covered in the signatures of famous writers. The inn sign depicts a popular bagpipe player of the mid 17C. The song he wrote during an outbreak of plague in 1679 still lives in the Viennese mind:

> *"O, du lieber Augustin,*
> *'s Geld ist hin,*
> *'s Mensch ist hin,*
> *O, du lieber Augustin,*
> *alles ist hin!"*
> *(Oh, my darling Augustin,*
> *there's no money,*
> *there are no more people,*
> *Oh, my darling Augustin,*
> *there's nothing more!)*

In the song, Augustin gets drunk and falls into a mass grave, but he has absorbed so much alcohol that he is safe from infection. The words of this little ditty revived the courage of the inhabitants of the town devastated by plague. In his *Second Quartet*, Arnold Schönberg borrowed the melody of this legendary song, illustrating the ability of Viennese artists to turn suffering into art.

The small **Griechengasse** possesses several Gothic remains, including an old 13C Gothic tower at No 9. The façade at No 7 displays a Virgin in a niche above a wrought-iron Rococo lantern. In the courtyard, there is another Gothic tower; the Turkish inscriptions on the wooden panels date from the 1683 siege. The name of this street evokes the Greek merchants who settled in this quarter in the 18C.

City Centre and the Ring

3 BIS/MICHELIN

Fleischmarkt: *Der liebe Augustin*

At No 9 Fleischmarkt, **Wohnhaus "Zur Mariahilf"** is a house with a late 17C façade featuring a *Virgin with Child* dating from the 16C. The plaque on the right is a reminder of the law of 8 May 1912 which required carriages to be preceded by somebody on foot to warn passers-by of the imminent arrival of a horse-drawn vehicle in the narrow Griechengasse.

At No 14, the fine green Jugendstil façade belongs to an office block built in 1899 by F. Dehm and Joseph Maria Olbrich, architect of the famous Secession pavillion *(see Secessiongebäude)*. The wall plaque commemorates Johann Herbeck (1831-1877), who was Kapellmeister and director of opera and theatre at Court.

At No 1, "Residenzpalast", another Jugendstil building, is more austere, although elegantly set off by gold banding. Arthur Baron built it in 1910. A plaque states that this site was also the birthplace of Franz Schalk (1863-1931), a pupil of Anton Bruckner and co-director, with Richard Strauss, of the National Opera.

As well as the last part of the Ring, the nearest sights are: Stephansdom and the tour around Stephansdom, the districts of Hoher Markt, Belvedere (equivalent to Landstrasse District) and Prater (equivalent to Leopoldstadt District).

The key on the inside front cover explains the abbreviations and symbols used in the text or on the maps.

FREYUNG District★

Local Map page 5, **HJR**
Underground: Schottentor (U2), Herrengasse (U3)
Tram: Schottentor-Universität (1, 2, 37, 38, 40, 41, 42, 43, 44, D)
Bus: Teinfaltstrasse (1A), Michaelerplatz (2A), Herrengasse (3A)

THE ARISTOCRATIC DISTRICT

One might think that the presence of the Hofburg gave rise to the numerous palaces around Freyung, but in fact the former Babenberg and Formbach residences preceded the Hofburg. The Baroque period gave birth to most of the palaces in the Innere Stadt or 1st District. However, while the Church had an archbishop's palace built near the cathedral *(see Dom- und Diözesanmuseum)*, and the Crown commissioned the construction of the Leopoldinischertrakt in the Hofburg, the aristocrats of the Empire built themselves palaces in the "Aristocratic District"; Herrengasse, or Lords' Street, links Freyung to Michaelerplatz, its name recalling its aristocratic past.

A place of asylum and a choice location

Freyung – A "place of asylum" is the literal meaning of the name of this triangular square. Formerly, it was a centre of festivities, and round it were only the Scottish monastery *(see Schottenstift below)* and its church. This Benedictine monastery granted the right of asylum to any fugitive from justice, except murderers. In the 17C and 18C, the present palaces were built around Freyung: Ferstel (No 2), Harrach (No 3), Kinsky (No 4), and Schönborn-Battyány (No 4 Renngasse) *(see below)*.

In the centre is the **Austria-Brunnen**, a fountain by Ludwig Schwanthaler and Ferdinand Miller (1846). Its allegorical figures represent the four main rivers of the Austrian Empire: the Po, Elbe, Vistula and Danube. It is said that Alma von Goethe, the poet's grandaughter, was the model for the figure of Austria; she died at the age of 17.

Schottenkirche – *Freyung bei 6*. Since its founding in 1177, the church of Our Lady of the Scots *(for the origin of the name, see Schottenstift below)* survived several destructive episodes. The present building is the result of 15C alterations and Baroque refurbishments by Andrea d'Allio and Silvestro Carlone between 1643 and 1648. The most characteristic feature of the church is undeniably its fine onion-shaped bell tower.

Inside, the 4th chapel on the left houses the greatly venerated and oldest statue of the Virgin in the city (about 1250). Other works of note are *The Assumption and the Martyrdom of St Sebastian* by Tobias Pock (about 1655) and *The Departure of the Apostles Peter and Paul* by Joachim von Sandrart (1652).

This church was the setting on 15 June 1809 for Joseph Haydn's memorial service *(see inset, Haydn-Museum)*.

Freyung seen from the Southeast by Canaletto

City Centre and the Ring

★Schottenstift – *Freyung 6.* In the days when missionaries set sail from the island of Iona in Scotland and from Ireland to convert the Germans on the Continent, this country was called New Scotland. Hence, the Irish Benedictine monks who came from Ratisbon to Vienna became known as Scotsmen. In 1155, in the reign of Henry II Jasomirgott, they founded the monastery which is still known today as Abbey of the Scots.

After 17C alterations, the monastery buildings underwent a complete renovation from 1826 to 1832 by Josef Kornhäusel. They house a famous college, which included Victor Adler, Johann Nestroy, Johann Strauss and the last emperor of Austria, Karl I, among its students.

Museum im Schottenstift ☉ – *Entrance through No 1 Schottenhof. 1st floor.* This art gallery contains some fine 17C still lives by Christian Luyckx, Alexander Coosemans and Nicolaas van Veerendael, as well as paintings by Peter Paul Rubens *(Christ as Salvator Mundi)*, Christian Seybold *(Self Portrait,* about 1755), Giovanni Battista Pittoni *(The Sacrifice of Abraham,* about 1720), David Vinckboons *(Alpine Landscape,* 1602), Jan Provost *(Jonas Hurled in the Waves,* 1465), Tobias Pock *(Coronation of the Virgin,* about 1655), Joachim von Sandrart *(Celestial Glory,* 1671). The star exhibit is the **Schottenaltar★★** (altarpiece of the Scots) dating from about 1470; it was created by the master craftsman who took his name. This late Gothic work occupies a room specially designed for it and comprises 19 panels (originally 24). One of its most interesting features is the way it conveys a picture of medieval Vienna. For example, in *The Flight into Egypt (see illustration),* the fortified city walls, Kärntnerstrasse and, in the background, the cathedral with its south tower are all clearly visible. Those who know the city well can amuse themselves by identifying silhouettes of buildings still visible today, such as the Romanesque tower of Peterskirche (St Peter's Church). Others will enjoy the perusal of scenes from the lives of Christ or the Virgin in a Viennese context, as in the first panel of the series, *Christ's Entry into Jerusalem.*

Schottenhof – Between 1869 and 1886, the Court of the Scots harboured a famous resident at No 3: Franz Liszt who stayed here when he gave recitals in Vienna. The shady terrace of Café Haag is very pleasant in summer.

At No 7 of this square is "Schubladkastenhaus", the "chest-of-drawers house", a Viennese nickname due to its resemblance to Biedermeier furniture. It is the former monastery priory built in 1774 by Andreas or Franz Zach. At No 4 Renngasse is the **Schönborn-Battyány palace**, which underwent alterations by Johann Fischer von Erlach at the end of the 17C. It belonged to the great Hungarian Battyány family, one of whose members, Charles Joseph, served as general under Prince Eugène of Savoy.

MUSEUM IM SCHOTTENSTIFT, Wien

Schottenstift: *The Flight into Egypt*

Palais Kinsky – *Freyung 4*. Johann Lukas von Hildebrandt built this mansion for the Imperial Count Daun between 1713 and 1716. It is a remarkable, and arguably the finest, example of Baroque civil architecture in the city. The splendid **façade★** displays a rich assortment of escutcheons, statues, huge pilasters, varied pediments and sculpted motifs. Above the monumental porch with its telamones is a pointed concave pediment.

A great patron of the arts, Prince Ferdinand Kinsky distinguished himself at the battle of Aspern (1809) and received the Order of Maria Theresa from Archduke Karl. He died at the age of 30 after falling from his horse in his estate in Weltrus, in Bohemia. This colonel was at the height of his fame in 1809, when he decided to detain in Vienna a certain Ludwig van Beethoven summoned to Kassel by Jerome of Westphalia. Together with Joseph von Lobkowitz and Archduke Rudolf, Kinsky offered the German composer a life annuity of 4,000 florins to keep him in Austria. Unfortunately for the great composer who dedicated his *Mass in C major* to the "noble prince", the Austrian currency devalued in 1811.

Palais Harrach (**P³**) – *Freyung 3*. Ferdinand Bonaventura Count Harrach commissioned this palace built between 1696 and 1699 to plans by Domenico Martinelli. It displays an elegant façade and the interior houses the Museum Shop and **Arts Centre** of the Kunsthistorisches Museum. Temporary exhibitions of a high standard take place there regularly. They provide an opportunity to see the majestic décor of the rooms which escaped bomb damage in 1944, particularly the chapel designed by J.L. von Hildebrandt.

Palais Ferstel (**P²**) – *Freyung 2 and Herrengasse 14*. In 1860, Heinrich von Ferstel built this palace which bears his name; he was the architect of the Votivkirche, Universität and Österreichisches Museum für Angewandte Kunst (Austrian Museum of Applied Arts) on the Ring. The building housed the National Bank and the Stock Exchange before recent restoration work saved it from collapse.

Freyung Passage is a small and elegant shopping arcade linking Herrengasse to Freyung. It has an attractive interior courtyard containing the Donaunixenbrunnen (fountain of the Danube sprites) by Anton Dominik Fernkorn (1861). In the palace is the Café Central *(see below)*.

Kunstforum (**M¹⁴**) ⓘ – *Freyung 8*. The Arts Forum of the Bank of Austria stages large thematic exhibitions. Gustav Peihl designed the gallery in 1987; the gilt metal ball above the entrance is a hommage to Josef Maria Olbrich's Secession pavilion *(see Secessiongebäude)*.

South of the square, take Heidenschuss. Before reaching Am Hof square, notice the Jugendstil façade of No 9 Bognerstrasse which is an extension of Heidenschuss.

The shopping arcade in Palais Ferstel

3 BIS/MICHELIN

Am Hof and the old Jewish quarter

Am Hof – There was once a Roman camp on the site of this square, which has always been one of the liveliest in the city. From the 12C to the 15C, it was a setting for tournaments. Its name, "At Court", refers to the fact that Henry II Jasomirgott, first Duke of Austria, settled there when he chose Vienna as his ducal capital in 1156.

Mariensäule – The Virgin Mary's Pillar in the centre of the square dates from 1667. The statue of the Virgin is by Balthasar Herold. It stands on a pedestal flanked by armoured cherubs fighting the scourges attacking the city: War (a lion), Plague (a basilisk), Famine (a dragon) and Heresy (a serpent).

Römische Baureste ⓘ – *Am Hof 9*. Traces of the Roman camp are visible.

Feuerwehrmuseum ⊙ – *Am Hof 7*. There are about 400 exhibits in the Fire Service Museum, tracing the history of firefighting (vehicles, equipment, uniforms, pictures, etc.)

Kirche "Zu den neun Chören der Engel" (K⁸) – *Am Hof bei 13*. The church of the Nine Choirs of the Angels is a former Jesuit church. Its chief attraction is its early Baroque façade (1662) which has never undergone alterations and is by the Italian architect Carlo Antonio Carlone. The remarkable design of the balcony was ahead of its time. Emperor Franz II appeared on it to announce the end of the Holy Roman Germanic Empire, on 6 August 1806. Hideous neon lighting spoils the view of the interior of the church, which contains an interesting high altar by Johann Georg Däringer (1798) and a fresco by Andrea Pozzo on the ceiling of St Ignatius' chapel (4th chapel on the right). There are other interesting

Am Hof: Close-up of the fire station

sights on the square. At No 13, the Collalto palace (1671) displays its pointed pediments; supposedly, it was this palace rather than Schönbrunn which was the setting of Mozart's first concert at the age of 6. At No 12, a Baroque house (about 1730) with a façade in the style of J.L. von Hildebrandt. At No 10, Bürgerliches Zeughaus or the burghers' former arsenal is now the headquarters of the Fire Brigade; above the Neoclassical pediment of the façade by Anton Ospel (1732) are **sculptures** by Lorenzo Mattielli *(see illustration)*.

Southeast of the square, take Drahtgasse.

Judenplatz – During the 13C, the Jews obtained permission to settle in Vienna, acquire property and engage in commerce. They built a synagogue, hospital, school and baths on the site and near *(Schulhof)* this square; its present name evokes their residence in Vienna. In 1783, Mozart occupied Nos 3 and 4, soon after his marriage to Konstanz Weber. At No 11 is the rear façade of the former Chancellery of Bohemia *(see Böhmische Hofkanzlei)*. At No 2, the façade of the "Haus zum Grossen Jordan" has a relief depicting the Baptism of Christ in the Jordan, because the owner of the house following the expulsion of the Jews in 1421 was called Jordan. The allusion to purification on the relief is sadly edifying.

The Bohemian Hussite heresy constituted a threat to northern Lower Austria in 1420. One year later, on 12 March 1421, Viennese Jews suffered persecution. Baptised by force or driven from the city, they abandoned the medieval ghetto; at Erdberg, 210 of them were burned alive.

Take Kurrentgasse, a charming street featuring the pink and white façade of No 12, with its attractive porch (about 1730). At the end of the street, take the first on the right for Schulhof.

★**Uhrenmuseum der Stadt Wien (M¹⁷)** ⊙ – *Schulhof 2*. The Clock and Watch Museum lies behind the church of the Nine Choirs of the Angels (Zu den neuen Chören der Engel). It occupies three floors and traces the aesthetic and technical development of timepieces from the 15C to the 20C. The museum has 12,000 exhibits and its vast collections range from the clepsydra to the computer watch or the Biedermeier *Laterndl*. A certain number of exhibits have won the museum a reputation for excellence throughout Europe. *1st floor*: the clock (1699) from Stephansdom (St Stephen's cathedral, Room 1); an astronomical wall clock (1663) of Austrian manufacture (Room 2, *see illustration in Admission times and charges)*; a clock (1752) by Louis Monet, a splendid **astronomical clock★** (1769) made in Vienna by Brother David a Sancto Cajetano (Room 4). *2nd floor*: a turnip watch (about 1760) by Nicolas Nicot (Room 10). *3rd floor*: a clock (1905) signed Josef Hoffmann (Room 13); Jaeger-Lecoultre's Atmos clock (1955) powered by changes in temperature (Room 15); a fob watch for the blind (1800) by Breguet and an aviator's watch (about 1940) by Adolf Lange (Room 16).

Puppen- und Spielzeugmuseum (M¹⁶) ⊙ – *Schulhof 4, 1st floor*. The 4 rooms of the Doll and Toy Museum specialize mainly in antique porcelain dolls. Of special interest are those in the Queen Anne (about 1750), Empire (about 1800) and Biedermeier (1840-1880) styles.

South of Schulhof, turn right into Seitzergasse then turn left into Bognergasse. At the end of it, turn right for Kohlmarkt.

Around the Hofburg

After leaving Graben *(see under this heading)* on the left, one enters **Kohlmarkt** (the former coal market), a pedestrianised street leading to Hofburg lined with some of the most luxurious shops in the city. At the corner of Wallnerstrasse, at No 6, is the Thonet shop; its bistro chair enjoys worldwide renown. Farther along on the same side, at No 14, is the tearoom Demel's, one of Vienna's major institutions. Following its foundation in 1785 on Michaelerplatz by Christoph Demel, it moved to the Kohlmarkt in 1857; after just a taste of one of their pastries, it is easy to see why Demel's was supplier of confectionery to the imperial court. Still on the right at No 16 is the Manz bookshop which Adolf Loos designed in 1912 (it has undergone several alterations since then).

On the left at No 9 is Artariahaus (1902) by Max Fabiani. This building is an important milestone in the history of the Viennese Secession movement, since it is a precursor of the Looshaus *(see below)*. Joseph Haydn lived in Grosses Michaelerhaus (1720) at No 11.

Take Wallnerstrasse.

Wallnerstrasse – This street is almost as elegant as Herrengasse *(see below)* running parallel to it; it boasts fine edifices such as: the Lamberg palace (No 3), nicknamed Kaiserhaus because Emperor Franz I held audience there; the Esterházy palace (No 4) *(undergoing restoration)*, built between 1809 and 1813 to designs by the Frenchman Charles de Moreau, and the residence of Otto von Bismarck in 1892; the Caprara-Geymüller palace (No 8) built by the Italian Domenico Egidio Rossi for Enea Silvio Caprara about 1698 and purchased in 1798 by the banker Jakob Geymüller; its Pompeiian drawing room is on view at the Historisches Museum der Stadt Wien *(see under this heading)*.

At the end of Wallnerstrasse, bear left for Herrengasse.

Herrengasse – The busy but serene "Lords' Street" links Freyung to Michaelerplatz. The palaces bordering it evoke its aristocratic past. At present, it is the location of some major administrative organisations: the Ferstel palace (No 14, *see above*); Landhaus of Lower Austria (No 13), a palace dating from the 16C and rebuilt in the 19C, which was the seat of the Diet of this province; the palace of the Lower Austrian Government (No 11); the Mollard-Clary palace (No 9) which houses the Niederösterreichisches Landesmuseum *(see below)*; the Innenministerium (Ministry of the Interior) in the former Modena palace (No 7) dating from the 16C, its façade remodelled in the early 19C by Ludwig Pichl and Giacomo Quarenghi; the Wilczek palace (No 5, 1737), home of poets Franz Grillparzer and Joseph von Eichendorff.

Palais Mollard-Clary – *Herrengasse 9*. The Museum of Lower Austria was located in the former Mollard-Clary palace (1689), with its rocaille salons. The collections are soon to be transferred to St. Pölten.

In the courtyard, there is a well, covered with a beautiful wrought iron grille (1570).

Café Central – *Herrengasse 14*. This café reopened in 1986. It was a famous meeting place for artists and intellectuals such as the writers Peter Altenberg (immortalised in a papier maché sculpture near the entrance), Franz Werfel and Stefan Zweig, or the politician Léon Trotsky, who founded *Pravda* in Vienna.

★ **Michaelerplatz** – West of St Michael's Square is the elegant St Michael's wing *(see Michaelertrakt)* of the Hofburg, at the far end of Kohlmarkt. For anyone visiting Vienna, this square is an essential tourist attraction. In the centre are Roman remains uncovered during digs in 1992; they will soon be two thousand years old. At No 2, **Café Griensteidl** is the descendant of the establishment of the same name which opened in 1847. This café boasted the privilege of being the original literary café. Its patrons were so intent on remaking the world that it was nicknamed the "delusions-of-grandeur café". Until 1897, it was a centre for young writers such as Hugo von Hofmannsthal, who made it his intellectual home. The new café has an unimpeded view of Michaelertrakt.

At No 3, Adolf Loos built the **Looshaus** from 1909 to 1911 for the firm of Goldman & Salatsch. This building, listed in 1947, is one of his best-known works. It made a considerable impact, since from its position in the Innere Stadt opposite the Hofburg, it epitomised the difference between the architecture of the old town and the new. During its construction, there was controversy both among the public

City Centre and the Ring

and the city councillors, who wanted to clothe the "indecent nudity" of the upper section. The dispute grew so heated that the police closed the building site. Finally, the city council tired of these complications and Loos' inflexibility and allowed the architect to finish his house "without eyebrows". It seems that Franz-Josef avoided looking at it by keeping the palace curtains drawn. Today, the Raiffeisenbank Wien occupies the Looshaus; the counters on the ground floor are open to the public, and the floor above opens for temporary exhibitions.

Michaelerkirche ⊙ – *Michaelerplatz 1*. St Michael's Church was the former Court parish church and dates from 1220. It has undergone many alterations. Its octagonal tower dates from 1340, the spire from 1598 and the Neoclassical façade from 1792. Before the entrance, on the right of the church *(access by a pedestrianised passage)*, there is a fine carved stone relief of the *Mount of Olives* (1494).

There were additions to the church in the 14C and renovations in the 16C. The interior is a mixture of styles, including Gothic: the choir (1327) and remains of frescoes, particularly on the triumphal arch; Renaissance: Georg von Liechtenstein's tombstone (1548) against the last pillar of the right side aisle; Baroque: David Sielber's great organ (1714), Michelangelo Unterberger's *Fall of the Angels* (1751) in the right arm of the transept and the high altar (1781) by Jean Baptiste d'Avrange, with carved figures by Johann Martin Fischer and Jakob Philipp Prokop and above it a remarkable **Fall of the Angels★** by Karl Georg Merville (1782). This group is the last religious work in Baroque style of Viennese origin *(see illustration in the Introduction, Painting)*.

The entrance to the crypt lies next to the north side altar with an altarpiece by Franz Anton Maulbertsch (1755). An ossuary and some open coffins emphasize the lugubrious atmosphere. It is also the burial place of Pietro Trapassi (1698-1782), known as Metastasio, official Court Poet and a protégé of Maria Theresa *(3rd coffin on the right)*.

Cross the square for Schauflergasse.

Bundeskanzleramt – The former Privy Court Chancellery houses the Office of the Federal Chancellor. It was built to plans by J.L. von Hildebrandt and underwent several alterations. On 28 June 1914, after Franz Ferdinand's assassination at Sarajevo, the ultimatum to Serbia was written here. Here too, in the corner reception room, Kurt von Schuschnigg broadcast his famous "May God protect Austria!" in 1938 *(see below for the reason)*.

The assassination of Dollfuss or towards the Anschluss – As Chancellor, Engelbert Dollfuss had established an authoritarian, Christian, anti-Marxist and anti-Semitic government, totally opposed to the National Socialist party in Germany, because it wished to uphold the independence of Austria. On 25 July 1934, he was murdered by a local SS group, during an attempted putsch at the chancellery. He had made the mistake of asking for support from Mussolini, who willingly gave it to him to guard against the presence of Germany on the Brenner Pass. This partly explains, without justifying it, the lack of reaction internationally to this murder; Dollfuss had lost the sympathy of the western powers, particularly after the violent events of February 1934 *(see Karl-Marx-Hof)*. After Dollfuss' death, Von Papen came to Vienna to set up the *Anschluss*. The new chancellor, Von Schuschnigg, was a cleric and a monarchist; despite his courage, Hitler's expansionist policies triumphed over Von Schuschnigg's short-lived national union. On 14 March 1938, Hitler marched into Vienna and annexed Austria.

Turn right into Bruno-Kreisky-Gasse.

Minoritenplatz – Several palaces surround the square, including the Lichtenstein palace (No 4, *see Bankgasse below*) and Strahemberg (No 5) palace, by an unknown architect (mid 17C).

Minoritenkirche ⊙ – Work began on the church of the Friars Minor in the first half of the 14C. Joseph II gave it to the Italian community of Vienna. After Baroque refurbishments in the 17C and 18C, the building regained its Gothic appearance at the end of the 18C. The chevet is flanked by an octagonal tower which Turkish attacks damaged in 1683. On the right side is an elegant ribbed gallery. The central porch displays a fine *Crucifixion* (1350) allegedly by a Franciscan friar, "Brother Jacob". The interior is striking with its almost square design and its three aisles of equal height, transforming it into a hall-church. On the left wall is a massive mosaic copy by Giacomo Raffaelli of Leonardo's *Last Supper*. Napoleon commissioned it in Milan as a replacement for the original fresco which he wished to transfer to Paris. Next to it, the bas-relief of the Virgin is by A. Rosselino (1427-1478). Against the left pillar of the nave is a 15C fresco of St Francis of Assisi, which has been taken down. Gothic fragments of the building are on view on the ground floor of the Historical Museum of the City of Vienna *(see Historisches Museum der Stadt Wien)*.

Take Petrarcagasse for Bankgasse.

Bankgasse – This is another street lined with splendid palaces. At No 2, the Battyány palace (about 1695) is in the style of Johann Bernhard Fischer von Erlach. At Nos 4 and 6, the Hungarian Embassy concealed behind a communal façade

(1784) by Franz Anton Hillebrand occupies the Trautson and Strattmann-Windischgrätz palaces. At No 9, Stadtpalais Liechtenstein was originally built for Count Kaunitz. Three architects worked on it: Domenico Martinelli, Antonio Riva and Gabriel de Gabrieli from 1694 to 1706. The façade is a magnificent creation with its monumental portal and sculptures by Giovanni Giulani.

Continue behind Burgtheater and bear right into Oppolzergasse, at right angles to Schreyvogelgasse.

Dreimäderlhaus – *Schreyvogelgasse 10. Closed to the public.* The "House of the Three Maidens" is a pretty Neoclassical residential house dating from 1803. Some people claim that it gets its name from the fact that Franz Schubert kept three mistresses there, the daughters of the master glassworker Franz Tschöll. Unfortunately for Schubert, this is sheer fiction.

Return up Schreyvogelgasse and turn right into Mölkerbastei.

★ **Pasqualatihaus** ⊙ – *Mölkerbastei 8. 4th floor.* This late 18C mansion bears the name of its owner, Josef Benedikt, Baron Pasqualiti. It houses one of the three museums in Vienna commemorating Ludwig van Beethoven *(see also Beethoven-haus in Heiligenstadt and Eroicahaus in Oberdöbling, in the Grinzing District).* There are numerous memorials to Beethoven in the capital.

In 1804 and from 1813 to 1815, the composer lived in two rooms on the 4th floor, with an unimpeded view, as it was before the construction of the Ring. There he wrote the opera *Fidelio*, first performed at the Theater an der Wien, the Fourth, Fifth and Seventh Symphonies as well as the piano concerto in G major Opus 58. The museum displays various objects and documents relating to the composer of the immortal *Ninth Symphony*. Among other mementoes, there are facsimiles of scores, including *Fidelio* (1805), a facsimile of a signed letter to Josephine Gräfin née Brunswick, a lock of hair, a Streicher piano made in Vienna, Beethoven's death mask and several portraits including an oil painting (1805) by W.J. Mähler. It is possible and pleasant to listen to extracts from his works *(earphones)*, such as the Corolian overtures and the opening to his only opera, *Fidelio*.

Besides the first part of the Ring, the nearest sights are: the Hofburg, the tour around Stephansdom, the Hoher Markt and Kapuzinerkirche Districts, as well as the Alsergrund and Josefstadt Districts.

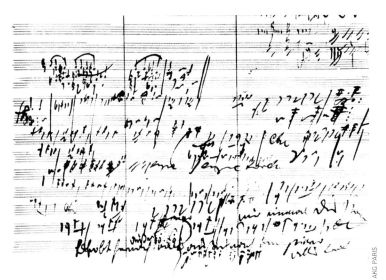

AKG PARIS

A signed manuscript of Beethoven's *Fifth Symphony*

*The **Practical information** section at the end of the guide lists:*

– information on travel, motoring, accommodation, recreation;
– local or national organisations providing additional information;
– the calendar of events;
– admission times and charges for the sights described in the guide.

HOFBURG★★★

Local map page 5, **JR**

Underground: Herrengasse (U3), Volkstheater (U2, U3)
Tram: Burgring (1, 2, D, J), Dr. Karl-Renner-Ring (1, 2, 46, 49, D, J)
Bus: Burgring (57A), Dr. Karl-Renner-Ring (48A), Heldenplatz (2A), Michaelerplatz (2A, 3A)

A TOWN WITHIN A TOWN

The imperial palace, favourite residence of the Habsburgs, became progressively larger over the centuries. There are no traces of the original building, a quadrilateral bristling with towers built in the second half of the 13C. This fortress had been built as a defence against the Turkish and Hungarian attacks upon Vienna, which continued until the end of the 17C. In their efforts to turn it into a palace, sovereigns continually enlarged and embellished their residence. This accounts for the juxtaposition of widely differing styles in this varied assortment of buildings.

Among the oldest are the Hofburgkapelle (chapel, mid-15C), Schweizertor (Swiss gate, mid-16C), Amalienhof (16C), and Stallburg (stables, 16C). In the 17C, Leopold I had the Leopoldinischer Trakt (Leopold wing) built. At the beginning of the 18C, Karl VI commissioned major alterations from the greatest Baroque architects in the empire, Johann Bernhard and Josef Emmanuel Fischer von Erlach and Johann Lukas von Hildebrandt. They built the Reichskanzleitrakt (Chancellery Wing), Winter-reitschule (Winter Riding School) which now houses the Spanish Riding School, and Prunksaaltrakt (now the National Library); the Albertina dates from the same period. Following the erection of Michaelertrakt (St Michael's Wing, completed in 1893), work started on Neue Burg after the construction of the Ring; its completion just before 1914 marked the end of the monumental history of the imperial palace. Despite numerous alterations, the Hofburg has retained the austerity of its military origins; in 1287, enraged by a wrong decision from the councillors, the Viennese besieged the castle to the great displeasure of the future Albert I.

This is indeed a town within a town: squares, gardens and buildings lie at the very heart of the Austrian capital, covering a total area of 240,000m²/287,037sq yds.

The description of the Hofburg is divided into two parts, since it is hard to envisage the palace as one entity. The first part, "The Louvre of the Habsburgs", describes its exterior architecture and the squares dividing it; the second, "Memories of the Habsburgs", gives an account of the museums and buildings open to the public.

The Louvre of the Habsburgs

History records in the *Continuatio vidobonensis* that in 1275, Ottokar II Przemysl, King of Bohemia and Duke of Moravia, built an impregnable castle in Vienna on the site of the present Schweizerhof. It is probable that even in the 15C this castle included state apartments. It is known that Sigismund of Luxemburg, King of Hungary, resided there in 1422 with some church dignitaries; four years later, John I, King of Portugal also stayed there. When, in 1533, Ferdinand, King of Bohemia and Hungary, moved the central administration of the States of Prague to Vienna, it became necessary to enlarge the palace and endow it with apartments fit for the future Ferdinand I. In fact, it became the residence of all the sovereigns thereafter. This heralded the birth of the Hofburg, a colossal creation in stone, symbolising the Austro-Hungarian empire and conjuring up an era when the House of Austria ruled from Castile to the West Indies.

Severe and full of majesty, the Hofburg resembles the Louvre in some ways: both date from the Middle Ages; both were not merely powerful strongholds; they were and are still centres of culture and city life (museums, shops, government offices). More spread-out than the Louvre, the Hofburg provides remarkable vistas of the courtyards between various parts of the Alte Burg and the Neue Burg, or of the buildings around the palace.

The view of the Neue Burg from Volksgarten, particularly at night (see illustration), is one of the most impressive in the Hofburg. However, it is preferable to approach the palace from Michaelerplatz.

★**Michaelerplatz** – *See Freyung District* – This square does not form part of the Hofburg, but it is through that one reaches the imperial palace when arriving from the town centre via Kohlmarkt. This is the same route that the emperor and his family took on their way back to their apartments or audience chambers.

★**Michaelertrakt** – The semicircular façade of St Michael's Wing faces towards Michaelerplatz. Although J.E. Fischer von Erlach had prepared plans for it, it was not built until between 1888 and 1893. This followed Emperor Franz-Josef's decision to link the Reichskanzleitrakt (Chancellery Wing) and the Winterreitschule (Winter Riding School); the old Burgtheater had moved to a new building on the ring and therefore no longer prevented the construction of Michaelertrakt (St Michael's Wing). Drawing inspiration from the colonnade of the Louvre, the façade displays two monumental fountains adorned by statues symbolising naval power (Rudolf Weyr, 1895) on the left and military might (Edmund Helmer, 1897) on the right. **The Michaelertor★** is a gateway flanked with groups depicting the Labours of Hercules. Its superb wrought-iron gates open into the rotunda. The outline of the **dome★** of St Michael's Wing is among the most elegant and famous views in Vienna.

Michaelerkuppel – There is a splendid view of the steeple of St Michael through the wrought-iron tracery of Michaelertor. There are also niches with statues representing the imperial mottoes of Karl VI, *Constantia et fortitudine* (Perseverance and courage), Maria Theresa, *Justitia et clementia* (Justice and mercy), Josef II, *Virtute et exemplo* (Courage and example), and Franz-Josef, *Viribus unitis* (United strength). The rotunda leads to the Kaiserappartements, Hofsilber- und Tafelkammer, Esperanto-Museum and Spanische Reitschule *(see below)*.

In der Burg – The former Franzenplatz was once the setting for horse races and tournaments. In its centre stands a statue of the Emperor Franz II by Pompeo Marchesi (1846). A Latin

A fountain in Michaelertrakt

inscription on the base is a quotation from his will: "My love to my peoples".

To the south of this inner courtyard is **Schweizertor★**, the Swiss gate built in 1552 (by Pietro Ferrabosco?) inspired by Michele Sanmicheli's gates in the town walls in Verona. He had succeeded in combining defensive purpose with formal majesty. This Renaissance gate, named after the Swiss guard manning it in 1748, replaced a drawbridge across the moat, traces of which are still visible along Alte Burg. The cartouche bears the name of Ferdinand I, ruler of Germany, Hungary, Bohemia, Spain, Austria and Burgundy.

Amalientrakt – The Amalia Wing, named after the empress who lived there in the 18C, was built in 1577 by Pietro Ferrabosco and completed in 1610 by Hans Schneider and Antonio de Moys. It was originally detached from the other buildings. Empress Elizabeth's apartments and those occupied by Tsar Alexander *(see Kaiserappartements)* are open to the public. The palace surrounds Amalienhof, a trapezoid courtyard with a fine ornate gate.

Leopoldinischer Trakt – The Leopold Wing was the headquarters of Count Starhemberg who resisted the Turks during the 1683 siege. It was built in the reign of Leopold I to link the Amalia Wing to the rest of the Hofburg. Building work began about 1660 to designs by Filiberto Lucchese but the wing was burnt down in 1668 and was rebuilt by Giovanni Pietro Tencala. This wing, which accommodated Marie-Theresa and her husband, Franz-Stefan, now houses the department of the President of the Federal Republic of Austria. His personal office is Josef II's former study.

Reichskanzleitrakt – In 1723, J.E. Fischer von Erlach began the Chancellery Wing opposite Leopoldinischer Trakt. The architect died in April of the same year. The façade was not completed until 1730, closing off In der Burg courtyard. J.L. von Hildebrandt designed the wing on Schauflergasse which dates from 1723. Franz-Josef's apartments are open to the public *(see Kaiserappartements)*.

Schweizerhof – The Swiss Courtyard is the oldest part of the Hofburg, forming the very heart of the Alte Burg or old palace. In the mid-16C, Ferdinand I turned Alte Burg into a Renaissance palace. Traces of its style are still visible around the window frames on each of the four façades. The courtyard leads to Hofburgkapelle and Schatzkammer *(see under these headings)*.

Take the arched passageway at the southeast corner of the courtyard.

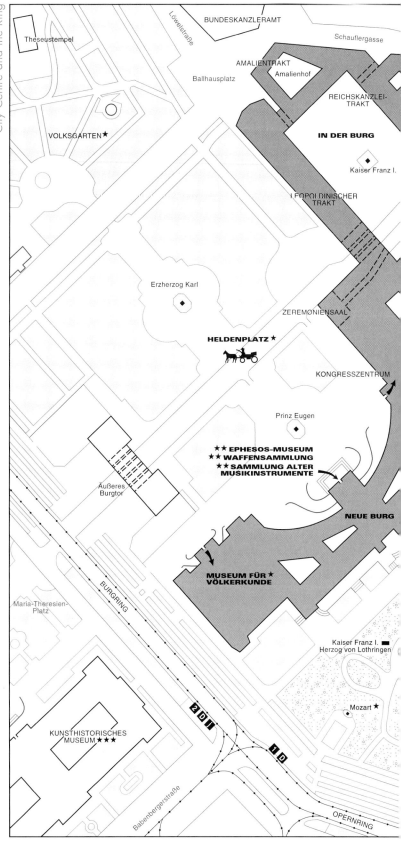

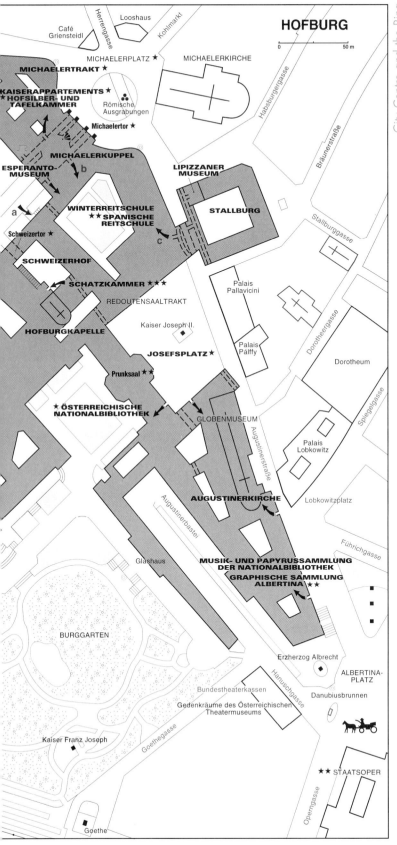

HOFBURG

0   50 m

Café Griensteidl

Herrengasse

Looshaus

Kohlmarkt

MICHAELERPLATZ ★

MICHAELERKIRCHE

MICHAELERTRAKT ★

Habsburgergasse

Bräunerstraße

KAISERAPPARTEMENTS ★
★ **HOFSILBER- UND
TAFELKAMMER**

Römische Ausgrabungen

Michaelertor ★

MICHAELERKUPPEL

b

**ESPERANTO-
MUSEUM**

**LIPIZZANER
MUSEUM**

a

**WINTERREITSCHULE
★★ SPANISCHE
REITSCHULE**

STALLBURG

Stallburggasse

Schweizertor ★

c

SCHWEIZERHOF

SCHATZKAMMER ★★★

Palais
Pallavicini

Dorotheergasse

REDOUTENSAALTRAKT

Kaiser Joseph II.

HOFBURGKAPELLE

Palais
Pálffy

Dorotheum

JOSEFSPLATZ ★

Prunksaal ★★

Spiegelgasse

★ **ÖSTERREICHISCHE
NATIONALBIBLIOTHEK**

GLOBENMUSEUM

Palais
Lobkowitz

Augustinerstraße

AUGUSTINERKIRCHE

Lobkowitzplatz

Augustinerbastei

Führichgasse

Glashaus

**MUSIK- UND PAPYRUSSAMMLUNG
DER NATIONALBIBLIOTHEK**
**GRAPHISCHE SAMMLUNG
ALBERTINA ★★**

BURGGARTEN

Erzherzog Albrecht

**ALBERTINA-
PLATZ**

Hanuschgasse

Bundestheaterkassen

Danubiusbrunnen

Gedenkräume des Österreichischen
Theatermuseums

Goethegasse

Kaiser Franz Joseph

★★ **STAATSOPER**

Operngasse

Goethe

★ **Josefsplatz** – This well-proportioned square is one of the finest in Vienna. It resembles a main courtyard and owes its name to the equestrian statue of Josef II in the centre (Franz Anton Zauner, 1806). During the 1848 revolution, this monument served as a rallying point for supporters of the Habsburgs.

At No 1 and 2 is the present Österreichisches Nationalbibliothek *(see also under this heading)*, the former Court Library. The Fischer von Erlach dynasty of architects built it (1723 to 1726). Its main façade, with alterations by Nikolaus Pacassi, is very effective; the masonry base with its splayed ridges pierced by an undecorated portal is reminiscent of the Renaissance; the Ionic order of pilasters on the upper storeys evokes the French C17 pre-Classical style; the attic and roof are Austrian. The decorative features at this level are well worth close study; quadrigas and immense golden globes borne by telamones emerge into view. Behind this façade is a magnificent hall of state, the Prunksaal.

At No 3, the Redoutensaaltrakt (Redoute Chamber Wing) was the setting for court masked balls. Its façade by N. Pacassi (1770) harmonises with that of the National Library. The two ballrooms, built to designs by Jean-Nicolas Jadot de Ville-Issey (about 1748) were decorated by Ferdinand Hetzendorf von Hohenberg in 1760. On 27 November 1992, a fire entirely destroyed the small room. Every year, the Kaiserball takes place in the large room with its coffered ceiling resting on 24 marble Corinthian columns. The elite of Viennese society attend this ball.

The fourth side of the square is closed off by the Pallavicini (No 5) and Pálffy (No 6) palaces. F. Hetzendorf von Hohenberg, architect of the Schönbrunn Gloriette built the first of these in 1784. It has a fine portal with caryatids and an attic adorned with statues, both by F.A. Zauner. It was the residence of a great patron of music, Count Fries, whose enthusiasm precipitated his downfall. The building no longer bears his name, which however is preserved for posterity on the frontispiece of Beethoven's *Seventh Symphony*. The second palace, built in 1575, was the setting for Mozart's first production of *The Marriage of Figaro*; it now houses Österreichhaus (Austria House).

Stallburg – *Reitschulgasse 2.* A glassed-in arcade separates this palace from the Winterreitschule (Winter Riding School); Ferdinand I had it built, between 1558 and 1565, for his son, Archduke Maximilian. When Maximilian ascended the throne, he lived in the Hofburg and the Maximilian palace was converted: the ground floor of the three storeys of galleries around the Renaissance courtyard became stables for the horses of the Court. Then, from 1593 to 1766, the first floor housed the imperial pages. Since Karl VI's reign, the stables have been home to the Lippizaners of the Spanische Reitschule; a museum was opened there in 1998 *(see Lipizzaner Museum)*.

3 BIS/MICHELIN

Winterreitschule – Opposite Stallburg is the Winter Riding School, used for performances by the Spanish Riding School. It was built by J.E. Fischer von Erlach from 1729 to 1735 *(interior: see Spanische Reitschule)*.
Return to In der Burg to reach Heldenplatz via the arched passageway.

★**Heldenplatz** – In 1809, the parade ground on the site of fortifications dismantled by Napoleon became the Heroes' Square after the unveiling of two equestrian statues designed by Anton Dominik Fernkorn. One depicted Prince Eugène of Savoy, the victor of the Turks in the 17C, while the other was of Archduke Karl, who defeated Napoleon at Aspern in 1809.
Standing with one's back to Volksgarten, the buildings seen from left to right are: the Amalia Palace and Leopold Wing *(see Amalientrakt and Leopoldinischer Trakt above)*, the façade of the Hall of Ceremonies built by the Belgian architect Louis Montoyer in 1806, Kongresszentrum (Congress centre) built by the same architect from 1802 to 1806, and Neue Burg *(see below)*. The fan-shaped façade of this palace overlooks the square. The view extends past the shady Volksgarten to the steeple of Neues Rathaus.
Southwest of the square, Äusseres Burgtor is a monumental gateway opening onto the Ring; Luigi Cagnola began it in 1821 and Pietro Nobile completed it in 1824. In 1934, Rudolf Wondracek converted it into a Heldendenkmal, a monument commemorating the victims of the First World War; after the Second World War a memorial was erected there to members of the Austrian resistance.

Neue Burg – The new imperial palace dating from between 1881 and 1913 is in the style of the Italian Renaissance. The architects, Karl Hasenauer and Gottfried Semper intended to complement it on the northwest side by a similar wing, but this was never built. They had in fact planned to construct a gigantic imperial forum, but Franz-Josef was satisfied with this impressive wing bordering the Ring. Beneath the colonnade in the gallery, statues between the bays represent outstanding figures from Austrian history. The interior of Neue Burg was not completed until 1926; it houses the following museums: Ephesos-Museum, Waffensammlung, Sammlung Alter Musikinstrumente, Museum für Völkerkunde *(see below)*.
Historical fact: it was from the balcony of Neue Burg that Adolf Hitler proclaimed the annexation of Austria in 1938. Literary event: Thomas Bernhard recounted this episode in his play *Heldenplatz*, produced in Vienna in 1988. It stirred deep feelings among both press and public, to say the least.

The gardens of the "imperial forum" – After Napoleon's departure in 1809 and the dismantling of the town walls which he had ordered, it was decided to extend the imperial city. The centre was already densely developed in the centre. The

City Centre and the Ring

public park and imperial gardens were laid out on the sites that had been cleared by Napoleon's engineers. The imperial garden later became known as the palace garden. With these new open spaces, Vienna began to lose its defensive character. This finally disappeared, when, in December 1857, Franz-Josef signed the order for the dismantling of the ramparts.

Burggarten – *See under this heading (Ring)*

Volksgarten – *See under this heading (Ring)*.

Souvenirs of the Habsburgs

★Kaiserappartements ⊙ – *Michaelerkuppel.* The imperial apartments are a long succession of rooms which have a certain sameness. They occupy the first floor of the Reichskanzleitrakt and Amalientrakt (Chancellery wing and Amalia wing). Of the 2,600 rooms in the palace about twenty are open to the public. Maria Theresa's rooms and those of her son Josef II (Leopoldinischer Trakt) are now used by the President of the Republic and his departments. The **Kaiserstiege** (imperial staircase) leads to the apartments.

Archduke Stefan's apartments – They are named after the Palatine of Hungary who resided there from 1848 to 1867 after the King of Rome, the son of Napoleon and Archduchess Marie-Louise. The **Speisezimmer** (dining room) is hung with Audenarde tapestries (*The Labours of Hercules*, 16C) and the **Cerclezimmer** (conversation room) displays Brussels tapestries *(Scenes from the Life of Emperor Augustus*, 17C). Both these rooms immediately convey a sense of the decorative unity achieved in the white and gold interiors of the second half of the 19C. The walls of the **Rauchsalon** (smoking room) are covered with Brussels tapestries (*Scenes from the History of Greece and Rome*, 17C). In it are a marble bust of Maximilian I and, on the table, *The Singer's Curse*, a bronze group by Wilhelm Seib inspired by a ballad by the German poet Ludwig Uhland.

Emperor Franz-Josef's apartments – A Trabant, or non-commissioned officer from the imperial bodyguard, was always on duty in the **Trabantenstube** (Trabants' room). It now displays a scale model of the imperial palace during the Middle Ages and a marble bust of Karl V by Karl Costenoble. Twice a week, people waited in the **Audienzsaal** (audience hall) to petition or thank the emperor. Since the beginning of the century, the 80 lights on the Bohemian crystal chandelier have run on electricity, illuminating frescoes by Peter Krafft of scenes from the life of Franz I. In the smaller **Audienzzimmer** (audience room) is the lectern on which lay the list of audiences; near it, the emperor awaited his petitioners. The last portrait of Franz-Josef aged 85 by Heinrich Wassmuth rests on the easel; on the walls are portraits. From left to right they represent Franz I, Ferdinand I, Franz-Josef aged 43, Ferdinand II attacked by the Protestants in 1619. In the **Konferenzzimmer** or council chamber, oil paintings by Anton Adam represent the battles of Temesvár and Komorn in 1849; on the end wall is a portrait of Franz-Josef aged 20. Franz-Josef learned of the tragic death of his son, Crown Prince Rudolf *(see Mayerling)*, in his **Arbeitszimmer**, or study, which contains Elizabeth's portrait by Franz Xaver Winter-

Fotostudio Otto/Museen der Stadt Wien

Johann Strauss the Younger and his Orchestra playing for the Court Ball, by Theo Zarche

halter, and, on the side walls, paintings of the battle of Custozza in 1849 and of the popular Marshal Radetzsky; Johann Strauss the Elder dedicated a famous march to him and his apartments were in a wing of the Alte Burg nearby; the concealed door in the wall leads to the chamberlain's room. In the **Schlafzimmer** (bedroom), with its painted iron bedstead, are several interesting items: four prints of Elizabeth; an oil painting of Archduchess Sophia with her son Franz-Josef aged 2; a miniature on Augarten porcelain of Franz-Josef aged 23 and Sissi aged 16. Beyond the bedchamber are two rooms which were never used after Sissi's death in 1898: **grosser Salon** and **kleiner Salon**; in the main drawing room are two magnificent **portraits★** of Elizabeth and Franz-Josef by F.X. Winterhalter, and in the small drawing room a portrait of his brother Maximilian, shot in Mexico in 1867 by republican revolutionaries.

Empress Elizabeth's apartments – These rooms were successively occupied by Ferdinand I, Elizabeth (from 1864 to 1898) and Karl I (from 1916 to 1918). The **Wohn und Schlafenzimmer der Kaiserin** served as a drawing room and bedroom (the iron bed was taken out every morning). In the **Toilettenzimmer** (bathroom) exercise rings (at the same level as the passage into the next room) convey the amount of care the empress, an excellent horsewoman, took of her physique and her figure; a wood carving by Anton Dominik Fernkorn shows her aged 8, and four watercolours depict Achilleion Palace, which she had built on Corfu. Notable among the objects (Louis XIV furniture, porcelain statuettes by Herman Klotz, Sèvres porcelain vases, etc.) in the **grosser Salon** is Antonio Canova's marble bust (1817) of Elisa Bonaparte, Napoleon I's older sister. The **kleiner Salon** was dedicated to the memory of the empress after her assassination in Geneva in 1898: the display cabinet contains a small allegorical group realised just after her death; there is also a fine **portrait★** of her as Queen of Hungary by Georg Raab. Finally, the **grosses Vorzimmer**, or grand antechamber, is adorned with paintings of Maria Theresa's sixteen children; the life-size statue of Empress Elizabeth aged 50 is by Herman Klotz.

Tsar Alexander's apartments – These became known as Tsar Alexander I of Russia's apartments during the Congress of Vienna in 1815. From 1916 to 1918, Karl I used them as an audience chamber and study. In the **Eingangzimmer** (antechamber) are portraits and busts of Karl I and his wife Zita of Bourbon-Parma. The **Empfangsalon** (reception room) is hung with Gobelin **tapestries★** woven in Paris between 1772 and 1776 after cartoons by François Boucher; they and the furniture were a present to Emperor Josef II from Louis XVI and his wife Marie Antoinette, daughter of Maria Theresa. In the **Speisezimmer** (dining room), the table is beautifully laid as in Franz-Josef's day: in accordance with Spanish court etiquette, all the cutlery is placed on the right of the plate; there are six glasses for white wine, champagne, red wine, liqueur, water and dessert wine respectively. The last room, **kleiner Salon**, is a memorial to the two unfortunate heirs to Franz-Josef's throne, Prince Rudolf who committed suicide at Mayerling and Archduke Franz-Ferdinand assassinated at Sarajevo; on the wall hangs a portrait of Stéphanie of Belgium, Rudolf 's wife, by Hans Makart.

★Hofsilber- und Tafelkammer ⊘ – *Michaelerkuppel. As the rooms are not always clearly identified, numbers referring to items in the display cases appear in brackets in italics.* Objects forming part of the Court porcelain and silver collections were in use until the fall of the Habsburgs in 1918.

The imperial table services include magnificent pieces such as the gilded bronze **Mailänder Tafelausatz★★** (Milan centrepiece) *(138-142)* commissioned in 1838 from Luigi Manfredini's Milanese workshop by Archduke Rainer, viceroy of the kingdom of Lombardy-Venetia, for a table 30m/98 ft long and seating 100 guests. The dancers were inspired by Canova's marble sculptures; the central decoration bears the emblems of Lombardy (stone crown) and Venetia (corno). About 1808, Eugène de Beauharnais, viceroy of Italy commissioned the **"Grand Vermeil"**

A Portrait of Sissi as Queen of Hungary, by Georg Raab

Kunsthistorisches Museum

banqueting service★ *(126-130)* designed by the Parisian Martin-Guillaume Biennais. Five goldsmiths worked on it, among whom was Eugenio Brusa, a Milanese craftsman who made the soup tureen *(126)*. This service for 140 people bears the arms of Napoleon, King of Italy. There are also some admirable porcelain services. The following were a present from the French Court to the Austrian Court: the "Green Ribbon" service (Vincennes and Sèvres, 1756-1757) *(185-187)*; a service on a green background (Sèvres, 1777) *(188-189)*; a service decorated with golden ears of corn (Sèvres, 1778) *(190)*. There are also a Japanese-style tea service (Vienna, about 1825-1850) *(46)* and a dessert service (Herbert Minton & Co., 1851) *(191-193)* by the Frenchman Joseph Arnoux, which Queen Victoria gave to Emperor Franz-Josef. Its "jelly or cream stand" *(192)* is noteworthy: the two-tiered dessert dish is surmounted by a group of *putti* in biscuit ware, apparently eager to savour the jelly and cream of which the English are so fond.

Other pieces are also of great interest: the romantic neo-Gothic style *Habsburger-service* (Vienna, 1821-1824) *(194-197)* with plates adorned by castles in *grisaille* enhanced with matt gold; silverware by Mayerhofer and Klinkosch (Vienna, 1836-1890) *(14-28)*; a fine soup tureen from the gold service (Vienna, 1814) *(35)* used during the Congress of Vienna; a collection assembled by Charles-Alexandre de Lorraine *(106-125)*, brother of Emperor Franz-Stefan and the Lobmeyer imperial glass service (Vienna, 1873) *(173)* engraved by Peter Eisert who devoted three years' work to it.

Esperanto-Museum ⊘ – *Michaelerkuppel. Entrance by the Batthyany staircase.* This is a very small museum on the international language invented in 1887 by the Polish linguist L.L. Zamenhof. A display of posters for various international congresses, photographs and books (including the latest editions), precedes a library of about 17,000 volumes that has been administered by the National Library since 1928. Beginners' manuals are on sale.

Hofburgkapelle ⊘ – *Schweizerhof.* The chapel is the only remaining medieval building around Schweizerhof. It was built between 1447 and 1449 in Frederick III's reign, then in the 17C and 18C underwent Baroque alterations. In 1802, it regained its Gothic interior. The building may not appeal to visitors because of these numerous alterations .

The renowned *Wienersängerknaben* (Vienna Boys' Choir) developed from the choir created by the Court to sing during services in the chapel. They perform here for Sunday mass *(see Practical information)*. Religious reasons apart, the choir is the only significant attraction in this church.

★★★**Schatzkammer** ⊘ – *Schweizerhof 1.* Karl VI moved the imperial treasury into the Alte Burg (his monogram and the date 1712 can be seen on the wrought-iron entrance gate). It is a unique and priceless collection, combining the Crown jewels (rooms 1 to 8 and 9 to 16) and the ecclesiastical treasury (rooms I to V). This treasury is not a systematic collection; it is designed to guarantee the safekeeping of the royal emblems of the Habsburgs and the sacred relics of the Holy Roman Germanic Empire. Undeniably, it is one of the highlights of a visit to Vienna.

Room 1 – These emblems of Habsburg sovereignty over the Archduchy of Austria were used during the ceremony of accession to the throne of the hereditary states corresponding to present-day Austria. Frederick III elevated the duchy of Austria into an archduchy in the mid-15C; the title of archduke set the Habsburgs apart from other Christian princes.

The sceptre and orb (Prague, 14C), the hand of Justice (17C) and the archducal mantle (Vienna, 1764) woven in gold and silver are the most outstanding items of regalia.

Room 2 – After the death of his father-in-law, Sigismond, Duke Albert V inherited the kingdoms of Hungary and Austria and was elected Holy Roman king under the name of Albert II in 1438. This title persisted until the end of the Holy Roman Empire in 1806. The emblems of this status were kept in Nürnberg rather than Vienna, which explains why the rulers had their own private insignia

---

A.E.I.O.U.

Apart from the Emperor Frederick III who thought of this emblem without explaining it, nobody knows what A.E.I.O.U. signifies. It dates from the birth of the House of Habsburg, at the coronation of Frederick, Duke of Styria, in 1440. There have been several interpretations of which *Austria Est Imperare Orbi Universo* (Austria shall rule the world) is the most likely. According to another version, the letters stand for *Austria Erit In Omne Ultimum* (Austria shall survive forever). During the occupation by the King of Hungary, Mathias Corvinus, the Viennese wryly adopted quite a different interpretation: *Aller Est Ist Österreich verloren* (Above all, Austria is lost).

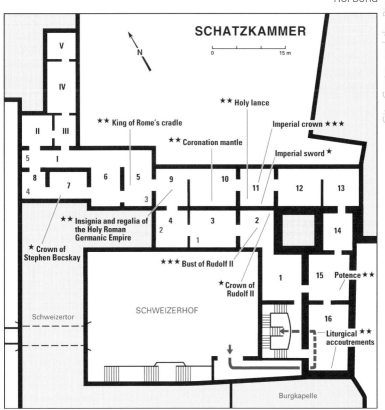

SCHATZKAMMER

0   15 m

★★ Holy lance

★★ King of Rome's cradle

Imperial crown ★★★

★★ Coronation mantle

Imperial sword ★

★★ Insignia and regalia of the Holy Roman Germanic Empire

★★★ Bust of Rudolf II

★ Crown of Stephen Bocskay

★ Crown of Rudolf II

Potence ★★

Schweizertor

SCHWEIZERHOF

Liturgical ★★ accoutrements

Burgkapelle

made, including the famous "family crowns" symbolising the imperial character of their rank. Although most were melted down, the **Kaiserliche Hauskrone of Rudolf II**★★★ is still existant. This magnificent imperial crown was made in Prague by the Antwerp jeweller Jan Vermeyen in the early 17C. It consists of a hoop with 8 lilies, symbolising royal status, an arched band evoking an ancient helmet symbolic of imperial power and a bishop's mitre representing divine law. The 4 embossed gold bas-reliefs adorning the mitre depict Rudolf II, a weak and incompetent emperor, as a victorious general (imperator) who was thrice crowned: in Germany (Augustus), Pressburg (Rex Hungariae) and Prague (rex Bohemiae). Emperor Matthias commissioned a sceptre and orb to match the crown from his court jeweller Andreas Osenbruck (Prague, 1615). This regalia became a symbol of constitutional power when Franz II, anticipating the demise of the Holy Roman German Empire, proclaimed Austria a hereditary empire in 1804 and assumed the title of Franz I, Emperor of *Kaiserreich Österreich* (there is a portrait of him by Friedrich von Amerling, to the left of the entrance). The bronze **bust**★ of Rudolf II by Adrian de Vries (1607) is noteworthy.

Room 3 – In 1830, Ferdinand was crowned King of Hungary. For his coronation, he wore a sumptuous red velvet mantle with a train embroidered with gold and an ermine collar (1) (as in F. von Amerling's painting). Also on display are ceremonial robes, chains and insignia of various orders, such as the Order of St Stephan (Hungary, 1764) and the Order of Leopold (Austria, 1808).

Room 4 – During the Congress of Vienna (1815), Metternich negotiated the award to Austria of the provinces of northern Italy, soon to become the kingdom of Lombardy-Venetia. Since Lombardy's only crown (supposedly made of iron and at present kept in Monza cathedral) seemed too modest, ceremonial robes were created in Vienna for Ferdinand I, including a blue velvet mantle with train (2). There is a herald's tabard to match, bearing the Visconti serpent (Milan) and the lion of St Mark (Venice).

Room 9 – The **insignia and regalia of the Holy Roman German Empire**★★. The empire, founded by Charlemagne in 800, was dissolved on 6 August 1806. The regalia served for the crowning of emperors in Rome, Aix-la-Chapelle and Frankfurt, and for the last time at Josef II's coronation in 1764. In 1423, this treasure was placed in the church of the Holy Spirit in Nürnberg to protect it fom the Hussites. It was transferred to Vienna in 1796 as Napoleon's troops were approaching, then returned briefly to Nürnberg in accordance with Hitler's wishes.

Room 5 – This contains mementoes of the "Aiglon", Napoleon's son, and his mother Marie Louise. One of the more remarkable exhibits is the **cradle of the King of Rome**★★, a gift from the City of Paris, executed in silver-gilt (280kg) from a sketch by the painter Pierre-Paul Prudhon. Above the cot, the goddess of fame stands on a celestial globe, holding a laurel wreath surmounted by a star, symbolizing Napoleon, while an eaglet (*aiglon* in French) watches from its perch; the frame displays small mother-of-pearl pillars embellished with a pattern of golden bees, the imperial emblem which Napoleon substituted for the monarchical Bourbon lilies. The following are of interest: **Marie Louise's portrait**★ (**3**) by Baron François Gérard (1812), two miniatures by Jean-Baptiste Isabey (1810), a silver-gilt trivet presented by the City of Milan on the birth of the King of Rome, and a glass case displaying mementoes of the Emperor Maximilian of Mexico (including his gold sceptre, dated 1863).

Room 6 – Children of the imperial family were baptised on the day of birth. Clothes and accessories were sumptuous: the most remarkable exhibits are a solid gold ewer and basin (Spanish, 1571), a wedding gift to Archduke Karl and his wife Maria from the States of Carinthia. The neo-Baroque cupboard contains 139 keys used to lock the coffins of the Habsburgs *(see Kaisergruft)* – 2 gold keys served to lock them, the remaining 139 being in the possession of the Capuchin monks who watch over the last sleep of the imperial family.

Room 7 – In 1918, following Karl I's abdication, the Habsburgs took most of their personal jewellery from the Schatzkammer with them into exile. The remaining pieces give some idea of the value of the collection once in the imperial treasury, for instance the *La Bella* (416 carat balas ruby, about 1687) set in an enamel mount in the form of a two-headed eagle and the *Smaragdgefäss*, a Columbian emerald (2,680 carats, 1641), the largest in the world, cut into an unguent pot by Dioniso Miseroni of Prague. The golden rose, a papal decoration, was a gift to Franz I's fourth wife, Carolina Augusta. Two fine pieces of Turkish workmanship are also on view: a sabre inlaid with gold (2nd half of 17C), used by Karl VI and Maria Theresa, and the **Crown of Stefan Bocskay**★, a gift from Sultan Achmed I of Constantinople, when his vassal the Grandduke of Transylvania was elected King of Hungary in 1605 (to "purify" the gift, he had a small cross added in front).

Room 8 – 16C treaties classified two specially valuable items as "inalienable heirlooms" which could neither be sold nor taken out of the country. The first is an antique **agate bowl**★ (**4**) cut from a single block (75cm/30ins wide), probably during the 4C in Constantinople; some believed that it was the Holy Grail, because they thought they could read Christ's name in the finely veined chalcedony. The second is a narwhal tooth (243cm/8ft), which people took for the horn of a unicorn. In medieval times, the unicorn symbolised power or God's sword (representations of them occurred as handles for sceptres or crosiers), or virginity (hence the tale of the virgin and the unicorn).

Room I – About 1680, Leopold I commissioned from the Augsburg goldsmith Philip Küsel a **miniature copy of the Mariensäule**★ (column of the Virgin, (**5**) situated on Am Hof square *(see under this heading)*. It is of silver-gilt adorned with over 3,700 precious or semi-precious stones (amethysts, chrysoliths, emeralds, garnets, rubies, etc.) Also of interest is the wooden crucifix (about 1630) by Leonhard Kern, a Baroque sculptor from southern Germany.

Room II – This contains medieval and Renaissance objects including: Louis I of Hungary's reliquary cross (about 1370) set with precious stones and bearing the arms of the king; a purse of Russian embroidery said to have belonged to St Stephen (late 11C – early 12C), the oldest item in the sacred treasury; a reliquary in the form of a pendant (mid-14C) known as Charlemagne's "monile" (necklace).

Room III – An ebony *tempietto* (temple-reliquary) displays an ivory figure of Christ by the Munich sculptor Christoph Angermair (between 1613 and 1620). Also of interest are two crucifixes, one in the style of Jean Boulogne from Douai, known as Giambologna (Florence, about 1590), and the other by Guglielmo della Porta (Rome, 1569).

Room IV – The nails of the Crucifixion form part of the instruments of the Passion. The Schatzkammer houses one of them which purportedly pierced the right hand of Christ. In accordance with the value of the contents, the reliquary is set with emeralds, sapphires and semi-precious stones. However, this casket seems relatively modest compared to Leopold I's two small reliquary altars (Milan, between 1660 and 1680). Three large glass cases display altarpiece ornaments of Meissen porcelain by Johann Joachim Kändler; Augustus III, King of Poland and Prince Elector of Saxony, commissioned it in 1737. This is the only group of its kind of this size.

Room V – This contains 18C and 19C works, including a splendid series of 22 reliquary busts (14 are in solid silver) by the Viennese Josef Moser. The following are also noteworthy: *St Francis of Assisi* and *St Theresa of Avila* (1765) by Laurent

Delvaux from Nivelles, artist to the Austrian court; a monstrance with one of St Peter's teeth, a gift from Pope Pius IX after a failed assassination attempt in February 1853 by a Hungarian tailor, János Libényi, on the life of Emperor Franz-Josef, who was protected from the blade by his collar stud.

Room 10 – This contains ceremonial garments belonging mostly to the Norman kings of the Hauteville dynasty, who ruled Sicily in the 12C. The Hohenstaufens acquired them on the marriage of Constance to Emperor Henry VI in 1186. A **coronation mantle★★**, one of the few items with a date, bears an Arabic inscription stating that it was embroidered in 1133 in Palermo for King Roger II (King of the Normans in southern Italy, Constance's father). In the centre of the red silk, a stylised tree of life divides a scene showing a lion (heraldic emblem of the Norman house) striking down a camel (symbol of the heathen East). Other garments are noteworthy: an indigo blue tunic (of the same period as the mantle); a white dress embroidered in gold (dated 1181) and an eagle dalmatic (early 14C Chinese damask). A ceremonial sword of investiture served for the ennobling of the patricians of Nürnberg; it was made in Sicily for Henry VI's son, Frederick II.

Room 11 – The finest piece in the jewellery collection of the Holy Roman German Empire is the **imperial crown★★★**. It was probably made in the monastery of Reichenau island (lake of Constance) for the coronation of Otto the Great in Rome on 2 February 962 – the hoop is a later addition bearing the name (encrusted in pearls) of Konrad II, also crowned in Rome in 1027. To the ordinary mortal, this crown was the emblem of imperial sovereignty; it also symbolises, by its octagonal shape, the celestial city of Jerusalem: there are 8 plaques, including 4 with figures in *cloisonné* enamel (Christ, David, Solomon, Ezekiel). Each of the two axial plaques is decorated with 12 precious stones: the 12 apostles and the 12 tribes of Israel. Below the cross added in the 11C, the upper part of the brow-plate bears a blue heart-shaped sapphire; this replaced the *Scholar*, a sparkling opal which disappeared about 1350. The imperial cross (1024) consists of gold plaques on a wooden core; this jewelled crown rests on a silver-gilt foot added in 1352 and at the back are figures of the apostles, symbols of the Evangelists and the Lamb of God. The **Holy Lance★★** (9C) is an amazing relic. Otto I the Great carried it at the battle of Lechfeld (955) which brought the invasions to an end. According to the traditions of the time, it had belonged to Constantine the Great and would guarantee invincibility for its bearer. Later, people began to believe it was the same lance that had pierced Christ's side; below the point there is a slit containing an iron rod, supposedly a nail from the Crucifixion. The **imperial sword★** (renovated about 1200, 11C scabbard), once considered St Maurice's sword, was in Aachen cathedral until 1794. A bearer held it, point upwards, facing the emperor. Other items of interest are: a processional cross, the imperial Gospel-book on which the emperor swore his oath, St Stephen's purse and the imperial sword which the monarch wore.

Room 12 – On view are leather boxes (Prague and Nürnberg, 14C and 15C) for transporting the crown jewels, and a glass case containing reliquaries with saints' relics (St John the Baptist's tooth, a fragment of the cloth from the Last Supper, etc).

Room 13 – Tunics and coats of arms of heralds from the duchy of Burgundy.

Room 14 – By her marriage to Emperor Maximilian I in 1477, Mary of Burgundy brought to the House of Habsburg the treasures of the dukes of Burgundy, whose portraits are on display (copies): Philip the Bold, John the Fearless, Philip the Good, Charles the Bold and Philip the Fair. In a glass case is the *Ainkuhrn*, the unicorn's sword (mid-15C), which acquired its name from its narwhal tusk scabbard. Philip the Good's chalice is made of rock crystal mounted in gold, diamonds and rubies.

Rudolf II's crown

The imperial crown

101

Room 15 – On his third marriage in 1430, Philip the Good founded the Order of the Golden Fleece. When there was no male heir the title passed to the husband of the heiress until her son came of age. Charles V left control of the Order to his son Philip II with the Spanish throne, after having given his Austrian States to his brother Ferdinand. In 1712, Charles VI demanded the Order with the Spanish crown and succeeded in having the Order's treasures returned to Vienna. Since then, there have been two Orders of the Golden Fleece, each disputing the legitimacy of the other (Napoleon founded a third in 1809, but abandoned the project in the face of objections from holders of the *Legion of Honour*). The **potence★★** (mid-15C), the armorial chain of the heralds of the Order, consists of a double gold chain with 52 removeable enamel shields corresponding to the members of the Order; a gold ram hangs from it. Nowadays, the Austrian branch is led by the head of the House of Habsburg: its members swear the oath of allegiance on the Cross of the Order (French is the official language, although France only recognises the Spanish branch of the Order).

Room 16 – Before leaving the Schatzkammer, visitors should not miss the **liturgical accoutrements★★** of the Order of the Golden Fleece, which include some of the most valuable examples of medieval textile art: two altar-frontals, a chasuble and two dalmatics, dating no later than 1477. They illustrate the art of "painting with a needle", showing the influence of Flemish masters such as Robert Campin and Rogier van der Weyden.

★★Spanische Hofreitschule ⊙ – *Attending Morgenarbeit (training sessions) or Vorführungen (parades) at the Spanish riding school is the only way of visiting the Winterreitschule (Winter Riding School).*

The Spanish riding school is one of the few places left in the world where one may see a display of *haute école* dressage, an art dating from the second half of the 16C. Beneath a coffered ceiling, two tiers of galleries surround an all-white room (57m x 19m/186ft x 62ft). This was the setting for numerous brilliant occasions, such as the banquet for the wedding by proxy of Archduchess Marie Louise and Napoleon I, the festivities of the Congress of Vienna and the debates of Austria's first constitutional assembly. The room was originally designed for show-jumping competitions and tournaments that enabled the nobility to display their prowess; since 1894, it has been reserved for performances of the Spanish riding school.

Vorführungen – *3 entrances according to the location of the seat: Innerer Burghof* (**a**), *Michaelerkuppel* (**b**) and *Josefsplatz* (**c**) *(Shown on ticket).* This famous and splendid spectacle to the accompaniment of music attracts a wide and cosmopolitan audience. It is essential to reserve seats in advance (unless one buys from an agency at a higher price). The riders wear white gloves, black two-cornered hats trimmed with gold, brown double-breasted coats with brass buttons, off-white buckskin breeches and knee-high glossy black riding boots. At the start and end of each display (7 in all), the riders silently salute, slowly doffing their two-cornered hats to Karl VI's portrait hanging in the imperial box facing the doors through which they make their entrance *(apart from the 1st display, by young stallions)*. It is customary not to wear a hat during the show. The performance (1 h 20) may seem somewhat long to those who do not understand the equestrian art of dressage, since its appeal lies in the impeccable manoeuvres rather than dramatic entertainment. However, even a layman could not fail to respond to its highlights, the unforgettable 4th and 6th displays *(Arbeit und die Hand and airs above the ground)*, where traditional exercises impress by their precision and lightness. There is no music and the 3 chandeliers are unlit during *Morgenarbeit* (the training session). This may provide less stimulus to a tourist's imagination.

Lippizaner horses – The stallions of the Spanish riding school take their name from the stud farm founded by Archduke Karl in 1580 in Lipizza (Slovenia), near Trieste. In 1920, they were brought from there to Piber castle, west of Graz (Styria), which now houses the national stud farm.

The present Lippizaners are the descendants of six great sires: *Pluto*, born in 1765 (Danish breed); *Con-*

An Equestrian Ballet

In *haute école* dressage, riders teach their horses a repertoire of "airs" or movements. Most of them stem from Renaissance military exercises.
Piaffe: the horse trots on the spot; this is its starting position. **Courvet:** the horse jumps several times with its front legs off the ground. **Croupade:** a jump where the horse raises its front and hindlegs, folding them under its belly. **Levade:** an exercise where the horse rises on its hindlegs, its hocks nearly touching the ground. **Pirouette:** the horse turns on the haunches at the walk or the canter. **Capriole:** the horse rises with all four feet off the ground at the same height and kicks out; it is the supreme movement, the high point in the show.

Spanish Riding School

ONAT

versano, born in 1767, and *Neapolitano*, born in 1790 (Neapolitan breed); *Maestoso*, born in 1773, and *Favory*, born in 1779 (Lippizaner thoroughbreds); *Siglavy*, born in 1810 (Arab breed). All stem from an old Spanish strain, famous at the time of Caesar. They begin their training when they are three years old; they are born bay or black and do not turn white until between the ages of four and ten. Exceptionally, a horse may keep its dark colour. This earns him special consideration and the title of "brown Hofburg bay".

Bereiter – It takes ten to fifteen years for a rider to become a trainer. After learning to ride without spurs, a young rider acquires further skills by riding an old, experienced horse. After five years' practice, the rider is now a novitiate trainer and may take part in the performances. He is then presented with a young horse which he must bring up to the level of "school horse". Once he completes this stage, he becomes a trainer; later, after training several horses and schooling some for jumping exercises, he acquires the title of master trainer.

Lipizzaner Museum ⊙ – *Reitschulgasse 2*. Since 1998, the Stallburg *(see under this heading)*, or palace of the Stables, has housed the Lipizzaner Museum. This exhibition, which is made up mainly of documents, exhibits and uniforms, also illustrates the training of the famous stallions which originate from the Spanish school. There is a brief audio-visual programme (in the basement) about the national stud farm where these superb horses are raised, and some of the stables can be viewed through a window.

★**Österreichische Nationalbibliothek** – *Josefsplatz 1 and 2*. The imperial court library, which became the Austrian National Library in 1920, dates from the 14C. Various departments of the national library occupy numerous buildings of the Hofburg. It was Karl VI who brought these magnificent collections together; previously, they had been scattered throughout Vienna. The national library inventory numbers 6,500,000 entries and nearly 2,500,000 printed works, about 8,000 incunabula – books printed before 1501 –, over 35,000 manuscripts, etc. Some are very valuable such as *The Vienna Dioskurides*, a Byzantine manuscript from the beginning of the 6C, or the *Gutenberg Bible*, or Forty-Two-Line Bible, printed in 1455-56. Emperor Karl VI used to say that this priceless collection was available to anyone except "fools, chatterers, idlers and stable boys". He therefore inscribed in the study of the Camera Praefecti (Director General) "Enter without payment, but depart enriched".

The staircase bears Roman remains from Dacia (present Romania) and southern Styria; it leads to the **Prunksaal**★★ ⊙, a magnificent hall of state by Fischer von Erlach, father and son, which is one of the finest examples of a Baroque library. The decoration is worthy of the splendid 200,000 works collected here. The room 78m/255ft long, 14m/45ft wide and 20m/65ft high contains, among others, 15,000 volumes (acquired by Josef II) from the library of Prince Eugène of Savoy *(below the cupola)*. There are two storeys of shelves concealing studies with secret entrances. In the cupola above, a *trompe l'œil* fresco by Daniel Gran (1730) depicts the apotheosis of Karl VI. The celestial and terrestrial globes (diameter 110cm/43ins, late 17C) are by Vincenzo Coronelli, and the statues in honour of Karl VI and the Habsburgs are by Peter and Paul Strudel (about 1700).

Globenmuseum der Österreichischen Nationalbibliothek ⊙ – *Josefsplatz 1, 3rd floor.* The museum of globes contains a fine collection consisting of over 200 items, including works by Rainer Gemma Frisius, Johann Gabriel Doppelmayr, Matthäus Greuter, Gerhard Valk and other famous geographers. Particularly noteworthy are: 2 terrestrial (1541) and celestial (1551) **globes** made in Louvain by Gerhard Mercator, who was the first to make a flat orthomorphic projection of the earth; 2 terrestrial globes (1602 and post 1621) by the Dutchman Willem Janszoon Blaeu (his son's maps often appear in Vermeer's paintings, as in *The Artist's Studio*, a famous painting in the art gallery of the Kunsthistorischesmuseum); 2 terrestrial (1688) and celestial (1693) globes by V. Coronelli, a Venetian geographer who worked at Louis XIV's court and who won fame by dedicating his globes to the Pope, the Emperor of the Holy Roman German Empire and the King of France.

The map collection *(closed to the public but open to researchers)* contains unique items, such as a valuable map of the world which Sancho Gutierrez created (1551) for Karl V, Prince Eugène's famous 46-volume atlas by Blaeu and Van der Hem, and the **Peutinger table**, the only existing copy (12C) of a Roman map (4C).

Augustinerkirche – *Augustinerstrasse 3. Undergoing restoration.* Formerly the court church. The Augustinian church was built during the first half of the 14C in the Hofburg by Dietrich Ladtner von Pirn (consecrated in 1349). It was used for great court weddings: Maria Theresa and François Étienne of Lorraine in 1736; the marriages by proxy of Marie Antoinette and Marie Louise, in 1770 and 1810 respectively (Napoleon's former opponent, Archduke Karl, represented him); Elizabeth of Bavaria and Franz Josef in 1854; Stephanie of Belgium and Crown Prince Rudolf in 1881.

In 1784, Ferdinand Hetzendorf von Hohenberg refurbished this edifice, with its austere exterior, and restored the original Gothic appearance, concealed behind Baroque decoration. It is the oldest three-aisled hall-church in the capital. One of the most impressive monuments is the **Christinendenkmal★**. Antonio Canova created the cenotaph of Maria Christina between 1805 and 1809: statues of Virtue, Felicity and Charity are shown advancing towards a 5m/16ft high pyramid of Carrara marble. On its summit, the spirit of Felicity holds a medallion portraying Maria Theresa's favourite daughter. On the right, the base of an equestrian monument displays French inscriptions "to the signal loyalty and valour of the Tour-dragoon regiment, acknowledged by the emperor and king" and "whoever meddles with it will smart for it". Georgkapelle is a chapel built by Otto the Merry in the 14C for the knights of St George; it houses the remains of the imperial Count Daun who defeated the Prussians at Kollin during the Seven Years' War. Leopold II's marble tomb is empty, since his body lies in the Kapuzinergruft (Capuchin crypt) *(see Kaisergruft)*. Near St George's Chapel is the Loretokapelle (chapel of Our Lady of Loreto) with a fine 18C wrought-iron gate leading to the Herzgruft, a crypt in which the hearts of all the Habsburgs since Emperor Matthias have been kept in 54 small silver urns; one of them contains the heart of the *Aiglon*, Napoleon I's son. The organ comes from Schwarzspanierkirche (the Black Spaniard church) which was destroyed in a storm; the first performance of Anton Bruckner's *Mass in F minor* was given here in 1872.

★★**Graphische Sammlung Albertina** – *Augustinerstrasse 1; 3rd floor. Closed at least until 2001 for renovation; see also Albertina in the Akademiehof.* The remarkable Albertina collection of graphic art owes its name to its founder, Duke Albert of Saxe-Teschen (1738-1822), son-in-law of Empress Maria Theresa through his marriage to her daughter, Maria Christina. It was founded in 1768 and has occupied the former Tarouca palace since 1795. In the early 19C, Louis Montoyer made major alterations to the building. The Albertina of today results from the amalga-

National Library: Prunksaal

G. De Laubier/FIGARO MAGAZINE

mation in 1920 of the collection of Duke Albert, an enlightened connoisseur, and the engravings from the imperial library originally assembled by Prince Eugène of Savoy. The museum now contains 45,000 drawings and watercolours, 60,000 books and about 1.5 million engravings, all of which constitute what is undoubtedly the world's largest collection of graphic art.

The **Dürer collection** belonged to Rudolf II who assembled it through purchases from the artist's heirs and the Cardinal Granvelle inheritance. It includes celebrated works such as *Praying Hands*, *The Hare* and *Madonna with Animals*. There are also other masterpieces here, by some of the greatest names in the history of art: Baldung Grien, Brueghel the Elder, Chagall, Cranach the Elder, Fra Angelico, Gainsborough, Goya, Holbein, Klimt, Kubin, Claude Lorrain, Makart, Mantegna, Michelangelo, Nolde, Picasso, Raphael, Rembrandt, Reynolds, Rottmayr, Rubens, Schiele, Tintoretto, Titian, Van Dyck, Veronese, Leonardo da Vinci, and Watteau. This is not a comprehensive list, but it gives an idea of the exceptional quality of this museum. The public eagerly awaits its reopening.

Musiksammlung der Nationalbibliothek ⊘ – *Augustinerstrasse 1, 4th floor.* (Collection of musical instruments). Small temporary exhibitions take place in the reading room. The collection includes musical archives of the Court and National Opera as well as **autographed manuscripts★** by Roland de Lassus, Josef Haydn, Wolfgang Amadeus Mozart (*Requiem*), Franz Schubert, Anton Bruckner, Gustav Mahler, etc.

Papyrussammlung der Nationalbibliothek ⊘ – *Augustinerstrasse 1.* One room houses some of the documents of the Egyptian papyrus collection from the National Library. It was a gift from Archduke Rainer and results from excavations in Fayoum. The capital, Arsinoe, was nicknamed "crocodile city". The documents on display (from 1600 BC to 1400 AD) include one of the oldest musical scores in existence, Euripides' *Choruses of Orestes* (180 BC).

Schmetterlinghaus ⊘ – The butterfly house (33° C) is decidedly not as elegant as its neighbour, but its butterfly collection is both amazing and delightful. It is in fact unexpected to stroll in the midst of tropical butterflies that flutter from plant to plant, sometimes coming to rest on the hat or shoulder of visitors, unaware of their sudden powers of attraction. Notices in German, English and French specify their names.

City Centre and the Ring

★★ Ephesos-Museum ⊙ – *Neue Burg. Entrance by Heldenplatz.* The Ephesus Museum has been housed in Neue Burg since 1978. It possesses a series of finds made by Austrian archeologists working on the ancient trading city on the coast of Asia Minor (1895 onwards). Only Istanbul and London have similarly magnificent collections. There is a remarkably good display of architectural fragments, reliefs and sculptures, with explanatory reconstructions, models and photographic documents. This includes objects from excavations in Samothrace, in the Aegean Sea. On a staircase from the ground floor there are fragments of an altar of Artemis, the Artemision, from the temple of Diana of Ephesus (4C BC); since the Renaissance, it has been considered one of the seven wonders of the world. Erostratus set fire to this temple in 356 BC.

The mezzanine displays one of the two major works in the collection: **the frieze from the Parthian monument★★**. The senate erected this monument around 170 to celebrate the Roman army's final victory over the Parthians ending the war that had been waged between 161 and 165. It is in honour of Emperor Lucius Aurelius Verus (died in 169), the adoptive brother and son-in-law of Marcus Aurelius. During the wars of conquest, his headquarters were in Ephesus, capital of the Asian province since 129. This marble monument 40m/43yds long (originally 70m/76yds) probably formed the exterior decoration of a huge altar. The frieze consists of five scenes *(start at the end of the right-hand wall, from No 59)*: adoption of Verus by Antoninus Pius in 138 *(59-64)*; Verus in combat *(see illustration)*; Verus as emperor with personifications of the principal cities of the empire *(69-76; Alexandria in 69, Ephesus in 70, Rome in 72, Ctesiphon in 75, capital of the Parthian empire)*; his coronation by the gods of Olympus *(77-80)*; and his apotheosis *(81-83)*. On the same floor, there is a fragment of an octagonal tomb with Corinthian columns built in the second half of the 1C for a young girl of 20, and a superb wooden model of Ephesus (1/500).

On the first floor, a collection of bronze and marble sculptures surrounds the extraordinary **Ephesian Athlete★★** *(129)*, a Roman copy of a Greek original of 340/330 BC. This 1.92m/6 ft tall athlete is shown cleaning his strigil, a curved blade used to scrape the sand of the arena from the athlete's oiled body. The **Boy with a Goose★** *(147)* is a marble copy of a 3C BC Hellenistic original; during this period, artists represented children as they really were, whereas Greek archaic and classical art gave children the features of young adults. The following exhibits are also noteworthy: an Ionic capital bearing a five-branched lamp *(139)*, *Hercules Fighting the Centaur (141)*, a satyr's head *(143)*, fragments from the library of Celsus *(156-162)* founded by the consul Tiberius Iulius Aquila, a head presumably of Homer *(166)* and a portrait of Hadrian *(171)* made in 123 during one of the emperor's visits to Ephesus.

On the same floor, on the other side of the staircase, there are finds from Samothrace which was colonised in the 8C BC by the inhabitants of Samos, an island off Ephesus. The collection comprises Victory figures, pediment sculptures, capitals and friezes. These architectural remains also include pieces *(247-268)* from the rotunda of the temple built between 289 and 281 BC by Arsinoë, wife of King Lysimachos of Macedonia.

★ Waffensammlung – *Neue Burg. Entrance through Heldenplatz.* After major renovation work, in 1998 the superb Collection of Arms and Armour of the Imperial Palace reopened its rooms and galleries for the pleasure of the public. Some readers may be surprised by the use of the term "pleasure" in relation to a collection associated with war, but the wealth of the exhibits is quite surprising, with in particular an incredible range of armour, some of which may be described as true works of technical and imaginative art.

The collection grew from the 15C and 16C collections of two impassioned enthusiasts, the archdukes Ernest of Styria (1377-1424) and Ferdinand of Tyrol (1527-1595), which were added in 1806 to the armoury of the Habsburgs, and is probably the most interesting of its kind in the world. Visitors will find complete suits of armour, fully jointed, most of which originate from Milan and the major centres of southern Germany which are famous for their quite remarkable examples.

Gallery – Before the gallery itself, in the room devoted to equestrian tournaments, there is a magnificent wooden ceremonial saddle (1439), made in southeast Germany for Albert II, displaying motifs and ivory figures.

There are so many suits of armour on display that we only have space to mention a few remarkable examples, some of which are indeed truly spectacular; they also give us the opportunity to flavour our description by the use of the colourful technical vocabulary associated with armour. The armour in rooms 1 and 2 includes work by Lorenz Helmschmied and Konrad Seusenhofer which is some of the finest in the collection. Emperor Frederick II's equestrian armour (Augsburg, 1477) is near the **harnesses★** belonging to the future Maximilian I (Augusburg, about 1477) and to Sigismund of Tyrol (Augsburg, about 1485); the ceremonial sollerets (heel protectors) of the long pointed shoes belonging to these exhibits indicate their ceremonial character within the European courts of the 14C and 15C.

Room 3 constitutes what may be described as the star attraction, with the so-called **"costume" armour★★★** (Brunswick, about 1526) of the Duke of Prussia Albert of Brandenburg (1490-1568), which is trimmed with a pleated metal skirt and a grotesque helmet with hooked nose, the **pleated skirt armour★★** (Innsbruck, about 1512) of the future Charles V (1500-1558) made by Konrad Seusenhofer, the **helmet★** (Innsbruck, around 1529, by the same silversmith) of Archduke Ferdinand I, whose ventail is shaped like the snout of a fox, the equestrian armour (Augsburg, around 1526) of the future Ferdinand I (1503-1564) by Kolman Helmschmid, the famous son of the Augsburg silversmith Lorenz, who also made the metal garment with the bouffant sleeves of Wilhelm von Roggendorf (1481-1541), the knight's armour (Augsburg, 1544) of Philippe II of Spain (1527-1598) by Desiderus Helmschmid and Ulrich Holzmann, and the splendid **breastplate★** (Nuremburg, about 1555) of Nicolas IV Radziwill (1515-1565), Chancellor of Lithuania, fashioned by Kunz Lochner, and last but not least the grotesque sallet (helmet) made in Nuremberg in about 1530.

Room 4 houses the **ceremonial armour★★** (Milan, about 1570) of Alexandre Farnèse (1545-1592), duke of Parma and of Plaisance, by Lucio Piccinino, who placed a bird on top of the helmet, and the **breastplate★** (France, about 1570) of the King of France Henri III, when he was King of Poland. In room 6 visitors will find the remarkably well preserved **armour and shield★** (Syria-Egypt, about 1500) of an Egyptian prince, fashioned by the silversmith Ali; and amongst the many exhibits in room 7, the finely chiselled breastplate (Augsburg, about 1571) of Archduke Ernest (1553-1595) by Anton Peffenhauser is worth close scrutiny.

★★Sammlung Alter Musikinstrumente ◯ – *Neue Burg. Entrance through Heldenplatz. Free headphones are available at the desk.* As a musical city, Vienna needed to have a Museum of Ancient Musical Instruments. Following reorganisation, it has acquired a network of infrared headphones enabling visitors to hear musical extracts relating to the period and the theme of the room they enter. This is why we strongly recommend them to visitors, despite the fact that at present the commentaries are solely in German. Among the exhibits is the 16C collection of Archduke Ferdinand of Tyrol then kept in Ambras Castle in Innsbruck, and a series of instruments from Catajo Castle near Padua. This accounts for the great historical value of the Renaissance section in this wing of the Neue Burg facing Burggarten.

Equipped with headphones, visitors can spend just over an hour absorbing the evolution of musical instruments from the early 16C onward. The selection below concentrates on instruments of historical or aesthetic significance. Further details: in the rooms, a red sticker on the label indicates that one can hear a sound recording of the instrument; a green sticker indicates that one may play the instrument; a green dotted line on the ground indicates a change of recording.

Room IX: Music in the reign of Maximilian I – A rare example of a **rebec★** (Venice, 15C); a lira da braccio, a kind of viol (Verona, 1511) with, on the back, a carving of a man's head in the middle of a woman's body; a small spinet or spinetto (Italy 2nd half of the 16C); a trumpet by Anton Schnitzer (1598), who worked in Nürnberg, a city famous in the Renaissance for its manufacturers of musical instruments; four recorders (16C); a harp (Italy, 16C), a medieval instrument still in use during the Renaissance; *Perseus and Andromeda*, a painting after Piero di Cosimo (after 1513).

Room X: Music in Ambras and Catajo castles – A serpent (Italy, 16C), the ancestor of the ophicleide, with a zoomorphic socket for the mouthpiece; a **harpsichord★** (Venice, 1559) with painted decoration dating from about 1580. Ferdinand of Tyrol's **cittern★★** (Brescia, 1574). This remarkable work of art is played with a plectrum and the archduke chose the decoration: there is a portrayal of Lucretia at the top wearing real pearl earrings. The **claviorganum★** (South Germany, late 16C) is the oldest existing example of its kind. A viola da gamba by Antonio Ciciliano (Venice, towards 1600) is noteworthy, as is Kaspar von der Sitt's table (Passau, 1590), its stone top carved with musical notes and heraldic motifs; and *The Lute Player* by Annibale Carracci (about 1600).

Room XI: Musical composition in the reigns of Ferdinand III, Leopold I and Josef I – Note a lute with its case (Venice, 1626) by Vendelinus Venere, whose real name was Wendelin Tieffenbrucker. He came from Füssen, a town of lute-makers specialising in ivory. Also a harp (Italy, 17C) with a fish-shaped frame; Emperor Leopold I's clavicytherium (Vienna, end of the 17C) by Martin Kaiser from Füssen – note the vertical lines of the case and the tortoiseshell, ivory and mother-of-pearl decoration.

Room XII: Josef Haydn – A baryton which belonged to Haydn by Daniel Achatius Stadlmann (Vienna, 1732); a harpsichord (Antwerp, 1745) by Joannes Daniel Dulcken, the principal Flemish manufacturer of harpsichords; a pianoforte or Hammerflügel (Ratisbon, 1798) by Christof Friedrich Schmahl.

Room XIII: Wolfgang Amadeus Mozart – **Six trumpets★**, magnificent instruments of partially gilt silver (Vienna, 1741 and 1746) by Franz and Michael Leichamschneider; the delicate coils on the mouthpiece are noteworthy. A "glasharmonika" (first half of the 19C), an instrument invented in 1761. On the wall, *Franz-Stefan and Maria Theresa* from the studio of Martin van Meytens (about 1755) and *Marie Antoinette* probably by Franz Xaver Wagenschöm (undated), depicting the future queen of France seated at a clavichord. The 18C or early 19C pianofortes had little in common with the modern piano as regards design, if not aesthetics. They did not possess the metal frame, crossed strings and felt-covered hammer heads of modern pianos, and they differed between each manufacturer. When about 1770, Johann

Andreas Stein invented the "Austrian mechanism", instruments acquired a musical tone, which delighted Mozart. Stein settled in Vienna, and his son-in-law, Andreas Streicher, improved the mechanism of the pianoforte, much to the enjoyment of Beethoven in later times.

Room XIV: Ludwig van Beethoven – A piano-organ by Franz Xaver Christoph (Vienna, about 1785). A pianoforte by Johann Jakob Könnicke (Vienna, 1796). A double-pedalled harp by Sébastien Érard (Paris, about 1810). Johann Nepomuk Mälzel's metronome (Paris, 1815), the first of its kind. A rosewood pianoforte by Josef Brodmann (Vienna, 1815). A pianoforte by Konrad Graf (Vienna, about 1820) with mother-of-pearl keys. *Napoleon, Emperor of the French* after François Gérard (after 1804). *Franz II* by Johann Baptist Lampi.

Room XV: Franz Schubert – Lyre-guitar by Jacques Pierre Michelot (Paris, about 1800). Guitar by Giovanni Battista (Naples, about 1801). A pianoforte by André Stein (Vienne, 1819). The modest pianoforte on which Schubert played and composed at the home of the painter Rieder. *Portrait of Schubert as a Young Man* (Vienna, about 1814).

Room XVI: Robert Schumann, Johannes Brahms, Franz Liszt, Anton Bruckner – Aluminium violin by Anton Dehmal (Vienna, end of 19C); its tone was unconvincing. Grand pianos by the manufacturers Graf (Vienna, 1839), Streicher (Vienna, 1840), Streicher and Son (Vienna, 1868), Bösendorfer (Vienna, 1875). *Franz Liszt at the Keyboard*, photogravure by Josef Danhäuser (2nd half of the 19C).

Room XVII: Dance music in Vienna – Zither (Austria, 19C). Zither by Frank Nowy (Vienna, about 1950). The term comes from the Greek *kithara* from which guitar also derives. It covers a range of instruments with strings which are plucked or set in vibration by a plectrum; in central Europe, the resonance box is usually trapezoidal.

Room XVIII: Gustav Mahler, Richard Strauss, Hugo Wolf – A pianino by Kaspar Lorenz (Vienna, about 1860). A **piano by Ludwig Bösendorfer★** (Vienna, about 1867); the case is of ebony and is magnificently inlaid with precious woods and metals, from a preparatory design by Theophil von Hansen, the architect of the Musikvereinsgebäude (Friends of Music building); the presence of the double-headed eagle in the decoration is evidence that the instrument was made for Emperor Franz-Josef. *Richard Strauss* by the Viennese portrait painter Wilhelm Victor Krausz (Vienna, 1929), showing the German composer, aged 65, conducting at the Opera. *Hugo Wolf* by Karl Rickelt (1895).

Linke Seitengalerie: the 20C – A cembalo by Paul de Wit (Leipzig, 1912). *Self Portrait* by Arnold Schönberg (Vienna, 1910). Grand piano by the firm of Bösendorfer (Vienna, 1958), made for the Brussels World Fair. The tour ends with a synthesizer dating from 1913, when Jorg Mager discovered how to analyse and reconstitute sound electronically.

★ **Museum für Völkerkunde** ⊘ – *Neue Burg. Entrance through Heldenplatz.* The ethnographic museum displays, on the ground floor, collections of artefacts from Africa and the Far East. On the first floor, there are permanent exhibitions devoted to Polynesia and the antiquities of the New World. The museum possesses over 150,000 objects which the Habsburgs bought over the centuries or which ethnologists working for the Court collected on expeditions.

On the ground floor, the collection of **Benin bronzes★** comprises a fine series of court portraits from this ancient kingdom set up in the 12C in the southwest of present-day Nigeria. The art of Benin consists of brass plaques (16C and 17C) which adorned the palaces of the *obas* – monarchs who reigned over the entire Gulf of Guinea – and fine sculptures on ivory (18C and 19C). In the Japanese section is the complete armour of a samurai (17C) and a katana sabre dated 1478; the Chinese section contains a splendid red lacquer screen made in Peking about 1760.

On the first floor, the Polynesian exhibition is well documented by audio-visual presentation *(German commentary)*. It includes the collections of Captain James Cook which Franz I purchased in London in 1806. Particularly noteworthy are the ceremonial paddles from Easter Island and a model (59cm/23ins) of an oracular shrine made in Hawaii, probably for

Oracular shrine (Hawaian Islands)

the British explorer. The antiquities of the New World comprise interesting Mexican items. After the conquest of Mexico, Hernán Cortez sent many of these to Karl V, who then gave them to his brother Ferdinand. There is a splendid exhibit in the case at the end: the **feathered crown of Montezuma**★★ *(its purchase by the museum is uncertain, which is why there is no picture of it in this guide)*. It owes its name to the Aztec Emperor killed in 1520 while fighting the Spanish troops; this headdress of quetzal, cotinga and cuckoo feathers is unique. The section contains various objects covering many periods and cultures: ceramics (mainly anthropomorphous), stone sculptures, jewelry, model of the ritual temple of Teotihuacan (a site covering a total area of 32km²/12sq miles), death masks, feather shields, obsidian mirror, fabrics, weapons, etc.

The nearest sights are: the Freyung, Kapuzinerkirche and Staatsoper Districts, the Ring and, close to Neue Burg, the magnificent Kunsthistorischesmuseum (Art History Museum).

HOHER MARKT District

Map pages 5-6, **JKR**
Underground: Schwedenplatz (U1, U4), Stephansplatz (U1, U3)
Tram: Schwedenplatz (1, 2, 21, N), Salztorbrücke (1, 2)
Bus: Hoher Markt (1A, 2A, 3A)

Together with the Fleischmarkt District, this forms the historic centre of the city. It displays Roman and Romanesque remains, a fine Gothic church and some splendid creations of the Baroque period.

Hoher Markt – In the Middle Ages, it was the site for public executions by hanging and also for the pillory. Today, the square features the canopy over the **Vermählungsbrunnen** (the "Virgin Mary's marriage fountain", 1732) by Josef Emmanuel Fischer von Erlach with a sculpture by Antonio Corradini. The buildings around the long rectangular square date from the post-1945 reconstruction of the city, which accounts for the mediocrity of the architecture.

On the archway over Bauernmarkt is the **Ankeruhr** *(see illustration)*, a magnificent clock which Franz von Matsch made in 1913 to link the two buildings of the Anker Insurance Company. Every hour, a different historical figure appears by the clock-face: Marcus Aurelius at 1am and 1pm, Charlemagne at 2am and 2pm, Duke Leopold and Empress Theodora of Byzantium at 3am and 3pm, Walter van der Vogelweide at 4am and 4pm, Rudolf I and his wife Anna of Hohenberg at 5am and 5pm, Johann Puschbaum at 6am and 6pm, Maximilian I at 7am and 7pm, the mayor Von Liebenberg at 8am and 8pm, Count Rüdiger von Starhemberg at 9am and 9pm, Eugène of Savoy at 10am and 10pm, Maria Theresa and Franz Stefan at 11am and 11pm and Joseph Haydn at noon. This is when all the figures file past to the accompaniment of music.

Römische Ruinen ⊙ – *Hoher Markt 3 (entrance in the passage)*. In Roman times, Hoher Markt was the site of a forum. Excavations under the square have uncovered the remains of two houses (2C and 3C) belonging to officers (carved stones, pottery, tiles, paving).

North of the square, turn left into Tuchlauben and go past Schultergasse.

N e i d h a r t - F r e s k e n ⊙ – *Tuchlauben 19. 1st floor*. The oldest secular frescoes (about 1400) in Vienna are on display in a building with a Baroque façade dating from 1716. These medieval frescoes were on the wall of the banqueting hall of a house which later disappeared during the various refurbishments at this address. Their discovery occurred in 1979 during building work in an apartment. Their significance and their quality prompted the city authorities to finance their restoration.

3 BIS/MICHELIN

Hoher Markt : l'Ankeruhr

Though sometimes fragmentary, the scenes are identifiable. Starting with the first of the series opposite the entrance, there are: a peasant quarrel with a fortified castle in the background; a ball game and some lovers symbolising summer; the theft of a mirror, its somewhat frivolous iconography evoking the delights of Court life; a snowball fight, which some see as an eggfight; a sleighride, probably a frequent occurrence during the medieval Viennese winter; picking violets or spring's awakening; a circular dance, where the flower in the dancer's right hand also symbolises spring; a banquet representing autumn, a time of festivities. These charmingly naïve paintings drew inspiration from the songs of Neidhart, hence their name. Neidhart von Reuental was a poet and troubadour at the Babenberg Court in the early 13C.

Retrace your steps and turn left into Schultergasse, where Johann Berhard Fischer died at No 5. Then turn right into Jordangasse for Wipplingerstrasse.

Böhmische Hofkanzlei (H) – *Wipplingerstrasse 7.* Johann Bernhard Fischer von Erlach designed the main façade of the former Bohemian Chancellery between 1708 and 1714. The telamones on the portals are the work of Lorenzo Mattielli *(see illustration)*, a specialist in this genre. In 1750, Maria Theresa commissioned Mathias Gerl to enlarge the palace; he greatly admired the work of the older master, hence, unlike the rear of the building visible from Judenplatz, today's splendid façade underwent no alterations.

Altes Rathaus – *Wipplingerstrasse 6 and 8.* The former town hall dates from 1316 and was the house of a burgher, Otto Heimo. The municipal authorities confiscated it after his part in a plot against the Habsburgs. In the Baroque period (1699), the building was refurbished by an unknown architect. In 1883, the municipal authorities moved into the new city hall on the Ring *(see Rathaus)*.

Near No 8 in an interior courtyard is **Andromeda-Brunnen★**, the lead fountain of Andromeda by Raphael Donner (1741). Framed by cherubs, this small masterpiece lies between the wrought-iron balustrades of the coping and the balcony. It depicts Perseus' rescue of Cassiopea's daughter, about to fall victim to a marine monster, now harmlessly spouting water. The superior quality of the relief and the masterly treatment of the different planes recall the naturalism of the Florentine goldsmith Lorenzo Ghiberi.

Continue along Wipplingerstrasse for Hohe Brücke.

Hohe Brücke – Spanning Tiefer Graben, the "deep ditch" where a tributary of the Danube (the Alsbach) once flowed, is a pretty Jugendstil bridge (1903) with elegant metal lampposts by Josef Hackhofer.

Descend the staircase and take Tiefer Graben to the right. Turn right into Am Gestade for the church of the same name.

★**Maria am Gestade** – *Salvatorgasse bei 12. Entrance by the south gate.* In the mid-12C, a church known as Our Lady on the Strand stood on a terrace overlooking the main branch of the Danube. At the end of the 14C, a Gothic edifice

Telamones on the facade of the Böhmische Hofkanzlei

replaced it; this is the present church, which has undergone recent restoration. Its popular name is Maria-Stiegen-Kirche (Our Lady of the Steps) and it is the Czech national church in Vienna.

The late Gothic west façade is tall and narrow (33m x 9.7m /108ft x 31ft). Below, the portal beneath its canopy displays sculptures (about 1410) representing St John the Evangelist and St John the Baptist; above is a pediment, flanked by pinnacles, with a wide stained-glass window between. The seven-sided tower bears a fine pierced **spire**★; following damage during the Turkish siege of 1683, it was rebuilt in 1688. The interior is unusual in that the nave and choir are of equal length. Particularly noteworthy are the **stained-glass windows** (14C and 15C) in the choir and the statues against the pillars of the nave.

Before going into the street along the right side of the church, take a look at the fine Baroque portal (1720) of "Zu den sieben Schwertern" house. Go past Stoss im Himmel to Salvatorgasse.

Austellung Der Österreichische Freiheitskampf (**M**[21]) – *Wipplingerstrasse 8. Entrance through No 5 Salvatorgasse.* The former town hall houses the archives of the Austrian resistance. On the ground floor, an exhibition covers the period from 1934 to 1945 and commemorates those who opposed National Socialism first by a patriotic front, then by underground resistance after Hitler proclaimed the annexation of Austria.

This permanent exhibition mainly consists of photographic documents. It evokes the assassination of Dollfuss, the reign of terror, the exile of some (including Robert Musil and Joseph Roth), the clandestine activities of the armed resistance as well as Mauthausen concentration camp in Upper Austria, where about 200,000 inmates lived in constant fear of death. Some 3,000 members of the resistance were executed during Hitler's régime, nearly 140,000 Austrians perished in the camps and 600,000 others lost their lives during World War Two, fighting in the ranks of the Wehrmacht or during air raids. The principal purpose of this museum is to act as antidote to any form of neo-Nazi propaganda.

Salvatorkapelle (**K**[4]) – *Salvatorgasse 5. Entrance through Altes Rathaus.* The Holy Saviour Chapel displays on Salvatorgasse a remarkable doorway with decoration in the Lombard Renaissance style. It dates from 1520 and is a copy, the original being in the Historisches Museum der Stadt Wien.

At the end of Salvatorgasse, take Marc-Aurel-Strasse on the left then Sterngasse on the right. Turn left for Ruprechtsplatz.

Ruprechtskirche – *Ruprechtsplatz.* According to tradition, St Virgil, Bishop of Salzburg, founded this church in 740. This would make it the oldest church in the city. It displays some Romanesque features. The nave and foot of the tower date from between 1130 and 1170, and the choir and portal from the 2nd third of the 13C. The church was completed in the first half of the 15C.

Its Romanesque bell tower and great roof lend it originality. Its modern stained-glass windows are by Lydia Roppolt. Rupertskirche is the French parish church of Vienna.

The nearest sights are: Stephansdom and the tour around Stephansdom, the Fleischmarkt and Freyung Districts, the first section of the Ring as well as the Prater District (which corresponds to the Leopoldstadt District).

KAPUZINERKIRCHE District★

Local map page 5, **JR**
Underground: Stephansplatz (U1, U3), Karlsplatz (U1, U4)
Tram: Oper (1, 2, 62, 65, D, J)
Bus: Albertinaplatz (3A), Michaelerplatz (2A)

The Church of the Capuchins with its famous crypt watches over the eternal sleep of the Habsburgs. It is close to the Hofburg, Opera and the shopping streets of Graben and Kärntnerstrasse. The church's sober and discreet façade attracts less attention than the fine fountain in Neuer Markt. Despite its lack of vitality, this small group of sleepy streets does however possess attractions for anyone interested in the history of the city.

Start the tour with Lobkowitz palace, practically oppposite Albertina Platz described in Staatsoper District.

Lobkowitz Palace (**P**[5]) – *Lobkowitzplatz 2.* Count Philip Sigismund Dietrichstein had this Italienate edifice built from 1685 to 1687 to plans by Giovanni Pietro Tencala. In 1709, Johann Bernhard Fischer von Erlach modified it. He added the attic and a gate showing the influence of the high altar which the architect had

Profile of a patron of the arts

Following the example of the Hildenburg-Hausens and the Esterházys who were patrons to Gluck and Haydn respectively, the Lobkowitz family played a leading role in Austrian music. Like all the aristocrats of his time, Prince Josef Lobkowitz was a rich man in touch with the art of music. He financed an entire orchestra and turned his palace into a veritable academy of music, attracting famous virtuosos and singers. Thus, Beethoven received an invitation to improvise on a quartet by Ignaz Pleyel who had just arrived from Paris and was highly enthusiastic about the German genius. Beethoven was not under the patronage of Lobkowitz but he had a priority contract with him (as in the first performance of the *Eroica*). Musical evenings at the Lobkowitz Palace drew the luminaries of the empire, as the prince never ceased to encourage new talent. As soon as a foreign composer came to Vienna, Lobkowitz would summon soloists and tenors so that they could play as soon as possible the works of his imminent guest.

designed the preceding year for the Franciscan church in Salzburg. In 1753, Wenzel von Lobkowitz bought the palace, where in 1804 or 1805 the first performance of Ludwig van Beethoven's Third Symphony was held, in the great hall called *"Eroica-Saal"* *(see also Eroicahaus)*.

Sensational music – It is hard to imagine the sensation which Beethoven's symphony must have caused among the small, select audience listening to it beneath the Baroque panelling of the palace. Public concerts were few and far between. Accustomed to Josef Haydn's gentler and less emotive music, the audience must have been overwhelmed. In fact, on the day after the concert, one of the listeners wrote: "Beethoven's music will soon reach the point where nobody can enjoy it at all". A great patron of music, Josef Lobkowitz (aged 32 in 1804) knew better *(see inset)*.

Österreichisches Theatermuseum ⊘ – The Austrian Theatre museum dates from 1923 and has been housed in the palace since 1991. It traces the evolution of theatre design from the Baroque period to the present day. Models show stage sets which made an impact on the Viennese theatre, such as *Anthony and Cleopatra* by William Shakespeare (Burgtheater, 1878) or *Lucia di Lammermoor* by G. Donizetti (Staatsoper, 1978). However, the exhibition is fairly small. It is preferable to see some of the temporary exhibitions which take place regularly in the museum, owing to the exceptional size and variety of its collections (100,000 sketches, drawings and etchings, numerous oil paintings, 700,000 photographs, 1,000 costumes, 1,000 models, library of 70,000 volumes). The museum has an annexe nearby *(see Österreichisches Theatermuseum: Gedenkräume, Staatsoper District)*.

Enter Führichgasse and turn left towards Neuer Markt by Tegetthoffstrasse.

Neuer Markt – This square was once the setting for the flour market, tournaments and the horseplay of *Hanswurst*, the Viennese equivalent of Mr. Punch. Owing to the predominance of 18C buildings, particularly Nos 13 and 16, it has retained a Baroque ambiance: Kupferschmiedhaus (No 13, 1796); Hatschiererhaus (No 14, 1665); Maysederhaus (No 15, 2nd half of the 18C, former home of the violinist and composer Josef Mayseder); Hufschmiedhaus (No 16, 1770 façade). No 2 was the site

R. Decharps/MICHELIN

Donner-Brunnen: The Fisherman with the Harpoon

of Josef Haydn's town residence from 1792 to 1797, where he composed the imperial Austrian national anthem in 1795-1796. It begins with the famous "God save the emperor" *(see Kaisergruft below)*.

In the centre of "New Market" is **Donner-Brunnen★★**, a fountain which Georg Raphael Donner built between 1737 and 1739 in response to a commission from the municipal authorities. The statue of Prudence stands in the centre of a high plinth, an allegory representing the concern and wisdom of the city authorities. Cherubs and fish spouting water are grouped around it. The figures on the edge personify the tributaries of the Danube: the rivers Traun (young fisherman with harpoon), Enns (bearded old ferryman), Ybbs and March (two nymphs), symbols of the four provinces adjoining the capital. Shocked by the nude figures, Maria Theresa had them removed in 1770 – at the time, this was the first secular group to adorn a square. Franz II replaced them with bronze copies in 1801. The original lead statues are in the Barockmuseum (Museum of Baroque Art) in the Belvedere. Unfortunately, to deter vehicles from parking, ugly white spheres now surround the fountain.

Kapuzinerkirche – *Neuer Markt.* The church of the Capuchins was built between 1622 and 1632 and dedicated to Our Lady of the Angels. It underwent several alterations before recovering its original appearance in 1936. In accordance with the rules of mendicant orders, the interior decoration is very austere. In a niche on the façade, a modern statue (1935, Hans Mauer) represents the Capuchin Marco d'Aviano, papal legate to Charles de Lorraine's army. He celebrated Mass on the summit of Kahlenberg on the morning of the last battle against the Turks in 1683 *(see Kahlenberg)*.

★★KAISERGRUFT OR THE HABSBURG PANTHEON ⊙

"The crypt of the Capuchins, where my emperors lay in their stone sarcophagi, was closed.

A friar came to me and asked:

"What do you want?"

"I want to see the sarcophagus of the Emperor Franz-Josef."

"God bless you", said the Capuchin, making the sign of the Cross over me.

"God save the Emperor!", I cried.

"Hush!", said the monk.

Joseph Roth, *The Crypt of the Capuchins.*

Kapuzinergruft – *Entrance on the left of the church.* Emperor Matthias founded the imperial crypt in 1618. It contains the tombs of twelve emperors, seventeen empresses and over one hundred archdukes, 138 members of the imperial family in all. The coffins contain their embalmed bodies; the entrails are in the catacombs at Stephansdom and the hearts in Augustinerkirche. Three emperors are buried elsewhere: Ferdinand II (in Graz), Frederick III (in the cathedral) and Karl I (in Madeira). Archduke Franz-Ferdinand and his wife, assassinated at Sarajevo on 28 June 1914, are not buried in Vienna but in Arstetten castle in Lower Austria. For any-

Eternity through the small door

Accompanying the plain wooden coffin, the chamberlain would knock at the small double door of the Leopold crypt. The Capuchin, waiting in the crypt, would ask "Whom do you bring?", and the chamberlain recited a long list of titles belonging to the emperor or empress, who had ruled over the vast Austro-Hungarian empire. "We do not know this person!" replied the Capuchin. At this point, the chamberlain again enumerated the titles. Once more this met with a refusal from the Capuchin. After the third rejection, the chamberlain became humbler: "We accompany a poor sinner, who begs for eternal rest", at which the Capuchin finally said: "We recognise him as our brother and we welcome him here."

one who is not Viennese, this multitude of tombs may seem a little macabre. However, as one visits the nine vaults arranged in chronological order, lugubrious feelings give way to respect in the presence of these last remains of the Habsburg empire.

Gründergruft (Founders' crypt) – The remains of Emperor Matthias and his wife Anna lie here.

Leopoldsgruft (Leopold crypt) – The 12 children's coffins it contains have given it the name of the "Crypt of Angels ". It contains the tombs of Ferdinand III (**1**) and Leopold I's wife, Elenore of Pfalz-Neuburg (**2**) by Balthasar Ferdinand Moll.

City Centre and the Ring

Karlsgruft (Charles crypt) – Johann Lukas von Hildebrandt designed the sarcophagi of Leopold I (**3**) and Josef I (**4**). **Balthasar Ferdinand Moll** designed the sarcophagus of **Karl VI★**, a splendid work of art displaying the coats of arms (crowning the skulls in the corner) of the Holy Roman German Empire, Bohemia, Hungary and Castile; above it is an allegory of Austria in mourning by the sculptor Johann Nikolaus Moll *(see illustration)*. Also of note are the fine veiled faces of the female mourners

at the corners of the sarcophagus of Elizabeth-Christina, Karl VI's wife who bore the nickname of "white lily" because of her pale complexion.

Maria-Theresia-Gruft (Maria-Theresa crypt) (**A**) – The Frenchman Jean-Nicolas Jadot de Ville-Issey designed this vault for François de Lorraine and Maria-Theresa. The architect conceived a domed mauseolum with an oval cupola, in the centre of which is the **double sarcophagus★★** by Balthasar Ferdinand Moll. The artist cast in lead an impressive bed of state bearing the imperial couple, symbolically face-to-face; before them an angel proclaims the triumph of faith, ready to blow his trumpet for the Last Judgment. At the corners are the crowns of the Holy Roman German Empire, Hungary, Bohemia and Jerusalem (a helmet encircled by thorns). In front is the coffin of their son, Josef II. A niche contains the tomb of Countess Fuchs-Mollard, Maria-Theresa's governess; although she was not of royal blood, the high esteem in which she was held by the empress accounts for her presence in the Habsburg crypt.

Franzensgruft (Franz crypt) (**B**) – The last emperor of the Holy Roman German Empire, Franz II, rests in a copper coffin by Pietro Nobile, with the tombs of his four wives around him.

Ferdinandsgruft (Ferdinand crypt) (**C**) – Among the numerous coffins in this room are those of Ferdinand I (**5**) and his wife Marie-Anne of Savoy (**6**).

Toskanagruft (Tuscan crypt) (**D**) – This vault contains the coffins of Leopold II (**7**) and his wife Maria Ludovica of Spain (**8**), and of members of the two collateral branches who reigned in Tuscany and Modena until 1860 (Archduke Franz-Ferdinand, born in 1863, was the heir of the last duke of Modena).

Close-up of Karl's VI sarcophagus

Pratt-Pries/DIAF

114

Neue Gruft (New crypt) – Below a concrete ceiling (1961), this crypt houses the sarcophagi of Maximilian, shot in Mexico by republican revolutionaries under Juárez in 1867, and of Marie Louise, Empress of the French. The coffin of her son lay in Franzensgruft until it was moved to the Invalides on 15 December 1940, precisely 100 years after his father's funeral.

Franz-Josef-Gruft (Franz-Josef crypt) (**E**) – Franz-Josef was the last Habsburg emperor to be buried in Kapuzinergruft. On either side of his coffin are the tombs of Elizabeth of Bavaria, assassinated in Geneva in 1898, and of their son Rudolf who died in mysterious conditions at Mayerling *(see under this heading)* hunting lodge in 1889. Sissi's coffin is permanently adorned with flowers, in particular a floral wreath bearing a ribbon in the national colours of Hungary (green, red, white).

Gruftkapelle (crypt chapel) – The last tomb in Kapuzinergruft is that of Zita of Bourbon-Parma, who died in exile in Switzerland in 1989. The chapel also contains a monument in memory of her husband Karl I, the last Habsburg sovereign.

The "pewter plague" – Contrary to the quotation from Joseph Roth *(see above)*, the sarcophagi are metal. Until the end of the 18C, they were made of pewter; later sarcophagi are copper. Oxidation, "the pewter plague", attacks 17C and 18C sarcophagi and requires expensive and regular maintenance.

Near Neuer Markt fountain, enter Plankengasse.

From this little street, there are three very different views which are all of interest: opposite is the yellow façade of the Evangelische Kirche built in 1784 by Gottlieb Nigelli; on the right *(near Seilergasse)*, Hans Hollein's modern Haas-Haus *(see Stephansplatz)*; behind, the elegant Donnerbrunnen *(see Neuer Markt above)*. Also noteworthy, at No 4, are the decorative details on the three façades of the Secession apartment house "Zum silbernen Brunnen" built of reinforced concrete in 1914.

Carry on along Plankengasse and turn right into Dorotheergasse. At the end is Café Hawelka (No 6), a veritable Viennese institution.

★ **Jüdisches Museum der Stadt Wien** ⊘ – *Dorotheergasse 11*. Since 1993, the City of Vienna Jewish museum has been housed in the Eskeles palace (second half of the 18C), a Baroque building which belonged to several aristocratic Austrian families.

Hanukkah lamp

JÜDISCHES MUSEUM, Wien

The Jewish community – The records of Upper Austria first mention the presence of Jews towards 903-906. 13C Vienna authorised a Jewish settlement within its walls, mainly on the site of present-day Judenplatz *(see Freyung District)*. In 1624, Ferdinand II allowed them land for their exclusive use near the Danube; soon it had a population of more than one thousand. In 1670, acting against the advice of his Treasurer, Leopold I expelled the Jews, who had to leave the city within a few weeks. *Unterer Werd* then became Leopoldstadt (present-day 2nd District) and the synagogue was turned into a church.

The Jews had obtained permission to play an important role in the finances of the country *(see inset "Court Jew", Prater District)*. In 1867, Franz-Josef granted them total emancipation. On the one hand, this ensured him the lasting loyalty of the

Jewish community. On the other hand, it led to a massive influx of Jews into the capital. Unfortunately, at the beginning of the 20C, they had to confront the anti-Semitism of Karl Lueger's Christian-Democrats. According to Adolph Hitler, he was "the most outstanding mayor of all time". This more than slightly negative ambiance lies at the root of the Zionism of Theodor Herzl, a Viennese by adoption. It also encouraged the excellent education of the young Jewish population, whose intellectual achievements soon transcended frontiers. There are many examples, such as Sigmund Freud, Joseph Roth, Arthur Schnitzler, Arnold Schönberg and Ludwig Wittgenstein, a list which is by no means comprehensive. The annexation of Austria in 1938 had catastrophic consequences, namely *Kristallnacht* (the Night of Broken Glass) from 9 November to 10 November 1938. At least 60,000 Viennese Jews died during the Second World War.

Tour – On the first floor, the "historical exhibition" is an impressive holographic display of thought-provoking images relating to the Jewish community in Vienna. It features large, bare glass panels displaying their contents only if observed from the correct angle. They trace the painful, still recent past of the descendants of Abraham, a nightmare which became only too real and which hopefully will never recur. Most of the documents describe the everyday life of the community, in particular in the former Leopoldstadt ghetto. In the centre of the room, a plinth displays the principal dates of Jewish history in Vienna, from 903 to date.

The 2nd floor features temporary exhibitions; the painted wooden coffered ceilings are noteworthy. The display cases on the 3rd floor contain religious objects mainly from the Max Berger collection.

Take Dorotheergasse in the opposite direction.

Dorotheum ⊙ – *Dorotheergasse 17.* It is impossible to overlook the pink façade of this institution. On the site of the church and the cloister which gave it its name, the Dorotheum is one of the largest auction houses in the world. "Tante Dorothee" occupies several neo-Baroque buildings dating from 1898 to 1901 and designed by Emil von Förster. In the courtyard *(Klosterneuburger Hof, Dorotheergasse 15)* is a fragment of mural from Dorotheerkirche (16C).

Some articles can be bought in advance. Furniture, carpets, works of art, jewellery, ornaments, books, stamps, clothes etc. are all auctioned in the rooms of this former pawnbroking institution which Josef I founded in 1707 *(see Practical information).* The Dorotheum has 13 branches in Vienna alone, and subsidiaries in the main Austrian towns, as well as in Prague.

Return and turn left into Stallburggasse, then immediately to the right into Bräunerstrasse.

Bräunerstrasse – At No 3 is a house with a Rococo façade dating from 1761. Johann Nestroy was born there on 7 December 1801. He was an actor, opera singer, painter, moralist and theatre director.

It is possible to extend the tour by going to Graben and Peterskirche, from where there is a small tour (see Around Stephansdom).

The nearest sights are: Hofburg, the Freyung and Staatsoper Districts, Stephansdom (the cathedral).

Join us in our constant task of keeping up-to-date.
Please send us your comments and suggestions.
Michelin Tyre PLC
Tourism Department
The Edward Hyde Building
38 Clarendon Road
WATFORD - Herts WD1 1SX
Tel: 01923 41 5000

KUNSTHISTORISCHES MUSEUM★★★

Map page 5, **HS**
Underground: Babenbergerstrasse (U2)
Tram: Burgring (1, 2, D, J)
Bus: Babenbergerstrasse (2A)

PRINCELY COLLECTIONS

The Habsburgs assembled the collections of the Museum of Art History, which are among the greatest and most extensive in the world.

The highlight of the museum is undeniably the Art Gallery, a collection of immense richness, both by its intrinsic value and its diversity. It is unusual in that, unlike the great British or German national museums, it did not grow in a systematic way. Rudolf II collected the works of Brueghel the Elder or Dürer; Archduke Leopold Wilhelm, Governor of the Low Countries, admired Memling, Tintoretto and Titian, and Teniers the Younger was the director of his gallery; Karl VI liked Rembrandt, Hals and Van Dyck. Prior to them, Ferdinand I wrote in his will that "vases, vessels, statues, jewels and antique coins should remain united and indivisible with the first-born of the dynasty". The collections grew over the centuries and occupied successively Stalburg, the Belvedere, then at the end of the 19C the Ringstrasse; they draw strength from their weakness: despite numerous historical omissions, the treasures they contain are incomparable.

Sections – The Kunsthistorisches Museum comprises ten sections. The building houses five *(see Ring, Burgring)*, while the others are in exterior annexes: Schatzkammer (Hofburg), Sammlung alter Musikinstrumente (Hofburg), Ephesos-Museum (Hofburg) and Wagenburg (Schönbrunn).

The Kunsthistorisches building contains 5 departments spread throughout 4km/2 miles of corridors: Ägyptische Sammlung (Egyptian and Near Eastern collections), on the mezzanine floor *(right side)*, in rooms I to VIII; Antikensammlung (Greek, Etruscan and Roman antiquities) on the mezzanine floor *(right side)*, in rooms IX to XVIII; Sammlung für Plastik und Kunstgewerbe (sculpture and decorative arts), on the mezzanine floor *(left side)*, in rooms XIX to XXXVI; Gemäldegalerie (art gallery), on the first floor, the Flemish, Dutch and German Schools in rooms IX to XV, and cabinets 14 to 24 *(left side)*, the Italian, Spanish and French Schools in rooms I to VII, and cabinets 1 to 13 *(right side)*; Münzkabinett (cabinet of coins and medals) on the 2nd floor, in rooms I to III.

Room VIII on the 1st floor is reserved for interesting temporary thematic exhibitions. The admission charge is included in the ticket to the museum.

Outstanding exhibits – Even a keen connoisseur of art might not have enough time to see everything in a museum of such range and quality. After having come so many miles to visit Vienna, it would be a pity to miss a masterpiece only a few feet away. Our selection is a reliable one. Works of outstanding calibre are indicated in bold lettering. The appreciation of a few select works is preferable to an exhausting trek round the whole edifice.

As in many museums, certain works are in course of restoration, others are on exhibition abroad; this leads to some rotation in the choice of exhibits. Our selection cannot take account of all these changes. Some works may, therefore, not be on view during the visit.

★★Ägyptische Sammlung (Egyptian and Near Eastern collections)

ROOMS	CONTENTS	SELECTION
I	Worship of the dead: sarcophagi; canopic jars; uschebtis.	Sarcophagus of Nes-Shu-Tefnut (about 300 BC; *papyrus columns*★ (18th dyn.).
II	Ceramics	
III	Animal worship: mummies; zoomorphical deities.	Ichneumon (6C-4C BC), mongoose relief.

Old Kingdom (*c* 2600-2130 BC). Middle Kingdom (*c* 2040-1650 BC). New Kingdom (*c* 1550-945 BC). Late Age (*c* 712 BC-641 AD).

IV	Writing	Khonsu Mes'Book of the Dead (about 1000 BC). Cylinder-seals.
V	Late Age sculptures	Lion from Ischtar gate, Babylon (6C BC); bust of a man (end 4C BC); sphinx of Wah Ib Re (end 4C BC).

117

VI	Everyday life: furniture; jewellery; tools.	Necklace and bracelet (end 5th dyn., gold and pottery); head of a woman (13C BC); Tell el-Yahudiya decorated tiles (12C BC).
VI A	Old Kingdom	Funeral chapel of Prince Kaninisout's mastaba (5th dyn.).
VII	Middle and New Kingdoms: sculptures	Hippopotamus (11-12th dyn.; head of Sesostris III (12th dyn); tomb of Hori (13th dyn.); **Sebek Em Sauf**★★ (13th dyn.); Horus and Horembeb (18th dyn.); Tjenuna (18th dyn.); Khai-Hapi (18th dyn.); **head of Thoutmosis III**★ (18th dyn.).

Kunsthistorisches Museum

A blue ceramic hippopotamus

Sebek Em Sauf is a votive figure representing a spokesman for the city of Thebes, capital of Upper Egypt. The funerary head symbolised the body of the dead person, at a time when mummification was not yet current.

The 4th dynasty funerary head is one of the major works in this collection. It comes from the site of Giza, where there were a number of Austrian digs from 1912 to 1929; it was found buried beneath the entrance of an underground funeral chamber. Scientists cannot agree as to the purpose of this limestone head with an idealised face.

| VIII | Old Kingdom | **Funerary head**★★ (4th dyn.); Ka Pu Ptah and Ipep (5th dyn.); Ba'Ef Ba (5th dyn.); Itjef and his wife (6th dyn.) |

★★Antikensammlung (Greek and Roman antiquities)

| IX | Cyprus and Asia Minor | Treasure of Dolichenus (early 3C) discovered in Lower Austria in 1937; over 100 objects from a temple. |
| X | Greece and Rome: sculptures | **Youth of Magdalensberg**★ (16C copy); head of Artemis; (2C BC); Artemis (3C); **sarcophagus of the Amazons**★ (2nd half of 4C BC); **portrait of Aristotle**★ (Roman copy); fragment of Parthenon frieze (about 440 BC). |

Experts once identified the youth of Magdalensberg as a 1C Roman sculpture; it is in fact a cast from the original found in Carinthia in 1502, which mysteriously disappeared.

| XI | Greece and Rome: sculptures | Relief of Mithra (2nd half 2C); sarcophagus depicting a lion hunt (2nd half 3C BC). |

XII	Greek bronzes	Disc with dolphin (about 500 BC); Herakles (4C BC); *head of Zeus*★ (1C BC).
XIII	Etruria	Bronze helmets; bucchero vases; Athena of Rocca d'Aspromonte (5C BC).
XIV	Greece: ceramics and terracotta	*Douris cup*★ (about 500 BC); skyphos from Brigos (about 490 BC); series of lecythi; Tanagra figurines; *Ptolemaic cameo*★ (9 layers of onyx, 3C BC).
XV	Rome: cameo collection; sculpture; mosaics; glass	*Gemma Augustea cameo*★★★ (1C); eagle cameo (1C BC); *Gemma Claudia*★ (1C); busts of emperors.

A cameo is a gem carved in relief. This art is of Egyptian and Oriental origin. The Greeks brought it to perfection with their polychrome cameos. The Romans appreciated this technique and from the 1C BC, imported artists and gems from as far as India. The *Gemma Augustea* enjoys world renown and commemorates the military victories of the first Roman emperor, visible at the top on his throne facing a goddess representing Rome.

Kunsthistorisches Museum

Gemma Augustea cameo

XVI	Late antiquity: sculpture and jewellery	Portrait of Eutropios (2nd half 5C)
XVII	Early Christian art.	Treasure of Szilágysomlyó (about 400, Romania); pair of fibulae (5C).
XVIII	Early Christian art.	*Treasure of Nagyszentmiklôs*★ (Bulgaria, 9C – present-day Romania).

The treasure of Nagyszentmiklôs was discovered in 1799 and comprises 23 ceremonial vases belonging to a tribal chief; it amounts to nearly 10kg of pure gold. Several influences are present in this collection: Persian-Sassanid, Graeco-Roman and Byzantine.

★★Sculpture and decorative arts

The Habsburgs' passion for collecting was proverbial. Thanks to their knowledge and their artistic flair, they amassed over the years a collection defying imagination. It comprises the art galleries of Archduke Ferdinand II at Ambras Castle near Innsbruck, Rudolf II in Prague, Archduke Leopold-Wilhelm in Vienna and the imperial treasury; grouped together in 1891, they formed a uniquely wide-ranging collection of very high quality.

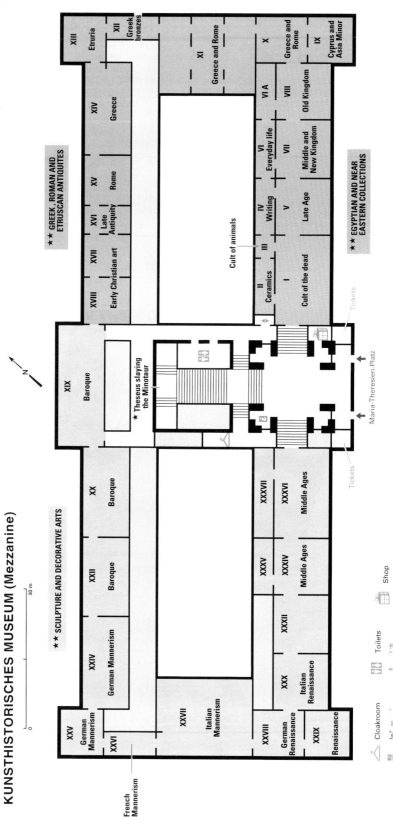

KUNSTHISTORISCHES MUSEUM (Mezzanine)

★★ SCULPTURE AND DECORATIVE ARTS

★★ GREEK, ROMAN AND ETRUSCAN ANTIQUITES

★★ EGYPTIAN AND NEAR EASTERN COLLECTIONS

N

XIII Etruria

XII Greek bronzes

XI Greece and Rome

X Greece and Rome

IX Cyprus and Asia Minor

XIV Greece

VI A

VIII Old Kingdom

XV Rome

XVI Late Antiquity

VI Everyday life

VII Middle and New Kingdom

IV Writing

V Late Age

XVII Early Christian art

XVIII

III Cult of animals

II Ceramics

Cult of the dead

Tickets

XIX Baroque

★ Theseus slaying the Minotaur

Maria-Theresien-Platz

Tickets

XX Baroque

XXXVII

XXXVI Middle Ages

XXII Baroque

XXXV

XXXIV Middle Ages

XXIV German Mannerism

XXXII

XXV German Mannerism

XXVI

XXVII Italian Mannerism

XXX Italian Renaissance

XXVIII German Renaissance

XXIX Renaissance

French Mannerism

Cloakroom   Toilets   Shop

0   30 m

120

It encompasses a multitude of items displayed in rotation. Only a few of them feature in the text, as an illustration of each aspect of this extraordinarily rich little world.

At present, only rooms XIX to XXVII are open to the public. However, the text mentions certain exhibits of exceptional interest, in the rooms closed to the public. These exhibits do not have a room number. Both in the text and throughout the visit, the sequence is not chronological.

German Renaissance, Mannerist and Baroque styles – Two silver gilt bowls (Nürnberg, about 1510) illustrate the evolution in modelling from the late Gothic period to the early Renaissance; it is evident from his studies and sketches that Albrecht Dürer played a part in this transition. The "automaton with trumpets" (Augsburg, 1582) is a small mechanical organ with 9 pipes and 11 moving figures, of ebony and silver incrusted with enamel and copper. The **equestrian statue of Joseph I★★** overcoming the demon of Discord is a brilliant ivory sculpture by Matthias Steinl (Vienna, 1693). The king is portrayed at the age of 15; the sculpture has two matching counterparts: the equestrian statue of Leopold I, the victor of the Turks, and the statue of Karl receiving the Spanish crown *(room XX)*. The **Bust of Emperor Leopold I★** *(see illustration in the Introduction, Sculpture)* by Paul Strudel (1695) belongs to a series of six portraits commissioned by the Elector Johann Wilhelm, brother-in-law of the emperor shown here *(room XIX)*. The bezoar set in an enamelled gold vessel is a delicate work by Jan Vermeyen (about 1600); bezoar is an accretion of indigestible matter in the intestines of certain animals, such as the llama and the antelope. The *Battle of the Amazons* is a cedar wood carving by Ignaz Elhafen (about 1685); it represents one of the 12 labours of Hercules *(room XX)*. In Prague, Adriaen de Vries created the **Bust of Emperor Rudolf II★★** (1603), the great Habsburg patron of the arts; the pedestal is noteworthy, with its figures of slaves and an imperial eagle *(room XXIV)*. A silver dish by Christoph Jamnitzer is in the shape of an ornamental basin representing Cupid's triumphal procession (Nürnberg, about 1605); this item is in keeping with the Prague Court's preference for elaborate decoration *(room XXIV)*. The **ewer★** (1602) of Seychelles coconut is a natural *objet d'art* by Anton Schweinberger; this masterpiece of the goldsmith's skill encloses what was once considered seafood *(room XXIX)*. A jug is a fairly commonplace object; however, this example carved in amber in Königsberg in the early 17C is out of the ordinary, consisting of different transparent layers *(room XXV)*. Clement Kicklinger was a craftsman from Augsburg who made some unusual objects, including another natural *objet d'art*, an ostrich egg in a setting decorated with coral *(room XXIV)*.

French Mannerist and Baroque styles – The *bust of Archduchess Marie Antoinette★* is by Jean Baptiste Lemoyne and represents the dauphine during the year of her marriage (at the age of 15); her husband's grandfather, Louis XV, commissioned it as a gift to Maria Theresa *(room XX)*. There are several Limoges enamels in a showcase: plates and dishes (mid-16C) by Pierre Reymond *(room XVI)*. A gold "Mercury goblet" is set with enamel, emeralds and rubies (about 1560) and surmounted by a statuette of Mercury holding an enamel ring; the contrast between the smooth surfaces and series of details is typically French in style *(room XXIV)*. Richard Toutain made the onyx ewer incrusted with gold, enamel, emeralds and diamonds in Paris about 1570 as a gift from Archduke Ferdinand to King Charles IX of France.

Italian Renaissance and Mannerism – The *bust of Isabella of Aragon★★* (?) dating from about 1488 is by Francesco Laurana *(see illustration)*, an itinerant artist from Dalmatia; presumably, he sculpted the portrait during a stay in Naples; the polychrome marble and subtle tones make this an outstanding work. Benvenuto Cellini made the gold and partly

Isabella of Aragon (?) by Francesco Laurana

Kunsthistorisches Museum

City Centre and the Ring

Saltcellar by Benvenuto Cellini

Kunsthistorisches Museum

enamelled *saltcellar*★★ in Paris between 1540 and 1543 for King Francis I *(see illustration)*. Resting on its ebony pedestal, this masterpiece of the goldsmith's art represents Neptune holding a trident and the Earth; the boat is for the salt and the temple for pepper *(room XXVII)*. *Emperor Karl V and Queen Maria of Hungary* are two fine busts (1555) by Leone Leoni, who engraved the papal and imperial coinage in Milan *(room XXVII)*. His son Pompeo Leoni created the painted silver *Head of Philip II* resting on an earthenware bust (1753) by Balthasar Moll *(room XXVII)*. Mercury (about 1585) is a famous work by Giovanni Bologna from Douai, a Flemish sculptor working in Italy under the name of Giambologna *(room XXVII)*. The *small altarpiece*★ is a typically Florentine piece of work set with hard gemstones. It was made in the late 16C for Archduke Ferdinand I of Medici and represents Christ and the Woman of Samaria. The frame of rock crystal is by Gian Ambrogio Caroni. *The Flagellation of Christ* by Alessandro Algardi is a Roman work dating from about 1630 of gold, bronze, agate, lapis lazuli and marble *(room XXII)*.

Kunsthistorisches Museum

Aquamanile in the shape of a gryphon

Middle Ages – An *aquamanile in the shape of a griffon*★ (early 12C) is of gilded bronze incrusted with silver and niello; during Mass, this jug was used for washing the hands. The griffon is a mythical animal, half eagle, half lion, symbolising the duality of Christ and the dual power of the Church *(see illustration)*. The Wilten chalice made in Lower Saxony about 1160 is a sacred vessel of silver gilt and niello. An onyx cameo of Poseidon (early 13C) in an early 19C gold setting was made in southern Italy, which is interesting since its subject foreshadows the Renaissance. There are two sets of painted playing cards: *Ambraser Hofjagdspiel* (mid-15C) where the 54 designs depict a court hunt and *Hofamterspiel* (1455) depicting court activities. The limestone Madonna of Krumau (about 1400) is from Bohemia; typical of International Gothic are the Virgin's graceful swaying stance and the delicately carved folds of the robe.

To reach the picture gallery on the first floor, take the main staircase. On the landing is **Theseus slaying the Minotaur★** which Napoléon commissioned from Antonio Canova for the Corso in Milan. Franz I of Austria bought the work.

The **stairwell★** is magnificent. Its ceiling features the *Apotheosis of the Renaissance*, a fresco by the Hungarian artist Mihály von Munkácsy. On the left is Leonardo da Vinci talking to the young Raphael *(on the steps)*, and, just above, Veronese engaged in painting; Michelangelo is behind the balustrade, while Titian advises a pupil before a female model. The 12 lunettes depicting great Renaissance artists are by Hans Makart. Figures between the columns are the work of Franz Matsch and the brothers Ernst and Gustav Klimt.

Kunsthistorisches Museum

The staircase with *Theseus Slaying the Minotaur* by Antonio Canova

★★★ The Picture Gallery

Rather than an inventory capable of wearying the reader, the following is a selection of outstanding works with biographical details of some of the artists. This presentation has the advantage of highlighting the major features of the art gallery; it also reflects the spirit that inspired this princely collection, when the Habsburgs showed irrepressible enthusiasm for the Arts.

Room IX – Michiel Coxcie (1499-1592), *The Expulsion from Paradise* (about 1550), and also the works of Hans Vredeman de Vries (1527-about 1605), Franz Floris (1515-1570) and Jan Mostaert (about 1475-about 1555).

Cabinet 14 – Jan van Eyck, **Cardinal Nicolo Albergati★★** (about 1435), a dignified realistic portrait, and *The Goldsmith Jan de Leeuw* (1436). Jean Fouquet, **The Court Jester Gonella★** (about 1440/45). Hugo van der Goes **Diptych: The Fall of Man and the Lamentation★★** (about 1470/75). Rogier van der Weyden, **Triptych: the Crucifixion★** (about 1440). Hieronymus Bosch (about 1450-1516), by whom another Viennese museum has a major work *(see Akademie der Bildenden Künste)*, *Carrying the Cross* (about 1480/1490). Gerard David (about 1460-1523), *The Archangel Michael* (about 1510). Joos van Cleve, *Virgin with Child* (about 1530) and **Lucrezia★** (1520/25).

Jan van Eyck (about 1390-1441) – With his brother Hubert, he perfected the new technique of painting in oils. They were the pioneers of the new painting which evolved from the Gothic tradition into the art of the Flemish primitives.

Jean Fouquet (about 1425-about 1480) – During his stay in Italy, his talent attracted the attention of Pope Eugenius IV who commissioned him to paint his portrait. According to a contemporary Italian artist, he was "a good master, especially in his portrayal from life".

Hugo van der Goes (about 1440-1482) – This artist of melancholy temperament assimilated the achievements of Jan van Eyck. He suffered mental illness and retired to an Augustinian monastery near Brussels as a lay brother. More than any other artist, he knew how to express the personality of his subjects.

Rogier van der Weyden (about 1400-1464) – After J. van Eyck's death, he was the leading representative of Flemish painting, although he was born in Tournai, which was French at the time. He was official painter to the city of Brussels, hence the translation of his name which was originally Rogier de la Pasture ("of the meadow").

Joos van Cleve (about 1485-1540) – He travelled to Germany, France and probably Italy, integrating these experiences with Flemish tradition. His portraits earned him lasting fame.

Cabinet 15 – Joachim Patenier (about 1485-1524), *The Baptism of Christ* (about 1515). Herri met de Bles (about 1510-about 1550), *Landscape with St John the Baptist (1535/40)*. Jan Gossaert (about 1478-1532), called Mabuse because born in Maubeuge, *St Luke Painting the Virgin* (about 1520).

Room X – One cannot fail to respond to this room with its unique assembly of paintings! 14 paintings by Brueghel out of a total of 45 in the world. Among this collection, from which copyists are often working, are: *The Tower of Babel*★★, *The Battle of Carnival and Lent*★★ (1559), *Children's Games*★★ (1560), *The Ascent to Calvary*★ (1564), *Peasant Dance*★ (1568/69) and *Peasant Wedding*★ (1568/69). One of the most remarkable features in many of the paintings is the near absence of a sky. *Hunters in the Snow*★★★ (1565) is an undeniable masterpiece, part of a series of 6 of which 5 are still existant, including 3 in this museum. The cycle began with the first days of spring and ended with this scene showing the peasants returning home after hunting. Even more than the subject itself, it is the handling and cool colours that convey the chilly wintry atmosphere.

Brueghel the Elder (about 1527-1569) – Peeters Brueghels probably came from a village called Brueghel, in Dutch Brabant or in the Limburg Kempen (in present-day Belgium). He soon signed his name Bruegel, a spelling to which he adhered right to the end. *Bruegel de Oude*, i.e. the Elder, served his apprenticeship in Antwerp, then travelled to Messina before returning in 1554 to Flanders, which was then the richest country in Europe. In 1563, he settled in Brussels and married Marie Coecke, daughter of Pieter Coecke, court painter to Charles V. He founded a family which produced 26 painters. His eldest son was Peter Brueghel the Younger (1564-1638), his youngest son was Jan Brueghel (1658-1625) who acquired the nickname of "Velvet" in the 18C.

Hunters in the Snow by Pieter Brueghel the Elder

Room XI – Jacob Jordaens (1593-1678), *The Feast of the Bean King* (before 1656). Frans Snyders, (1579-1657), *Fish Market* (about 1618).

Cabinet 16 – Albrecht Dürer, *Madonna with Pear* (1512), **Portrait of a Young Venetian Woman**★ (1505), *The Martyrdom of the Ten Thousand Christians* (1508), and **The Adoration of the Holy Trinity**★★ (1511). This altar has an unusual feature: there is a self-portrait of the painter in the lower right-hand corner and he is the only person in the painting with his feet on the ground; the inscription he is holding makes it clear he is the artist.

Albrecht Dürer (1471-1528) – Germany's most illustrious artist enjoyed great renown during his lifetime, especially as an engraver. He had learned how to use an engraver's chisel in the studio used by his father, a goldsmith from Nürnberg, originally from Hungary. The German Romantics considered him to be the supreme example of German genius in the realms of art.

Cabinet 17 – Albrecht Dürer, *Portrait of Emperor Maximilian I*★ (1519) and *Portrait of Johann Kleberger* (1526). Martin Schongauer (about 1450-1491), **The Holy Family**★ (about 1480). Lucas Cranach the Elder, **The Crucifixion**★★ (1500/01), **Judith with the Head of Holofernes**★ (about 1530). Hans Baldung Grien (about 1485-1545), *The Three Ages* (1509-10). Leonhard Beck (about 1480-1542), *St George and the Dragon* (about 1515). Bernhard Strigel (about 1460-1528), *Emperor Maximilian I and his Family* (1516). Albrecht Altdorfer, **The Nativity**★ (about 1520). Wolf Huber (about 1485-1553), *The Humanist Jakob Ziegler* (after 1544).

Martin Schongauer (about 1450-1491) – The son of an Augsburg goldsmith, he trained in Colmar, where he was born, in a milieu rich with Flemish influences. His work

Judith with Holoferne's Head
by Lucas Cranach the Elder

comprises engraving on copper, a technique in which he excelled, and painting. His painting is notable for great attention to detail.

Lucas Cranach the Elder (1472-1553) – This friend of Luther produced his first paintings in Vienna. His work has been labelled either pathetic or sophisticated. He worked at the Court of Wittenberg and painted portraits of Protestant princes, but it is sometimes difficult to distinguish his work from that of his assistants.

Albrecht Altdorfer (about 1480-1538) – A member of the Danube School, this citizen of Ratisbon specialised in scenes from the Passion and landscapes, which soon became empty of any human figures. The Romantics prized his works.

Cabinet 18 – Hans Holbein the Younger, *Jane Seymour*★ (1536) and *Dr. John Chambers, Physician to King Henry VIII* (1543). Jakob Seisenegger (1505-1567), *Emperor Charles V* (1532).

Hans Holbein the Younger (1497-1543) – A native of Augsburg, he died in London. His first patron was the burgomaster of Basel, Jacob Meyer. In England, he became famous among the aristocracy at Court through his portraits which combine impassiveness with great plasticity.

Cabinet 19 – Giuseppe Arcimboldo, **The Fire**★ (1556). Roelant Savery (1576-1639), *Landscape with Animals* (about 1618). Georg Flegel (1566-1638), **Still Life with a Bunch of Flowers**★ (1632), a composition of unusual subtlety.

Giuseppe Arcimboldo (about 1527-1593) – The museum has 4 allegorical paintings *(Fire, Water, Summer, Winter)* by this artist who attained the rank of Count Palatine. His technical brilliance is unusual in Mannerist art but his style found great favour in the Germanic Empire.

KUNSTHISTORISCHES MUSEUM (1st floor)

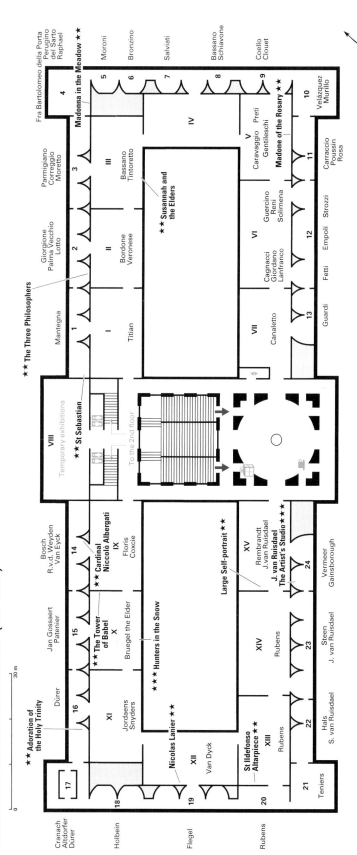

★★ The Three Philosophers

★★ Madonna in the Meadow

Fra Bartolomeo della Porta
Perugino
Raphael

Moroni

Bronzino

Salviati

Bassano
Schiavone

Coello
Clouet

4

5

6

7

8

9

Velázquez
Murillo

10

Madone of the Rosary ★★

Caravaggio Preti
Gentileschi

V

Carraccio
Poussin
Rosa

11

Parmigiano
Correggio
Moretto

3

Bassano
Tintoretto

III

★★ Susannah
and the Elders

IV

Giorgione
Palma Vecchio
Lotto

2

Bordone
Veronese

II

Guercino
Reni
Solimena

VI

Empoli Strozzi

12

Mantegna

1

Titian

I

Cagnacci
Giordano
Lanfranco

Fetti

Canaletto

VII

Guardi

13

VIII

Temporary exhibitions

★★ St Sebastian

To the 2nd floor

Bosch
R.v.d. Weyden
Van Eyck

14

★★ Cardinal
Niccolò Albergati

IX

Floris
Coxcie

Jan Gossaert
Patenier

15

★★ The Tower
of Babel

X

Bruegel the Elder

★★★ Hunters in the Snow

Large Self-portrait ★★

Rembrandt
J. van Ruisdael

XV

J. van Ruisdael ★★★
The Artist's Studio

24

Vermeer
Gainsborough

Dürer

16

Jordaens
Snyders

XI

Nicolas Lanier ★★

Steen
J. van Ruisdael

23

Rubens

XIV

Hals
S. van Ruisdael

22

Rubens

★★ Adoration of
the Holy Trinity

Cranach
Altdorfer
Dürer

17

Holbein

18

Flegel

St Ildefonso
Altarpiece ★★

XIII

Van Dyck

XII

19

20

Rubens

21

Teniers

Lift   Shop   Toilets   Café

126

Room XII – This room is devoted to Anthony van Dyck, containing some exceptionally fine portraits and religious works: *Study of a Female Head* (about 1620), *Portrait of a Young General* (about 1624), **Nicolas Lanier**★★ (1628), *Samson and Delilah* (1628/30), **Venus at Vulcan's Forge**★ (1630/32), *Prince Rupert of the Palatinate* (1631/32) and *Jacomo de Cachiopin* (1634).

Anthony van Dyck (1599-1641) – He was a painter of exceptional talent, although some historians have stressed a certain lack of assiduity. It is of course true that Rubens' former assistant enjoyed luxury and that his behaviour was apt to be capricious. However, the secret of his success depended on two things: study and discipline. He was a portrait painter who tried to delve into the soul of his models rather than flatter them, even if they were kings or princes.

Cabinet 20 – This and the two following rooms concentrate on Peter Paul Rubens. One must visit Vienna to grasp the achievements of one of the most famous painters in the history of art. *The Lamentation* (1614) and *St Jerome dressed as a Cardinal* (about 1625)

Room XIII – *The Triumph of Venus* (1635/37), **Self Portrait**★ (1638/40) and **The Little Fur**★★ (1635/40), which represents Helen Fourment, Rubens' wife. The **Ildefonso Altar**★★ (1630/32) dates from the time when Rubens was Court painter in the Low Countries. Although the shape of the triptych is medieval, Rubens is at the pinnacle of his art. Coudenberg Abbey in Brussels sold it to build a church for 15,000 livres. This gives an indication of how much the Viennese Court appreciated Rubens.

Room XIV – *Vincent of Gonzagua* (1604/05), *The Annunciation* (1609), *The Assumption of the Virgin Mary* (1611/14), *The Miracles of St Francis Xavier* (1617/19) and *Young Girl with Fan* (1612/14).

Peter Paul Rubens (1577-1640) – A dominant figure in Baroque art, he was a prolific painter, famous during his lifetime, since he was also a diplomat. His lasting prestige rests upon his powerful style and his designs in warm colours, both precise and monumental. In the late 20C, it is easy to qualify his paintings as pompous. However, one should remember that his grandiose style heralded the Baroque era in the northern countries and that his influence was decisive.

Cabinet 21 – David Teniers the Younger, **Archduke Leopold Wilhelm in his Gallery**★ (about 1651).

David Teniers the Younger (1610-1690) – This master of St Luke's corporation in Antwerp was an eclectic painter, who settled in Brussels. There, Archduke Leopold Wilhelm made him the director of his art gallery. His successor, Don Juan of Austria, retained his services.

Cabinet 22 – Frans Hals (about 1580-1666), *Portrait of a Man* (1654/55). Salomon van Ruysdael (about 1600-1670), *Landscape with Fence* (1631).

Cabinet 23 – Isaac van Ostade (1621-1649), *Stopping by the Inn* (1646). Jacob van Ruisdael (about 1628-1682), *River Landscape with Cellar Entrance* (1649). Aert van der Neer (about 1603-1677), *Fishing by Moonlight* (about 1669).

Cabinet 24 – Thomas Gainsborough (1727-1788), *Suffolk Landscape* (about 1750). Johannes Vermeer, **The Artist's Studio**★★★ (1665-66). To achieve this view of his studio where we see him from behind, the artist used a camera obscura. This is his most ambitious painting, where he developed an almost Pointillist technique, bathing his work in exquisite light.

Johannes Vermeer (1632-1675) – This Dutch painter's reputation rests upon a relatively small number of paintings. His work depicts scenes of everyday life, which he transcends by adding a timeless dimension to workaday images. His work did not revolutionise painting. However,

The Artist's Studio by Johannes Vermeer

through his mastery of light and texture and his subtle palette, Vermeer became one of the most remarkable masters of the 17C and in the whole of art history.

Room XV – Jacob van Ruisdael (about 1628-1682), *The Great Forest* (1655/60). Ludolf Bakuyzen (1631-1708), *Amsterdam Port* (1674). Rembrandt van Rijn, *Portrait of the Artist's Mother as a Prophetess* (1639), *Portrait of Titus, the Artist's Son* (1656/57), and a very interesting series, including: **Small Self Portrait**★ (about 1657) and **Large Self Portrait**★★ (1652). The latter dates from a period of financial difficulties and does not depict the artist in the splendid attire of his youth. He wears a simple jacket, and all the light illuminates his face, as if to stress the ravages of time.

Rembrandt (1606-1669) – Few painters have achieved such universal appeal as Rembrandt, the son of a Dutch miller. This highly successful artist is intriguing, nevertheless, because of the disparity between his life and his art. He painted his most serene pictures soon after his wife's death, and his happiest painting is his last self portrait, now in Cologne. He gives rise to many questions, to which, hopefully, there may never be any answers.

Cross the hall diagonally for room I.

Room I – The museum possesses numerous paintings by the Venetian School. This room is devoted to Titian and contains many of his masterpieces, including *The Virgin of the Gypsies (1510)*, *The Virgin with Cherries* (1516/18), *Bravo* (about 1520), **Woman with Fur**★ (about 1535) and **Ecce Homo**★ (1543), a painting with the signature and date on the palace steps.

Titian (about 1490-1576) – As the embodiment of the High Renaissance, this painter enjoys universal renown. His work displays vivacity, energy, psychological insight as a portrait painter and grandeur. He was exceptionally long-lived for the time. His earlier naturalistic vision developed into a Mannerist technique which gave free rein to an expressionism bordering on the dramatic. At sixty, he was still innovative, executing commissions from princes and producing work imbued with a new spirituality.

Cabinet 1 – Andrea Mantegna, **Saint Sebastian**★★ (1457/59). Cosmè Tura (about 1430-1495), *Christ's Body held by Angels* (1460/70).

Andrea Mantegna (1431-1506) – His work is of particular significance in the history of art. It combines Tuscan perspective, Venetian dramatic flair and Roman echoes of classical mythology. Anyone wishing to understand Italian Renaissance painting should study the work of this painter from Padua.

Cabinet 2 – Palma Vecchio, *Virgin with Child surrounded by Saints* (1520/25). Giorgione, *Young Woman* (1506) and **The Three Philosophers**★★ (1508/09), a major contribution to the history of Venetian painting. According to Vasari, his "new manner" was to paint "without a preliminary sketch on paper", a technical change of the utmost importance. Lorenzo Lotto, **Portrait of A Young man against a White Curtain**★ (about 1508), *Gentleman with Lion's Paw* (1524/25) and *Triple Portrait of a Goldsmith* (1525/35).

Giorgione (about 1477-1510) – Details of his life are brief, but his fame is great, owing mainly to the celebrated *Tempest* in the Academy Gallery in Venice. It is known that this "quite excellent" artist, according to Baldassare Castiglione, frequented humanist circles in Venice, particularly musicians and poets.

Lorenzo Lotto (about 1480-1556) – Another Venetian painter, he is less famous among the general public. He was an independent spirit of daring temperament, a tormented artist of great distinction. His greatest ambition was to develop a highly eclectic style, without drifting into Mannerism. This was his achievement.

Room II – Veronese, *The Anointment of David* (about 1555), *The Raising of the Youth of Nain* (1565-70) and *The Adoration of the Magi* (about 1580).

Room III – Tintoretto, *Loranzo Soranzo* (1553), *Sebastiano Venier* (1571/72), **St Jerome**★ (1571-1575) and **Suzannah and the Elders**★★ (1555/56). This typically Mannerist painting displays various influences and represents the peak of Venetian art. The composition is full of contrasts (light-dark, youth-age, proximity-distance) and depicts a scene from the Old Testament.

Tintoretto (1518-1594) – Jacopo Robusti was the son of a dyer, and he was small, hence his nickname. He was of affable temperament and transmitted this name to his descendants. It is said that his studio displayed a sign saying: "Michelangelo's drawing, Titian's colours".

Cabinet 3 – Corregio, *Ganymede* (1530) and *Jupiter and Io* (1530). Moretto (about 1498-1554), *Portrait of a Young Woman* (about 1540). Parmigiano, **Self Portrait in a Convex Mirror**★ (1523/24) and *Portrait of a Man* (1525/30).

Parmigiano (1503-1540) – Francesco Mazzola was born in Parma and came under the influence of Corregio. He was very precocious, producing mature works at the age of 16. The self-portrait in Vienna is the first of a series tracing the psychological development of this artist who died young and in exile.

Cabinet 4 – Perugino (about 1450-1523), *The Baptism of Christ* (about 1500). Fra Bartolomeo della Porta, *Presentation in the Temple* (1516). Andrea del Sarto (1486-1530), *Lamentation* (1519/20). Raphael, **Virgin in the Meadow**★★ (1505), a painting typical of the Florentine High Renaissance, in its balance and harmony. It is also known as *Madonna of the Belvedere*.

Raphael (1483-1520) – For a long time, Raffaello Sanzio enjoyed a reputation as the greatest painter of all time. He is certainly the spiritual master of those who prized form above colour. Although his appeal waned after the birth of Impressionism, his powerful and lasting influence must be the envy of any creative artist. His paintings of the Virgin assured his immortal popularity.

Cabinet 5 – Giovanni Battista Moroni (about 1520-1578), *The Sculptor Alessandro Vittoria* (1552).

Cabinet 6 – Bronzino (1503-1572), *The Holy Family with St Anne and the Young John the Baptist* (1545/46).

Cabinet 9 – Alonso Sanchez Coello (about 1531-1588), *The Infante Don Carlos* (1564). François Clouet (about 1510-1572), *Charles IX of France* (1569).

Cabinet 10 – The department of Spanish painting is famous for its portraits of infantes and infantas by Velázquez: **The Infanta Margarita Teresa in a Pink Dress**★ (1653/54), **The Infanta Margarita Teresa in a Blue Dress**★ (1659) and *The Infante Philip Prosper* (1659). Bartolomé Esteban Murillo (about 1617-1682), *The Archangel St Michael*. Juan Bautista del Mazo (about 1612-1667), *Portrait of the Artist's Family* (1664/65).

Diego Rodrígues de Silva y Velázquez (1599-1660) – The creator (Velazquez in English) of Las Meninas became in 1633 Chief Marshal of the palace in Madrid. He painted portraits of the royal family, before travelling to Italy on the king's behalf. About 1650, his encounter with the Venetian Cinquecento transformed his painting.

Cabinet 11 – Annibale Carracci, **The Lamentation**★ (1603-1604) and *Christ and the Samaritan Woman* (about 1605). Salvator Rosa, *The Return of Astraea* (1640/45).

Annibale Carracci (1560-1609) – Brother of Agostino and cousin of Ludovico, Annibale belonged to a leading family of painters. In 1595, Cardinal Farnese summoned the Bolognese artist to Rome. His pictorial knowledge benefited from this. Unfortunately, after 1605, mental illness prevented him from working.

Room V – Orazio Gentileschi (1563-1639), *Rest during the Flight into Egypt* (1626/28). Maria Preti (1613-1699), *The Incredulity of St Thomas* (1660/65). Caravaggio, **David Holding the Head of Goliath**★ (1606/07) and **The Virgin with a Rosary**★★ (1606/07). Here, dramatic flair reaches perfection: the realism and intensity of the scene almost induce the viewer to take part in the distribution of rosaries by St Dominic on the left.

Caravaggio (1571-1610) – Michelangelo Melisi had a difficult personality. Brawls and periods in prison punctuated his life in Milan, then he fled to Genoa. In 1606, he killed his opponent in a game of real tennis. He had to flee to Rome, then Naples, from where he left for Sicily. Feverish and exhausted, he died on a beach in Porto Ercole. He ranks among the greatest Italian painters. Many consider him the greatest Baroque painter.

Room VI – Guercino, **The Return of the Prodigal Son**★ (about 1619). Guido Reni (1575-1642), *The Baptism of Christ* (1622/23). Giovanni Lanfranco (1582-1647), *The Virgin Appearing to St James and St Anthony* (about 1624). Francesco Solimena (1657-1747), *Descent from the Cross* (1730/31). Luca Giordano, **The Fall of the Rebel Angels**★ (about 1655). Guido Cagnacci (1601-1663), *Cleopatra's Suicide* (1659/63).

Guercino (1591-1666) – His real name was Giovanni Francesco Barbieri. His career as a painter dates from his meeting with Ludovic Carracci. The latter encouraged him to develop his original naturalistic style and produce grand, luminous paintings.

Luca Giordano (1634-1705) – At the age of twenty, this Neapolitan artist rushed to Rome to display his virtuosity. He was in such a hurry to reach his goal that people nicknamed him *Luca fa presto*. He travelled throughout Italy then left for Spain in answer to Carlos II's summons. He was a prolific artist of great significance to anyone wishing to understand early 18C painting.

Cabinet 12 – Domenico Fetti (about 1588-1623), *The Return of the Prodigal Son* (1620/23). L'Empoli (about 1551-1640), *Susannah Bathing* (1600). Bernardo Strozzi (1581-1644), *The Lute Player* (1640/44) and *The Prophet Elias and the Widow of Zarephat* (about 1640).

Cabinet 13 – Francesco Guardi (1712-1793), *The Miracle of St Dominic* (1763).

Room VII – Hyacinthe Rigaud (1659-1743), *Philipp Wenzel, Count Sinzendorf* (1728). Josèphe Sifrède Duplessis (1725-1802), *Christoph Willibald von Gluck* (1775). Canaletto, ***View of Vienna from the Belvedere★*** (1758/61), *Freyung from the Southwest* (1758-61) *(for illustration, see Freyung District)*.

Bernardo Bellotto (1721-1780) – Bellotto was the nephew of the great Canaletto and is known under the same name as his uncle in Germany and Austria. He was among the greatest exponents of the *vedute* school of painting. He worked in Dresden, Vienna, Munich and Warsaw.

Cabinet of Coins and Medals

At present this department is closed to the public. It has a collection of 500,000 items, which makes it one of the world's largest numismatic collections. Emperor Maximilian I founded it and the museum has an inventory dating from 1547 in Ferdinand I's reign. The collection of coins and medals continued to increase in size under successive emperors. Karl VI was interested in it and encouraged contemporary artists to engrave coins. Franz I acquired rare coins and medals.

Kunsthistorisches Museum

A florin bearing the effigy of Maximilian I

The nearest sights are the Ring, Hofburg and Staatsoper, as well as the Mariahilf, Neubau and Wieden Districts (Karlsplatz area).

RATHAUS

Local map page 5, **HR**
Underground: Rathaus (U2)
Tram: Rathausplatz/Burgtheater (1,2,D), Rathaus (J)
Bus: Teinfaltstrasse (1A)

Neues Rathaus ⊘ – *Rathausplatz 1*. Facing Burgtheater, the "New City Hall" was constructed from 1872 to 1883 by Friedrich von Schmidt to replace the old one *(see Altes Rathaus)*, still visible in Wipplingerstrasse. The architect decided upon a neo-Gothic style evocative of the Middle Ages when most of the large cities acquired their borough charters. Brussels City Hall (1402-1455) on the magnificent Grand-Place was his inspiration.

The building is the seat of the administrative and legislative authorities of the Land (the Regional Assembly) and the City of Vienna; these functions have been amalgamated under the same administration since 1922 when Vienna acquired the twin status of federal and regional capital. As soon as one starts walking along one of the streets bordering it (Felderstrasse or Lichtenfelsgasse), one becomes aware of the colossal bureaucracy behind the majestic and impressive walls of this monumental building. The figures speak for themselves: an area of 14,000m²/16,744sq yds, 7 interior courtyards, a central tower 98m/321ft high, two lateral towers "only" 61m/200ft high. At nightfall, this tower lights up; it is surmounted by the *Ratshausmann* (the man from the town hall), a copper figure of a knight by Alexander Nehr, carrying the town banner (it weighs 1,800kg/4,000lb and measures 3.4m/11ft).

The tour starts with the Stadtbureau *(entrance through Friedrich-Schmidt-Platz)* in the former foyer and continues through the reception rooms (listed historic monuments), which include the great Festsaal (assembly hall), 71m/77yds long and 17m/55ft high, where the book fair takes place in November. The Gemeinderatssitzungssaal (debating chamber) is lavishly decorated with rare woods and a large chandelier designed by the architect. The roter Salon (red room) with its Venetian chandeliers is the mayor's reception room.

In July, the Arkadenhof (central courtyard) of the town hall is the setting for the "Jazzfest" *(see Practical information)*.

Rathauspark – Rudolf Sieböck, director of the city's gardens, laid out the attractive City Hall park in 1872-1873. It features statues of people who left their mark on the history of the city. The following **eight sculptures★** stand on either side of the avenue dividing the park in two. Starting at the south end of the park, on the Ringstrasse side, there are: *Henry II Jasomirgott* (by Franz Melnitzky) who chose Vienna as his ducal capital, *Rudolf IV the Founder* (by Josef Gasser) who founded Vienna University, *Ernst Rüdiger Count of Starhemberg* (by Johann Fessler) who bravely resisted the Turks in 1683, *Johann Bernhard Fischer von Erlach* (by Josef Cesar), the most brilliant court architect, *Leopold VI the Glorious* (by Johann Preleuthner) who granted Vienna its first authenticated city charter in 1221, *Niklas Count Salm* (by Matthias Purkartshofer) who resisted Suleyman the Magnificent in 1529, *Leopold Count Kollonitsch* (by Vinzenz Pilz), the bishop of Wiener Neustadt who gave moral support to the inhabitants in 1683, and *Josef von Sonnenfels* (by Hanns Gasser), Maria Theresa's counsellor who abolished torture.

The park also contains several monuments: To the south, the *Johann Strauss und Josef Lanner Denkmal* (by Franz Seifert and Robert Oerley, 1905) which reconciles the famous rivals of the Viennese waltz – in this case, Johann Strauss the Elder –, the *Ratshausmann*, a recent copy (1986) of the one above the immense belfry of the City Hall and the *Karl Renner Denkmal* (by Alfred Hrdlicka and Josef Krawina, 1967), in memory of the father of the Second Austrian Republic of which he was president from 1945 to 1950. To the north, there is the *Ferdinand Georg Waldmüller Denkmal* (by Josef Engelhart, 1913), a memorial to a Biedermeier painter who frequently depicted the countryside around Vienna, and the *Karl Seitz Denkmal* (by Gottfried Buchberger, 1962), a popular Social-Democrat mayor of Vienna from 1923 to 1934.

In July, a giant cinema screen is set up in front of the Town Hall. Open-air concerts also take place here. During Advent, a large Christmas market occupies the central avenue in the park and the trees are adorned by red fairy lights, creating a magical and seasonal ambiance.

Besides the Ring which it faces, the Rathaus is near several sights: Hofburg, the Freyung District in the town centre, and the Alsergrund, Josefstadt and Neubau Districts.

B. Kaufmann

The spire of the Rathaus (Town Hall) from Heldenplatz

The RING★★

Ringstrasse forms a ring, the symbol that took Vienna into the modern world in the mid 19C and a reminder of the wedding ring which its last great emperor gave to his bride, Sissi, whom he welcomed on 22 April 1854 at Nussdorf landing stage, north of the city.

Some three and a half years later, on 20 December 1857, Franz-Josef signed a letter ordering the demolition of the ramparts around the town centre *(Innere Stadt)* to make way for a circular throroughfare lined with public buildings and rented accommodation.

The Ring represented a new Vienna with a neo-Absolutist regime gradually giving way to constitutional monarchy. It was a city in the process of throwing off the shackles of its old fortifications and opening up to growing industry and a "second society" of newly rich industrialists. It had economic hegemony and a programme of urbanisation comparable in Europe only to Haussmann's Paris. Finally, it was a secular middle class Vienna, without clergy or aristocracy.

Ringstrasse is 4km/2 miles long and nearly 60m/196ft wide lined with ailanthuses, linden and plane trees. The buildings vary in style but are all of historic interest. This "historicism" was a source of pride to the ruling Liberal party and exemplified the eclecticism of the small group of architects responsible for the Ring. It was this grandiose historicism which, later, became anathema to the Secession movement. The architects erected a prestigious and fantastic façade of neo-Gothic towers, neo-Classical pediments, neo-Renaissance attics and neo-Baroque ornamentation to the strains of a Strauss waltz. However, social contrasts in the city were as acute as in modern New York, then in its infancy. Slums abounded. This accounts for the large housing estates built after the proclamation of the Austrian Republic. These, together with the Ring, contributed to the reputation of Vienna as a monumental city, an image which it cannot and will not forsake.

The Ring is the last heritage of a dynasty about to die out after having ruled over 52 million people. It was a "total art" project *(Gesamtkunstwerk)* which took over three decades to develop. Since then, it has remained unchanged. Exploring it is a form of time travel.

Do not explore the Ring by car, because of the heavy traffic and the one-way system. The best method is on foot or cycling. Going by tram is an alternative (circular line Nos 1 or 2) in inclement weather. An evening stroll along the floodlit Ring is undoubtedly one of the most outstanding memories anybody can carry away from Vienna.

Italian raid on Vienna

At dawn on 9 August 1918, the *Serenissima* squadron took off from Venice. At its head was a 2-seater Caproni carrying the pilot, Captain Palli, and Gabriele d'Annunzio. The squadron flew over the Julian and Noric Alps and reached Wiener Neustadt safely. By 9.30 a.m., the *Serenissima* was flying over Vienna in a clear sky with perfect visibility. The squadron started to descend on the city and came so close that the Ring was visible with its throng of people. The capital was defenceless; it was time to attack.

Instead of bombs, a shower of leaflets fell out of the aeroplanes, bearing the colours of the Italian flag. The main one bore the title *Donec at metam*: "To the very end". The message from the poet of Lake Garda favoured Entente, evoking the sword of Damocles which threatened the imperial capital. D'Annunzio could now return home. At 12.40, he landed in Venice to loud acclaim from cheering supporters of his raid in the cause of peace.

People rarely listen to poets; moreover, D'Annunzio belonged to the armed forces. On 24 October, the Italian victory of Vittorio Veneto sent the Hapsburg dynasty toppling to the ground. On 11 November, Karl I abdicated.

THE GIANTS OF RINGSTRASSE

Schottenring (HJP)

This section takes its name from the 1276 Schottentor or "Gate of the Scots" *(for the origin of the name, see Schottenstift)*. Anton Bruckner lived at No 5 from 1877 to 1895. No 14 was the birthplace of Stefan Zweig, on 28 November 1881. No 23 (façade with nail-head ornamentation) is one of Otto Wagner's first achievements (1877).

Ringturm – *Schottenring 30*. Built between 1953 and 1955, Erich Boltenstern's Ring Tower lacks elegance. For many Viennese it evokes the difficult post-war period when Vienna had to rise from a mass of ruins. At the time, its modernistic style showed the inhabitants that the city was recovering its pride.

Fotostudio Otto/Museen der Stadt Wien

Building Ringstrasse

Deutschmeisterdenkmal – *Schlickplatz*. This building commemorates the Hoch- and Deutschmeister, formerly the regiment of the city of Vienna. Behind it is Rossauerkaserne, a curious building (1869) which an Imperial army colonel (Pilhal) and major (Markl) built in the Windsor style.

Börse – *Schottenring 16*. Theophil von Hansen was one of the Ring's most prolific architects (Parliament, Academy of Fine Arts). With the assistance of Carl Tietz, he built the Stock Exchange in a neo-Renaissance style from 1874 to 1877. Thus, this edifice was not the site of the famous "Black Thursday" stock market crash which marked the end of Viennese Liberalism in 1873. The main hall underwent restoration after a fire in 1956.

Votivkirche ⊙ – *Rooseveltplatz* – Although part of the Ring, the votive church is set back from the line of buildings. Its name commemorates Franz-Josef's escape from an assassination attempt. On 18 February 1853, a Hungarian named Libényi stabbed the emperor in the back of the neck. A metal collar stud saved his life. The idea of building this church came from Archduke Maximilian, Franz-Josef's brother. Architect Heinrich von Ferstel (University, Museum of Applied Arts) erected it between 1856 and 1879 on the slopes of the Schotten stronghold, which in a way connects it to Schottenring.

With the Prater Ferris wheel and the cathedral spires, the two traceried spires (99m/324ft) of this neo-Gothic church are among the architectural landmarks on the Viennese horizon. The Viennese architect sought inspiration for his design in the 14C German Gothic style, particularly Cologne cathedral. Inside, in the Taufkapelle is the tomb and **recumbent figure★** of Count Salm, who resisted the siege of Vienna by Suleyman the Magnificent in 1529. It dates from 1530 and is from the studio of Loy Hering. In the south arm of the transept, the "Antwerp" altarpiece is a fine late Gothic woodcarving by the Flemish school dating from 1520. The stained-glass windows illustrate the history of the Austrian Catholic church; they date mainly from 1966.

Dr.-Karl-Lueger-Ring (HPR)

Universität – *Dr.-Karl-Lueger-Ring 1*. Next to the neo-Gothic Votivkirche, Heinrich von Ferstel designed a building in a style reminiscent of the Italian Renaissance, the period seen as the Golden Age of Knowledge. Founded by Rudolf IV on 12 March 1365, this is one of the oldest German-speaking universities, second only to Prague. Formerly, it stood on Dr.-Ignaz-Seipel-Platz *(see Alte Universität)*. The building (1884) comprises 8 inner courtyards surrounding a central courtyard, "Arkadenhof" (3,300m²/3,946sq yds). In the centre is Kastaliabrunnen, a fountain by Edmund Hellmer (1904). Originally, the University entrance displayed frescoes by Gustav Klimt. People disliked his work because of the nude figures on some panels (the frescoes disappeared during the Second World War).

Beneath the arcades of the central courtyard are busts of famous University professors, including: Anton Bruckner, Theodor von Billroth, Sigmund Freud, Karl Landsteiner (1930 Nobel prize for medicine) and Gerhard van Swieten.

City Centre and the Ring

Opposite, behind the memorial to the mayor Andreas von Liebenberg (1890) is **Beethovenhaus** *(see under this heading)*.

Rathaus – *See under this heading.*

Café Landtmann – *Dr.-Karl-Lueger-Ring 4.* Franz Landtmann built this famous Viennese café in 1873. The clientele consists of prosperous middle class people, politicians and actors from the Burgtheater. Sigmund Freud enjoyed smoking his cigar in this comfortable ambiance.

★Burgtheater ☺ – *Dr.-Karl-Lueger-Ring 2. Guided tour only (in German).* The Burgtheater opposite the City Hall opened in 1888, replacing the Court theatre on Michaelerplatz, which Maria Theresa had founded in 1741. In 1776, Josef II made it a national theatre, and for many decades it remained the leading German-speaking theatre. Since then, to play in the Burgtheater has remained the crowning achievement of any actor's career. Numerous actors played there, including: Ewald Balser, Hedwig Bleibtreu, Klaus Maria Brandauer, Annemarie Düringer, Käthe Gold, Elfriede Jelinek, Werner Kraus, Adolf Rott, Hugo Thimig, etc.

Gottfried Semper (in charge of the exterior) and Karl Hasenauer (in charge of the interior) designed it in 1874 and completed it in 1879. The building is in a late neo-Renaissance style with neo-Baroque elements. It is of respectable size: 136m /446ft long, 95m/311ft deep and 27m/88ft high. On the convex façade of the central section, there is a statue of Apollo flanked by the muses Melpomene and Thalia (by Karl Kundmann), over a frieze depicting Bacchus and Ariadne (by Rudolf Weyr). The first floor windows display 9 busts by Viktor Tilgner: in the centre, Goethe, Schiller, Lessing (Germany); on the right, Halm, Grillparzer, Hebbel (Austria); on the left, Calderon, Shakespeare, Molière (other European countries). The two wings contain monumental staircases. One was for the Court, the other for the public.

The tour *(30min)* of the interior *(entrance on the left, opposite Café Landtmann)* is less interesting than the Staatsoper tour. Nevertheless, it affords an opportunity of appreciating the early works of Gustav Klimt. With his brother Ernst and Franz

Maria-Theresien-Platz and Kunsthistorisches Museum

Matsch, he produced the ceiling **frescoes★** above the staircases *(lit by night, therefore partially visible from outside)*. He himself painted two scenes: *Romeo and Juliet (right staircase)*, and *Theatre at Taormina (left staircase)* which portrays Salome. The semicircular foyer is 60m/196ft long and provides a fine **view** of the City Hall *(particularly at night)*. On its walls hang portraits of famous actors and actresses. The auditorium was rebuilt to designs by Michael Engelhart following Second World War air raids and can now accommodate about 1,500 people.

There is an amazing story about the fire which gutted the auditorium in 1945. In 1888, soon after the opening of the theatre, G. Semper met with numerous criticisms, directed mainly at the deplorable acoustics. He retorted that "every theatre requires reconstruction after 60 years, unless it burns down before then." He was wrong by only three years!

Dr.-Karl-Renner-Ring (HR)

Parliament ⊘ – *Dr.-Karl-Renner-Ring 3*. Theophil von Hansen designed this rather pompous edifice with its large dimensions and its strict academic resemblance to a Greek temple. Although the architect spent some time in Athens, this does not really explain why he chose this style as a setting for meetings attended by delegates from the various countries in the Austro-Hungarian empire. However, Hansen wished to allude to ancient Greece, the country which invented democracy.

Two long wings ending with small neo-Classical pavilions stand on either side of the projecting part of the building. This consists of a *pronaos* behind 8 Corinthian columns bearing a triangular pediment. Its richly decorated tympanum displays Franz-Josef granting the Constitution to the 17 peoples of his empire (by Edmund Hellmer). The double flight of steps leading to the building features statues of historians from classical antiquity. On the left, Greeks: *Herodotus* (by Karl Schwerzek), *Polybius* (by Alois Düll), *Thucydides* (by Richard Kauffungen) and *Xenophon* (by Hugo Haerdtl). On the right, Romans: *Sallust* (by Wilhelm Seib),

Caesar (by Josef Beyer), Tacitus (by Karl Sterrer) and Livy (by Josef Lax). In front of Parliament, almost on the Ring, is Karl Kundmann's **Pallas-Athene-Brunnen**★, dating from 1902. This work represents the Greek Pallas Athena or Roman Minerva, goddess of wisdom and intelligence. With gilded helmet, bearing a shield, the daughter of Jupiter stands above 4 figures symbolising the rivers Danube, Inn, Elbe and Moldau.

The legislative Assembly – "Austria is a democratic republic. Its laws emanate from the people". This is article 1 of the 1920 federal constitution. On 27 April 1945, the Declaration of Independence stipulated: "Article 1: the Austrian democratic Republic is restored and must function in the spirit of the 1920 constitution. Article 2: The Anschluss imposed on the Austrian people in 1938 is null and void." The 1920 federal Constitution was mainly the work of Hans Kelsen who also coined this definition of democracy "the most precise approximation of the idea of liberty in a real social context."

The Austrian Parliament has two chambers: the Nationalrat and the Bundesrat (national Council and federal Council). Together, they constitute the Republic's legislative body. The **Nationalrat** passes federal laws and has the power to dismiss the federal government or one of its members; at present, it has 183 deputies elected for 4 years by direct universal suffrage and secret ballot (proportional representation). Like the Diets of the Länder and the governments of the 9 federal Länder, the **Bundesrat** represents the federal state. This means that each bill of federal law from the first chamber must be passed by the second chamber; 64 deputies are delegated to represent the Diets of the Länder. The two chambers come together to form the federal Assembly, occasionally meeting in joint session. The president of the Bundesrat is elected for 6 years. In theory, he has the right to veto a law and dissolve Parliament.

★**Volksgarten** – Louis de Rémy designed the city's first public garden from 1819 to 1823 on the site of the fortifications which Napoleon blew up in 1809 before leaving the city. The "People's Garden", which counterbalances Burggarten (see under this heading), was so-called because it was open to the public. It offers fine views of the neighbourhood and has benches where it is pleasant to sit between museum visits.

The gardens enclose two monuments: one commemorates Empress Elizabeth (by Friedrich Ohmann), the other is a memorial to the poet Franz Grillparzer (by Karl Kundmann).

Theseustempel – In the middle of the rose gardens stands an 1823 replica of the Athens Theseion by Pietro Nobile. He built it to protect Theseus Killing the Minotaur by Antonio Canova (see the stairwell of the Kunsthistorisches Museum). This small Doric edifice requires restoration.

Burgring (HR)

On the right is the vast Maria-Theresien-Platz with its two gigantic symmetrical and identical buildings housing the Natural History Museum (Naturhistorisches Museum, architect, Gottfried Semper) and the Art History Museum (Kunsthistorisches Museum, architect, Karl Hasenauer). These architects, who designed the Burgtheater (see above), built this complex between 1872 and 1891.

★**Naturhistorisches Museum** ⊙ – Burgring 7. Entrance Maria-Theresien-Platz. The collections in the Natural History Museum date from the reign of Franz I and thus predate the opening of the museum in 1889, during Franz-Josef's reign. The museum galleries display the exhibits systematically, showing them off to advantage in this purpose-built building.

Mezzanine – The **Mineralogical department**★★ (Rooms 1 to 5) has some remarkable specimens, including a 1m/3ft long quartz crystal from Madagascar, a large salt obelisk from the Rónaszék mines weighing about 1,680kg – 3,5lbs, a 1-ton block of salt from the Wielicka mines, a topaz weighing 117kg – 258lb from Brazil, the famous **bouquet of precious stones**★ (1760) which Maria Theresa gave to her husband François-Étienne of Lorraine, and some meteorites and aerolites like the 909kg – 2,003lb stone that fell in Australia in 1884.

The Geological (Room 6) and Paleontological (Rooms 7 to 9) sections are under restoration at present. Room 10 contains casts and the largest known skeleton of a tortoise. The foyer houses some skeletons from the Ice Age, including a rhinoceros, an ibex, mammoth's tusks and a glyptodont from Argentina. The **iguanodon** is a cast from the Brussels Natural Science Museum, the impressive skeleton of a specimen discovered in Bernissart in Belgium.

The Prehistorical section (Rooms 11 to 15) displays exhibits found in Austria. There is a copy of the famous chalk figure of the **Willendorf Venus**★ about 25,000 years old, funeral objects from the **Hallstatt graves** (Hallstatt period 1,000-500 BC) and objects from the La Tène period (500 BC to the Roman conquest).

The Anthropological section (Rooms 16 and 17) traces the evolution of man through numerous skulls (Australopithecus Gracilis, Homo Erectus, Homo Nean-derthalensis, Homo Sapiens etc.); their classification may puzzle some visitors. The children's section (Room 18) displays farm animals.

1st floor – The Zoology department consists of large sections. The museum has a superb collection of naturalised birds, including zigzag herons (born in Brazil 150 years ago), and also extinct species such as the moa and the dronte.

Maria-Theresien-Denkmal – *Maria-Theresien-Platz.* The sculptor Kaspar Zumbusch made this monument in 1888; it is nearly 20m/65ft high. It represents Empress Maria Theresa holding the Pragmatic Sanction in her left hand. The 4 allegories at the upper corners of the plinth symbolise Power, Wisdom, Justice and Mercy.

★★★ **Kunsthistorisches Museum** – *See under this heading.*

Äusseres Burgtor – *See Heldenplatz.*

★★★ **Hofburg** – *See under this heading.*

Opernring (JS)

Burggarten – Like Volksgarten *(see above)*, the Palace garden stands on the site of the fortifications which Napoleon destroyed in 1809 before leaving the city. Franz I had it laid out between 1816 and 1819. Courtiers at the imperial palace soon called it the "promenade". It has been open to the public since 1919 (apart from the lawns). There are several statues in this little park: the **Mozart Memorial**★ (1896 by Viktor Tilgner) with reliefs showing a scene from *Don Giovanni* and *Mozart with his Family*; the equestrian statue of Franz I (1781, by Balthasar Ferdinand Moll); the Franz-Josef monument (1903, by Josef Tuch); and a bronze originally from Wiener Neustadt, installed here in 1957.

Glashaus – *Under restoration.* This imperial glasshouse consists of glass and steel set in a stone structure with graceful Jugendstil motifs. Friedrich Ohmann built it between 1901 and 1905.
At the south corner of Burggarten is the Goethe memorial (1900, by Edmund Hellmer).

Schillerdenkmal – Robert-Stolz-Platz opens into Schillerplatz, a former market which in 1876 received the name of the great German dramatist. His statue by the Dresden sculptor Johann Schilling shows him standing next to Goethe, with allegorical figures representing the four ages of man around them.
Theophil von Hansen built the neo-Renaissance edifice housing the Academy of Fine Arts in 1876. Adolf Hitler sat, and failed, the entrance examination for this institution in 1907. It provides training for painters, sculptors, decorators, architects, restorers and curators. Friedensreich Hundertwasser and Fritz Wotruba taught there.

★★ **Gemäldegalerie der Akademie der Bildenden Künste** ☉ – *Schillerplatz 3.* The Art Gallery of the Academy of Fine Arts displays paintings with a certain lack of discrimination in a succession of unattractive rooms. However, visitors cannot fail to respond to the artistic and historic merit of many of the exhibits. This selection concentrates on a few magnificent paintings, which are also of major importance. Far from being an inventory, this is a list of works selected on the basis of personal preference.
The first room contains many treasures, including works by the masters of the German Renaissance such as Lucas Cranach the Elder. It is easy to see why this painter is so famous, when one looks at one of his early paintings, such as *St Francis receiving the Stigmata*, or the admirable and enigmatic **Lucretia**★★ (1532), Tarquin's legendary wife who stabbed herself rather than live with the shame of rape. There are examples of various schools (German, Danubian, Flemish, Dutch, Swiss): Dirk Bouts, *The Coronation of the Virgin Mary* (between 1450 and 1460), Hans Baldung Grien, *The Holy Family* (about 1512), Joos van Cleve, *The Holy Family* (about 1515), Ambrosius Holbein, *Death of the Virgin* (about 1518), Hans Maler, *Portrait of Moritz Weltzer von Eberstein* (1524).
Hieronymus Bosch's great *Triptych of the Last Judgment*★★★ (1504-1508) is a masterpiece in the full sense of the word. In fact, it is close to perfection. The Last Judgment is the only theme in Christian art to be depicted on successive levels. This is why the triptych is the most suitable representational form for it. This one illustrates *The Last Judgment* and *The Seven Deadly Sins (central panel)*; *The Fall of the Angels, The Creation of Eve, The Temptation, The Expulsion from Paradise (left wing)*; *Hell and its Laws (right wing)*. There are *grisaille* representations of St Bavo and St James on the underside of the wings.

Heaven and Hell, land of the dead – *Peter's Apocalypse* (2C) is the first Christian work to describe the tortures of Hell. In Christian art, Paradise is a cool welcoming place for the blessed and elect who resisted temptation by the Devil. They stand naked, because they are clothed in light and will no longer know

Akademie der Bildenden Kuenste/AKG PARIS

The *Last Judgement* triptych by Hieronymus Bosch (close-up)

disease, old age or death. Hell, on the other hand, is a dark furnace with flames failing to burn the damned who will never escape their torments. It is the destination of the proud, envious, gluttonous, lascivious, irascible, lazy and avaricious.

Hieronymus Bosch (about 1450-1516) – His paintings represent hybrid creatures, which seem to spring from the capitals of the most ancient churches. In its iconography, Bosch's work belongs to the Middle Ages. However, he was a contemporary of Leonardo da Vinci. The work of Bosch, a painter who denounced human folly, should be seen against the background of the philosophy of his day. Bosch is closer to Thomas More than to the Christian establishment in the throes of religious crises and racked by scandals in the early 16C.

After viewing painting from northern Europe, one comes to Italian painting, with a *Virgin with Child and Angels* (about 1480) from Sandro Botticelli's studio, and *Tarquin and Lucretia* (about 1575), one of Titian's last pictures. Then, there is Spanish painting with **Boys Playing Dice**★ by Bartolomé Esteban Murillo. Illustrious examples of Baroque painting from the southern Netherlands are in evidence: Anthony van Dyck, *Self Portrait*★ (about 1614), Jakob Jordaens, *Portrait of the Artist's Daughter* (about 1640), and Peter Paul Rubens' 6 oil studies for the frescoes (destroyed by fire in 1618) in the Jesuit church in Antwerp.

Besides producing much manner and genre painting, the Dutch school of the 17C was also responsible for some fine landscapes and portraits. This collection features: **Portrait of a Young Woman**★★ (1632) which Rembrandt painted at the age of 26, *A Social Gathering* (1635) by Pieter Codde, **Portrait of a Delft Family**★ (about 1660) by Pieter de Hooghe, and *Small Still Life* (1671) by Willem van Aelst. The Dutch school also included painters in the Italian manner who unlike their contemporaries painted in the open air. Among them were Jan Both, *Utrecht about 1615*, and Thomas Wijck, *Harbour Scene* (1650).

The group of 18C paintings has an irresistible appeal. Yet the **Eight Views of Venice**★ (between 1742 and 1780) by the famous Francesco Guardi should not divert attention from the two paintings by Pierre Subleyras: *Portrait of Virginia Parker Hunt* (after 1746) and *The Artist's Studio* (about 1747) which bears on the back a self portrait, discovered after restoration in 1968. Some works with an Austrian theme or artist are at the end of this series of rooms, notably the *Portrait of Maria Theresa* (1759), a *Self Portrait* (after 1731) by Martin van Meytens and *Odysseus and Circe* (1785) by Hubert Maurer.

Finally, it would be regrettable to leave the gallery without seeing the *Bouquet of Flowers* (about 1720) by Jan van Huysum, the *Cupboard Panel: Trompe l'oeil* (1655) by Samuel van Hoogstraten, the *Mourning Mother* by Rogier van der Weyden, **Still Life with Flowers and Fruit**★ (1703) by Rachel Ruysch, a Dutch female painter who was a pupil of Willem van Aelst, and the **Mourning Mother**★ by Dirk Bouts, whose paintings have a luminous and often ascetic quality.

★★**Staatsoper** – *See under this heading.*

Kärntnerring (JKS)

Imperial Hotel – *Kärntnerring 16.* This is probably the most prestigious hotel in the capital. Since 1873, it has occupied the palace of the Duke of Wurtemberg who had the edifice built in 1865 (raised in 1928). Richard Wagner and his family stayed here when he conducted *Tannhäuser* and *Lohengrin* in 1875 and 1876; President Mitterrand also stayed here on his visits to Vienna.

Café Schwarzenberg – *Kärntnerring 17.* This is one of the city's most pleasant cafés in the great tradition of Viennese coffee houses, with its Edwardian ambiance.

Parkring (KRS)

Stadtpark – This vast public garden (114,000m²/135,660sq yds) opened in 1862. Rudolf Sieböck, architect of the imperial gardens, laid it out and Josef Selleny designed it. There are two bridges over the Wien which flows through the middle. At night, illuminated fountains light up the central lake.

It contains several statues of the city's famous painters and musicians, such as Friedrich von Amerling (1902, by Johannes Benk), Hans Makart (1898, by Viktor Tilgner), Anton Bruckner (1899, by V. Tilgner), Franz Lehár (1980, by Franz Coufal), Franz Schubert (1872, by Karl Kundmann) and Robert Stolz (1980, by Rudolf Friedl). However, it is the famous **monument to Johann Strauss the Younger**★ which most often appears in tourist brochures on the attractions of the Habsburg capital. It was the work of Edmund Hellmer (1921). It consists of a marble arch adorned by nymphs framing the gilded bronze figure of the celebrated violinist. In the late 19C, the *Kursalon* was one of the cafés famous for music-hall performances. Now, it is the setting for waltz recitals, between Easter and October.

Colloredo Palace – *Parkring 6.* This palace belonged to the Colloredo family. One of its members was the Prince-Archduke Jerome of Salzburg who quarrelled with Wolfgang Amadeus Mozart after being an insensitive employer *(see Deutsch-hordenhaus, inset "My happiness starts today").*

Stubenring (LR)

★★**Österreichisches Museum für Angewandte Kunst** ⊙ – *Stubenring 5.* When it was founded in 1864, the Austrian Museum of Applied and Decorative Arts was unusual in that it had no permanent collections. Its purpose was primarily educational: to develop the aesthetic sensibilities of the public without having recourse solely to the heritage of the past. In 1868, drawing inspiration from the Victoria and Albert Museum in London, the Museum für Angewandte Kunst began working closely with the *Kunstgewerbeschule* (School of Arts and Crafts). This reflected the trend of the time, which tried to encourage a close relationship between art and industry, as in the English *Arts and Crafts* movement. Thus, the museum has always favoured projects in the sphere of design, notably developments such as the *Wiener Werkstätte*.

The Museum of Applied Arts

139

Since 1871, it has occupied a neo-Renaissance building by Heinrich von Ferstel which in 1909 acquired an extension by Ludwig Baumann. Following restoration work begun in 1989, the museum reopened its doors in 1993. In keeping with its educational aims, the museum developed a remarkable **museology★★**. Famous contemporary artists have created settings to show the splendid collections to their advantage *(numbers in brackets refer to the numbers of the rooms)*.

Romanesque, Gothic, and Renaissance (1) – Designer: Günther Förg, German painter. The bold cobalt blue on the walls is a happy choice which sets off the exhibits splendidly. There are some magnificent objects such as a pearwood folding stool (Salzburg, early 13C), a maple cabinet (south Germany, late 16C) and Urbino majolica ware (16C). The room contains some even more edifying objects, starting with the *sacerdotal ornaments★* (embroidered linen and silk vestments and antependium, about 1260) from the Benedictine convent of Göss in Styria, which form the oldest collection in existence. Then, there is a painted cherrywood *table top★★* (Swabia, late 15C), which is one of ten existing examples and allegedly from a convent in Ulm; it depicts scenes from the Passion and the legend of St Ursula.

Baroque, Rococo and Classical (2) – Designer: Donald Judd, American minimalist artist. The sobriety of the décor suits the exhibits, notably furniture including a cabinet signed J.N. Haberstumpf (Cheb, 1723) which belonged to Karl VI. In the centre is a reconstruction of the porcelain room of the Dubsky palace at Brno (porcelain from the Viennese Du Paquier factory, before 1730). On one of the walls hang two *inlaid panels★* (Neuwied, 1179) by David Roentgen for the palace of Charles of Lorraine in Brussels. Also noteworthy is the **centrepiece** from Zwettl monastery (Viennese porcelain, 1768) consisting of 60 figurines and vases made for the abbot's jubilee festivities.

Renaissance, Baroque and Rococo (3) – Designer: Franz Graf, Austrian painter. In one of the two cases displaying glass there is some 16C Venetian glass. The extensive lace collection includes a *chasuble* also from Venice (late 17C).

Empire and Biedermeier (4) – Designer: Jenny Holzer, American artist. A long column of chairs precedes a striking cherrywood *writing desk★* (Vienna, towards 1825). The display cases contain silver, china and glass, in particular a travelling service (1811) which Napoleon ordered upon the birth of his son, the future Duke of Reichstadt, and stemless glasses (about 1830, with a French inscription) with enamelled decoration depicting the capital's most prestigious sites.

Historicism, Jugendstil and Art Deco (5) – Designer: Barbara Bloom, American artist. A superb shadow show traces the history of the Viennese **chair**, with special emphasis on the *Thonet★* dynasty. The retrospective ends with other masters of the genre: A. Loos, J. Hoffmann, and J. Frank.

Orient (6) – Designers: Gang Art, a group of Viennese artists. The *carpet★★* collection of the MAK is one of the most famous in the world, mainly because of its Egyptian, Persian and Turkish exhibits. Particularly noteworthy are the hunting carpet (first half of the 16C) from Kashan in central Persia, and the unique silk Mameluke carpet (early 16C); both belonged to the imperial family.

20C design and architecture (3) – Designer – Manfred Wakolbinger, Viennese sculptor. This room on the first floor concentrates on art applied to architecture, or the relation between art and function through the designs of Nils Landberg, Walter Pichler, Philippe Starck or Frank Gehry.

Jugendstil and Art Deco (1) – Designers: Eichinger oder Knechtl, Viennese designers. This is a fine and varied collection of **glass** and **furniture** bearing the signature of masters such as Josef Hoffmann, Charles Rennie Mackintosh, Kolo Moser, Henry van de Velde and Otto Wagner. One of the most impressive exhibits is the *series of drawings★★* (1905-1909) by Gustav Klimt for the dining room of Stoclet House in Brussels: 9 tempera cartoons for the mosaic decoration of the famous mansion which J. Hoffmann built for the engineer and businessman Adolphe Stoclet. The materials for this mosaic by the *Wiener Werkstätte* cost 100,000 crowns at the time, a veritable fortune.

Wiener Werkstätte (2) – Designer: Heimo Zobernig, Austrian sculptor. Anyone fond of decorative art should visit this room, if only because it contains the archives of the **Wiener Werkstätte★★**: a collection of sketches by all the artists in the association, as well as factory marks, cartoons, photographs, etc. In the display cases are numerous items of silver, jewelry and bookbinding, most of them signed Josef Hoffmann or Dagobert Peche.

Contemporary art – Designer: Peter Noever, Austrian designer and curator of the department. The purpose of this section is to display, through a collection begun in 1986, the links uniting "fine art" and "applied art", despite the differences between them.

In the museum basement, there is a study collection divided into sections: furniture, textiles, metalwork, ceramics. This apparent jumble should not confuse the visitor. It features objects of high quality. The presentation aims at contrasting the exhibits with each other.

In the centre, the Far East room has a superb display of items originating from European collections, when orientalism was so fashionable as to influence continental art, or imported from Asia in the early 20C to illustrate the evolution of art in that part of the world.

Regierungsgebäude – *Stubenring 1*. Formerly the War Ministry, this huge government building is 250m/272yds long. At the top, its bronze eagle has a wingspan of 16m/17yds. The edifice (1912) by Frans Neumann is heavy and slightly decadent in style. It is a voluminous stone mausoleum which one may compare to the Post Office Savings Bank opposite *(see Postsparkasse)*.

The Radetzky monument in front of the façade commemorates the famous marshal and war minister. As a mark of his admiration, Franz-Josef wanted him to be buried in Kapuzinergruft (crypt of the Capuchins). This monument (1892) is by Kaspar Zumbusch (moved from Am Hof square).

Urania-Sternwarte ⊘ – *Uraniastrasse 1*. At the corner of Stubenring and opposite the Danube canal, is this building (1910) by Max Fabiani. Some consider it the prototype of Adolf Loos' *Raumplan*: to treat space in terms of volume rather than area. This principle was applied for the first time in 1922 in the Rufer house (Schliessmanngasse 11).

Concerts take place in the large auditorium. After destruction during the Second World War, the cupola *(3rd floor)* was reconstructed in 1957. It contains an observatory.

Franz-Josefs-Kai which closes off the loop of the Ring is not a tourist attraction. The nearest sights are: the Fleischmarkt District, in the town centre, and the Belvedere and Prater Districts.

STAATSOPER District★

Local map pages 5-6, **JKRS**
Underground: Karlsplatz (U1, U2, U4)
Tram: Oper (1, 2, 62, 65, D, J)
Bus: Oper (59A), Karlsplatz (4A)

★★STAATSOPER, THE FIRST PUBLIC BUILDING ON THE RING

Emperor Franz-Josef opened the Vienna State Opera House, then known as Hofoper, on 25 May 1869. The first performance was of Wolfgang Amadeus Mozart's *Don Giovanni*. Very soon, from its position at the crossroads of Kärntnerstrasse and the Ring, it attracted people of fashion and right until the eve of the First World War was one of Viennese society's favourite sites. In June 1944, J. Goebbels, the Third Reich's Minister of Propaganda, ordered the closure of German theatres. The ironies of history are often appreciated a posteriori: the last performance at the Vienna Opera House before compulsory closure was ... *The Twilight of the Gods* by Richard Wagner. It took place less than a year before the air raid of 12 March 1945, when fire gutted it, destroying the auditorium and stage. After reconstruction, it rose phoenix-like from its ashes on 5 November 1955, opening with *Fidelio* by Ludwig van Beethoven. Since 1956, it stands facing the unfortunate Opernringhof, a building from which it is best to turn away and instead admire the fine neo-Renaissance façade of the Opera House, which has thrilled, and will continue to thrill, to the most moving singing voices in the world.

The origins of opera and ballet in Vienna

Orfeo was the first opera performed on Austrian soil, in 1614 in Salzburg. Many emperors with Italian wives began to appreciate opera. It was the Mantuan princess Eleonora of Gonzagua, wife to Ferdinand II, who initiated the first examples of drama set to music. Gradually, most entertainment for the imperial family included madrigal recitals which progressively developed into lavish Court operas. Contrary to the Venetian tradition, these entertainments were not open to the public. In 1652, the Court celebrated the birth of the Infanta Margarita-Teresa of Spain with a performance of *La Gara* at which non-members of the imperial family were present. In 1666, Leopold I commissioned Ludovico Burnacini to build the Theater an der Cortina, which opened with *Il Pomo d'Oro* by Antonio Cesti. It could accommodate nearly a thousand people (owing to its wooden interior, it was destroyed as a fire hazard in 1683). Under his direction lasting from 1658 to 1705, about 400 performances of operas and ballets took place in Vienna.

Salome (Mara Zampieri) by Richard Strauss

A symbolic institution – With its indisputed international reputation, Austria's most illustrious theatre, so dear to the heart of the Viennese, has counted outstanding figures among its directors: Gustav Mahler (1897 to 1907), appointed despite Cosima Wagner's reluctance, and who began his directorship with a performance of *Lohengrin*; Felix Weingartner, Richard Strauss (1919 to 1924), Clemens Krauss, Karl Böhm (1943 to 1945 then from 1954 to 1956), Herbert von Karajan (1956 to 1964), Lorin Maazel (1982 to 1984) and Claudio Abbado (1986 to 1991). Bruno Walter was assistant artistic director in the years preceding the Anschluss. During his decade as director, G. Mahler gave the Opera its present status. By producing 184 operas and reforming the conception of the most renowned series (Mozart, Wagner) with faultless stringence, he raised Vienna's Opera House to an eminence which was the envy of the musical world. Many a Viennese singer has forgone a worldwide career to remain with the Staatsoper and its music-loving public.

The Vienna State Opera has a permanent company and its own orchestra and training school, the Viennese Philharmonic, divided into two teams – this orchestra is somewhat misogynist since there are no women in it; female harpists if any are not members. It is one of the few opera houses in the world able to show a different work every night, almost the whole year round. The season starts on 1 September and ends on 30 June. There are no operas or ballets on Christmas Day, Good Friday, on the day or eve of the debutantes' ball *(see below)*, on 18 May (the date of the Mahler concert) or when Johann Strauss' *Die Fledermaus* is performed on 31 December and 1 January. During the musical season, some sixty operas are staged, all of them performed in the original language of the libretto (unlike the Volksoper). There are three price categories: A, operas starring world-famous singers; B, operas with "normal" singers; C, ballets. Seats are on sale a month before the performance *(see Practical information)*. An unchanging Staatsoper tradition allows standing spectators to buy tickets for as little as 20 or 30 schillings. These tickets, which are restricted in number, are on sale on the evening of the performance and often require a long wait, at the end of which only the first in the queue or those keen to watch an opera such as *Die Meistersinger von Nürnberg* by Richard Wagner *(5 1/4 hours)* on their feet, will be rewarded.

Gustav Mahler by Auguste Rodin

Decisive influences of Mahler and Karajan – After being conductor of the Hamburg Stadttheater, G. Mahler became director of the Viennese Imperial Opera in May 1897, one year after Bruckner's death and a month after Brahms' death on the day of the creation of the Secession. Under his guidance, orchestration gradually abandoned austerity in favour of expressionism, and he was particularly interested in performing works he conducted himself. This conscientious curiosity, unusual for the time, modified an essential aspect of opera: thereafter, singers concentrated also on acting.

When in 1956 Karajan became director, he also made his personality felt by instilling new life into the dramatic style which had lost all spontaneity over the years. He introduced to the Opera a policy of co-production with La Scala in Milan and left behind him an organisation based on the repertory system. However, this may now be a weak point for the Staatsoper, which no longer has time for in-depth study of the works in its repertoire.

The building ⊙ – *Entrance under the arcades, on the Kärtnerstrasse side*. A rumour that eventually became a legend had it that one of the architects hanged himself in 1868, driven to suicide by criticisms and Franz-Josef's alleged remark that the opera "looked about to sink into the ground". According to the same rumour, the other architect died of grief after his friend's death. In fact, Eduard van der Nüll was a depressive and August Siccard von Siccardsburg died following an operation two months after his colleague's suicide. The former was in charge of decorating the edifice, while the latter directed the construction. However, in artistic matters it is certain that the emperor usually restricted himself to making bland all-purpose compliments. The building, begun in 1861, displays in the Ring a stone façade in the French Renaissance style (left intact after the air raid and subsequent fire in 1945). It represents the peak of what is known as Romantic Historicism. Its loggia displays five bronze statues by Ernst Julius Hähnel: Heroism, Drama, Fantasy, Humour and Love.

The tour of the interior *(3/4 hour)* starts with the interval rooms. The Gobelins room features modern tapestries by Rudolf Eisenmenger depicting Mozart's *Magic Flute*. The **Schwind Foyer★** (undamaged in 1945) takes its name from the painter Moritz von Schwind whose frescoes represent scenes from operas; among the busts of composers and conductors, that of G. Mahler by Auguste Rodin (1909) is noteworthy. Otto Prosinger decorated the marble room. Once exclusively reserved for the Court during the intervals, the tea room (undamaged in 1945) is adorned by silk draperies stamped with the imperial initials. Nowadays, this room is only used for press conferences, interviews with famous singers or receptions paid for by the few spectators willing to disburse a substantial sum *(20,000 schillings, champagne and tickets not included)* in order to await the start of a performance or pass the time during the interval in luxurious surroundings. From it, one descends the superb **grand staircase★** (undamaged in 1945). The lunettes are decorated with allegorical reliefs painted by Johann Preleuthner (light Opera, Ballet, Opera) and statues of the seven liberal arts by Josef Gasser. It leads to the auditorium. Erich Boltenstern, in charge of its reconstruction, did not restore the rich Italienate decoration of the theatre designed by the two original architects. Abandoning all ornamentation and discarding the ribs of the last balcony and the columns which obstructed the view, he designed a horseshoe-shaped auditorium for over 2,200 spectators and 110 musicians.

A formidable technological feat – The lighting, air conditioning and machinery of the opera uses the same amount of electricity as a town of 30,000 inhabitants. A total of almost 2,000 people work in shifts at the Opera House; some 100 of them are employed as stagehands and dressers. Due to space restrictions, the scenery has to be stored at the Arsenal depot, 4km/2,5 miles away. The vans transporting it have their own entrance at the back of the building and the scenery is moved automatically on stage by means of lifts 22m/72ft long. The huge ultramodern stage (1,500m²/16,145sq ft, 50m/164ft deep, 45m/147ft high) is able to cope with the needs of today's productions with an array of the latest machinery, hydraulic jacks, lifts, cranes and a 45 tonne turntable. Every day, the scenery from the previous night is replaced by the sets required for the current day's performance. Before this, the scenery for a rehearsal is often introduced to accustom the singers to the dimensions of the stage. The Staatsoper is a permanent building site.

Opernball – In Vienna the season starts on 31 December with the *Kaiserball* which takes place in the Hofburg. However, the most prestigious of them all is undoubtedly the *Opernball* or debutantes' ball, created in 1877 to celebrate the entry of aristocratic young girls into high society. It takes place on the last Thursday of carnival *(Fasching)* in February. For this occasion, the auditorium of the Opera converts into a ballroom by means of a fitted floor; thousands of carnations are specially flown in from the Riviera to adorn the boxes for this, the most fashionable night (until 5am) of the year. Anyone may attend provided he has a ticket...which will cost about 2,700 schillings (standing), to which he should add 10,000 schillings for a table for 6, and up to 170,000 schillings for a box.

143

ADDITIONAL SIGHTS

Albertinaplatz – Behind the Opera is this large square dominated by the Erzherzog Albrecht-Denkmal by Kaspar Zumbusch, an equestrian statue of Archduke Albert, who defeated the Italians at Custozza in 1886. The foundation wall consists of the remains of a former bastion of the city fortifications. Backing on to it is the Danubiusbrunnen, or Danube fountain (1869). It was designed by Moritz Löhr, while its allegorical sculptures were by Johann Meixner; the central group represents the rivers Danube and Wien. This square leads to the Burggarten or imperial gardens *(see Hofburg)*.

Gedenkräume des Österreichischen Theatermuseums ⓥ – *Hanuschgasse 3; take the entrance on the left and go to the first floor.* These rooms commemorate ten personalities who left their mark on Austrian theatre *(documentary in German, 20 mins)*. Some of the most well-known are the sculptor Fritz Wotruba (1907-1975) and the impresario Max Reinhardt (1873-1943), born in Baden as Max Goldmann, who had to emigrate to New York in 1938. Among the works on display are portraits of M. Reinhardt by Emil Orlik, as well as *Nuda Veritas* (1899) by Gustav Klimt in the room dedicated to Anna Bahr-Mildenburg (1872-1947), a famous singer of R. Wagner's operas.

Philharmonikerstrasse – In this street is the *Sacher* hotel (No 4), a veritable institution frequented by diplomats and opera singers. Built between 1874 and 1876 by Wilhelm Frankel for the restaurateur Eduard Sacher, on the site of the former Court theatre, it evokes the memory of Anna Sacher who was almost as famous as the hotel. Towards the end of the 19C, she served her illustrious guests, smoking a cigar *(see below)*. The tea room with its red velvet décor once attracted men of letters such as Arthur Schnitzler who alluded to the hotel's private dining rooms in his *Farewell Supper*. Today, gourmands come to savour the famous *Sachertorte*.

The *Sacherbuben* – Anna, Eduard Sacher's widow, was not just the promoter of the family *torte*; she acted as financial sponsor for the impoverished scions of good Viennese families who frequented the hotel. This was so well known that these young people awaiting their inheritance acquired the nickname of *Sacherbuben*, or "Sacher's rascals".

Kärntnerstrasse – *See also Around Stephansdom*. Below the junction of Kärntnerstrasse and the Ring is Operngasse, a passage with several shops. At No 51, opposite the right side of the Staatsoper, is the imposing façade of the Todesco palace, built between 1861 and 1864 in a neo-Renaissance style by Ludwig Förster and Theophil Hansen for the banker Eduard Todesco. Eminent politicians such as Anton Schmerling and playwrights such as Hugo von Hoffmannsthal met there (the palace had its own theatre).

Malteserkirche (K⁶) – About 1200, Leopold VI summoned to Vienna the order of Knights Hospitaller of Malta who built a chapel (1265) of which a few traces remain at No 37. The Empire style façade of the Church of Malta is still visible.

Pratt-Pries/DIAF

The Opernball

Inside the church are the coats of arms of many of the families connected with the order. On the left is the memorial (1806) to Jean de la Valette, Grand Master of the order. He distinguished himself on the island of Malta during the Turkish attacks of 1565. In 1530, Charles V granted the island to the order who remained there until 1793. The *St John the Baptist* on the high altar was by Johann Georg Schmidt (early 18C). Opposite the church is the famous shop Lobmeyr (No 26) founded in the 19C and managed by the 5th generation. Its crystal chandeliers are for luxurious display in public places (Staatsoper, Kremlin, etc.) At No 41, the Esterházy palace (mid-17C, refurbished in the 18C) first belonged to the imperial counsellor Adam Antonius Grundemann von Falkenberg before passing to Count Moritz Esterházy-Galantha-Forchtenstein in 1871. Since 1968, it has housed the *Casino Wien* and its *Black Jack Café*; it underwent complete restoration in 1991.

Annagasse – This delightful, narrow street at the corner of the Esterházy palace is bordered by attractive buildings: at No 4, the fine façade of Kremsmünsterhof (17C); at No 6, Herzogenburgerhof, its Baroque façade dating from 1730; at No 8, Täubelhof, also known as Deybelhof, built about 1730 to a design by Johann Lukas von Hildebrandt and modified in 1789 by Andreas Zach; at No 14, "Zum blauen Karpfen", a house which owes its name to the blue carp, still visible, that was the inn sign on Georg Kärpf's tavern about 1700 (the façade was refurbished in 1824 by Karl Ehmann who added a frieze of *putti*); at No 18, the building known as "the Roman Emperor" house.

Annakirche – *Annagasse 3b*. Build in Gothic style in the 15C and remodelled in Baroque style between 1629 and 1634 by a pupil of Andrea Pozzo, Christian Tausch, the little church of St Anne displays several interesting works: the ceiling frescoes (1748) and the altarpiece on the high altar *(The Holy Family)* by Daniel Gran, as well as the delicately carved wooden statue representing the Holy Parenthood (about 1510) and attributed to Veit Stoss (a Nürnberg artist) or to the Master of the Mauer altar, near Melk. Although the Madonna occupies the place of honour everywhere in Austria, there is also a special devotion to St Anne. She often features as one of three figures in the Holy Parenthood: the grandmother holds the Virgin Mary on one arm and the Infant Jesus on the other.

Turn left into Seilerstätte and again left into Johannesgasse.

Ursulinenkirche und Kloster (**M**[18]) – *Johannesgasse 8*. Empress Éléonore summoned the Ursulines from Liège in 1660. They commissioned an architect unknown today to build their convent and their church between 1665 and 1675. The barrel-vaulted sanctuary contains an altarpiece by Johann Spillenberger, *The Martyrdom of St Ursula* (1675).

Sammlung Religiöse Volkskunst ⊘ – The museum of popular religious art houses a reconstructed chemist's shop (first half of the 18C) and a small collection of sacred art including naïvely carved objects which often possess real charm. Room 1 contains a realist painting (1747) from northern Tyrol of *Christ the Apothecary*.

Johannesgasse – At No 15 nearly opposite the church stands the Savoysches Damenstift (1688), the Ladies of Savoy foundation. In a niche of the façade there is a lead statue of the Virgin Mary by Franz Xaver Messerschmidt (1768) better known for his grimacing heads *(see Österreichisches Barockmuseum)*. At No 6, the Hofkammerarchiv (Archives of the Court treasury) had dramatist Franz Grillparzer as its director from 1832 to 1856 (his study on the 4th floor is open to the public). No 5 is the fine Questenberg-Kaunitz palace (1701), after a design by Johann Lukas von Hildebrandt; Talleyrand stayed there during the Congress of Vienna.

It is possible to extend this tour by going to Himmelpfortgasse via Kärntnergasse (see Around Stephansdom).

The nearest sights are: the Hofburg, the Kapuzinerkirche and Karlsplatz Districts, Stephansdom, the Ring.

STEPHANSDOM★★★

A SYMBOL OF THE CITY

Stephansdom★★★ (St Stephen's Cathedral) is unique. With its vast roof of glittering poly-chrome tiles, it emerges from the compact old city, an elegant silhouette with its mighty south tower soaring to the skies. According to the 19C writer Adalbert Stifter, it has "the simplicity of a mountain", an image which also applies to Vienna, because the cathedral lies at the heart of this Baroque city. This stone edifice has shared the vicissitudes of Viennese life for over eight centuries.

An incomplete masterpiece

The first building on this site was a simple three-aisled Romanesque basilica, erected between 1137 and 1147, the date of its consecration by the Bishop of Passau, who administered the city. In accordance with the wishes of Friedrich II the Warrior, the last of the Babenbergs, another basilica soon replaced it, about 1230. In 1258, a fire destroyed a large part of it, although it left intact the present west front, the Riesentor (giants' portal), Heiden (pagan) towers, and the west rood screen. After swift reconstruction, the church was again consecrated in 1263 in the reign of Ottokar II Przemysl.

In 1359, Duke Rudolf IV of Habsburg wished to refurbish the cathedral in the Gothic manner, a style first seen in 1140 in the ambulatory of St Denis minster, in Paris. He laid the foundation stone of the present three-aisled nave. It was another hundred years before the completion of the vaulting. From this period date the Bischofstor (bishops' doorway) (north) and Singertor (singer's doorway) (south), and the south tower, the famous *Steffl* so dear to the Viennese, completed in 1433. In 1469, at the request of Emperor Frederick III, the pope raised Vienna to the status of an episcopal city. St Stephen's then became a cathedral.

After the completion of the work carried out under Anton Pilgram, head of the guild of stonemasons of St Stephen's cathedral from 1510 to 1515, the Baroque style made its appearance in 1640 with the construction of a high altar by the brothers Johann and Tobias Pock. The cathedral was damaged during the Turkish siege and deteriorated further during the French occupation in 1809. At the end of the Second World War (March 1945), it was hit by shells fired by German regiments retreating before the Red Army and the rafters were set alight. After skilful restoration from 1945 to 1952, the cathedral regained its indestructible brilliance.

However, it is still incomplete: construction of the north tower began in 1467, was interrupted in 1511 and was never finished.

Exterior

West front – Framing the Romanesque façade are the 66m/216ft high octagonal Heidentürme or towers of the Pagans. Its chief attraction is the **Giants' Doorway★★** (Riesentor, *see illustration in the Introduction, Architecture*). It acquired its name after the discovery during construction work in 1230 of an enormous bone. According to tradition, the bone belonged to a giant drowned during the Flood; in the 18C people realised that it was in fact the shin bone of a mammoth, and the relic was removed from its position hanging in the doorway. The tympanum displays a Christ in Majesty between two angels; in accordance with western iconography, this is a portrayal of Christ as teacher, wearing a philosopher's tunic, holding the Gospels in His left hand and blessing with the right those about to enter the cathedral. In the past, this doorway was opened only for ceremonial occasions; it was at this entrance that the Babenbergs meted out justice. On the left of the doorway, two metal bars are embedded in the wall. They served as measures; the shorter one was an ell (the usual measure in old Vienna) and the other a two-foot rule.

North façade – The left pillar of the Adlertor (Eagle Doorway) includes an iron handle which once bore the name of "asylum ring"; anyone grasping it automatically came under ecclesiastical jurisdiction. Johann Puschbaum began the Adlerturm (Eagle Tower) in 1467; incomplete, it should have reached the same height as the south tower. It houses the *Pummerin*, an impressive bell weighing 21t.

Nobody knows why work on the Adlerturm came to a stop. Possibly, the troubles of the Reformation were a factor. However, according to a legend, Puschbaum fell in love with the daughter of the cathedral's architect, Johann von Prachatitz. He promised to give his daughter to his collaborator, provided the latter managed to finish the tower in one year. Aware of the impossibility of the task, Puschbaum asked the devil for help. The devil agreed, provided the masterbuilder never spoke the name of God or the Virgin. Now, one day while Puschbaum was working on the scaffolding, he caught sight of his betrothed and could not refrain from attracting her attention by calling: "Mary! Mary!". The devil immediately sent the scaffolding hurtling down. As the architect had died, the workmen refused to continue building the accursed tower.

At the corner of the chevet is the Capistrano pulpit (1738), in memory of St John Capistrano, an Italian Franciscan monk canonised for his part in the evangelisation of Central Europe. It was here that the remains of **Wolfgang Amadeus Mozart** received absolution on 6 December 1791.

Bischofstor (Bishop's Doorway) was the women's entrance, hence its nickname of "fiancées' doorway". It was the work of Gregory Hauser.

The east end – It features a bust with the nickname of *"Zahnwehherrgott"*, or "God with toothache", dating from about 1440. There is also a relief (1502) of *Christ on the Mount of Olives*.

South façade – St Stephen's Tower★★★ also bears the name of *Steffl*, a diminutive of Stephan. It was begun in 1359 and reached completion in 1433. Soaring to a height of 137m/449ft above the ground, it is a masterpiece of the German Gothic School, and undeniably the finest spire in the German world, together with that of Freiburg cathedral, in Germany. The masterbuilder's triumph lies in the way he completed the transition from the square section of the tower to the octagonal section of the spire. He achieved this by increasing the number of gables, pinnacles, finials and crockets in a filigree which lightens the potentially heavy superstructure *(see illustration in the Introduction, Architecture)*.

The Singertor (Singer's Doorway) was the men's entrance. It was the work of Johann Puschbaum.

The roof – An unforgettable landmark of old Vienna, the cathedral roof displays a magnificent expanse of glazed tiles with zigzag motifs, always a delight to tourist photographers. It is a tapestry of about 250,000 tiles, with the two-headed eagle on the southeast. Beneath the roof are metal rafters dating from 1945; previously, they consisted of one thousand larch trunks five storeys high.

Interior

The late Gothic nave of this hall-church radiates an unusual serenity, perceptible to a visitor immediately upon entering, despite the crowds of tourists. In the words of the Secession architect, Adolf Loos, who eschewed ornamentation, it is "the most majestic church nave in the whole world". It is 170m/552ft long and 39m/127ft wide.

Points of artistic interest – *See map.* The cathedral vaults with liernes look down on some fine works and interesting monuments. In the Tirna chapel (or Holy Cross chapel) is the tomb of Prince Eugène of Savoy *(for information about him, see Belvedere)*, a simple sword blade embedded in the ground. On the third pillar in the north aisle is the splendid **pulpit★★** (about 1515) by the master sculptor Anton Pilgram, who portrayed himself in a window at the foot of the pulpit. This late Gothic masterpiece displays busts carved in the round of the Fathers of the Church: St Ambrose, St Jerome, St Gregory and St Augustine. Carved details illustrate the symbolic significance always present in medieval religious art. Along the banister, toads and frogs represent evil thoughts, while the lizards

Close-up of the pulpit: Anton Pilgram

B. Kaufmann

City Centre and the Ring

H. A. Jahn/VIENNASLIDE

Frederick III's tomb

pursuing them symbolize good thoughts. Any medieval monument reads like a book; the imagery is carved in stone. Another remarkable work by Pilgram is decidedly in the Renaissance spirit of anthropocentric art: his self portrait at the foot of the **organ case★** (1513) by the north wall; the organ itself was removed in 1720. The artist holds a masterbuilder's set square and compass.

At the end of the north aisle are Rudolf IV the Founder's cenotaph, with an angel from the Annunciation, and on the Wiener-Neustädter Altar in the apsidal chapel known as the "Virgin's choir" is the **Wiener Neustadt altarpiece★**. It dates from 1447 and displays figures carved in the round. When it is open, *The Coronation of the Virgin* is visible on the upper level, and on the lower level a *Virgin with Child* with St Barbara and St Catherine; when it is closed, the panels illustrate scenes from the Passion. The brothers Johann and Tobias Pock made the black marble high altar in 1640; the altarpiece, executed on pewter, represents the Stoning of St Stephen. The right apsidal chapel, the "Apostles' choir" contains **Frederick III's tomb★★** carved

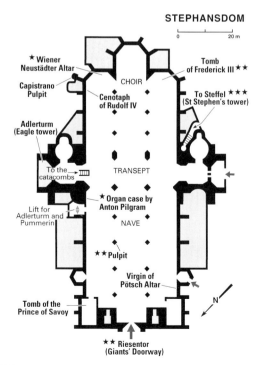

STEPHANSDOM

0   20 m

★ **Wiener Neustädter Altar**

Capistrano Pulpit

CHOIR

Tomb of Frederick III ★★

Cenotaph of Rudolf IV

To Steffel ★★★ (St Stephen's tower)

Adlerturm (Eagle tower)

To the catacombs

TRANSEPT

Lift for Adlerturm and Pummerin

★ **Organ case by Anton Pilgram**

NAVE

★★ **Pulpit**

Virgin of Pötsch Altar

Tomb of the Prince of Savoy

N

★★ **Riesentor (Giants' Doorway)**

from red Salzburg marble, first by Nikolaus van Leyden from 1467, then by his pupils *(see Neuklosterkirche at Wiener Neustadt)*. The artist represents the struggle between good and evil: noxious animals try to enter the emperor's tomb and disturb his sleep, while on the surround, figures symbolising goodness restrain them.

At the other end of the south aisle is a canopy housing the Maria Pötsch altar, which takes its name from a village in north Hungary. This naïve painting on two maple panels is an object of great veneration. In 1696, a peasant saw real tears in its eyes and the emperor had the miraculous icon brought to Vienna. It was held responsible for Prince Eugène's victory over the Turks.

Cathedral towers ⊘ – It is possible to climb the south tower (343 steps) to the watch room, at a height of 73m/239ft. Access to the 60m/196ft high platform on the north tower is by lift. On a clear day, it offers a wide panoramic **view**★★ over Vienna, the Kahlenberg Heights and the Danube plain to the east.

The North tower, Adlerturm, contains *Pummerin*, the 21t bell which rings at New Year. Originally cast (1711) from 180 bronze canons captured from the Turks in 1683, this monumental bell used to be in the south tower. After its destruction in 1945, it was rebuilt in 1951. The 9 provinces of the country donated it in 1957. It is now in the north tower, because the south tower had suffered damage from vibrations of the clapper against the *Pummerin*'s bronze sides.

Catacombs ⊘ – *Guided tour only; ask the guide to translate his comments into English.* They extend beneath the choir and Stephansplatz. Vast and on several levels, they comprise an old (14C) and a new (18C) section.

The Cardinals' crypt is still in use. The **ducal crypt** dates from 1363 in the reign of Rudolf IV, who was buried there at the age of 26, after dying from the plague in Milan. His wife Catherine of Bohemia lies at his side. Niches display urns containing the entrails of the imperial family, in accordance with Spanish Court ceremonial. The embalmed bodies are in Kapuzinergruft *(see Kaisergruft)*, while the hearts are in Augustinerkirche.

After passing the cathedral foundations (6m/19ft thick in places), one reaches the former city cemetery with about 16,000 graves. This extends into the area of the mass grave for victims of the 1714 plague, its opening sealed down to avoid contamination. Later, prisoners had the task of cleaning and tidying this somewhat putrid necropolis.

★★ STEPHANSPLATZ

Time has preserved the small dimensions of St Stephen's Square which contrast with the vast cathedral and its soaring 137m/449ft spire. Now almost exclusively a pedestrian zone, it displays on the west side pale red paving stones; these indicate the site of St Mary Magdalene chapel, where the funeral Mass was once celebrated. Fire destroyed this edifice in 1781.

Virgilkapelle ⊘ – Standing on the site of the former St Mary Magdalene chapel, is the Virgil chapel. It was discovered during the construction of the *Stephansplatz* underground station in 1973. There is a view of it through a window from the station (Museum in die Station Stephansplatz).

The cathedral and Haas-Haus

Bartl/ÖSTERREICH WERBUNG

★**Dom- und Diözesanmuseum** ⊙ – *Stephansplatz 6 or Wollzeile 4. Entrance though Zwettler Hof.* Giovanni Coccaponi was probably the architect of the archbishop's palace (1640). Adjacent to it is the cathedral museum, the creation of Cardinal Theodor Innitzer in 1933, in the former courtyard of Zwettl abbey dating from the 14C. Besides a fine picture and sculpture collection, it has a display of the most precious items in the cathedral treasury, and constitutes an ideal ending to a visit to Stephansdom. In a succession of rooms, the museum features exhibits ranging from the Baroque period to the early Middle Ages *(numbers in brackets correspond to the numbering of the exhibits).*

In the first rooms are numerous paintings and a few sculptures from the Baroque period: *Christ Bound to a Pillar* (mid-17C) *(126),* an unusual *St Mary Magdalene* carrying a skull (about 1670) *(128),* *God the Father and the Holy Ghost* (1724) *(134)* and *Glory of St Charles Borromeo* (1728) *(135)* by Johann Michael Rottmayr, *Virgin with Child* (about 1725) *(139)* by Martino Altomonte, *Virgin with Child Appearing to St Anthony of Padua* (1744) *(142)* by Michelangelo Unterberger, *Holy Parenthood* (1775-1780) *(151)* by Martin Johann "Kremser" Schmidt, *St Catherine of Sienna* (late 17C) *(155)* by Tanzio de Varallo.

Then there are many Gothic works, including a superb fragment from a stained-glass window, the **Thurifer Angel**★ or incense-bearing angel (about 1340) *(59),* from the cathedral, a fine *Virgin with Milk* (post 1537) *(73),* a painting from Lucas Cranach the Elder's studio, a *Virgin with Child* (about 1320) *(76)* and an *Entombment* (early 17C) *(121)* both from Thernberg church in Lower Austria. In the

Erzbischöfliches Dom und Diözesanmuseum

A Syrian vase

end room are the **Ober St Veit altar piece**★ (about 1507) *(69)* by one of Dürer's pupils, Hans Schäufelein, *The Mocking of Christ* (about 1505) *(70),* **Ecce Homo**★ (1537) *(72)* by Lucas Cranach the Elder, depicting Christ's presentation at the temple with Pilate saying to the crowd "Here is the man", and a carved group *The Birth of Christ* (about 1500) *(100).* Before leaving the room, one may note the two series of seven painted panels, one dating from the end of the 14C and the other from the beginning of the 15C *(62).* The two rooms of the treasury contain old and rare items, including in particular **Rudolf IV's shroud**★ *(3),* of gold silk brocade made in Persia (early 14C), and **Duke Rudolf IV's portrait**★★ (about 1360) *(2, see illustration in the Introduction, the Habsburg Empire).* He was the founder of the cathedral and Vienna University. Like the portrait of the King of France, John the Good (d. 1365) in the Louvre, this tempera portrait is one of the earliest in the history of western art. There is also a sardonyx cameo (3C, the cross and stole being later additions, probably about 1365) *(1),* six enamelled plaques (1160-1170) *(5)* from a reliquary, two glass **Syrian vases**★ (about 1280 and about 1310) *(6),* a reliquary of St Andrew's cross (1440) *(8),* a reliquary containing St Stephen's skull (1741) *(12),* a Carolingian Gospel (late 9C) *(13)* depicting the four Evangelists, a monstrance from Stephansdom (1482) *(17),* two monstrances in the shape of a tower (1508 and 1515) *(18 and 19),* a **chasuble**★ (about 1400) *(24),* its Latin cross embroidered in high relief with the *Crucifixion* in the centre.

After going through a room containing liturgical accessories including the Maria Pötsch monstrance (Hungary, about 1680) *(44),* one reaches the old chapel. On its walls hangs *The Virgin with St Elizabeth, St Joseph, and St Francis of Assisi* (1856) *(174)* by Leopold Kupelwieser; the principal exhibit is the **Passion altar piece**★ *(193),* made in Antwerp about 1460; its shutters (no longer there) used to be opened only on feast days.

Haas Haus – *Stephansplatz 12.* Opposite such a historic site, the architect Hans Hollein had no qualms about building a structure of blue-grey marble and glass, which reflects the Gothic arches of the cathedral. When it opened in 1990, this building caused a controversy. It houses shops, cafés, a restaurant and offices, and symbolizes the rebirth of architectural creativity in a city where practitioners of this art include the best artists of the turn of the century.

People who object to it fail to understand that by his bold treatment of volume, Hollein has restored vastness to the junction between Stephansplatz and Stock-im-Eisen-Platz. By following the old curving lines of the area, he has opened up the view of the Gothic church visible on arrival from Graben.

All the sights in the town centre are near Stephansplatz. However, the most convenient itinerary is the tour around Stephansdom.

Tour around STEPHANSDOM★★

Metro: Stephansplatz (U1, U3), Herrengasse (U3)
Bus: Graben-Petersplatz (1A, 2A)

According to one's inclination, this historical tour may take the form of a pleasant stroll through the city, from Peterskirche (St Peter's church) to Stephansdom (St Stephen's cathedral) by roundabout routes; alternatively, the visitor may prefer a faster pace, his steps gliding briskly to the rhythm of a waltz.

GRABEN AND KÄRNTNERSTRASSE

After a visit to the church with the finest Baroque interior in the centre of Vienna, the tour starts with two historic streets in the town centre. They are now elegant pedestrianized shopping streets. In summer they are teeming with musicians and singers; in winter, they are dotted with groups of carol singers and kiosks selling mulled wine.

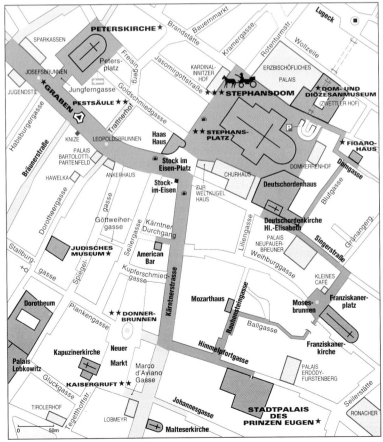

B. Kaufmann

Peterskirche

★ Peterskirche ⊘ – *Petersplatz*. St Peter's church was built from 1702 to 1733 by Gabriele Montani then Johann Lukas von Hildebrandt on the site of what was thought to be a Carolingian church; it may well have been the first Viennese parish church (first documentary evidence: 1137). It lies near the imperial apartments in the Hofburg. Empress Elisabeth often used to come and pray here in complete privacy, ensuring the doors were locked to the public.

Exterior – Rising from a restricted site, the edifice is typically Baroque with sinuous lines and austere decoration. The west front displays two towers obliquely framing a central concave section. In front of this stands Andrea Altomonte's porch, built between 1751 and 1753, surmounted with lead figures by Franz Kohl (pupil of Georg Raphael Donner), allegories of Faith, Hope and Charity. The east end is adorned by statues by Lorenzo Mattielli, a sculptor from Vicenza (very active in Dresden in the last ten years of his life): *St Peter* and *St Michael* (below).

Interior – The **interior decoration★** is sumptuous to the last detail, as on the pews in the short nave which follow the oval line of the dome. The latter gives visitors the illusion of entering a much larger edifice. It displays a fresco of the Assumption by Johann Michael Rottmayr (1714), a brilliant artist famous in Austria for the decorated dome of St Charles Borromeo church *(see Karlskirche)*. Under this imposing structure lit by eight windows lie the side chapels, their altarpieces by eminent artists of the period. Starting from the left, there are chapels dedicated to St Barbara (Franz Karl Remp), St Sebastian (Anton Schoonjans), and the Holy Family (Martino Altomonte); on the right are chapels dedicated to St Anthony (Martino Altomonte), St Francis de Sales (J.M. Rottmayr), and St Michael (Martino Altomonte). On the left of the chancel, the gilded pulpit designed by Matthias Steindl (about 1716) matches the monumental altar by Lorenzo Mattielli on which a gilded wood group *(Sturz des hl. Johannes Nepomuk in die Moldau)* represents St John Nepomuceno's fall into the Moldau (about 1729). The saint was a canon of Prague cathedral; he was the Queen of Bohemia's confessor. He was martyred by drowning in 1393 for refusing to betray the secret of the confessional to King Wenceslas IV (he is now called upon to ward off the dangers of false testimony). Finally, the choir is adorned by a *trompe l'oeil* dome by Antonio Galli-Bibiena and stuccowork by Santino Bussi (about 1730); the high altar is also by Antonio Galli-Bibiena, while the altarpiece is by Martino Altomonte.

★ Graben – Graben, once a Roman moat, is now a pedestrianized street lined with smart shops and is busy by day and night. After the filling of the moat around 1200, it was the flour and vegetable market until the 17C. In the 18C, a Baroque century if ever there was one, it became a haunt of those known as "the nymphs of Graben". From the 1870s – namely when the Ring began to attract industrialists and bankers – this road and neighbouring Kärntnerstrasse assumed their present commercial role.

Wider than a street, Graben is a long square leading to Stock-im-Eisen-Platz and Stephansplatz, where the cathedral suddenly comes into view. To appreciate the elegant architecture, it is best to hurry past the enticing shop window displays of Viennese goods: at No 21, Alois Pichl created Sparkassen in a neo-Classical style (1838); at No 17, Ernst von Gotthilf built a Jugendstil façade (1906) on the site of a house where Mozart lived from September 1781 to July 1782 and where he composed *Die Entführung aus dem Serail (The Abduction from the Seraglio)* in "a beautifully furnished room"; at No 13 (beyond Bräunerstrasse), is the little shop *Knize* designed by Adolf Loos between 1910 and 1913; at No 11 is Graben's last Baroque building, the Bartolotti-Partenfeld palace (1720); at No 10 (between Dorotheergasse and Spiegelgasse) is Ankerhaus built by Otto Wagner in 1894. Adolf Loos designed the public toilets in 1905. Since the 15C, two fountains have adorned Graben. The present ones have been ascribed to L. Mattielli, who made the sculptures in Peterskirche, but this is mere supposition. The lead figures are certainly by Johann Martin Fischer (1804): *The Flight into Egypt* on Josefsbrunnen; *The Discovery of St Agnes' Veil (see Klosterneuburg)* on Leopolds-brunnen.

The Graben

Pestsäule★★, the Plague Pillar, also known as *Dreifaltigkeitssäule* (Trinity Pillar) dates from 1693. Emperor Leopold I built it in response to a vow made during the plague of 1679. Matthias Rauchmiller began this Baroque monument in 1682, Johann Bernhard Fischer von Erlach and Paul Strudel continued it after his death (1686) and Lodovico Burnacini completed it. The figure of Emperor Leopold I kneeling in prayer crowns the complex upward winding scrolls of sculpture.

Stock-im-Eisen-Platz – The "tree-trunk set in iron" square owes its name to the tree-trunk standing in a niche at the corner of Graben and Kärntnerstrasse. According to a mid-16C tradition, apprentice locksmiths hammered a nail into the tree-trunk before setting off on their journey round Austria.
From this square there is a striking view of the architectural contrast between the glass Haas Haus (1990) and the weathered stone of Stephansdom *(see Stephansplatz)*.

Kärntnerstrasse – *See also Staatsoper District* – In the mid-13C, *strata Carinthi-anorum* marked the start of the road to Carinthia (Kärnten) via Styria (Steiermark). During the Middle Ages this road extended to Trieste and Venice. However, the buildings on this street date from the 18C or later, excepting some fragments of the Malteserkirche or church of the Knights of Malta *(see Staatsoper District)* and architectural unity suffered from Second World War bombings. The street was reduced in size about 1860. Since 1973 most of it has become a pedestrian precinct, filled with a lively crowd of busy Viennese and tourists ambling under the lime trees, gazing at shop windows.

American Bar – *Kärntner Durchgang 10* – A. Loos built this small bar (4.45m x 6.15m/14ft x 20ft) in 1908. A listed monument since 1959, it is one of the artist's major works, notable for its meticulously designed interior (mahogany, leather, copper, marble, onyx and mirrors). In it is a copy of the portrait of Peter Altenberg (by Gustav Jagerspacher), a friend of Loos who put the painting there himself. For many years, a landscape hung in place of the original. In his book *My Life*, Oskar Kokoschka recalled the decoration of the sign, *"pieces of blue, white and dark crimson glass, as in a Western"*, and the atmosphere in the bar *"where you sipped your drink like a disenchanted reveller"*. This description does not fit the present clientèle.

In 1896, Eduard Veith decorated the façade of No 16 Kärntnerstrasse with mosaics. Their pre-Secession style recalls those on some Venetian palaces. They represent the five Continents (restored in 1959).

THE "SAVIOUR OF CHRISTENDOM"

When in 1683, the Christian princes came to the aid of the Viennese besieged by the Turks, the King of Poland's army included a French nobleman who was to become justly famous, **Eugène of Savoy**. This renegade eliminated the Ottoman menace with the Peace of Karlowitz (1699), then the Treaty of Passarowitz (1718). He acquired two magnificent Viennese residences for winter *(see below)* and summer *(see Belvedere)*.

Himmelpfortgasse – In this narrow street, named "Heaven's gate" after an old convent, is *Ronacher*, a recently restored building from the end of the 1880s. This theatre once featured Josephine Baker; it boasts one of the finest auditoriums in the city and was the first to stage variety shows in German. As well as Prince Eugène's winter palace *(see below)*, the fine Baroque Erdödy-Fürstenberg palace also stands on this street (No 13). Its 1720 façade and magnificent portal adorned by telamones is reminiscent of the entrance to the former Bohemian Court Chancellery *(see Böhmische Hofkanzlei)* designed by J.B. Fischer von Erlach more or less during the same period.

★**Stadtpalais des Prinzen Eugen** – *Himmelpfortgasse 8 (the palace now houses the Ministry of Finance; it is only occasionally open to the public)*. Prince Eugène of Savoy, who defeated the Turks several times between 1697 and 1716, appointed J.B. Fischer von Erlach to build the winter palace (from 1695 to 1698) then replaced him with J.L. von Hildebrandt (from 1702 to 1724). The prince had his apartments decorated with a sumptuousness equal to that of Schönbrunn. He died there in April 1736, in a room with panelling and blue ceilings adorned by gold arabesques. However, with apparent indifference, Emperor Karl VI was not present at his funeral; he spent the day in Laxenburg. Eugène of Savoy's embalmed body is in the cathedral *(see Stephansdom)*. His heiress, Anna Victoria of Savoy-Soissons, rapidly squandered the fortune of her illustrious relation.

Unfortunately, the view of the long palace façade is somewhat restricted by the narrowness of the street. It is a sober and, for Vienna, relatively smooth façade. An order of Ionic pillars adorns it, bearing an entablature adorned by statues. The portal features low bas-reliefs, attributed to L. Mattielli, since the narrow street does not allow for traditional telamones or caryatids, although the Erdödy-Fürstenberg palace displays them *(see above)*. Go through the double doors *(ask permission from the porter)* to view the interior courtyard and fountain as well as J.B. Fischer von Erlach's **Grand staircase**★★. This is often mentioned as one of the finest examples of Baroque art, owing to the four telamones by Giovanni Giuliani exuding formidable power, beneath the absent-minded gaze of a nonchalant Hercules in his alcove. Considering the general lack of space, the effect is impressive.

> ### Celestial palaces supported on the shoulders of telamones
>
> There are numerous palaces in Vienna from the Baroque period. This style favoured eloquent decoration. The highly expressive telamon, or atlante, was often used to lend strength and power to the architecture of aristocratic residences.
>
> It is a colossal statue of a man designed for support. The word "atlante" comes from the Greek *Atlas*, a mythological god. A brother of Prometheus, Atlas sided with the Titans and rebelled against Jupiter (the Greek Zeus). After their defeat, he was condemned to support the sky on his shoulders.

MOZART IN VIENNA

Wolfgang Amadeus Mozart arrived in Vienna in 1781. Like Ludwig van Beethoven, he lived in various residences – 18 in the present first district. This tour ends near the cathedral where he married Konstanz Weber on 4 August 1782; this area comprises significant dwellings where the musical genius from Salzburg stayed: his first and last address, and the house which is now a memorial museum.

Rauhensteingasse – Mozart's last residence stands in this street. On 30 September 1790, he moved into No 8, in the house known as *Kleines Kaiserhaus* (small imperial house).

It was here that he composed several of his masterpieces such as *The Magic Flute* and *La Clemenza di Tito*. Before his death on 5 December 1791, at five minutes to one in the morning, he started writing the *Requiem* commissioned by Count Walsegg-Stuppach via the memorable "messenger in grey"; Franz Xaver Süssmayr completed the work at the widow's request. The neglected Mozarthaus needs restoration.

Franziskanerplatz – In the centre of this attractive square is **Mosesbrunnen**, the Moses Fountain, by the sculptor J.M. Fischer (1798). At No 3 is the tiny Kleines Café, built in the 1970s in "retro" style.

Franziskanerkirche – The church of the Order of St Francis (1603-1614), or church of St Jerome, displays a curious façade inspired by south German architecture: a Renaissance pediment adorned with statues stands above

Fotostudio Otto/Museen der Stadt, Wien

A silhouette of Mozart

windows shaped like Gothic arches and a Renaissance portal added in 1742. Inside, the Gothic-style arches overlook a fine canopied high altar by Andrea Pozzo *(Virgin with Child, 1707)*, a *Crucifixion* by Carlo Carlone (4th chapel on the right, mid-18C), a painting by Johann Georg Schmidt known as "Wiener Schmidt" depicting St Francis (4th chapel on the left, 1722) and an organ carved by Johann Wöckerl (1643).

Singerstrasse – There is much to see in this street which leads to Stock-im-Eisen-Platz and possesses many Baroque palaces. Among them is Neupauer-Breuner palace (1715-1716) with its fine doorway at No 16. Deutschordenhaus (House of the Order of German Knighthood) and its treasures is of particular interest.

Deutschordenhaus – *Singerstrasse 7*. The House of the Order of German Knighthood contains the treasures of its knights. Founded by the burghers of Bremen and Lübeck during the siege of Acre in 1191, this order of hospitallers became a military order in 1198. In 1244, it acquired a definitive rule distinguishing between three categories of members: knights, priests and domestics. Under the leadership of its Grand Master, it prospered until the defeat of its knights at Tannenberg in 1410. After a period of decline, it won renown fighting the Turks in 17C Hungary.

Napoleon dissolved the order in 1809, but it survived in Austria until 1938. Since the Second World War, it has devoted itself to charitable works in Germany, Austria and Italy.

In the famous film *Alexander Nevsky* by the Russian director Sergei Eisenstein, there is a somewhat distorted portrayal of the order which needs amending. Made in 1938, the film focuses on the order's colonisation and Germanization of Lithuania and Estonia, analogous at that time to the Nazi threat to Europe.

★ **Schatzkammer des Deutschen Ordens** ⊙ – *A small guidebook is supplied to English-speaking tourists free of charge*. Assembled by the Grand Masters, the collection in this treasure chamber is varied and comprises unusual items such as the *Tigermuscheln* (tiger's shell) spoons (17C, Room 2) or the "grass snake's tongue" saltcellar (1556, Room 2) supposedly capa-

R. Dechamps/MICHELIN

A fresco in the Sala Terrena

155

ble of detecting poisoned food. The following exhibits are noteworthy: a ceremonial ring in solid gold and a ruby set with diamonds (Room 1), the **chain of the Order★** (about 1500, Room 1) with sword-shaped links joining 12 shields, Grand Master Westernach's coconut goblet (16C, Room 2), a **clock★** (about 1620, Room 3) supported by Hercules and indicating the position of the sun and moon, and a series of weapons including a Persian sabre (about 1600, Room 3) adorned by 30 rubies and 13 turquoises.

Deutschordenkirche Hl. Elisabeth ⊘ – *Singerstrasse 7*. Built between 1326 and 1395, St Elizabeth's church is almost totally surrounded by the buildings of the order. It is a Gothic edifice with alterations in the Baroque style dating from between 1720 and 1722. The interior features a fine southern Dutch **altarpiece★** *(Crucifixion, Flagellation and Ecce Homo, 1520)* by the Mechlin sculptor Nicolas van Wavere, which was until 1864 in the church of Our Lady of Gdansk. About 1722, the walls were hung with coats of arms of the knights of the order.

On the ground floor of Deutschenordenhaus is **sala Terrena**, a delightful little concert hall displaying Venetian style Baroque frescoes from the second half of the 18C. *(If it is closed, go to the interior courtyard to view it through the windows)*.

Domgasse – Since 1862, Kleine Schulerstrasse has been known as "small Cathedral Street". Vienna's first café opened there in 1683, at No 8; the sign *Zum roten Kreuz* "at the Red Cross" recalls this; it is on the building constructed on the site in the 18C. However, the street owes its current fame to the fact that Mozart stayed in Camesinahaus, now generally known as Figaro-Haus.

★ Mozart-Gedenstätte Figarohaus ⊘ – *Domgasse 5* – The great Mozart lived in this house from 29 September 1784 to 23 April 1787, namely less than three years during a period which could be qualified as "happy". It was one of his most productive periods. There, he composed *The Marriage of Figaro*, an opera which gave its name to the building – a good address at the time – and entertained numerous visitors, such as Josef Haydn, Lorenzo da Ponte and Johann Nepomuk Hummel, his pupil. In addition to musical extracts *(earphones)*, several objects and documents are of interest *(numbers in brackets are those used on the exhibits)*. Room 1: after joining a Masonic lodge in December 1784, Mozart composed the cantata *Die Maurerfreude* (Masonic Joy) (frontispiece of first edition, 4); contrary to received opinion, Antonio Salieri greatly respected his rival's music (lithography by K.T. Riedel, 9). Room 2: fine map of Vienna showing each of Mozart's 18 residences (10); his father, Leopold Mozart (engraving by J.A. Friedrich, 15); Josef Haydn (engraving by J.E. Mansfeld, 16) to whom Mozart dedicated six string quartets in 1785 (18); on the ground, two coins found between the floorboards during restoration work (Nürnberg Rechenpfennig and Bavarian Kreuzer, 25). Room 3: Pierre-Augustin Caron de Beaumarchais who wrote *La Folle Journée or the Marriage of Figaro* (anonymous engraving, 26); Michaelerplatz with the Burgtheater where three of Mozart's operas were first performed (engraving by C. Schütz, 33). Room 4: Leopold Mozart and his children Wolfgang and Maria Anna with whom he went on a European tour (engraving by J.B. Delafosse, 37). Room 5: portrait of Konstanz Mozart (anonymous pastel, 70); portraits of Mozart's sons, Karl Thomas and Franz Xaver (engraving after a painting by H. Hansen in Salzburg, 69). Room 6: facsimile of the letter Mozart sent his father informing him of his marriage to Konstanz (48); 6 scenes from *Die Zauberflöte* (The Magic Flute, coloured engravings by J. and P. Schaffer, 66); facsimile of a page from the handwritten score of the *Requiem* (67). Room 7: Mozart was small in height and apparently had a pale complexion, his blue eyes were framed by thick blond hair (6 portraits, 73 to 78).

The Viennese Marriage of Figaro – In 1785, Emperor Josef II forbade the performance of Beaumarchais' *The Marriage of Figaro*, because he thought the contents dangerous. Several years before the French Revolution, the play promoted the abolition of the aristocracy's privileges. In October that year, Mozart started composing an *opera buffa* in four acts which he completed in April 1786 and which was produced a month later with an Italian libretto by Lorenzo da Ponte, court poet. Although the librettist toned down some of the political edge, this version still had considerable impact on the Viennese public.

Stephansdom (St Stephen's cathedral) is nearby. Anyone who has not yet visited it should walk back up Domgasse and turn left into Schulerstrasse. After reaching the chevet of the cathedral, one may feel like the visitor to whom the great writer Adalbert Stifter alluded: "...as he went round a corner, the cathedral came suddenly into view. Like a mountain, it was simple and wonderful; his spirits rose at the sight..." *(see Stephansdom)*.

In addition to Stephansdom, the nearest sights are the districts in the town centre: Fleischmarkt, Freyung, Hofburg, Hoher Markt, Kapuzinerkirche, Staatsoper.

"My happiness starts today"

Following his arrival in Vienna from Munich on 16 March 1781, Wolfgang Amadeus Mozart decided on 9 May to leave the employment of Prince-Archbishop Colloredo in Salzburg. This event, which took place in Deutschordenhaus in Singerstrasse, is important in musical history because it was the first time a musician had rebelled against his servile condition. Some sixty years earlier, J.S. Bach had been imprisoned after seeking to leave the employ of the Duke of Weimar. That evening, at the age of 26, Mozart wrote: *"My happiness starts today"*. Thereafter, he had to ensure financial independence by giving lessons to Countesses Rumbeck, Zichy and Pálffy, as well as Frau von Trattner. This emancipation, inconceivable at the time, paved the way for the freedom of Beethoven, Schubert and Liszt after him. Everyone knows the tragic conditions surrounding the death of Mozart, who had the courage and audacity to face up to his destiny as a man of genius.

Beyond the Ring

ALSERGRUND★

With its numerous hospitals and convalescent homes, this district north of the town centre is a centre of medicine. It is also somewhat French in character, with the French Lycée (Liechtensteinstrasse 37a) and French cultural institute (Währingerstrasse 32). Many famous people lived there, including Ludwig van Beethoven, who was constantly moving house, Anton Bruckner, Sigmund Freud, Franz Schubert and the writer Heimito von Doderer. The Swiss artist Helmut Federle lives there today.

THE SPHINX OF VIENNA

★Sigmund-Freud-Museum (**HP**) ⊘ – *Berggasse 19. Underground: Schottentor (U2); tram: Schlickgasse (D); bus: Berggasse (40A).* This address has almost become a place of pilgrimage, since the founding father of psychoanalysis lived there from 1891 to 1938, that is for nearly half a century before leaving the Austrian capital for London, to escape the Nazis.

Biographical notes – 1856: birth in Freiberg, Moravia (Pribor) to Jakob and Amalia Freud. 1859: settles in Vienna. 1873: student at the faculty of Medicine. 1881: doctor of medicine. 1882: mar-

Sigmund Freud by Max Halberstadt

M. Halberstadt/Sigmund Freud Museum

riage to Martha Bernays, in Hamburg. 1883: doctor at Vienna general hospital. 1885: lecturer in nervous diseases; training period with Charcot in Paris. 1896: for the first time Freud uses the term psychoanalysis. 1910: founding of the Association of the Society of Psychoanalysts chaired by Alfred Adler. 1920: Freud becomes professor with tenure at the University. 1924: becomes "honorary citizen of the City of Vienna". 1933: in Berlin, the Nazis burn Freud's books. 1939: death of Freud in London; his ashes are placed in a Greek wine bowl from his collection of antiques.

The Freudian revolution – Before Freud, people viewed the unconscious as a negative force, a chaotic disorder clouding reason and disrupting conscience. Starting from research on the aetiology of neuroses, Freud evolved a revolutionary theory. Its impact on the history of ideas was as dramatic as that of the discoveries of the Polish astronomer, Copernicus, who revolutionised thinking with the theory that the planets moved round the sun. Freudian theory describes the psyche and develops a technique for the interpretation of dreams; as such, it is universal.

A great collector

Sigmund Freud possessed a remarkable collection of antiques. Thanks to the cooperation of Hans Demel, the director of the Kunsthistorisches Museum at the time, who deliberately undervalued them, Freud was able to take them with him into his London exile. These objects literally filled his Berggasse chambers. The eminent psychoanalyst found them instructive both for himself and his patients.

On his desk, he kept significant items, such as the bronze head of Osiris, ruler of the underworld, and a bronze statuette of Imhotep, architect of the Sakkara pyramid, associated with the god of healing. People said that every morning Freud would stroke a carved Egyptian alabaster baboon dating from the beginning of the Christian era. In ancient Egypt, the baboon symbolised Thoth, god of the moon who weighs the hearts of those who have just died.

This theory is the subject of a cult book, *The Interpretation of Dreams*, published in German in 1900 (in 1909 in English). For the first time, dreams had a coded meaning, which concealed the unconscious desires of the dreamer. The language and syntax of dreams were that of the neurosis which required analysis. Briefly, psychoanalysis is a means of communicating with the patient's unconscious and restructuring his personal history.

Freud had to face the ridicule and incomprehension of most of his contemporaries. However, with the support of followers such as A. Adler or Carl Gustav Jung, he was able to overcome difficulties and transform his doctrine into a movement. The modern view of the human psyche originated here, at No 19 Berggasse, in this impersonal, middle-class apartment house.

The apartment – *1st floor*. Dating from 1971, this museum occupies the apartment where Freud wrote his works; his study was on the ground floor. The famous couch is in the Freud Museum, in the London suburb of Hampstead. On the other hand, the furniture in the waiting room is back in Vienna, thanks to his youngest daughter Anna Freud, herself a psychoanalyst.

Most of the collection consists of photographic documents *(explanatory leaflets are available in English)*. There is a veritable panorama of photographs tracing Freud's life, from the Freiberg house to his departure to London and including family photographs, such as the snap of Freud with his daughter Sophia. An audio-visual documentary with a commentary by Anna Freud shows her father with his family, during rare moments of leisure in the Viennese suburbs. It is a touching and somewhat unexpected scene.

Victor Adler – This politician lived in the same building as Freud, from 1881 to 1889. He was born in Prague in 1852 and died in Vienna in 1918. He studied medicine in Vienna before becoming involved in the "condition of the working classes" and meeting Engels. Elected head of the Austrian Social-Democratic party in 1888, he founded *Die Arbeiterzeitung (Workers' Journal)* in 1899. He believed in the right to self-determination for the nationalities of the Empire and died on the eve of the proclamation of the Austrian republic.

SEVERAL ASPECTS OF ALSERGRUND

It would be impractical to describe a tour encompassing all the sights mentioned below. It would lead visitors into additional and tiring detours. The best plan is to select places of interest from the map of Vienna and its suburbs, and visit them either on foot, or by public transport, as shown after the address.

"The old Jewish cemetery of Rossau" *(Der alte Jüdische Friedhof in der Rossau)* founded in the 16C is now closed to the public (Seegasse 11). The convalescent home of Kuratorium Wiener Pensionistenheime Zentrale prevents access to it. Samuel Oppenheimer and Samson Wertheimer are buried there *(see Prater district, inset "Court Jews")*. However, if it is sunny, a walk along the embankments of the Danube is an attractive prospect. Of particular interest is **Rossauer Lände** (U4), the underground station which Otto Wagner erected on the quay at the turn of the century.

Servitenkirche – *Servitengasse 9. Tram: Schlickgasse (D); bus: Berggasse (40A)*. Carlo Canevale built the "Servants of our Lady" church, also called Annunciation church, between 1651 and 1677. It is the earliest edifice in Vienna to possess a central space of oval shape. It provides valuable evidence for foreign artistic influence in the early Baroque style in the Austro-Hungarian capital. One may reasonably suppose that it inspired the architects of Karlskirche and Peterskirche. Its rich interior attracts visitors. The stucco work was by Giovanni Battista Barberini and Giovanni Battista Bussi. On the left, the fine Baroque **pulpit★** (1739) displays carved figures by Balthasar Ferdinand Moll. Some of his masterpieces are visible in the Capuchin Crypt *(see Kaisergruft)*. Here, he created the four Evangelists *(lower level)* and the three theological Virtues *(upper level)*.

On the right is St Peregrine's chapel, dating from 1727. The frescoes in the cupola are the work of the Tyrolian artist Josef Adam Mölk (1766).

Museum Moderner Kunst (M⁴) ☉ – *Fürstengasse 1. Tram: Fürstengasse (D); bus: Bauernfeldplatz (40A)*. The museum of Modern Art occupies the summer palace of Johann Adam Andreas, Prince of Liechtenstein, former ruler of the territory on the Swiss border, which has remained a tiny sovereign state. Italian models inspired Domenico Martinelli, the creator of this somewhat austere Baroque building, which he began in 1700 and completed in 1711. The hall of state on the first floor displays frescoes by Andrea Pozzo *(for further information about him, see Jesuitenkirche)* entitled *The Apotheosis of Hercules*. The views of the park have unfortunately disappeared.

This museum of Modern Art has limited appeal. It displays the reserve collections of the famous Ludwig Foundation consisting of a hotchpotch of minor works, interspersed with a few paintings of real artistic merit (Ernst, Klee, Léger, Magritte, Rauschenberg). One feels like urging lovers of art to avoid it, but this would be unfair to the rare high-quality paintings in the palace. It is not very difficult to locate them.

Strudelhofstiege – *Between Strudlhofgasse and Liechtensteinstrasse. Tram: Sensengasse (37, 38, 40, 41, 42); bus: Bauernfeldplatz (40A).* The architect Johann Theodor Jager designed these picturesque steps with several flights in 1910. A fine example of urban art, it displays Jugendstil balustrades and candelabra. It was the setting of a famous novel by Heimito von Doderer, *Die Strudlhofstiege oder Melzer und die Tiefe der Jahren* (1951, not yet translated into English).

Bezirksmuseum Alsergrund (**M**[20]) ⊘ – *Währingerstrasse 43. Tram: Sensengasse (37, 38, 40, 41, 42).* This museum commemorates the writer **Heimito von Doderer** (1896-1966), a great Viennese writer who is practically unknown outside Austria. For a time he flirted with the ideas of National Socialism, but abandoned them after Hitler's *Anschluss*. He lived in Währingerstrasse.

Volksoper (**T**[2]) – *Währingerstrasse 78. Tram: Währingerstrasse/Volksoper (40, 41, 42). Bus: Währingerstrasse/Volksoper (40A).* The People's Opera was built in 1898 to mark Franz-Josef's fiftieth jubilee celebrations.
The company dates from 1903. At the Volksoper, unlike at the National Opera *(see Staatsoper)*, the libretti are always sung in German, although there is some discussion as to whether some operas will be performed in the original language. Performances of *Carmen* or *Don Giovanni* take place in the language of Goethe, without any indication of the original text. It is often young singers or conductors who perform in this opera house and the operas or operettas sometimes display an avant-garde spirit. The Volksoper also stages musical comedies such as *My Fair Lady*. It is the opera of the people, in the best sense of the word.

Müllverbrennung-Fern-wärme-Heizwerk (**S**) – *Heiligenstädter Lände. Underground: Spittelau (U4); tram: Radelmayergasse (D).* – This is the name, difficult for a foreigner to pronounce, of the incinerator which **Friedensreich Hundertwasser** decorated, north of Franz-Josef station. The gold-tipped chimney of this building is a landmark in the Viennese urban landscape. The incinerator is part of the new university complex which Kurt Hlawenicka and Company built between 1972 and 1990 (Faculty of Economic Science, Institutes of Zoology, Biology and Botany).

Waste incineration plant "clad" by Hundertwasser

THE MASTER OF LIEDER

"When I wanted to sing about love, I became sad; when I wanted to sing about sadness, it lead me to love". Franz Schubert wrote this famous sentence in 1822. It sums up the attitude of this composer, underrated in his time, who wrote over 1,200 pieces of music in less than twenty years.

★ **Franz-Schubert-Gedenkstätte "Geburtshaus"** (**M**[5]) ⊘ – *Nussdorferstrasse 54. Tram: Canisiusgasse (37, 38). Althanstrasse (D).* This museum, which opened in 1912, occupies a house formerly called *Zum roten Krebs* ("at the red crayfish"). Franz Peter Schubert was born there on 31 January 1797; his family lived in the rooms overlooking the inner courtyard. The future composer spent the first four years of his life there, before moving to No 3 Säulengasse *(see below).*
The Historisches Museum der Stadt Wien (Historical Museum of the City of Vienna) had the excellent idea of equipping the "great musician memorials" under its administration with a sound system enabling visitors to hear musical excerpts. Using headphones, one may listen to Schubert and select the music of one's choice.

Schubert's piano

Fotostudio Otto/Museen der Stadt Wien

The museum possesses numerous documents and mementoes. It displays the famous spectacles of the composer of *Der Tod und das Mädchen* (*Death and the Maiden*, Room 1), extracts from his diary (Room 1) and a lock of his hair in a medallion with an authentication certificate. Among the portraits, there are a signed zincograph by Leopold Kupelwieser (1821), a lithograph by Josef Teltscher (about 1825) and a Carrara marble bust (1893) by Carl Kundmann (Room 2). His guitar is also on view, dating from about 1820 and made by the Viennese craftsman Bernard Enzensperger (Room 4).

A prolific composer – Schubert was born and died in Vienna, a city which he rarely left. As an escape, he composed ceaselessly and worked continuously; he took his first lessons in counterpoint some weeks before his death. He was a great friend of Franz Grillparzer and admirer of Johann Wolfgang von Goethe and Friedrich von Schiller. Schubert was very disillusioned. A distant spectator of the festivities of the Congress of Vienna, he was a close observer of the failure of Metternich's policies, a period of conservatism known as *Vormärz*. By 1818, he had already composed nearly 600 pieces, having achieved in 1815 and 1816 an output greater than many composers produced in a lifetime. Surprisingly, he rarely met Beethoven, who lived in the city during the same period and died a year before him. From the depths of his solitude, Schubert composed 5 Masses, 10 symphonies, 15 operas and over 600 *Lieder*.

It was during his adolescence that Schubert began writing *Lieder*, a musical form present throughout his work. His childhood as a choirboy *(see Lichtentalkirche, below)* probably led him to explore this new genre which can be defined as a musical setting of a poem for one or more voices. His masterpiece is probably *Der Doppelgänger (The Double)*, which he composed at the age of 31 for a text by Heinrich Heine.

After leaving the museum, bear left and cross Nussdorferstrasse, then turn right into Säulengasse.

Schubert lived at No 3, *Zum schwarzen Rössel* ("The Black Horse") house, from 1803 to 1808. He moved back in 1813, spending 17 years of his short life there. It was where he composed, among other works, *Erlkönig (King of the Alders)* in 1815. The house is now a garage, formerly *Schubertgarage*.

Cross Nussdorferstrasse again and take the steps up to Liechtensteinstrasse. Cross it and enter Lichtentalergasse. Marktgasse is the second street on the left.

Lichtentalkirche (**K**[7]) – *Marktgasse 40*. This small church was the setting for Schubert's christening on 1 February 1797. It was also here that he played the violin and sang in public for the first time, before becoming a pupil at the choir school "K. und K. Stadtkonvikt". This comprised 130 pupils who sang on Sundays at the imperial chapel. Finally, the first public performance of one of his works was given in this church on 16 October 1814. It was the *Mass in F Major*.

163

A CENTRE OF MEDICINE

★**Josephinum** (**HP**) – *Währingerstrasse 25. Tram: Sensengasse (37, 38, 40, 41, 42)*. Josef II founded the former military academy of surgery and medicine known as the "Josephinum". Isidor Canevale built it between 1783 and 1785. In the main courtyard is a fountain by Johann Martin Fischer dating from 1787. Since 1920, the Josephinum has housed the Museum of the Institute of the History of Medicine.

Museum des Institutes für Geschichte der Medizin ⊘ – *First floor*. This museum is in two sections. First, there are two rooms displaying 19C instruments (including Karl Zeiss's first magnifying glass) and documents (photographs, engravings, etc.) Of interest is the display case dedicated to S. Freud, A. Adler and J. Preuer (manuscript of a letter by Freud). Then, there are three rooms containing life-size **anatomical preparations**★ modelled in wax under the supervision of Felice Fontana and Paolo Mascagni. Josef II commissioned this collection of figures, the "Anatomia Plastica", to make the study of anatomy easier for future military surgeons. A visitor will marvel at the astonishing precision of this unusual series of flayed wax torsos, incorporating muscles, nerves, ligaments and blood vessels, by the two Tuscan sculptors. The model of the Lunatics' Tower *(see Narrenturm below)* will be of interest to anyone who does not have time for a visit to the General Hospital.

Allgemeines Krankenhaus – *Alserstrasse 4*. At the end of the 18C, Josef II asked Isidor Canevale to build the Vienna General Hospital, taking as his model the Central Hospital in Paris. The hospital grew during the following century and now consists of a vast group of buildings around 13 inner courtyards *(many of them are under restoration)*.

Narrenturm – *Enter the hospital precinct and follow the signs*. The same architect constructed the strange and slightly weird "Lunatics' Tower". It is a massive cylinder of bricks reminiscent of the projects of contemporary French architects, such as Etienne-Louis Boullée and Jean-Nicolas-Louis Durand. Behind these narrow windows like arrow slits with bars, mental patients inhabited (until 1866) cells opening onto a corridor skirting a really sinister inner courtyard. People nicknamed it "Emperor Josef's Kugelhof".

Pathologisch-Anatomisches Bundesmuseum ⊘ – The museum of pathology and anatomy occupies several storeys of Narrenturm *(only the ground floor is open to the public; the rest is for the use of medical students)*. It contains an impressive display of the deformities of the human body.

After leaving the General Hospital by Alserstrasse, the visitor will be nearly opposite the Church of the Holy Trinity *(see Dreifaltigkeitskirche)*.

The nearest sights are: the Freyung District, in the town centre, the Grinzing and Prater quarters and the Hernals, Josefstadt and Währing Districts.

BELVEDERE Area★★

Landstrasse – 3rd District
Map pages 6-7, **KLS, FGUV**
Underground: Stadtpark (U4)/Wien Mitte (U3, U4)
Tram: Schwarzenbergplatz (1, 2, 71, D, J), Unteres Belvederes (71)
Bus: Schwarzenbergplatz (3A), Gusshausstrasse (4A)

"Asia begins at the Landstrasse", Metternich once said. Today, this diplomatic quarter is the most varied in the whole of Vienna. Famous inhabitants include Beethoven (Untergasse 5), Anton Bruckner (Oberes Belvedere), Gustav Mahler (Auenbruggergasse 2), Robert Musil (Rasumofskygasse 20), Adalbert Stifter (Beatrixgasse 18 and 48) and Richard Strauss (Jacquingasse 8 and 10).

★**Schwarzenbergplatz** – This vast square bears the name of Prince Schwarzenberg, supreme commander of the combined Austrian, Prussian and Russian armies during the campaigns of 1813 and 1814. His bronze equestrian statue (1857) by Ernst Julius Hähnel stands in the centre of the square.

French Embassy – Dating from between 1901 and 1909, this edifice was built to plans by the architect George Chedanne. For a long time, rumour had it that it was the Turkish embassy. This was not the case. The Art Nouveau building is like a corner of Paris in the city of Jugendstil and the Secession, its curving lines a distinctive feature in a land of geometric design.

Russen-Denkmal – The Russians renamed the square Stalinplatz. On it stands a monument commemorating the liberation of Vienna by the Red Army in 1945, identical to others in Bucharest, Budapest, Sofia and Warsaw. The Viennese resented it and nicknamed the soldier above the fountain "the unknown looter".

Schwarzenberg Palace – This is the work of two great Viennese architects of the Baroque period, Johann Lukas von Hildebrandt and Johann Bernhard Fischer von Erlach (1697-1723). In its time, the palace was among the first summer residences outside the city walls. Almost entirely destroyed in 1945, it has housed a hotel by Hermann Czech since 1985.

On the side of the main courtyard, the Schwarzenbergplatz side, the building displays a façade with colossal pilasters.

Schwarzenberggarten – The palace gardens are by Josef Emmanuel Fischer von Erlach. Like many Baroque gardens, this one displays a sumptuousness that is an extension of the reception rooms. This is why it conforms to a carefully designed conception. The statuary is not the work of minor artists; for instance, the group *The Rape of the Sabines* is by Lorenzo Mattielli.

THE ESTATE OF PRINCE EUGENE OF SAVOY

The "little Capuchin"

This is the nickname which his soldiers gave to Eugène of Savoy-Carignan (Paris, 1663 – Vienna, 1736), because he wore a simple brown tunic, instead of the magnificent military attire befitting his rank. Moreover, before Eugène became a brilliant army commander, his parents had intended him for the Church. Finally, he was small and ugly.

A fiery young man – He was the son of the Count of Soissons and Olympe Mancini, Cardinal Mazarin's niece, who lived the life of a "merry widow" in Brussels after her husband's death.

Eugène joined Louis XIV's army. Following a refusal to give him command of a regiment, he proudly enlisted in the service of Leopold I, at the age of 20. He joined the King of Poland's army, which the Pope had entrusted with the relief of the siege of Vienna by Kara Mustapha in 1683.

"Austria over all" – After rejection by the Sun King, the French nobleman achieved glory, when as supreme commander of the Austrian imperial armies he defeated the Turks at the battle of Zenta (1697). He then imposed on them the Peace of Karlowitz (1699) and the Treaty of Passarowitz (1718), which defined the furthest eastward expansion of the Habsburg Empire; these frontiers remained unchanged until 1918.

A field marshal at 25, the "Saviour of Christendom" became counsellor to Josef I, then prime minister under Karl VI. The prince was responsible for uniting the different kingdoms within the Empire. This policy resulted in the Pragmatic Sanction of 1713, by which Maria Theresa became sovereign in 1745. Eugène of Savoy had the satisfaction of imposing the Treaty of Rastadt on Louis XIV. The military commander was by now a veritable statesman. Covered in glory and riches, he acquired two magnificent residences, a winter *(See Stadtpalais des Prinzen Eugen)* and a summer palace, the Belvedere.

A man of culture – A lover of art and a great collector, he was largely responsible for Vienna's wide-ranging cultural influence during the 18C. For instance, the philosopher Gottfried Wilhelm Leibniz dedicated to him two of his works written in Vienna, *Principles of Nature and Grace* (1718) and *Principles of Philosophy* (1721); and it is the 15,000 volumes from his collection that form the nucleus of the majestic Prunksaal in the National Library.

The prince was just over fifty when he signed the Treaty of Rastadt in 1714. He decided to cease fighting against Louis XIV and enjoy the fruits of his exertions. He commissioned Johann Lukas von Hildebrandt to build two palaces linked to one another by a garden, on the gentle slope of a hill not far from the Carinthian gate *(next to the present Staatsoper)*. Some years later, as he was passing through Vienna, Montesquieu declared on seeing the Hofburg and the Belvedere: "It is pleasant to be in a country where subjects live in finer lodgings than their sovereigns."

Today, this magnificent example of late Baroque architecture is one of the loveliest, most coherent and best preserved in Europe.

★ UNTERES BELVEDERE

Tram: Unteres-Belvedere (71)

At an angle to Rennweg, the Lower Belvedere stands at the end of a great courtyard with an imposing gate displaying the cross of Savoy on its pediment. This wide palace reached completion in 1716. Of greater interest than the façade overlooking the courtyard, the façade facing the garden is a superb harmonious ensemble of pilasters and decorative sculptures, extending from the central building to the two wings with pavilions.

★**Museum mittelalterlicher Kunst** ⊙ – *Closed during alterations* – The Museum of Austrian Medieval Art occupies the Orangery, next to the Unteres Belvedere. The exhibits are mostly from the Gothic period, and are mainly religious works from the Schools of Vienna, Lower Austria and Styria (from the end of the 14C to the beginning of the 16C).

There are many significant items in this museum. This is a selection of some of the most interesting, on view when the museum reopens: the Romanesque Stummerberg crucifix, carved in oak at Stummerberg in the Tyrol about 1160; the *Holy Trinity*, *Christ Carrying the Cross* and the *Crucifixion* by the Master of the St Lambrecht votive altar; the altarpiece "of Znaim", made in Vienna between 1420 and 1440; a **Crucifixion**★ by Konrad Laib (1449), the central panel of an altarpiece in the style of the Salzburg School; scenes from the life of the Virgin and the Passion by Rueland Frueauf the Elder who created them for the Salzburg altarpiece (1490); *The Adoration of the Magi* and **The Deploration**★ by the Master of the Viennese altarpiece of the Schottenkirche (about 1469); several works by the Tyrolean painter and sculptor Michael Pacher, including *St Laurence before the Prefect of Rome* and the *Flagellation* (late 15C); *St Augustine* and *St Ambrose* by the Master of Grossgmain (late 15C), near Salzburg; *Ecce Homo* (1508), a painting which is already Renaissance in style, and **The Legend of Chaste Susannah**★ by the Carinthian artist Urban Görtschacher; two paintings of *The Visitation* and *The Virgin Walking up to the Temple* (about 1515) by Max Reichlich.

★★**Barockmuseum** ⊙ – The prince's summer residence is a majestic setting for the Museum of Austrian Baroque Art, which gives an excellent idea of painting and sculpture in 18C Austria.

Three rooms make an outstanding impact during a visit to this museum, putting many of the works described here very much in the shade. First, the magnificent **Marmorgalerie**★ or great Marble Hall, which houses the originals of the sculptures on the **Neuer Markt fountain**★★ *(see Donner-Brunnen)*. It is an impressive ensemble. The ceiling frescoes (1716) by Martino Altomonte commemorate Prince Eugène's Triumph; the *trompe l'oeil* architectural paintings are by the Bolognese painters Gaetano Fanti and Marcantonio Chiarini, who also painted the bedroom frescoes. The second gem in this museum is the **Groteskensaal**★ or antechamber with grotesque paintings and its series of **grimacing faces**★★ which Franz Xaver Messerschmidt carved

from 1770 in an amazingly avant-garde spirit. This German sculptor created precisely 69 *Heads of Characters* (in lead or stone). There are 49 in the museum, and 7 of them in this room. According to tradition, the artist drew inspiration for these studies in physiognomy by grimacing in front of a mirror. According to another version, Messerschmidt avenged himself on people who mocked him at Court by depicting them with eccentric expressions. Another German artist, Jonas Drentwett, is responsible for the decoration of the room, which shows the influence of frescoes from ancient Rome and Pompeii (with allegories of the four seasons and four elements). Finally, the **Goldenkabinett**★★ or "conversation chamber" (originally the prince's bedroom) contains the **Apotheosis of Prince Eugène**★ (1718/22) by Balthasar Permoser, who painted himself at the feet of his model, who himself appears as Hercules treading on Envy. The room sparkles with mirrors and panelling of gilded wood adorned by Chinese porcelain.

Fotostudio Otto/Österreich Galerie

Grimacing Head
by Franz Xaver Messerschmidt

Naturally, many of the exhibits in the museum's other rooms deserve full attention. In room 1, *The Wrath of Samson* (about 1740) by Johann Georg Platzer. In room 2, *Empress Maria Theresa* and *Emperor Franz-Stefan* (about 1760) by F.X. Messerschmidt). In room 4, *Mourning for Abel* (1692) by Johann Michael Rottmayr, the pair to this painting *The Sacrifice of Isaac* is in the Landesmuseum in Graz; *The Lamentation* (about 1692) by Peter Strudel; *Susannah and the Elders* (1709) by Martino Altomonte. In room 5 or the "dining room", **Christ on the Mount of Olives**★ (about 1750) by Paul Troger, with typically Baroque sharp contrasts between light and shade; *Venus at Vulcan's Forge* (1768) and the *Judgment of King Midas* (1768) by Martin Johann Schmidt. In the marble cabinet, the marble statue of François Étienne of Lorraine as Emperor Franz I (between 1770 and 1780) by Balthasar Moll. In the small drawing room, bronze reliefs with classical themes by Georg Raphael Donner: *Venus at Vulcan's Forge* and *The Judgment of Paris* (about 1735).

Beyond the marble hall are other important works. In the bedroom are sculptures by G.R. Donner: *Apotheosis of Emperor Karl VI* (1734), *Hagar in the Desert* (1739), *Jesus and the Samaritan Woman* (1739). On the walls of the gallery hang *The Family of Count Nikolaus Pálffy* (1753) by Martin van Meytens, *Emperor Ferdinand I* (about 1750) by Franz Anton Palko and the imposing **Napoleon's Passage over the St Bernard Pass★** (1801) by Jacques-Louis David. In the passage is a *Self-portrait* (about 1767) by Franz Anton Maulbertsch. The second gallery displays works, including his **Views of Laxenburg★** (1758), by Johann Christian Brand, an important Austrian landscape painter of great influence on Martin von Molitor and Michael Wutky. The 7 niches in the Marmorgalerie used to contain 3 statues from Herculaneum, a gift to the prince in 1713 from the general in command of the imperial troops in Naples, as well as 4 statues by Domenico Parodi. After the prince's death, the antique statues were sold in Dresden and Parodi replaced them by 3 other sculptures.

Bundesgarten Belvedere ⊙ – The Parisian Dominique Girard, designed this French style garden at the beginning of the 18C. This pupil of Le Nôtre was a landscape architect, specialising in hydraulics. To link the two palaces, he laid down ramps and terraces adorned by sculptures, flower beds, groves, pools, fountains and waterfalls. As was usual at the time, the composition of the Belvedere gardens featured some esoterical symbols. The lower section concentrates on the Four Elements, the middle evokes Parnassus, and the upper part is an allegory of Olympus. In the upper part, there are sphinxes, mythical creatures with the head and breasts of a woman and the body of a lion. Those familiar with classical literature will recall that this animal challenged travellers on the road from Delphi to Thebes to solve a riddle. Those who did not know the answer were thrown into the sea. Oedipus' correct answer sent the sphinx hurtling into the deep in a fit of fury.

At the top of the garden, there is a splendid **view★** reminiscent of a Canaletto. It is obvious why the prince named the edifice "Belvedere".

★★OBERES BELVEDERE

Tram: Schloss Belvedere (D)

J.L. von Hildebrandt's Masterpiece – *See illustration in the Introduction, Architecture.* The Upper Belvedere is of a later date (1722) than the Lower Belvedere (1716). It was the setting for celebrations given by the prince and consists of seven buildings under one roof; those who have travelled beyond the Bosphorus will recognise the Oriental touch. The main façade stands south, and is therefore not the first one visible from the terraced gardens, as one arrives from the Lower Belvedere. The south side displays accentuated divisions, and a central building; the carriages of the prince of Savoy's guests used to pass through its three-arched gateway. They had to drive through the south gateway, which today faces Landstrasse Gürtel, and round the vast pool reflecting the palace. The wrought-iron **gate** is a sumptuous Baroque work by Arnold and Konrad Küffner. Attentive visitors will be able to decipher the "S" of the House of Savoy and the cross of its blazon.

Interior decoration – Visitors enter through the basement on the north side, since Ferdinand Hetzendorf von Hohenberg sealed the windows of the porch on the south façade, when Archduke Franz Ferdinand, Franz Josef's brother, lived in the Belvedere. With its 4 Telamones (Lorenzo Mattielli) and its stucco clad vaults (Santino Bussi), the **vestibule★** opens on the right into a room displaying **frescoes** by Carlo Carlone *(The Triumph of Aurora)*. Above the sweeping staircase is the *piano nobile* where the Grosser Marmorsaal, a vast red marble ballroom occupies the whole height of the central building. Its ceiling features a fresco by Carlo Leone representing the Glory of Prince Eugène. This immense room was the scene of the signing, on 15 May 1955, of the State Treaty which brought to an end the Allied occupation of Austria. The room contains a facsimile bearing the signatures of Figl, Dulles, McMillan, Molotov, Pinay, etc. From one of the rooms on the first floor, the chapel is visible with frescoes also by C. Carlone; the altarpiece represents the Resurrection, by Francesco Solimena (1723).

A "Shadow Cabinet" – Following Rudolf's suicide at Mayerling, Archduke **Franz Ferdinand**, now heir to the throne, moved to the Belvedere in 1897. It became the haunt of Romanians, Czech aristocrats, Croats, eminent civil servants or a man like Karl Lueger, founder of the Christian Socialist party, an anti-parliamentary and anti-semitic movement. This is an important detail for most Jews were loyal to the monarchy. Finally, Hungarians in favour of the dynasty frequented it, but no liberal Hungarians, because the heir apparent thought Hungary wielded too much power from its position within the Dual Monarchy. The palace was the Opposition's headquarters. An attentive but brutal observer, Franz Ferdinand was impatient for

View of the Oberes Belvedere

power. His case summarized Austria's situation at the beginning of the century: hesitations and contradictions in the face of lack of systematic government by the emperor. His dream of an Ottoman Austria came to an end in 1914 in Sarajevo, a town which Eugène of Austria had occupied in 1697.

The composer Anton Bruckner died in a building adjoining the palace on 11 October 1896.

★★Österreichische Galerie Belvedere ⊘ – *Prinz-Eugen-Strasse 27.* This gallery contains a large number of major works illustrating the principal trends in 19C and 20C Austrian and international painting. The Neue Galerie in the Stallburg is closed. Its collections of European, non-Austrian, art are now on view in the Upper Belvedere. Lovers of Klimt, Makart, Romako or Schiele will be in their element.

As is often the case in large museums, certain paintings are removed for restoration, others are on loan to outside exhibitions, and some rotation of the paintings occurs. This selection cannot take all these changes into account. Some works may not be on view during your visit.

Major works – On the ground floor: *The Buffoon*★ (Dobner), *The Tiger Lion*★ (Kokoschka). On the first floor: *Eve*★ (Rodin); *Path in Monet's Garden at Giverny*★★ (Monet); *After the Bath*★ (Renoir); *The Lady at the Harpsichord*★, *The Five Senses*★ (Makart); *Empress Elizabeth*★★, *Admiral Tegetthof at the Naval Battle of Lissa*★, *Mathilda Stern*★ (Romako); *Still Life with Blue Bottle, Sugar Bowl and Apples*★ (Ensor); *The Plain at Auvers*★ (Van Gogh); *The Kiss*★★★, *The Bride*★★, *Adam and Eve*★, *The Purple Hat*★ (Klimt); *Death and the Maiden*★★, *Four Trees*★★, *The Family*★ (Schiele); *Laughing Self Portrait*★ (Gerstl). On the 2nd floor, *Young Girl with Straw Hat*★ (Von Amerling), *Parlour game*★ (Von Schwind).

Ground Floor – The right wing is used for temporary exhibitions. The left wing begins with the museum bookshop, which precedes the section on "Post-1918 art". This includes various artists such as John Quincy Adams *(Luise Eismer,* 1923), Max Beckmann *(Young Woman Reclining with Irises,* 1931), Oskar Kokoschka *(Mother and Child Embracing,* 1922; *Prague,* 1923; *The Tiger Lion,* 1926), Anton Kolig

(Portrait of the Artist's Wife with Flowers, 1913; *The Artists's Family*, 1928), Oskar Laske, Max Oppenheimer *(The Philharmonic)*.

There are also sculptures such as *Mrs H. Levy* (1923) by Charles Despiau, *The Buffoon* (1926) by Josef Dobner, and *Head of a Young Man* (1934) by Franz Hagenauer.

First floor — After coming up the staircase and entering the red marble hall, one sees on the left the "Historicism, Realism, Impressionism" section, and on the right the "Art about 1900" section. In chronological order, the tour begins with the section on the left.

The first room contains *The Judgment of Paris* (1887) by Max Klinger and *The Bad Mothers* (1894) by Giovanni Segantini, and two fine sculptures: *Eve* (1881) by Auguste Rodin, and *The Triumph of Venus* (1916) by Auguste Renoir. The next two rooms display fine Impressionist paintings by Edgar Degas, *Woman Emerging from her Bath* (1896-1911), Edouard Manet, *Lady with Fur* (about 1880), Claude Monet, *Path in Monet's Garden at Giverny* (1902), A. Renoir *After the bath* (1876), Camille Pissaro, *The Road to Gisors at Pontoise* (1894), as well as works by Carl Moll, *The Naschmarkt in Vienna* (1894) and Karl Schuch.

Born in Salzburg in 1840, **Hans Makart** died at the height of his glory 44 years later. His historical paintings ensured him rapid fame. However it is his portraits and monumental compositions that linger in the memory, conveying the society of the Ringstrasse. He organised on this street the famous silver wedding procession of the imperial couple, riding at its head on a white horse and wearing a wide-brimmed plumed hat.

His masterpiece is a painting which seems small in comparison to his usual monumental compositions which earned him the nickname of "prince of painters". This is *The Lady at the Harpsichord* (1871). *The Five Senses* (1872/79) form part of a series, from which 4 allegorical paintings are on view (smell, sight, hearing, touch). These reveal the admiration which Makart felt for Titian. *The Triumph of Ariadne* (1873): this huge painting is a project for a theatre curtain.

After a start as a historical painter, **Anton Romako** (1832-1889) worked in the shadow of Makart's success and developed a highly personal style, without any imitators or pupils. After the suicide of his two daughters in Rome, he died in tragic circumstances. His work was often not appreciated.

The *View of Gastein Valley I* (1877) forms part of a splendid series of 5 views. *Admiral Tegetthof at the Naval Battle of Lissa I* (1878/80): this oil painting on wood marked the painter's break with 19C historical painting, the theme of the hero has disappeared. *Empress Elizabeth* (1883): nobody can say for sure whether this is an example of Mannerism, irony, or dreamlike projection, but the portrait exudes a sense of unreality unique in a Court portrait. *Danse Macabre* (1882/85): a paint-

BILDAGENTUR BUENOS DIAS

The Kiss by Gustav Klimt

ing which is very close to Ensor's art. *Countess Maria Magda Kuefstein* (1886): halfway between an exact rendering and a sketch, this portrait is a surprising psychological study. *Mathilda Stern* (1886): this is as psychological as the preceding work and also shows an ambiguity characteristic of Romako.

The two last rooms in this section display works of diverse tendencies, such as the *Puddler* (1890) by Constantin Meunier, *Sancho Panza Resting under a Tree* (1860/70) by Honoré Daumier, *The Wounded Man* (about 1854) by Gustave Courbet, *Still Life with Blue Bottle, Sugar Bowl and Apples* (about 1880) by James Ensor, and the lascivious *Ensa* by Leopold Karl Müller. The red marble hall leads to the second section on this floor. The first room houses: *The Plain at Auvers* (1890) by Vincent Van Gogh; *Interior* (1907) by Egon Schiele; *Twilight* (1900) by Karl Moll; *Project for a Monument to Victor Hugo* (about

Empress Elizabeth by Anton Romako

Fotostudio Otto/Österreich Galerie

1886) and a bust of Gustav Mahler (1909) by A. Rodin. In the next rooms are: *Portrait of a Woman in Profile* (about 1910) by Kolo Moser; *Bettina Bauer* and *Mira Bauer* (1908) by Max Kurzweil; *Vivien* (1896) by the leading Belgian Symbolist painter, Fernand Khnopff; *Crouching Woman* (1900/01) by Max Klinger; *Young Man Kneeling* (1900) by George Minne.

The Viennese **Gustav Klimt** (1862-1918) has acquired a reputation as a "painter of women" or as the "Messiah" of the Secession. The characters he paints in a naturalistic manner often display angular bodies on an abstract surface. His painting which is erotic in form is sensual in substance.
Youthful works such as *Helen Klimt* (1898), *Portrait of Sonia Knips* (1898) and *Farm with Birches* (1900) give way to the creations of maturity. *Judith I* (1901): this Old Testament figure has undergone a metamorphosis, the master depicts her as a *femme fatale* expressing the frustration of the Viennese middle class. *Adele Bloch-Bauer I and II* (1907 and 1912): portrait I evokes the mosaics of Ravenna which Klimt first saw in 1903; the second portrait is of the frontal type typical of this painter. *The Kiss* (1907/08): even if there is little left to say about this work and although reproductions of it are arguably too numerous (leaflets, posters, postcards), the drawing and the contrast in the decoration still suggest passionate desire. *The Violet Hat* (1909) is a remarkable painting, and the biblical theme of *Adam and Eve* (1917) is an unusual choice for Klimt. *The Bride* (1918): an unfinished work exemplifying the transition from sketch to painting.
Also noteworthy are the 8 paintings in the same format, such as *Avenue in Schloss Kammer Park* (about 1912).

Born in 1890 in Tulln, in south Austria, **Egon Schiele** died in Vienna in 1918. After a period inspired by Klimt, he soon broke away from it, depicting bodies swamped in elaborate decoration which in Klimt's work was marginal to his figures. His work consists mainly of studies of models and self portraits (about a hundred), hence the description of his painting as "narcissistic".

Sunflowers I (1911): *this belongs to his series of anthropomorphic plants. Death and the Maiden* (1915): this extraordinary painting expresses his grief for Wally Neuzil, his favourite model and companion, from whom he parted to marry Edith Harms and who died of scarlet fever two years later. The dark man is a self portrait of Schiele and the young woman's hands are holding on by only one finger. *Woman with Two Children* (1915/17): longing for a family, Schiele here contrasts luminous colours with the melancholy of the faces. *Four Trees* (1917): this painting is one of his typical desolate and expressionist landscapes (one of the four trees has shed all its leaves), but this late work displays a warmer range of colours. *The Family* (1918): this last major painting is surprisingly realist in comparison to its predecessors. This portrayal of motherhood is Schiele's last work.

The first floor tour of late 19C and early 20C art ends with *Still Life with Lamb and Hyacinth* and *Portrait of the Artist's Mother* (1917) by Oskar Kokoschka, *Joseph Relating his Dreams* (1910) by Emil Nolde, *Woman against a Blue Background* (about 1908) by Alexei Jawlensky, *The Klinger Quartet* (1916) by Max Oppenheimer, *Fantastic Still Life* by James Ensor (about 1917) and *Laughing Self Portrait* (1908) by Richard Gerstl, a very solitary painter who committed suicide at 25 without ever having exhibited his works.

Second floor – *Closed at present*. Coming up the staircase, one sees on the right the "Classicism and Romanticism" section and on the left the "Biedermeier" section. History, mythology and religion: Friedrich Heinrich Füger *(Death of Germanicus)*, Johannes Peter Krafft *(Emperor Franz I's Entrance after the Treaty of Paris, 6 June 1814)*, Moritz von Schwind (*Parlour game, King of the Alders*, about 1830), Leopold Kupelwieser *(Journey of the Magi*, 1825).
Landscapes: Ferdinand Georg Waldmüller *(Panoramic View of the Prater*, 1849), Karl Blechen, Rudolf von Alt *(St Stephen's Cathedral from Stock-im-Eisen*, 1832), Kaspar David Friedrich *(Seaside in the Mist*, about 1807; *Rocky Landscape in Elbsandsteingebirge*, about 1822/23), Friedrich Gauermann *(Landscape near Miesenbach*, about 1830), Josef Anton Koch, Josef Rebell, Ludwig Ferdinand Schnorr von Carosfeld *(Large Pine near Mödling*, 1838), Franz Steinfeld, the poet Adalbert Stifter *(View of Vienna's City Suburbs*, 1839).
Portraits: Friedrich von Amerling *(Young Girl with a Straw Hat, Rudolf von Arthaber and his Children*, 1857), Moritz Michael Daffinger, Franz Eybl, Friedrich Heinrich Füger, François Gérard *(The Family of Count Moritz von Fries)*, Angelika Kauffmann, Johann Baptist Lampi the Elder, Ferdinand Georg Waldmüller *(Large Group of the Eltz Family)*.
Genre paintings: F.G. Waldmüller, *(Peasant Wedding at Perchtoldsdorf)*, Josef Danhauser *(Debauched Man)*, Peter Fendi *(Inquisitive Woman*, 1833), Friedrich Amerling *(The Fisherman's Son)*, Michael Neder *(The Coachman's Dispute)*, Karl Spitzweg, Karl Schindler.
Still life: F.G. Waldmüller, Franz Xaver Petter, Josef Lauer, Johann Knap.

EXCURSIONS AROUND THE BELVEDERE

Besides the Salesianerinnenkirche *(see below)*, there are some attractive sights on Rennweg. **Hoyos Palace** (No 3), the present Yugoslav embassy, is the work of Otto Wagner (1891). It is easy to recognize the Historicism, typical of this famous architect's early career and the decorative Rococo elements. At the corner of Rennweg and Auenbruggergasse (No 2) is the house where Gustav Mahler lived from 1898 to 1909, opposite the **Garde Kirche** (1763) by Nikolaus Pacassi, the former church of the Polish guard; it is now the parish church for the Polish community, attracting a large congregation every Sunday beneath its flat ribbed cupola.

Salesianerinnenkirche (**LS**) – *Rennweg. Tram: Unteres-Belvedere (71)*. A splendid gateway precedes the church of the Salesian Convent by the Italian architect Donato Felice d'Allio (1717-1730), with a dome soaring to 48m/157 ft. Its proportions are harmonious, particularly those of the façade completed by Josef Emmanuel Fischer von Erlach. However, it lacks the Baroque force of many of the city's churches.

Botanischer Garten – *Rennweg 14. Tram: Rennweg (71)*. Empress Maria Theresa founded the Botanic Gardens in 1754 with the assistance of her physician Gerhard van Swieten, to create a reserve of medicinal plants for Vienna University. Disappointed in herbal medicine, she had it turned into a botanic garden by Nikolaus von Jacquin. It now contains 9,000 species of plant and is a pleasant setting for a stroll.
In the upper section, a small gate links it to a garden dedicated to the cultivation of rare alpines *(Alpengarten)*.

Museum des 20. Jahrhunderts (**FV**) ⓧ – *Schweizergarten. Tram: Südbahnhof (D), Wildgansplatz (18)*; *bus: Südbahnhof (13A), Fernmelde-zentrum (69A)*; *train: Südbahnhof (S1, S2, S3, S15)*. There are two museums of modern, contemporary art in Vienna *(see also Museum Moderner Kunst)*. The Museum of the 20C houses temporary exhibitions of non-figurative work (sculpture and painting).
Karl Schwanzer constructed the building for the 1958 World Fair in Brussels. The Austrian pavillion was dismantled and reassembled in Schweizergarten. The ground floor is closed to meet the needs of its present purpose.
Entrance tickets give access to the park which displays works by Alberto Giacometti, Marino Marini, Henry Moore and Fritz Wotruba.

★**Heeresgeschichtliches Museum** (**GV**) ⏱ – *Arsenalstrasse. Tram: Südbahnhof (18,D); bus: Südbahnhof (13A, 69A); train: Südbahnhof (S1, S2, S3, S15)*. The Museum of Military History lies at the heart of the Arsenal, a pseudo-medieval fortress (1852/56) by Theophil von Hansen, one of the future pioneers of the Ring, and Ludwig Forster. Franz Josef commissioned the building one year after the 1848 revolution, when Metternich went into exile and the Court took refuge in Innsbruck. Of a Gothic-Byzantine-Moorish style, the museum is only one of 31 edifices in this Babylonian barracks; the building is undeniably the precursor of the Historicism which dominated the Ring. The museum traces the military history of the Habsburgs, from the end of the 16C until 1918.

To view the exhibits in chronological order, one enters through the **generals' room** leading up to the first floor. This three-naved neo-Gothic room houses statues of the most famous generals of the Empire.

From the Thirty Years' War (1618-1648) to Prince Eugène of Savoy – *First floor, left of the Hall of Fame.* In this section are numerous weapons (halberds, lances, muskets, armour), documents signed by Wallenstein and Tilly, 12 battle scenes by the painter Pieter Snayers, the **seal of Sultan Mustapha II**, the red standard of Prince Eugène of Savoy's 13th Dragoon regiment, as well as his breastplate, **Marshal's baton** and the funeral altar cloth for his Requiem Mass, in St Stephen's cathedral (Stephansdom).

The 18C (until 1790) – The room consists of 3 sections. The first covers the period from 1700 to 1740: on display are numerous standards and a pen-and-ink lifesize drawing (1700) by the future Karl VI of a cannon barrel *(below the window)*, the **tent of an Ottoman prince**★ and the **Belgrade mortar bomb** which caused the explosion of the powder magazine of that city during the Turkish occupation of 1717. Section 2 covers Maria Theresa's reign, the time of the War of Austrian Succession and the Seven Years' War (1756-1763): a showcase contains the "Albertina Manuscript", with a series of watercolour drawings (copies) from it illustrating the uniforms of the imperial and royal army from 1762; an oil painting depicts Marshal Count Daun who defeated the Prussians at Kolin in 1757. The third section deals with the reign of Josef II: *Field Marshal Gideon Ernst Freiherr von Laudon* is a major work (1878) by Sigmund L'Allemand representing the man who defeated Friedrich II at Kunersdorf and captured many standards.

Return to the Hall of Fame and cross the whole of the other wing on the 1st floor.

The Austro-French Wars (1792-1815) – There are many exhibits of interest, including flags, paintings by Johann Peter Krafft, the original model of the *Aspern Lion* by A.D. Fernkorn *(see Donaustadt)*, the Russian general Schuwalow's greatcoat which Napoleon wore to conceal his identity when he left Fontainebleau for exile on the island of Elba in 1814, the **Hercules balloon**★ captured at the battle of Würzburg on 3 September 1796; this montgolfier or hot-air balloon belonged to the first French aeronautical company and served for reconnaissance missions.

Archduke Karl Room – Anton Dominik Fernkorn is the sculptor of the statue of Napoleon's famous adversary; it is a replica of another statue of the victor of Aspern (1809), which is in Heldenplatz. The room also contains some family portraits (Johann Ender).

Radetzky Room – Marshal von Radetzky was governor of Lombardy and Minister of War. He distinguished himself by fighting the nationalist movements in Italy. Johann Strauss the Elder dedicated a famous march to him; it bears his name. There are many mementoes of him in this room.

Franz Josef Room – His equestrian portrait (1856) by Franz Adam dominates this section.

Sarajevo

A member of a secret society "the Black Hand", the Serb nationalist Gavrilo Princip shot the heir to the Austro-Hungarian Empire on 28 June 1914. **Franz Ferdinand** was visiting Sarajevo, and was aware that he ran a risk of assassination. As soon as they received news of the archduke's death, General Konrad and the War Minister, Krobatin decided to attack Serbia in a localized conflict; in actual fact, they wished to destroy the Serbian state which had become a threat since the Balkan wars of 1912-13. Assured of German support, Franz Josef approved their decision.

Events quickly came to a head. Austria declared war on Serbia on 28 July after the Austrian ultimatum had been rejected. Franz Josef had pulled the first thread in a complex tapestry of alliances and compromise which would rapidly unravel, triggering off the First World War.

Go down to the ground floor and bear left after the generals' room.

Franz Ferdinand and Sarajevo – Uniforms and objects from all nationalities of the Empire precede the Sarajevo room. This Bosnian city was the scene of the assassination of Archduke Franz Ferdinand and his wife Sophia Chotek *(see inset)*. The **car** in the tragedy is on display (one can see the impact of the bullet through the body-work of the Graef & Stift vehicle), together with the archduke's bloodstained uniform. A photographic report of the tragic event is visible in a corner of the room. The assassin, Gavrilo Princip, died in a Bohemian cell on 28 April 1918. He had been kept in chains throughout the world war which he had precipitated by pressing the trigger of his revolver.

The car in which the royal couple were assassinated in Sarajevo

Heeresgeschichtliches Museum

The End of the Empire and World War One – The most interesting items include pieces of heavy artillery, particularly a 38cm/15in canon and an Albatross B1 plane (1914).

Return to the generals' room and continue into the other wing.

The Navy Room – It may surprise some to learn that Austria was once a great naval power. Since the end of the 14C, Trieste and its port had belonged to the Empire, which extended to the Venetian and Dalmatian coasts at the beginning of the 19C. There are numerous scale models on view; of special interest is the 1:25 **model of a section of the Viribus Unitis★** (7m/23 ft), a ship which sailed the Mediterranean during World War One.

St. Marxer Friedhof (**CZ**) – *Leberstrasse 6-8. Tram: Litfassstrasse (71, 72); bus: Hofmannsthalgasse (74A).* On 6 December 1791, the remains of the musical prodigy were moved from the mortuary in Rauhensteingasse *(see Around Stephansdom)* to the cathedral *(see Stephansdom)* where the coffin received bene-diction. Then, owing to the severe weather, the forlorn cortège entered the tiny St Mark's cemetery, unaccompanied by Salieris or Van Swietens. Mozart was buried in a common grave, from which Austria can never recover the remains of its most illustrious son.

Today, Mozart's cenotaph is in Zentralfriedhof *(see under this heading)*, but St Mark's cemetery is noteworthy because of the supposed site of Mozart's grave.

★**Wiener Strassenbahnmuseum** (**CY M³**) ⊘ – *Erdbergstrasse 109. Entrance: Ludwig-Koessler-Platz. Underground: Schlachthausgasse (U3); tram: Schlacht-hausgasse (18, 72); bus: Erdbergstrasse (79A); Ludwig-Koessler-Platz (80A); Schlachthausgasse (78A, 80B, 83A, 84A).* This tram museum opened in 1922 and has recently undergone restoration. It is the largest of its kind in the world and is the home of the Viennese tram, with its red and white livery representing the city. It contains a full documentation on the development of public transport in Vienna (technical information, photographs, etc.), and also about a hundred trams and buses, in excellent condition and often restored. The horsedrawn trams are par-ticularly attractive; they disappeared after the invention of the overhead trolley by the German Siemens and the Belgian Van de Poele.

This museum organises trips in vintage vehicles *(see Practical Information)*.

Haus Wittgenstein (**GU**) ⊘ – *Kundmanngasse 19. Entrance: Parkgasse 18. Un-derground: Rochusgasse (U3); bus: Geusaugasse (4A).* The philosopher built this house in 1929 for his sister, Gretl, with the assistance of Paul Engelmann. Draw-ing direct inspiration from Adolf Loos' theories, the building is of a somewhat dry modernistic style. This exercise in minimalism was a reaction to Biedermeier Neo-classicism. Since 1975, the building has been the home of the Bulgarian Embassy. Temporary exhibitions are held there.

Ludwig Wittgenstein – Born in Vienna in 1889, he studied in Berlin, Manchester and Cambridge where he became Professor of Philosophy in 1929. Two phrases from his work *Tractatus* (1921) summarize Wittgenstein's philosophy: "To signify what cannot be said by presenting clearly what can be said" and "Whereof one cannot speak, thereof one must be silent". He had a large following in English-speaking countries and influenced philosophers of the Vienna Circle and the analytical School. He died of cancer in Cambridge in 1951.

Hundertwasserhaus (**GU F**) – *Kegelgasse 36-38, at the corner of Löwengasse. Closed to the public.* A painter and a cosmopolitan engraver, **Friedensreich Hundertwasser** started work in Paris. However, it was in Vienna that he expressed his conception of housing in a creation repudiating any form of architectural conformity. The city of Vienna sponsored this residential complex commissioned by the former mayor, Leopold Gratz; it was completed in 1985.

It avoids the monotony of conventional housing estates through the use of varied motifs, a wide range of materials (glass, brick, ceramic, roughcast of a different colour for each apartment), and sloping terraces laid out as hanging gardens. This example of low-income housing met with criticism in Vienna and praise abroad. It comprises 50 apartments and always attracts a large number of visitors and lovers of architecture. According to

Ch. Bastin et J. Évrard

Hundertwasserhaus

F. Hundertwasser, its design encourages a creative spirit and enables the individual to live in harmony with his environment. Two golden onion domes surmount the edifice, because "a Byzantine belltower on a house raises its occupant to the status of a king".

KunstHaus Wien (**GU G**) ⊘ – *Untere Weissgerberstrasse 13.* Also by F. Hundertwasser, this building consists of two sections, one of which houses a collection of works of art illustrating the diversity and originality of the artist: paintings, engravings, plans and models. Temporary exhibitions are staged in the other half of the museum.

The nearest sights are: the Ring and the Fleischmarkt District, in the town centre, the Karlsplatz and Prater Districts, as well as Favoriten and the central cemetery (Zentralfriedhof).

*The **Practical information** section at the end of the guide lists:*
– information on travel, motoring, accommodation, recreation;
– local or national organisations providing additional information;
– the calendar of events;
– admission times and charges for the sights described in the guide.

The 21st District (Floridsdorf) extends over the eastern section of the city; Donaustadt sometimes bears the name of "Transdanubia". It is still alive with the memory of the conflict between Napoleon and Archduke Karl. The silhouette of U.N. City dominates Donaustadt, a modern urban landscape which has nevertheless retained many areas of greenery.

Donauinsel – *Underground – Donauinsel (U1); tram: Floridsdorfer Brücke/ Donauinsel (31, 32). The Tourist Information Centres have a leaflet describing the tourist attractions in the island.* Danube Island arose after the creation of the supplementary New Danube canal. Straddling the 21st and 22nd Districts, Donauinsel is a narrow strip of land covering 700 hectares/1,729 acres and 21km/13 miles long. It specialises solely in **recreation activities**, except when the river is in spate.

The north end has everything to attract anyone going for a stroll, and also swimmers (beaches), devotees of water sports (pedalos, motor boats, windsurfing schools, yachting), cyclists *(access by the cycle path on Floridsdorf bridge)* and joggers (trim course).

The central and southern sections also boast numerous beaches; however, they are more popular *(access by Reichsbrücke and Praterbrücke)* with keen cyclists (mountain bike trails and cycle race track), roller skaters and even divers (one school) or fishermen *(permit compulsory)*. There is also water skiing and canoeing. The southern part of the island is a protected area and has a nature reserve harbouring fauna in the reeds on the river banks.

★**UNO-City** – *Underground: Kaisermühlen-Vienna International Centre (U1).* Since August 1979, Vienna has been the third city of the United Nations, after New York and Geneva. UNO City is also known as the Vienna International Centre.

UNO – The United Nations Organisation was founded by 51 states in San Francisco, on 26 June 1945. It consists of several autonomous bodies linked to UNO and generally active in the field of international cooperation. The two most important institutions in this huge political structure are the Security Council for the maintenance of peace, with restricted membership, and the General Assembly, which comprises all members (184 in 1993). The organisation also possesses an economic and social Council, which is active in the domains of economy, culture, education and public health. The former president of the Austrian Republic, Kurt Waldheim, was secretary general of UNO from 1972 to 1981.

UNO in Vienna (UNOV) – UNO employs 3,500 people from over 100 different countries. In the Austrian capital, there are: IAEA, International Atomic Energy Agency, with its head office in Vienna since 1956; UNIDO, United Nations Industrial Development Organisation, with its head office in Vienna since 1967; SCDHA, Social Centre for the Development of Humanitarian Affairs; UNCITRAL, United Nations Commission on International Trade Law; UNRWA, United Nations Relief and Works

B. Kaufmann

UNO-City

Agency for Palestinian refugees in the Near East; UNDPC, United Nations Development Programme for the international control of drugs; UNDP, United Nations Development Programme.

Buildings – The vast complex between the New Danube supplementary canal and the meander of the Old Danube comprises 3 buildings with concave façades arranged in a star shape; each consists of two double towers with a section forming a Y, around a circular building. The architect of this complex (1973 to 1979) is an Austrian, Johann Staber. It belongs to the Austrian state who rents it for 99 years for the symbolic sum of 1 schilling a year.

The site covers a surface of 180,000m²/215,262sq yds and the towers have a cubic capacity of 1,000,000m³/1,307,950cu yds; the façades are covered by 70,000m²/83,719sq yds of metal and 63,000m²/75,347sq yds of glass (there are 24,000 windows); 58 lifts are in operation, including 15 for documents and goods; 6,000 doors open into 80,000m²/95,679sq yds of offices, etc.

Next to UNO City is an international congress centre, Austria Centre Vienna. It dates from 1987 and numbers 14 conference and congress halls with seating for 9,500 people. It is also an exhibition centre.

Tour ⏱ – *Guided tour only (1 hour), in several languages.* This traces the history of UNO and describes the activities of all departments in Vienna, with the help of an audio-visual presentation.

★ **Donaupark** – In 1964, a former rubbish dump became the site for the international flower show. Next to UNO City, the Danube park is today the second largest public park in the city, covering 100 hectares – 247 acres; it is also one of the most attractive. A small train carries visitors round the gardens and the artificial lake, Irissee.

The park's main attraction is the **Donauturm** (Danube tower) which, at 252m/826ft, is the tallest building in Vienna. There are two fast lifts to the panoramic platform 165m/541ft from the ground and to two restaurants. From this revolving terrace it is possible to enjoy a 360° panoramic view which takes 26min, 39min or 52min to complete. The **view**★★ is magnificent.

From Aspern to Wagram

Causes of the conflict – 1808: The French Empire had never extended so far, from Hamburg to Naples, from the Vistula to Lisbon. In Paris, the Austrian ambassador had bellicose intentions and encouraged the "party of war" at the Viennese Court. His name was Metternich; in 1814, Napoleon wrote to his brother Joseph: "Do not trust this man".

Undoubtedly, Emperor Franz wished to erase the humiliations of Austerlitz. In Vienna, the party of war, with the support of Stadion, prevailed over the party of peace which had the support of Archduke Karl. Without declaring war, the Austrian armies mobilised in April 1809 (against Bavaria, Italy and Poland). Aware of the situation, Napoleon marched upon Germany, then Vienna, in short from the Rhine to the Danube.

Napoleon's first setback... – Four years after the first occupation of Vienna by the French, Napoleon entered the Habsburg capital once again on 12 May 1809 to suppress the Austrian uprising. On 20 May, after the construction of numerous pontoon bridges, since the enemy had destroyed every means of crossing the Danube, Masséna's 24,000 men positioned themselves on Lobau island, between the villages of **Aspern** and **Essling**. For his part, Archduke Karl had 95,000 men posted nearby; a French cavalry brigade reconnoitring as far as Raasdorf failed to notice them! The following day, Archduke Karl with 200 artillery units, made a surprise attack on the French emperor. Although they drove Masséna from Aspern, he remained in control of Essling. On 22 May, Oudinot came to reinforce Masséna; the French troops then numbered about 32,000, far less than the Austrians. Archduke Karl was exceptionally well informed on his opponents' position. He personally took part in the surprise attack in retaliation to Napoleon's vast offensive; his forces surrounded and cut off the French army from the pontoon bridge floating on the Danube in spate, which had served to supply the three divisions taking part. The Emperor had to retreat at 2 p.m., while the Young Guard pointlessly recaptured Essling, which had been lost. A cannonball wounded Marshall Lannes, Duke of Montebello, in the knees and he died as a result of the amputation. The Austrians lost 23,000 men, while Napoleon lost 21,000, including Oudinot, Saint-Hilaire and General Lassalle who was fond of saying that "a hussard who was not dead by thirty was nothing but a jackass!".

Opposite Aspern church, one may see today the *Aspern Lion*: wounded by a sword, the animal crushes the arms of France. This sculpture by Anton Dominik Fernkorn commemorates the 50th anniversary of an Austrian victory, which represented a check to Napoleon's advance. The German speaking and Anglo-Saxon public know it as the battle of Aspern, while French speakers call it the battle of Essling.

... followed by yet another victory – Defeat was psychological rather than military. In addition, failure was of short duration, since Archduke Karl and Napoleon met again on 5 and 6 July at **Wagram**, 4km/2.5 miles northeast of present-day Vienna, on the borders of the Marchfeld area. Despite diversionary tactics by the British at Walcheren and in Portugal, the Emperor inflicted a crushing defeat on the Austrians. Napoleon also imposed draconian terms on them: loss of Istria, Carinthia, Carniola and Trieste, which was a centre of contraband. At the end of the battle, Berthier, Prince of Neuchâtel, was created Prince of Wagram, and Masséna Prince of Essling.

The nearest sights are in the Prater District.

FAVORITEN✠

10th District

Map page 3, **BCZ**

Underground, tram and bus: details next to each sight

The 10th District lies south of the urban area, beyond Wieden as one comes from the town centre. Like its neighbours Simmering and Meidling, it is mainly a working class area.

Amalienbad – *Reumannplatz 23. Underground: Reumannplatz (U1); tram: Quellenstrasse/Favoritenstrassse (6); bus: Reumannplatz (14A).* This public bath complex can accommodate over 1,000 people. It forms part of the great architectural achievements of Austro-Marxist Vienna in the 1920s, known as Vienna the Red. The City architects, Otto Nadel and Karl Schmalhofer, built it between 1923 and 1926. At the time, it was among the most modern and largest in Europe. A visitor could, and still can, enjoy saunas, therapeutic baths, a swimming pool with a 30m/32yd long glass roof which on a fine day is opened in 4 minutes. The ceramics and mosaics decorating 2 small circular hot water baths transport the viewer straight into the Jugendstil era; it is a sight not to be missed for anyone visiting Amalienbad.

After suffering damage at the end of World War Two, the establishment underwent restoration and acquired another large pool in 1986.

Spinnerin am Kreuz – *Triesterstrasse. Tram: Windtenstrasse (65).* This late-Gothic medieval column (1452) is the work of Johann Puschbaum, the architect of the cathedral's Adlerturm. It marked the city's southern boundary, and therefore the end of the safe area of the city, at a point where, according to legend, a woman spent years waiting for her husband's return from the Crusades. This woman spent her time at her spinning wheel, spinning wool, hence the name of the column: "column of the spinner by the Cross". The reality was less romantic; it was the site for public executions.

At the Historisches Museum der Stadt Wien (Historical Museum of the City of Vienna), one can see a painting of the site at the beginning of the last century. This provides a good opportunity to see how much urbanisation has encroached, as everywhere else, upon the surrounding countryside.

3 BIS/MICHELIN

The Amalienbad swimming pool

George-Washington-Hof – *Unter-Meidlingerstrasse 1 to 12.* Next to Spinnerin am Kreuz is a housing estate typical of 1920s Vienna. Karl Krist and Robert Oerley built it between 1927 and 1930. It comprises 1,085 apartments divided between 5 blocks of buildings in the midst of gardens. At the time of their completion, these buildings bore the name of "neighbourhood units", a concept which has to be seen in the historical context of working-class Vienna after the dismembering of the Empire.

Wasserturm – *Windtenstrasse 3.* In the street at right angles to Triesterstrasse, near Spinnerin am Kreuz, this 19C red brick water tower displays a corbelled silhouette with a roof of polychrome tiles. Its purpose was to supply the capital with drinking water from the Alps. It closed in 1910. It now houses temporary exhibitions which afford an opportunity of seeing the pumps still in place.

Kurzentrum Oberlaa ⊙ – *Kurbadstrasse 14. Tram: Kurzentrum Oberlaa (67).* The Oberlaa thermal centre is a reminder that Vienna is also a spa. It lies at the southern tip of the district, not far from Zentralfriedhof. In 1934, oil prospectors found sulphurous waters on the site. The water is harnessed at a depth of 418m/1,371ft and reaches the surface at a temperature of 54° C – 138°F. Treatment is mainly for people with rheumatism, back pain and sciatica, as well as fracture patients. This convalescent and physiotherapy centre is open to the public and people often come in family groups to use the 4 swimming pools, saunas and jacuzzis.

Kurpark – This vast park to the north of the establishment is a pleasant place for walks, with about 25km/15 miles of footpaths, children's play areas and sports facilities. In the 1920s, this park was a location for filming the great Austrian productions.

The nearest sights are in the Landstrasse (Belvedere area), Liesing, Simmering (Zentralfriedhof), and Wieden (Karlsplatz area) Districts.

GRINZING District★★

Döbling – 19th District
Local map pages 2-3, **ABX**

The Döbling area is extensive, but little known to those who do not live in Vienna. It includes two districts with internationally famous names: Heiligenstadt, immortalized by Ludwig van Beethoven's will of the same name, and Grinzing famous for its vineyards.

The district has been divided into three, with directions indicating modes of transport for visiting each section from the centre of the town. It is however possible to visit all three sections successively by following the directions printed in italics. In this case, it is advisable to begin the itinerary with the diverse sights in Heiligenstadt, then go to Grinzing, the hillsides of Kahlenberg and Leopoldsberg and back to the city via Oberdöbling.

★HEILIGENSTADT

Underground: Heiligenstadt (U4) – Tram: Halteraugasse (D) – Train: Heiligenstadt (S40)

This old wine-growing village has been part of Döbling since 1892. One hundred years earlier, it had only three streets. Today, it consists of a lower urbanised section and an upper residential quarter. The area is pleasantly remote from the bustle audible along the Danube Canal, as one arrives from the centre of Vienna.
If the weather is fine, visitors in light-hearted mood may deviate from the tour and explore the Nussdorf vineyards *(see Introduction, Living in Vienna)*, a region less popular with tourists than Grinzing. It is a good opportunity for walking in Beethovengang *(see below, Beethoven the bucolic)*, alongside a brook, past Lehár-Schikaneder Villa *(Hackhofergasse 18)*. As its name suggests, past owners included Emanuel Schikaneder, librettist of *Die Zauberflöte (The Magic Flute)* and director of the Theater An der Wien, then, from 1932, the Hungarian composer Franz Lehár.

★**Karl-Marx-Hof** – *Heiligenstädterstrasse 82 to 92.* Facing the exit from the underground is the immense "red fortress". Vienna's Austro-Marxist council in power from 1919 to 1934 opened it on 12 October 1930 *(see Introduction, Architecture)*. This monumental ensemble is the most famous *Hof* of this period in the capital and it is known to architectural students throughout the world. It was built between 1927 and 1930 by Karl Ehn, a pupil of Otto Wagner, who was director of planning services in 1922. This "stronghold" numbers about 1,400 apartments for approximately 5,000 people. It comprised cooperative groceries, central laundries, kindergartens, a dental clinic, an infirmary and a workers' library. The complex lies on a long narrow stretch of land with an area of 156,000m²/186,574sq yds; buildings occupy 20% of it, while the rest is for garden areas. It is a striking display of archways over passages between courtyards and gardens, sculptures (Joseph Riedl) over the arches, blue flagpoles from which banners fluttered, and the red and ochre contrasting colour scheme of the rough-cast. The whole effect has led people to define it as proletarian *Ringstil*. Such critics may be correct from the point of view of form. However, they forget to mention that in Karl-Marx-Hof, just as in the similar Karl-Seitz-Hof (built by Hubert Gessner in Floridsdorf), there is no lift. Moreover, the largest 3 room apartment measures 60m²/71sq yds in total. This is a far cry from Ringstrasse.

During the three-day civil war which broke out in Vienna in 1934, militants from the Republikanischer Schutzbund retreated to communal dwellings, including Karl-Marx-Hof, 1km/0.5 mile long. Chancellor Engelbert Dollfuss ordered the army to dislodge them by force. According to official figures, there were 314 dead; the Social-Democrats, on the other hand, stated there were 1,500 victims and over 5,000 wounded. Bloodshed confirmed the nickname Red Vienna, which the city had gained because of its ideology. In 1938, the Austro-Fascist regime renamed the site Heiligenstädter-Hof, added a chapel and doubled the rent. In 1977, Karl-Marx-Hof became a historic monument. It is now a cultural tourist attraction, of artistic and historical interest.

Take bus 38A to Februar Platz (opposite the underground station) and alight at the Fernsprechamt Heiligenstadt stop. Walk back up Grinzingerstrasse and turn right into Nestelbachgasse to reach Pfarrplatz.

Karl-Marx-Hof

3 BIS/MICHELIN

St. Jakobskirche ⊙ – *Pfarrplatz 3*. This church has often been rebuilt on Roman and early Christian foundations. It has a simple façade of brick and rubble stone. In the interior, the left wall with 16C stained-glass windows displays a niche containing a relic of St Severin. In 1952, excavations revealed 2C Roman remains as well as a burial place and baptismal font dating from the 5C. It is now certain that the saint, who died on 8 January 482, was buried here fifteen centuries ago. Although his remains have been transferred to Naples, the village owes its name to the saint's erstwhile presence here: *locus sanctus* has become *Heiligen Stätte*, the holy place.

Outside the church, there is on the right a map listing and locating Beethoven's various residences in Heiligenstadt. In 1817, he lived at No 2 on the square, in a 17C house with its corner adorned by a wooden statue of St Florian on one corner; it is now a *Heuriger* of rather severe aspect.

Probusgasse begins nearly opposite the church.

Beethovenhaus ⊙ – *Probusgasse 6*. At the age of 27, the composer noticed the onset of deafness, which gradually grew worse. At 30, he mentioned it for the first time in a letter to his friend Karl Amenda: *"I cannot hear the high notes of the instruments"*. His doctor sent him at the age of 31 for treatment at Heiligenstadt spa, but he soon realized that there was no cure. At 32, he drew up the harrowing **"Heiligenstadt Will"**. The first lines describe his sense of desperation: *"Oh* *you men, who consider me hostile or inflexible, even a misanthrope, you deeply misjudge me! You do not know the hidden cause of all these symptoms..."* The letter was addressed to his brothers, but he never sent it.

Beethoven lived in this house (mid-18C) in 1802. In 1970, it was turned into a museum (engravings, facsimiles, Streicher piano). In one of the 8 glass cases there is a facsimile of the famous document which has been in Hamburg National University Library since 1888. On the end wall are 5 attractive engravings on wood by the Viennese painter Karl Moll (1907) showing the places where Beethoven lived in the region. Just in front is a plaster bust which the sculptor Josef Danhauser made (1827) after completing the composer's death mask *(the original mask is in the Historisches Museum der Stadt Wien)*. The street takes its name from the Roman emperor Probus (276-282) who allowed his *Vindobona* legionaries to plant the first vines in the region.

ONAT

Ludwig van Beethoven

Beethoven the bucolic – Following in the footsteps of Haydn and Mozart, Beethoven worked tirelessly to create works of genius. He frequently changed accommodation, so there are numerous places dedicated to him in and around Vienna (as far as Baden). Beethoven loved the countryside. In the summer, he stayed north of Vienna. It was there that he composed most of the *Eroica* (Third Symphony). In 1808, its rustic character inspired him to create the *Pastoral* (Sixth Symphony). Between Heiligenstadt and Nussdorf lies Beethovengang (Beethoven's promenade) along the banks of the Schreiberbach *(go down Eroicagasse from Pfarrplatz, the square including St. Jakobskirche)*. This serves as a reminder of the extent to which the composer enjoyed immersing himself in nature. *"As he gradually lost contact with the outside world, he focused more intensely on the world within."* (Richard Wagner).

In Grinzingerstrasse, take bus 38A at the Armbrustergasse stop and alight at Grinzing.

★GRINZING

Tram: Grinzing (38)

The first mention of Grinzing occurs in 1114. It is a delightful village on the outskirts of Vienna with low-roofed, brightly coloured houses; it is famous for its wine and *Heurigen*. As part of Döbling District, Grinzing now has to contend with the urban development which is gradually spreading towards the lower slopes of the Viennese forest. To remedy the situation, the village has been practising a pleasant subterfuge practised for several years: anyone may buy 1m²/1.25sq yds with a single vine, just like Leonard Bernstein, Jimmy Carter or the lovely Sophia Loren.

Village – It is situated at the foot of verdant, vine clad slopes and attracts many Viennese and tourists, who come to taste the new wine sold by the winegrowers, mainly on Sandgasse *(see Introduction, Living in Vienna)*. The village comes to life in the evening, recovering its usual calm with twelve strokes of the clock from the onion-shaped dome of Grinzinger Pfarrkirche (early 15C); this heavily restored church lies on Himmelstrasse. No 25 features a plaque in honour of Franz Schubert, "prince of *Lieder* who enjoyed staying in Grinzing". At No 29, another plaque evokes the memory of the Schrammelmusik player Sepp Fellner, the "Schubert of Grinzing". The celebrated conductor Karl Böhm occupied the elegant white Jugendstil building at No 41. He was a friend of Richard Strauss and director of the Vienna Philharmonic. Viennese music lovers held him in great respect and he became famous for his interpretations of German compositions (Mozart, Wagner etc.).

Return to the chevet of the church; bear right into Mannagettagasse which soon becomes Mannagettasteig, then turn right into An den langen Lüssen.

Churchyard ⊙ – *Consult the map on the right just beyond the entrance.* Gustav Mahler (block 6, row 7) is buried here next to his daughter Maria, who died at the age of 5. Josef Hoffmann designed the austere tombstone. Some yards away

3 BIS/MICHELIN

Grinzing

is the grave of his wife Alma (block 6, row 6), buried under his name despite two later marriages. In an anonymous grave lies the great writer Thomas Bernhard who died in 1989.

EXCURSIONS

From Grinzing to Klosterneuburg via Höhenstrasse

Only car owners will be able to go to Dreimarkstein and Klosterneuburg (see map of Vienna and its suburbs). Others should take bus 38A to the stops at Kahlenberg and Leopoldsberg. Enter Cobenzlgasse then turn left into Höhenstrasse, on the slopes of Wienerwald. Walk 500m/545yds.

From the *Cobenzl* café and restaurant at the foot of Latisberg, there is an interesting **view** of Vienna, particularly by night. It was on the way to this restaurant that, on 24 July 1895, Sigmund Freud suddenly realised the importance of dreams in the study of mental illness. Follow Höhenstrasse to the Gasthaus *Häuserl am Roan* on Dreimarktstein (alt. 454m/1,489ft). There is a fine view from the car park of the whole of Vienna and Wienerwald.

Return to Höhenstrasse for Kahlenberg.

The Most Beautiful Girl in Vienna

Alma Mahler: a legend. Born in the imperial capital in August 1879, Alma Mahler was the daughter of Jakob Emil Schindler, a famous landscape painter, and Anna von Bergen who, after her husband's death, married Karl Moll, a founder member of the Secession.

Towards the end of the century, the Habsburg regime was approaching its demise, but the city was a focus of European cultural life. At the end of the century, Alma was twenty, and was to become the muse of the greatest artists of the time. Gustav Klimt and the musician Alexander von Zemlinsky fell in love with her before her marriage in 1902 with Gustav Mahler, then director of the imperial Opera. After the composer's death in 1911, she had a stormy relationship with Oskar Kokoschka. She married the architect Walter Gropius in 1915, then the poet Franz Werfel in 1929.

The woman once known as the most beautiful woman in Vienna died in New York in December 1964.

The Great Wheel in the Prater

★**Kahlenberg** – The roof terrace (alt. 483m/1,584ft) of the restaurant provides a **view**★ of Vienna alive with the soaring spires of Stephansdom and Ringturm. In the foreground lie the Grinzing vineyards, while, to the right, are the slopes of Wiener-wald. On a clear day, there is a distinct view of the Gloriette over Schönbrunn Park, and, in the distance, of the massive black and white Alt-Erlaa tower blocks. Kahlenbergkirche dates from 1629. This church contains a replica of the Black Virgin of Czestochowa, which is greatly venerated in Poland and attracts the Polish community of Vienna. The façade displays a plaque in honour of John III Sobieski *(see below)*.

In 1809, many Viennese climbed "the bald hill" to watch the troop movements during the battles of Wagram (east of the city) and Essling (on the site of Donau-stadt or 22nd District).

A formidable observation post for the Christian army – In 1683, when Grand Vizier Kara Mustafa was about to capture Vienna *(see "Vienna, a city that nearly became Turkish" in Historical table and notes)*, John Sobieski, King John III of Poland, responded to Pope Innocent XI's appeal. With 65,000 men under his command, he joined the remains of the imperial army under Charles of Lorraine. On 12 September, the morning of the last battle, Marco d'Aviano, a Capuchin friar and papal legate, celebrated Mass on the top of Kahlenberg. Strengthened by the papal blessing, the army left this observation post with an unimpeded view and deployed to attack the forces of *Babi Ali*. At noon, the enemy began to give way. By nightfall, the Turks were defeated. In accordance with custom during periods of conflict, John III Sobieski's men were authorised to loot their opponents' camp.

Return to Höhenstrasse for Leopoldsberg.

★★**Leopoldsberg** – Leopold III of Babenberg built a castle for his wife Agnes, daughter of Emperor Henry IV, on this promontory at the tip of Wienerwald (alt. 423m/1,387ft). The Turks destroyed the stronghold in 1529, during Suleyman the Magnificent's unsuccessful siege of Vienna.

Opposite the small Leopoldskirche (1679-1693), a church that has often been rebuilt, there is a restaurant with a courtyard terrace. From a platform (relief map of Vienna in 1683), featuring the Heimkehrerdenkmal in memory of victims of the Nazis, there is an extensive **view**★★. In the foreground is the multicoloured tower built by the sculptor Friedensreich Hundertwasser for the incineration plant Müllverbrennung-Fernwärme-Heizwerk *(see illustration in chapter on Architecture in the Introduction)*. There is a view of the Prater, the Danube canal, UNO-City and the Donauturm, the meander of the Old Danube, the Wagram plain and, on the horizon, the Little Carpathians in Slovakia as well as the alpine profile of Leithagebirge at the edge of Neusiedlersee which lies astride the Hungarian frontier.

Return and proceed along Höhenstrasse to the small town of Klosterneuburg. From the slopes on the other side of the valley, the winding road offers fine views.

★**Klosterneuburg** – *See under this heading.*

Return to Grinzing to take tram 38 to the Silbergasse stop. Take Hofzeile leading into Döblinger Hauptstrasse.

OBERDÖBLING

Tram: Pokornystrasse (37)

Weinbaumuseum (**M¹**) ⊘ – *Döblinger Hauptstrasse 96.* This small museum in a medieval cellar contains documentation and objects relating to the history and tra-ditions of the Döbling District which includes Grinzing, Nussdorf and Sievering and is the winegrowing region of Vienna. Among the winegrowing equipment is a large winepress known as *Winzerkrone* (winegrower's crown), which dates from Maria Theresa's time.

Eroicahaus (**E**) ⊘ – *Döblinger Hauptstrasse 92.* – The four rooms where Beethoven lived in the summer of 1803 house some engravings and etchings relating to his work here on the *Eroica* (Third Symphony). It was also here that he wrote the famous *Triple Concerto* for piano, violin and cello (opus 56).

A portrait of Josef von Lobkowitz recalls that the first performance of the *Eroica* took place in the Lobkowitz palace *(see under this heading)*. This symphony was initially dedicated to Napoleon, whose portrait (lithograph by Franz Eybl) is visible. It then became *dedicata A Sua Altezza Serenissima il Principe di Lobkowitz* (dedi-cated to His Serene Highness the Prince of Lobkowitz, document No 22).

Those unable to drive to Klosterneuburg from Leopoldsberg may go to Franz-Josefs-Bahnhof and take Schnellbahn line S40: take tram 37 at Pokornygasse and alight at Nussdorferstrasse/Alserbachstrasse, then walk up Alserbach-strasse to the station.

The nearest districts with sights described in this guide are: Alsergrund, Hernals and Währing.

JOSEFSTADT
8th District
Local map page 7, **EU**
Underground: Lerchenfelderstrasse (U2), Rathaus (U2)
Tram: Rathaus (J), Langegasse (43, 44)
Bus: Theater i.d. Josefstadt (13A)

Beyond the Ring

This small district lies northwest of the town centre, close to Ringstrasse. It takes its name from Emperor Josef II and its attractive streets display many 18C façades. One can sense the presence of the University and the Law Courts by the number of students and lawyers in the local restaurants. Vienna's English Theatre with productions in English is also in this district (Josefsgasse 12). During his constant changes of lodging, Beethoven stayed in Josefstadt in 1819-20 (Auerspergstrasse). Another famous inhabitant was the author of *Verwirrung der Gefühle* (*Confusion of Feelings*), Stefan Zweig *(see Schönborn-park)*.

A good starting point for a tour of the district is Josefstädterstrasse *(see the plaque at No 12 relating the history of the district)*; this street lies on the site of an old Roman road and affords delightful views of the Vienna woods and the outline of Stephansdom.

Theater in der Josefstadt (**T¹**) – *Josefstädterstrasse 26*. This theatre so dear to Viennese hearts dates from 1788 and is still in operation. In 1822, it was rebuilt by Josef Kornhäusel, an architect responsible for the finest edifices in Baden *(see under this heading)*. For its reopening, Beethoven composed the *Consecration of the House*, and conducted it himself. This old theatre's reputation is due largely to the writer Hugo von Hoffmannsthal and to the producer Max Reinhardt *(see Gedenkräume des Österreichischen Theatermuseums)* whose portrait appears in a medallion on the façade.

Turn right into Piaristengasse.

Piaristenkirche Basilika Maria Treu (**A**) ⊙ – *Jodok-Fink-Platz*. The Church of Mary the Faithful belongs to the Piarists. This clerical order was founded in 1597 and settled in Vienna in the 17C. Its calling was to educate poor children in religious schools. Construction of the church began in 1716 and continued until the mid 18C. The architect was Johann Lukas Hildebrandt, the brilliant creator of many palaces. The fine façade is a blend of the Baroque and classical styles. A pediment rises above the central section with two bell-towers on either side, which did not reach completion until just before 1860. The whole composition has a real grace.

Inside, two large domes display Rococo frescoes by the celebrated Franz Anton Maulbertsch; they were his first major work (1753). He is also the creator of the *Crucifixion* (1772) in the chapel on the left of the choir. It may interest music lovers to know that it was on this church organ that Anton Bruckner sat his exams in composition.

Recently restored monastic buildings surround the square. In the centre stands a votive column crowned by a statue of the Virgin, one of the numerous Pestsäulen or plague columns in Vienna and the surrounding area. This one commemorates

Close-up of Piaristenkirche

the end of the 1714 epidemic, but is not as fine as those of Graben, Mödling, or Perchtoldsdorf *(see under these headings)*. At the corner of the square, *Piaristenkeller* (Piaristengasse 45) occupies the former monastery wine cellar.

Opposite Jodok-Fink-Platz, go down Maria-Treugasse and bear right into Langegasse.

Alte Backstube (**B**) ⊘ – *Langegasse 34* – Behind the attractive façade of this residential house, dating from 1697 and easily identifiable by the sandstone group *Zur Hl. Dreifaltigkeit* (Holy Trinity) over the entrance, is a former baker's shop that is now a café and museum. The old bakery, which produced bread from 1701 to 1963 is still visible, as well as many implements of former trades in the district.

Retrace your steps up Langegasse.

Schönborn-park – *Corner of Langegasse and Florianigasse. See also Schönborn Palace below.* The name of this park commemorates Count Friedrich Karl Schönborn-Buchheim (1674-1743). It is shady in summer and displays on Langegasse two magnificent Jugendstil wrought-iron gates. It offers play areas for children and numerous chairs for the benefit of tourists, who are invariably weary after exploring in summer a cultural capital such as Vienna. A bust (1974) by Leo Gruber represents the composer Edmund Eysler. On the other side of the park is Kochgasse where the writer Stefan Zweig lived at No 8 from 1907 to 1919.

Continue along Langegasse and turn left into Laudongasse.

Österreichisches Museum für Volkskunde (**M**⁷) ⊘ – *Laudongasse 15-19. Tram: Langegasse (43, 44), Laudongasse (5); bus: Laudongasse (13A).* The Austrian Folklore Museum is the only Viennese museum devoted to the popular arts and traditions of Austria and of the former provinces of the Empire, apart from the Museum of Religious Folk Art which is under the same administration *(see Sammlung Religiöse Volkskunst)*. The varied exhibits illustrate everyday life in the Austrian provinces from the 17C to the 19C. Among them are wood carvings, tools, models of rural housing, reconstructed rooms, furniture (often painted), costumes, pottery, etc. Some items are of particular interest *(numbers in brackets correspond to the numbering of the exhibits)*, as for example: the strange "**bird of self-knowledge**"★, a wood carving from the Tyrol dating from the mid 18C (1/0); an impressive Tyrolean mask dating from about 1900 (1/61); a raincoat made of rushes from Slovenia or Croatia dating from about 1900 (2/2); a painted cupboard from Upper Austria made in 1791 by Mathias Huember who decorated it with allegories of the seasons (12/1); a mechanical theatre from Vienna dating from about 1850 (14/14).

Schönborn Palace – The museum occupies a palace, a former country residence which from 1706 to 1711 Johann Lukas von Hildebrandt and Franz Jänggl refurbished to turn it into a summer palace for Friedrich Karl Schönborn-Buchheim. He was assistant chancellor of the Empire, soon to become Hildebrandt's benefactor. Half a century later, the building underwent another transformation, probably by Isidor Canevale, who added a Classical façade.

Return to Langegasse and turn right into Alserstrasse.

Dreifaltigkeitskirche (**K**¹) ⊘ – *Alserstrasse 17. Tram: Langegasse (43, 44).* Opposite the General Hospital *(see Allgemeines Krankenhaus)* is the Church of the Holy Trinity, often known as Alserkirche, dating from between 1687 and 1727. Hundreds of votive tablets illustrate the Viennese veneration for St Anthony *(in the cloister gallery and the chapel, south side)*. The north aisle houses an altarpiece by Martino Altomonte (1708); In the south aisle is a wooden crucifix (early 16C) from the studio of Veit Stoss, an artist from Nürnberg.

On 29 March 1827, the body of Beethoven was brought to this church *(see inset)*.

A Titan

Ludwig van Beethoven died on 26 March 1827. On 29 March, he was laid in state in the Dreifaltigkeitskirche before the funeral service, which the eminent poet Franz Grillparzer and Franz Schubert attended. Schubert declared later: "much water will flow into the Danube before people fully understand this man's achievements." Thirty thousand Viennese accompanied the lonely genius to his grave in Währing cemetery, to pay him a last tribute.

Besides Rathaus, opposite the Ring, the nearest sights are: the Alsergrund, Hernals, Neubau and Währing Districts.

KARLSPLATZ District★★

Wieden – 4th District
Map pages 5-6, **HJKS**
Underground: Karlsplatz (U1, U2, U4)
Tram: Karlsplatz (62, 65)
Bus: Karlsplatz (4A, WLB)
Departure of the tour by old tram

The imposing district of Wieden lies south of Innere Stadt, the inner city. Karlsplatz lies between these two districts and is the centre of all of Wieden's tourist and cultural attractions. Three famous composers lived there: Johannes Brahms (Karlsgasse 4), Franz Schubert (Kettenbrückengasse 6) and Johann Strauss the Younger (Johann-Straussgasse 4). Like Mariahilf, Neubau, Josefstadt or Alsergrund, this is a pleasant district to explore, with interesting examples of domestic architecture in the city's older residential areas. The urbanisation of Wieden dates mainly from the second half of the 19C.

Karlsplatz – St Charles' Square is a junction for underground and tram lines. Beneath its animated surface lies a long equally busy underground corridor lined with shops which links the U4 line to the Ring. It is a favourite haunt of haggard young people driven by despair.
In 1979, Sven Ingvar renovated this square bordered by large buildings. In the shady Ressel Park stands **Brahms' statue** by Rudolf Weyr.

A crossroads for Baroque, Historicist, Jugendstil and Secession styles

★**Wagner-Pavillons** – *Karlsplatz*. Facing each other, the two pavilions (1899) designed by Otto Wagner housed for a long time the entrances to the Vienna underground (one for each platform). In 1892, the architect was commissioned to design and build 36 stations for the 40km/24 miles of underground railway. Wagner saw this project as being of major importance for the creation of a modern city. The pavilions, restored in 1979, formed the highlight of this scheme. Wagner was so successful in his project that the buildings now embody the Viennese Jugendstil in all its refinement in contrast to the Historicism then prevailing on the Ring. They present a harmonious combination of dazzling white marble and green-painted prefabricated metalwork, a technique that was new at the time. The roof is made of corrugated copper. In keeping with the elegance of nearby Karlskirche, Wagner's buildings display delicate gold incrusted or embossed floral motifs (mainly sunflowers), which strike a Baroque note, with delicate floral motifs.
One of the pavilions serves as an exhibition centre, while the other is a café. From the terrace on the pavement there is an excellent view of the site.

Künstlerhaus – *Karlsplatz 5*. The architecture of the House of the Artists evokes an Italian Renaissance palazzo. It was the work of Andreas Streit and Friedrich Schachner (1881). At the entrance are marble statues of Velazquez, Raphael, Leonardo da Vinci, Michelangelo, Dürer, Titian, Bramante and Rubens.

Karlsplatz: Otto Wagner pavilion and Karlskirche

B. Kaufmann

185

Kärtner Durchgan: American Bar

Hüttelbergstrasse: Prima Villa

Linke Wienzeile: house with medallions

Bognergasse: Apothecary Angel

Michaelerplatz: Looshaus

The building houses a theatrical company and is also used for exhibitions organised by the Historisches Museum der Stadt Wien (Historical Museum of the City of Vienna). It was the setting for the famous exhibition "Vienna 1880-1938, Dream and Reality" which toured the world, displaying the best of Viennese art.

Musikvereinsgebäude – *Dumbastrasse 3. Closed to the public. See also Introduction, Life in Vienna.* Lovers of classical music will be familiar with the gilded décor of the Goldene Saal (Great Hall) in the Friends of Music building, since it is seen during the television broadcast in mondiovision of the New Year Concert which takes place annually on 1st January at 11 a.m. To attend this concert, one must not only apply a year in advance, but tickets for the seats are chosen by lot. This is always a festive event, and the public never fails to applaud in time to the rhythm of Johann Strauss the Elder's *Radetzky March* which traditionally closes the concert. The orchestra always performs, on these occasions, under the baton of a world-famous conductor.

P. Schramek/MUSIKVEREIN, Wien

Musikverein concert hall

The building is the home of the Vienna Philharmonic Orchestra which usually plays for the National Opera *(see Staatsoper, a Symbolic Institution)*, but it also performs 18 annual concerts in the Great Hall (2,044 seats). The Great Hall and the Brahms auditorium (600 seats) are home to two other orchestras: the Radio and Television Orchestra (O.R.F.) and the Vienna Symphony Orchestra. This institution's archives, the world's largest private collection, contain unique items, such as manuscripts of Ludwig van Beethoven's *Eroica*, J. Brahms' *Double Concerto*, Gustav Mahler's *Sixth Symphony*, and all Schubert's symphonies apart from the *Fifth*.
Founded in 1812, the Friends of Music Society commissioned Theophil von Hansen in 1866 to build this neo-Renaissance temple (completed in 1869), recognisable from Karlsplatz by its red and yellow colour scheme. The building houses the famous piano-making firm, Bösendorfer, which still pays the same rent as in 1914!

★**Historisches Museum der Stadt Wien** ⊙ – *Karlsplatz 8.* The Historical Museum of the City of Vienna opened in 1887; in 1959 it moved from the City Hall to these new Karlplatz premises built by Oswald Haerdtl in honour of the President of the Republic Theodor Körner. Covering a surface area of 3,600m²/4,305sq yds, the exhibition traces the history of the city from Neolithic times to the present. If one does not have too much time, it is possible to make a rapid tour of the exhibits illustrating the landmarks in the history of Vienna, including remarkable pictures by Waldmüller, Klimt and Schiele.

Ground Floor – On display are some precious architectural fragments evoking medieval Vienna, such as the three keystones from Minoritenkirche (early 14C), the *Beautiful Madonna* (about 1420) which used to adorn the south tower of the cathedral, the terracotta statue of *St John* (1430) from the cloister of St Dorothy *(see Dorotheum)*, and a statue of *St Michael* (about 1440) from the west front of the cathedral. There are also stained-glass windows (about 1390) from the ducal chapel, which no longer exists, including the **portrait of Rudolf I** (buried in Speier in Germany).

First floor – Among a series of engravings and paintings are a *circular plan of Vienna*★ by the Nürnberg artist Augustin Hirschvogel (1545), Maximilian II's armour made in Augsburg about 1550, a facsimile of the **Turkish map of Vienna** discovered during

The fascination of Jerusalem

Numerous were the pilgrims who left Vienna for Jerusalem. Among those participating in the Crusades and the quest for the Holy Sepulchre were St Colomba, the bishops of Utrecht and Ratisbon, Peter the Hermit, the Knight of Poissy, the priest Gottschalk, Godfrey of Bouillon – received in Melk by the Holy Margrave Leopold who did not go on a crusade himself –, the Duke of Bavaria, Archbishop Thiemo of Salzburg, the imperial Marshall Konrad, etc. Another of the pilgrims was Itha, Leopold's mother. Jerusalem exerted its fascination on her too and she did not return. According to legend, she succombed to the charms of the Emir of Mossul and preferred to stay in his harem rather than see the Danube and Wiernerwald foothills again.

the capture of Belgrade in 1688 and an attractive model of the old town dating from 1854, about 4 years before the razing of the fortifications. Of special interest are: *The Battle to Lift the Siege of Vienna before the City Gates* in 1683 by Franz Geffels; *View of the City* (1690) by Domenico Cetto; *Karl VI* (1716) by Johann Kupezky; *Franz I* (about 1740) and *Maria Theresa* (1744) by Martin van Meytens.

Second floor – This floor displays mementoes from the Napoleonic era, porcelain and glass exhibits from Viennese factories, a **Pompeiian drawing room**★ (about 1800) from the Caprara-Geymüller palace (Wallnerstrasse 8) and an admirable picture collection: **Love**★ (1895), *Pallas Athena* (1898) and *Emilie Flöge* (1902) by Gustav Klimt; *Lady in Yellow* (1899) by Max Kurzweil; *Landscape* (1901) by Adolf Boehm; *Arthur Roessler* (1910), **Self Portrait with Outstretched Fingers**★★ (1911) and *The Blind Mother* (1914) by Egon Schiele; *Portrait of Peter Altenberg* (1909) by Gustav Jagerspacher, which used to hang in the *American Bar (see under this heading)*. After the section on the 1848 revolution comes a collection of landscapes and portraits by Ferdinand Georg Waldmüller.

There is also a series of objects from the *Wiener Werkstätte*, as well as sculptures, including a bust of Gustav Mahler (1909) by Auguste Rodin and a bronze head of Adolf Loos by the Viennese artist Arthur Emmanuel Löwental. Of equal interest are a reconstruction of the dining room in the architect's apartment (No 3 Bösendorferstrasse), and of the flat of dramatist Franz Grillparzer (No 21 Spiegelgasse).

★★**Karlskirche** – *Karlsplatz*. **Johann Bernhard Fischer von Erlach** was 60 when he started building this church dedicated to St Charles Borromeo, following a vow by Emperor Karl VI during the plague epidemic of 1713. Von Erlach began work on the building in 1716; his son completed it in 1737. It is undeniably the finest Baroque church in the capital.

Exterior – *See also Introduction, Architecture.* According to tradition, it was on the Pincian hill in Rome that J. B. Fischer von Erlach had the unusual idea of combining Trajan's Column, the Roman portico of the Pantheon and St Peter's dome. The façade

Karlskirche

B. Kaufmann

3 BIS/MICHELIN

The dome in Karlskirche

used to stand in complete isolation near the slope of the old fortifications. At first sight this strange juxtaposition is startling, but visitors never fail to succumb to the typically Baroque strategy of disconcerting the better to charm.

On either side of the central staircase are two angels with outstretched wings, the one on the left represents the Old Testament and the one on right the New Testament. The stairs lead to a Corinthian *pronaos* over which is a triangular pediment decorated with a relief by Giovanni Stanetti, *The Cessation of the Plague*; above it is a sculpture of St Charles Borromeo by Lorenzo Mattielli. This central portico is flanked by two triumphal columns with spiral reliefs of the life of the saint, bishop of Milan, who distinguished himself during an epidemic which devastated the capital of Lombardy in 1576. The left-hand column evokes the saint's steadfastness and the other his courage: *Constantia et fortitudo*, Karl VI's motto. The presence of these columns in the façade was an idea that had been dear to J.B. Fischer von Erlach ever since his studies in Rome; he incorporated them in his first project for the entrance to Schönbrunn. Moreover, in Baroque art, columns do not usually support anything; there is no saint or emperor above these columns which end in a belvedere with a platform, faintly reminiscent of the minarets from which the muezzin called the faithful to prayer in Ottoman Islam which was such a threat to imperial Vienna.

Rising above a double terraced attic, the dome of St Charles Borromeo evokes St Charles Church of the Four Fountains (a church in Rome dedicated to the same saint); its lines are as elliptical though more graceful than those of Borromini's dome which preceded Karlskirche by some 70 years. Between the eight windows are engaged columns and twinned pilasters bearing a projecting raised entablature. Above each opening is an elegant skylight with an angled pediment and consoles. Above the copper dome is a lantern turret with narrow windows; on top are a globe and a gold cross. At the sides, the surbased pavilions of the side entrances play an essential part in the illusionism created by the architect: they widen the façade and counterbalance the vertical lines of the dome and columns. The whole **edifice★★** is outstandingly impressive.

Interior – The plan of the building is a combination of an ellipse and an inverted Latin cross. In the absence of a nave and owing to the relative lack of decoration, all attention is drawn to the huge oval **dome★★** with frescoes by **Johann Michael Rottmayr** *(see illustration in the Introduction, Painting)*. They represent the apotheosis of St Charles Borromeo (on the left, there is an angel setting fire to Luther's Bible on

KARLSKIRCHE

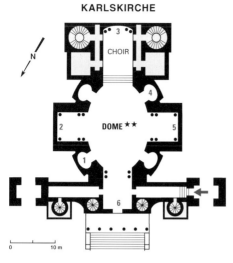

the ground). Admittedly, the decoration is austere: however, all the characteristics of the Baroque are present: indirect lighting, polychrome marble and soaring columns.

Starting clockwise, visitors see: a baptistry with a vault decorated in *trompe l'œil* style (**1**); an *Assumption* by Sebastiano Ricci (**2**); the high altar with scuptural decoration representing St Charles Borromeo's *Ascent into Heaven in the Company of Angels*, probably by J.B. Fischer von Erlach (**3**); *St Luke Painting the Virgin* by Jakob van Schuppen (**4**); *St Elizabeth of Hungary* by Daniel Gran (**5**). Before leaving, note the fresco above the organ loft (**6**), *St Cecilia among the Heavenly Choir*, by J.M. Rottmayr. Dominating the pool in front of the church is a sculpture by Henry Moore.

Technische Universität – *Karlsplatz 13. Closed to the public*. Johann Josef Prechtl founded the Technical University in 1815. Josef Schmerl von Leytenbach constructed the building from 1816 to 1818. It is an impressive Neoclassical edifice, which acquired several additions during the 19C and in the early 20C. Sculptures in the centre of the main façade are by Josef Klieber and represent Austrian inventors; among them is Josef Ressel who invented the ship's propeller and who gave his name to the park on Karlsplatz.

The ceremonial hall of the Technical University is the work of Pietro Nobile, dating from between 1835 and 1842.

Go to the west corner of the square.

Kunsthalle – *Treitlstrasse 2*. Dating from 1992, this orange and blue block with a transparent access ramp houses permanent and temporary exhibitions of contemporary art in all its forms *(for information, apply to the tourist office)*, organised by the City Council. The collections and activities of Kunsthalle will soon move to the Messepalast buildings *(see Neubau District)*. Since provisional arrangements tend to become permanent, it is possible that this ugly neighbour of the Secession Pavilion may spoil the surrounding urban landscape for some time to come.

Behind Kunsthalle, there is a view on the right of the Café Museum. Set at an angle to the left is the Secession Pavilion.

Café Museum – *Friedrichstrasse 6*. Belonging to the *Wiener Kaffeehäuser* tradition, the *Museum* is the work of Adolf Loos, but it has lost the original interior decoration. When it opened in 1899, Loos' contemporaries nicknamed it "Nihilism Café" because of its sober décor. Students and artists still frequent it.

Just in front of the Secessionsgebäude, a passage leads to the Akademiehof

★★ Albertina im Akademiehof ⊘ – *Makartgasse 3*. While closed for renovation *(see Graphische Sammlung Albertina)*, the Albertina has set up a temporary wing just two steps away from the Secessionsgebäude, since it would appear that it will be reopening much later than planned. Apart from temporary exhibitions dedicated to modern and historical engraving, this offshoot offers the opportunity to admire *(upstairs)* a series of historical masterpieces (from the 15C to 20C).

★★ Secessiongebäude ⊘ – *Friedrichstrasse 12*. Two days after its completion on 10 November 1898, the Secession Pavilion opened for the second exhibition by the group of the same name. This group, founded the previous year, was the creation of **Josef Maria Olbrich** and his friends, who repudiated academicism in any form. The building is a temple to these artists.

"Mahdi's Tomb" – This is the strange appellation which the Viennese gave to J.M. Olbrich's pavilion, in reference to an Assyrian toilet. Owing to the proximity of the Naschmarkt *(see below)* and the gilded dome on top of the building, it was also nicknamed "the golden cabbage".

Today the edifice has a certain familiarity, but at the end of the 19C it was incredibly modern, a provocative assault from the avant-garde: Olbrich had designed a white cube – later he wrote that he had found inspiration in the unfinished sanctuary of Segesta in Sicily. However, even if there were some bravado in building

For or Against, but Never Indifferent

Despite the prevalence of received ideas, the **Secession** received a favourable welcome from the Viennese, who were probably somewhat weary of the grandiloquent excesses of Ringstrasse Historicism. The Viennese did not greet the Secession with indifference.

Resistance to change took root among intellectual circles, particularly at the University, where 87 professors signed a petition protesting against the works of Klimt. Recognition, on the other hand, came from the ranks of the bourgeoisie and captains of industry. Director of a steel cartel and a friend of Mahler, Karl Wittgenstein was the patron of the arts Klimt, Hoffmann, Olbrich and their disciples had been waiting for. There were others such as Ferdinand Bloch-Bauer, August Lederer, Otto and Robert Primavesi *(see Villa Primavesi)*, or the Belgian Adolphe Stoclet.

Although this is not generally known outside Vienna, the Secession is still alive and well. The movement's activities ceased in 1938, but it was never dissolved. A professor at the College of Fine Arts, Edelbert Köb is responsible for its resurgence, with the assistance of a group of sponsors who created a foundation. It is thanks to this obstinate and generous man that it is possible today to admire Klimt's magnificent frieze.

such a pavilion, the architect did create elegant forms. This is particularly evident in this famous dome with its 3,000 gilded laurel leaves. This parody of historicism encapsulates all the humour and talent of the Secession.

"Der Zeit ihre Kunst, der Kunst ihre Freiheit" – This motto ("to each century its art, to art its freedom") features on the front of Olbrich's pavilion. It is an artistic declaration of war on the nearby Artists' Association *(see Künstlerhaus above)*. The pavilion is still an exhibition centre. The huge hall of this temple to art has zenithal lighting; it is functional in spirit, since the space can be modulated thanks to mobile partitions. To preserve it in good condition, the **Beethoven Frieze★★★** by Gustav Klimt is in the basement. The artist painted it on the theme of the *Ninth Symphony* for the 14th Secessionist exhibition (1902). Auguste Rodin came to see the frieze and declared it "tragic, divine and sumptuous". 34m/37yds long, it was in three private collections, before the Österreichische Galerie bought it in 1975 and, thanks to the energetic Edelbert Köb *(see inset)*, put it back in the pavilion which was superbly refurbished and restored by Adolf Krischanitz in 1986. Those who have already been to the Burgtheater will appreciate the extent of the artist's evolution since the theatre frescoes. Left of the entrance, the project begins with *Longing for Happiness* and its characters, and with *Weak and Suffering Humanity* represented by a couple imploring a knight in armour (it is said to be a portrait of Mahler) with Ambition and Pity on either side of him; it continues opposite the entrance with a richly detailed panel displaying successively *The Three Gorgons*, dominated by

Close-up of Secessiongebaüde

Sickness, Madness and Death, *The Giant Typheus*, *The Hostile Forces* of Impurity, Envy and Excess, *Sorrow* and *The Expectations of Mankind Flying over Hostile Forces*; it ends on the right again with *Longing for Happiness* flying over Poetry, the Arts with arms outstretched to a heavenly choir (Beethoven's *Hymn to Joy*), and *The Fulfilment of Happiness*, an allegorical illustration of a sentence by Schiller: "This kiss is given to the whole world".

Go into Linke Wienzeile.

Linke Wienzeile – This thoroughfare links Karlsplatz to Schloss Schönbrunn. The left *(linke)* side of this row *(zeile)* of buildings borders the Wien and runs through Rudolfsheim-Fünfhaus (15th) and Mariahilf (6th) Districts. After leaving the Secession pavilion, one continues upstream of the river, which has flowed underground at this point ever since arches were built over it in 1912. On the right of the river is a group of buildings of special interest.

Theater an der Wien – *Linke Wienzeile 6.* In 1801, the librettist of *The Magic Flute*, Emanuel Schikaneder, founded this theatre, which four years later was the setting for the first public performance of Ludwig van Beethoven's *Fidelio*. It was a fiasco. Towards the end of the century, the establishment became the home of Viennese operetta. People came to listen to Johann Strauss the Younger's music or Franz Lehár's *Merry Widow*.

Naschmarkt – Extending between Getreidemarkt and Kettenbrückengasse, this fruit and vegetable market has the reputation of being working-class, although its stalls display fresh, gourmet produce often from Central Europe *(naschen* means to eat with relish). As one approaches the underground station Kettenbrückengasse, prices fall and the scene becomes increasingly lively. On Saturdays, the south end of the market is specially colourful, because it is the setting for a flea market; the arrival of crowds soon attracts hordes of pickpockets.

Continue along Linke Wienzeile; Beethoven lived in a street at right angles to it, at No 22 Laimgrubengasse (from October 1822 to May 1823).

★**Two buildings by Wagner** – *Linke Wienzeile 38 and 40. Closed to the public. Underground: Kettenbrückengasse (U4).* Wagner wished to turn this thoroughfare into a road fit for emperors. The project never came to fruition, but in 1899 the famous architect built there two residential buildings incarnating Jugendstil ideals. Their façades are magnificent.
The entrance of No 38, the Medallion House, is at No 1 Köstlergasse. It displays two highly decorative corner façades. The golden stucco sparkles in the sunlight, sometimes impeding the view of Othmar Schimkowitz's *Criers* surmounting pilasters ringed with laurels, or of Koloman Moser's medallions, palm leaves and garlands. The building is in two horizontal sections, each with a different purpose, one for offices and shops, the other for apartments.
No 40, Majolikahaus (Majolica House), is of a similar structure to No 38. The building displays an architecturally austere façade covered in floral ceramic motifs, hence the name of the building. This façade is in the Jugendstil rather than the Secession style, since it is a spectacle in itself, with its polychrome rose spreading its branches between the regularly spaced windows.

Near the underground station, bear left into Kettenbrückengasse.

Schubert Sterbewohnung ☉ – *Kettenbrückengasse 6. Second floor. Underground: Kettenbrückengasse (U4); bus: Grosse Neugasse (59A).* From 1 September to 19 December 1828, Franz Schubert lived in the apartment of his brother Ferdinand, himself a composer. Franz moved there on the advice of his doctor, Ernst Rinna von Sarenbach, to take advantage of the cleaner air in the inner suburbs. He did not intend to stay long. He had left all his manuscripts at the home of his friend, Franz von Schober, in the city centre where he had been living previously. He was right, his stay in Kettenbrückengasse was short but fatal. Here is Schubert's last letter, dated 12 November.

"Dear Schober,

I am ill. For 11 days, I have not eaten or drunk and I totter weakly to and fro between my chair and my bed. Rinna is taking care of me. Whenever I try to eat anything, I cannot keep it down. Would you be kind enough to help me in this desperate situation. Among Cooper's [James Fenimore Cooper] novels, I have read: The Last of the Mohicans, The Spy and the Pioneers. If you have any other novels by him, I implore you to leave them at the café, care of Bogner's wife. My brother, who is conscience itself, will conscientiously bring them to me. Or anything else.

Your friend

Schubert".

Probably because he was worried about infection, Schober did not visit his friend, and Ferdinand was so "conscientious" that he claimed to be the composer of the *Deutsches Requiem* which his brother had written for him to ensure that he acquired the status of composer.

Tour – Although the apartment has been extended and turned into a museum, it still stirs the emotions. The composer of *Erlkönig* (King of the Alders) died in the room directly past the hall on the street side.

Among documents and items of interest *(numbers in brackets correspond to the numbering of the exhibits)*, are: a lithography by Josef Kriehuber representing Ferdinand *(1)*; a reproduction of the watercolour and lead sketch by Josef Teltscher, *Franz Schubert in Teltscher's Studio (5)* (about 1827); an Elwerkember piano that belonged to Ferdinand *(4)*; Franz's last letter *(8, see above)*; a silver toothpick belonging to Franz *(11)*; facsimiles of his last works *(16)*, including the string quintet in C major D 956, and his last work, the lied *Der Hirt auf dem Felsen*, D 965; a facsimile of the announcement of his death *(17)*; a drawing of Augustinerkirche where the funeral took place *(26)*.

The last sight in Wieden is at a distance from the preceding ones. It could be included in a visit to the Upper Belvedere.

Theresianum (**FV**) – *Favoritenstrasse 15. Closed to the public. Underground: Taubstummengasse (U1).* Empress Maria Theresa founded the College for Diplomats, which has occupied this building since 1946. The façade is monotonous; it was first constructed between 1616 and 1625, commissioned by Emperor Matthias. After its destruction during the 1683 siege, Ludovico Burnacini turned the castle into a palace in 1690. Karl VI died there. His daughter Maria Theresa presented it to the Jesuits who ran it as a school for young penniless noblemen: the Collegium Theresianum.

The nearest sights are: the Ring and the Staatsoper, in the city centre, as well as the Belvedere, Favoriten and Mariahilf Districts.

LIESING

District 23

Map p 2, **AZ**

Take the underground (line U4) and alight at "Hietzing" then take tram 60 and alight at "Maurer Hauptplatz" in Liesing; take the 60A bus and alight at "Kaserngasse". Walk down Maurer Lange Gasse on the right then turn left to walk up Georgsgasse.

By car, take Breitenfurter Strasse (road 12) and turn right at Atzgersdorfer Platz into Levasseurgasse then left into Endresstrasse; follow the signs after Maurer Hauptplatz where there is a wine press dating from 1800.

R. Dechamps/MICHELIN

Wotrubakirche

Wotrubakirche ⊘ – *At the end of Rysergasse.* The church Zur Heiligsten Dreifaltigkeit (Most Holy Trinity) is pleasantly situated on Sankt-Georgenberg, at the edge of the Wienerwald (Vienna Woods). Consecrated in 1976, it owes its unofficial name to its creator, Fritz Wotruba (1907-1975), a renowned Austrian sculptor also responsible for Arnold Schönberg's cube *(see Zentralfriedhof)*. Whether arriving from Rysergasse or Georgsgasse, a visitor will be struck by the sudden sight of 152 octagonal concrete blocks displayed asymmetrically. This massive composition forming a sculpture 15.5m/50ft high does not conform to the traditional view of a religious centre. The church, with room for a congregation of 250, contains a replica of the cross made by F. Wotruba for the castle chapel of Bruchsal in Baden-Württemberg.

Although it does not possess the remarkable spirituality of Notre-Dame-du-Haut church built by Le Corbusier in Ronchamp, France, Wotrubakirche is faintly reminiscent of the edifice created by the master of reinforced concrete. Both these works were built by atheists.

People travelling by car can go on to visit Perchtoldsdorf (see under this heading).

MARIAHILF
6th District
Map page 7, **EUV**

Underground: Babenbergerstrasse (U2), Gumpendorferstrasse (U6), Neubaugasse (U3), Westbahnhof (U6), Zieglerstrasse (U3)
Tram: Mariahilfergürtel (6, 18), Neubaugasse/Westbahnstrasse (49)
Bus: Neubaugasse (13A, 14A, Kaunitzgasse (57A)

This district lies in the southwest of the city centre. Along its north side, it shares with Neubau District the long commercial thoroughfare of Mariahilferstrasse. The Wien, which flows along the south side into the Danube Canal, gave the Austrian capital its name. Following the example of Döbling and the city centre, this district provided a home for Ludwig van Beethoven (Laimgrubenstrasse 22) from October 1822 to 17 May 1823. However, it was Joseph Haydn who left his mark on Mariahilf.

Walking along Mariahilferstrasse, remember that the sights in Neubau District are not far away. Looking at a map of Vienna should make it easy to combine visits to both these quarters and their sights, depending on individual tastes and inclinations.

Mariahilferstrasse – *This street contains two museums described elsewhere: Bundessammlung Alter Stilmöbel and Tabak-Museum (see under these headings).* This busy street links Westbahnhof to Messepalast, which the identical buildings of the Naturhistorisches Museum and Kunsthistorisches Museum separate from the famous Ring. No 45 in this street was the birthplace of the playwright **Ferdinand Raimund** (1790-1836). This poet instilled new life into old Viennese folk tales and his plays formed part of the Burgtheater's repertory. He committed suicide after being bitten by a dog which he thought was suffering from rabies. A tragic mistake.

Mariahilferkirche (**K²**) ⊘ – *Mariahilferstrasse 65.* This pilgrimage church replaces an older church which the Turks destroyed in 1683. In front of it stands a monument to Haydn. The church houses a replica of the statue of the Mariahilfberg Virgin which is said to work miracles. The original is in Bavaria. The architect of the church was probably Sebastiano Carlone. The building was not dedicated to the Our Lady of Succour until 1730. Inside, an organ case with a clock above it is noteworthy.

An adjoining chapel contains a crucifix from the "house of the ruffians" in Rauhensteingasse (1st District), from where those condemned to death left for execution on Hoher Markt.

A discreet death

In spring 1809, Napoleon's troops entered Vienna. **Haydn** was ill and the sound of cannonfire scarcely disturbed him. In protest, he would sit at his piano at midday playing *"Gott erhalte"*, the national anthem sung in every language of the Empire, including German, Hungarian, Italian, Polish, Romanian, Serbo-Croat, Slovakian, Czech and Ruthenian. While Napoleon moved into Schönbrunn, some French officers came to pay homage to the great composer. One of them, a captain of hussars, hummed a tune from *The Creation*. Haydn embraced him. He died five days later, on 31 May. When he heard the news, Napoleon ordered the posting of a guard of honour outside his house.

On 15 June, there was a memorial mass for Haydn in the Schottenkirche. Because of the French occupation of Vienna, hardly anyone attended it. One of the few who did was a certain Henry Beyle, better known as Stendhal, then an official in Napoleon's army.

---

*Walk round the church and down Barnabitengasse. Turn right for Esterházy-
park.*

Haus des Meeres (**M⁹**) ⊘ – *Esterházypark 6. Underground: Neubaugasse (U3);
bus: Kaunitzgasse (57A).* The House of the Sea is in an enormous concrete tower
(Flakturm) in the centre of this small park. This amazing structure is a practically
indestructible reminder of the Germans' presence from 1938 to 1945 *(for further
details, see Augarten).*
The museum occupies 4 floors in the tower. The reptile houses are on the 1st floor
and the aquariums on the two floors above. Although snakes and piranha fish are
probably a major attraction, some visitors might prefer the quieter beauty of the
vividly-coloured tropical fish *(3rd floor).*

*Return to Mariahilferstrasse keeping to the left side of the street and turn left into
Webgasse. Take the first street on the right, Schmalzhofgasse, then Haydngasse
on the left.*

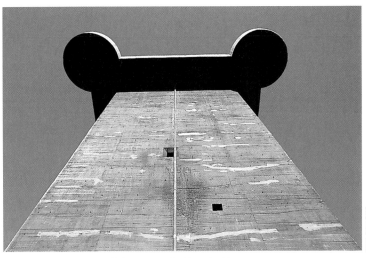

Flakturm, now the Haus des Meeres

★ **Haydn-Museum** (**M¹⁰**) ⊘ – *Haydngasse 19. Underground: Westbahnhof (U6),
Zieglergasse (U3); tram: Mariahilfergürtel (6, 18); bus: Brückengasse (57A).* "I like
this house [...] I would like to have it as a retreat for my old age, when I am a
widow", Haydn's affectionate wife wrote to her husband. At the time he was in
London, performing symphony concerts to much acclaim. He did not send the
money to his wife, but he bought the house on his return to Vienna in 1793. It
was in a new district, allegedly on the site of a windmill, in Kleiner Steingasse,
which in 1862 received the name of Haydngasse. He added a floor to this house
about which he said later: "it is indeed a retreat, but the widow living in it is
myself." Mrs Haydn had been the first of the two to die.
It was in this house that Prince Esterházy's musical director wrote his famous oratorios *The Creation* (1798) and *The Seasons* (1801). Since 1899, it has housed a
museum consisting of 6 rooms, including one commemorating **Johannes Brahms** who
settled in Vienna in 1869 (objects and mementoes from his apartment). The
exhibits evoke mainly the people and places that had the greatest impact on
Haydn's career. Besides musical excerpts *(earphones)*, there are also *(numbers in
brackets correspond to the numbering of the exhibits):* a facsimile (1) of the score
of *Missa in Tempora belli*; an engraving (24) from a watercolour by Balthasar
Wigand depicting the performance of *The Creation* at Alte Universität *(see
Akademie der Wissenschaften)*; a facsimile of the composer's last letter (41) on
1 April 1809, and his last visiting card (37), with its own melody; his deathmask
in a showcase; an interesting black lead drawing of Haydn in profile (51) by George
Dance dating from 1794, and a 1795 gouache portrait (52) by Johann Zitterer.
Also in the Mariahilf District are the Theater an der Wien and two buildings by
Otto Wagner at 38 and 40 Linke Wienzeile. There is a description of them among
the sights of the Karlsplatz area.

*Apart from the Ring, which is very close to the beginning of Mariahilfer-
strasse and which runs along one side of the Kunsthistorisches Museum, the
Mariahilf District is near the Karlsplatz area (corresponding to the Wieden
District) and the Neubau District.*

NEUBAU

Neubau lies between Gürtel and the Ring, between Josefstadt and Mariahilf Districts. It stretches along Mariahilferstrasse, a busy commercial thoroughfare with at No 88A a branch of Dorotheum *(see Kapuzinerkirche District)*. Croats and Hungarians once lived in this district of housing estates and residential houses.

Gustav Klimt lived there (Westbahnstrasse 36) and Josef Lanner, the famous composer of waltzes, was born there on 12 April 1801 (Mechitaristengasse 5)

While walking along Mariahilferstrasse, remember that the sights in Mariahilf District are nearby. A glance at a map of the city will make it easy to combine visits to both districts.

Messepalast – The 360m/392yd long Exhibition Hall is near the twin Naturhistorisches and Kunsthistorisches Museum. The architects, **Fischer von Erlach,** father and son, built it between 1719 and 1723. Before alterations in the mid 19C, it housed the former Court stables. In 1921, the authorities decided to use it for large trade fairs. At present, work is in progress to convert it into a Museum of the 20C.

Tabak-Museum ⊘ – *Mariahilferstrasse 2. Underground: Babenbergerstrasse (U2).* The Austrian national tobacco company administers this small museum. It was built in 1784 following Josef II's decision that tobacco should be a state monopoly. This very varied collection surprises visitors by the contrast between the magnificence (most of the pipes) and mediocrity (most of the paintings) of the exhibits in their antiquated setting. The following are notable: the ornate **Meerschaum pipes** (1873) in the first room, particularly the one representing 4 Continents supporting a figure of Europe; the opium pipes from China; the short-stemmed pipe (1893) depicting Christopher Columbus disembarking in America; the water pipes (about 1880). The adjoining theatre is a venue for music recitals or poetry readings.

Carry on along Mariahilferstrasse.

★**Kaiserliches Hofmobiliendepot** ⊘ – *Andreagasse 7.* Having been closed for several years, the Imperial furniture storehouse reopened in 1998, in the new pleasant and well-lit premises. This furniture collection is the Habsburgs' furniture depository. As fashions changed and styles fell out of favour, they changed their furniture just like anyone else, added to which the Imperial family travelled extensively, both in Austria and also in Bohemia and Hungary. After the fall of the empire, this storehouse created by Maria Theresa in 1747 became in 1924 a collection open to the public. The visitor is enticed through an overwhelming collection (163,000 items in a space of 6,000 m²) organised in sections which retrace the development of the furniture and its accessories. Although some rooms are more intesting than others, there are some striking periods which are bound to thrill the dormant interior designer in us all. This applies in particular to the "Laxenburg room", which houses furniture from this palace which is decorated in the Neo-Gothic and German Renaissance styles, to "Prince Eugène of Savoy's room", with its superb chintz Indian tapestries, and also the rooms dedicated to Maria Theresa, François II and Joseph II. Under no circumstances should the visitor miss the Egyptian study of the Empress Ludovica (wife of François I), the Turkish room which was used as a private study by Prince Rudolph when he was staying at the Hofburg, and the marvellous and interesting series of bedrooms furnished in the **Biedermeier** style *(see also the Decorative Arts in the Art section of the Introduction).*

Museum der Gold- und Silberschmiede (**EU M¹²**) ⊘ – *Zieglergasse 22. Underground: Zieglergasse (U3).* This small museum displays six centuries of handcrafted silver and gold.

Go along Zieglergasse and bear right into Lerchenfelderstrasse. Turn into the 3rd street on the right, Döblergasse.

WagnerHaus (**EU M¹³**) ⊘ – *Döblergasse 4. Tram: Strozzigasse (46); bus: Neubaugasse/Neustiftgasse (48A).* Otto Wagner completed Nos 2 and 4 in this small street in 1912. They contrast sharply with the two adjacent buildings he constructed on Linke Wienzeile *(see Karlsplatz District).* The later Döblerstrasse buildings are more geometrical and are typical of O. Wagner's second creative phase, when he favoured right angles and a certain restraint in his decoration.

The famous *Wiener Werkstätte* were also at this address and O. Wagner lived at No 4, where he died on 11 April 1918. Since 1985, it has housed the Otto Wagner archives from the Akademie der Bildenden Künste (Academy of Fine Arts).

Continue along Döblergasse and turn left into Neustiftgasse then right beyond Kellermanngasse.

Spittelberg District

St. Ulrichs-Platz (**EU**) – *Underground: Volkstheater (U2, U3); bus: St.-Ulrichs-Platz (48A).* This square and its church form a fine 18C Baroque ensemble. The most attractive façade belongs undisputably to No 2 (mid 18C), displaying an elegant and aristocratic gate leading into a pretty interior courtyard.Josef Reymund built **St Ulrich's church** ⓥ between 1721 and 1724 on the site of two 13C chapels. It was the setting for the marriage of the German composer Christoph Willibald Gluck and the christening of Johann Strauss the Younger.

Near the chevet of the church, turn left into Burggasse. The Spittelberg quarter starts near Stiftgasse.

★**Spittelberg quarter** – *Underground: Volkstheater (U2, U3); tram: Stiftgasse (49); bus: St.-Ulrichs-Platz (48A).* This was once the artists' quarter. In the 1970s, it attracted people on the fringe of society and since then has experienced a revival. Aware of the charm of these few streets, the town of Vienna refurbished the area, restoring most of the buildings and turning it into a pedestrian precinct.

Situation – The district forms a rectangle consisting of Burgasse, Stiftgasse, Siebensterngasse and Kirchberggasse.

Historical sketch – In 1683, the Turks decided to establish their artillery in this quarter, because it stands on a small hill. It was certainly a good strategic position, since Napoleon did the same at the beginning of the 19C, when he directed his cannons against the town.

Spittelberg was always a working-class quarter, a centre for artists, actors and street singers. Spittelberggasse was an alley where the army rabble came to forget the hardships and privations of barrack life. In 1787 for example, to his annoyance Emperor Josef II had to hasten back to his unit in the Hofburg after someone had surprised him with a charming lady living at No 13 Gutenberggasse.

The present – With its numerous shops, cafés and restaurants, the quarter now offers more cultural attractions. No 8 Stiftgasse (birthplace of the painter Friedrich Amerling) is a centre for musical or literary events, collective workshops for craft or restoration work, and exhibitions. Always lively, Spittelberg has remained a busy area: a craft market takes place there every Saturday from April to November; young people flock to the Christmas market, which is the most convivial in town.

Return to Burgasse towards the Ring.

Near Spittelberg, at the corner of Burggasse and Breitegasse is the smallest house in Vienna (1872); it is now a jewellery shop.

Continue along Burggasse.

Volkstheater – *Neustiftgasse 1. Underground: Volkstheater.* The popular theatre is the creation of two specialists in theatre architecture, Ferdinand Fellner and Hermann Helmer, who built it in 1889. This eclectic edifice offers a repertoire of contemporary and avant-garde plays.

NEUBAU

Turn left into Museumstrasse.

Palais Trautson – *Museumstrasse 7. Closed to the public.* Unfortunately this elegant Baroque palace is closed to the public. Johann Bernhard Fischer von Erlach designed it in 1710 and Christian Alexander Oedtl built it. Since 1961 it has housed the Ministry of Justice. The main body of the ornate façade is worthy of attention. At the top is a statue of Apollo playing the lyre. The influence of Palladio is visible in the handling of the whole structure and the neo-Classical pediment. Beyond the twinned-column entrance, on the left, are telamones which the Italian sculptor Giovanni Giulani fashioned for the magnificent staircase leading to the ceremonial hall. G. Giulani had Georg Raphael Donner *(see Neuer Markt)* as a pupil.

The palace was built for Johann Leopold Trautson. Empress Maria Theresa bought it in 1760 and installed the Hungarian royal guard in it.

Go up Neustiftgasse and take the first street on the right. One of the houses is Josef Lanner's birthplace (Mechitaristengasse 5).

Besides being near the Ring, separated from Messepalast and Volkstheater by Maria-Theresien-Platz, Neubau District is also close to the Mariahilf and Josefstadt Districts.

PENZING★

14th District

Map page 2, **AYZ**

Tram and bus: details next to each sight

Lying west of Vienna, the Penzing District is to the north of Hietzing. It is a quiet, residential quarter.

Technisches Museum (M²) – *Under restoration. Underground: Schloss Schönbrunn (U4); tram: Winckelmannstrasse (52, 58); bus: Anschützgasse (57A).* The Technical Museum of Craft and Industry faces the Auer-Welsbach park and will have had a complete overhaul by the time it reopens. Its collections date from the 18C and cover many areas such as agronomy, chemistry, mechanical engineering, textile industries, metallurgy, physics, telecommunications, etc.

★★Kirche am Steinhof ⊘ – *Baumgartner Höhe 1. Bus: Psychiatr. Krankenhaus (48A). Enter the hospital precinct, turn left then immediately right to walk up the avenue. Guided tour only, in German (45min).* Otto Wagner designed St Leopold's

Musseen der Stadt, Wien

Am Steinhof, a church designed by Otto Wagner

church for the new Lower Austria psychiatric hospital between 1904 and 1907. Symbolically, it occupies the top of the grassy hill (alt 310/1016ft) on which the hospital complex stands. It forms part of this development and faces north instead of the more usual east. It was Vienna's first modern church and is contemporaneous with the Postal Savings Bank, using the same method of construction *(see Postsparkasse):* its Carrara marble cladding lies on top of a simple brick construction. The enormous dome resting on a double tambour is a metal structure covered by copper tiles, which were originally gilded. The architect made use of these new technical devices to build a church which in its form brilliantly echoes the Baroque creations of Bernini and Fischer von Erlach.

Interior – Wagner defended and imposed his design for the interior not because of aesthetic considerations but by demonstrating its cost-effectiveness: the design of the stoups prevented any risk of infection, the floor sloping towards the altar was easy to clean, the pews had no sharp edges against which people might injure themselves, the staff could quickly intervene from any point in the church, the three entrance doors made segregation of the sexes easy. However, the decoration is somewhat precious, almost neo-Byzantine, the high altar, in particular, displays a gilded canopy that resembles a trellis of copper filigree. The angels adorning the canopy were from the *Wiener Werkstätte* studios after a design by Othmar Schimkowitz. Wagner himself designed the whole of the liturgical fittings; he chose Koloman Moser to make the **stained-glass windows**★ *(see illustration in the Introduction, Applied Arts)* based on the theme of mercy. Above the entrance is a portrayal of Paradise Lost which the saints in the side windows are seeking to regain; St John the Baptist leads those on the right, while Tobias conducts those on the left.

★**Wagner Villas** – *Hüttelbergstrasse 26 and 28. Tram: Bergmillergasse (49).* Built in 1888 on a hillside at the edge of the Vienna woods, the first ◷ of these two villas has a classical elegance, with its portico with Ionic columns. Wagner built this eclectic villa for his own use and lived in it until 1908. It looks as it has been transplanted from the Riviera. Originally, the wings were pergolas; they were altered and closed before the end of the century, thus destroying their contrast with the central mass. The present owner is the Symbolist painter Ernst Fuchs, who created the colours of the façade.

A quarter of a century later, the architect built next to it a villa in a more austere style, which in its severity recalls the building at Neubau *(see WagnerHaus).* Both date from the same period. Though in its more geometrical elegance, it differs from the first villa, the second does not dispense altogether with decoration. In particular, it displays a mosaic head of Medusa by Koloman Moser above the entrance.

The nearest sights are in Hietzing District, and in the magnificent Schloss Schönbrunn estate.

PRATER District★
Leopoldstadt – 2nd District
Map page 7, **FGTU**
Underground: Praterstern/Wien Nord (U1)
Tram: Praterstern/Wien Nord (O)
Bus: Praterstrasse (5A)

Just as the Eiffel tower symbolises Paris or the Atomium represents Brussels, the Riesenrad or Giant Ferris Wheel is an emblem of Vienna. Since 1897, this universal landmark situated in the 2nd District slowly raises its cabins above the Prater; this is the location of the famous scene in Carol Reed's film, *The Third Man,* which takes place on the Giant Wheel, in a Vienna laid to waste by the bombings of World War Two. Historically, the district owes its name to the expulsion of the Jews from Poland and the Balkans who lived there until Leopold I drove them out in 1670, less than half a century after Ferdinand II allowed them to settle there. *Unterer Werd,* as people used to say, became Leopoldstadt.

Before going to the Prater, those interested in memorabilia of Viennese musicians might enjoy visiting the house of Johann Strauss the Younger (see Strausshaus), not far from the Riesenrad.

From imperial hunting ground to public amusement park

The first mention of the Prater dates from 1403. In 1560, Maximilian II transformed the wide island between the Danube canal and the river into a walled imperial hunting ground. Joseph II, a liberal emperor, opened the Prater to the public in 1766. Within ten years, stalls and circus tents had made their appearance. From then on, the Prater became an amusement park. In 1771, it was the site of a fireworks display; in 1791, Blanchard flew from there in his balloon, in 1815, sovereigns descended from sumptuous carriages for the Congress of Vienna. It was a place for riding or promenading and was extremely popular in the hey-day of the Viennese waltz, the late 19C. At that time, the Prater was filled with cafés where people could sing or dance. Until the end of the Empire, this park was a fashionable and smart centre, where crinolines stopped twirling only to change partners.

★ Prater – Nowadays, this huge public park has become a focus of attraction for tourists with children. With its area of 1,287 hectares – 3,180 acres, it exists for the amusement of all, children and also adults if they are fond of football or harness racing. The Park consists of two sections: one is a fairground, while the other is a setting for trade fairs and sporting facilities. The first is known as **Wurstelprater** or "Mr. Punch's Prater", and *Volksprater* or "People's Prater". It is a vast fun fair, colourful and noisy, with rifle ranges, roller coasters, dodgem cars, roundabouts and sticky candy-floss.

5km/3 miles long with chestnut trees on either side, Hauptallee starts near Praterstern (Prater Star). It runs through the second part of the Prater from end to end. Although tarmacadamed, the avenue is closed to traffic. This former bridlepath leads to a roundabout on which stands the **Lusthaus**, a pleasure pavilion once belonging to Karl VI which underwent alterations by the French architect Isidore Canevale in 1785. Today, it is a café and restaurant. Trade fairs take place in the exhibition grounds of the Messegelände, and various parts of the park are a setting for numerous sporting events: the Krieau harness racing track dating from 1913 (September to June), the Ernst Happel football stadium, the Freudenau flat racing track (spring to autumn), a swimming pool, a tennis club, a golf links, and a large number of joggers' paths.

Behind the Giant Wheel, the **Liliputbahn** is a little train reaching the Stadion (football stadium) and swimming pool after a tour of 4km/2 miles.

★★ Riesenrad ⊘ – An English engineer, Walter B. Basset took eight months to build the Giant Ferris Wheel which started functioning on 21 June 1897. It was to be an advertisement for the British metallurgical industry. Basset built other Ferris wheels in Chicago, London and Paris, but only the Viennese one is still in operation. During World War One, it served as an observation post. After fire and bomb damage in 1944, it was rebuilt in 1947 with half as many cabins. It was a spectacular setting for the meeting of Harry Lime (played by Orson Welles) and Holly Martins (Joseph Cotten) in Carol Reed's film *The Third Man* (1949). The fifteenth *James Bond* film (1986) used some shots featuring it. It provides an interesting **view★** of Vienna.

Vienna Rapid, the local team

Presse-Sports

Facts and Figures: 64.75m/212ft high, 61m/200ft diameter, 430 tons, 8 pylons of steel girders, 120 wire cables, 1 complete rotation every 20 minutes, as the cabins move at a rate of 75cm/29ins per second.

Planetarium ⊙ – *Hauptallee; next to the Riesenrad*. In 1927, the Zeiss company founded the planetarium housing the small **Prater-Museum** ⊙. This traces the history of the Prater by means of a small exhibition of scale models and photographs. There is a scale model of the 1873 World Fair.

Fussball-Museum (**CY**) ⊙ – *Meiereistrasse 7. Access through main entrance.* Within the Ernst Happel Stadium is this modest Football Museum of trophies and photographic documents of the Vienna Rapid team (World Cup finalist in 1996). Entry to the stadium named after a leading Austrian trainer is on the other side of the museum. The building by Otto Schweitzer dates from 1931 and since refurbishment in 1956 can accommodate 75,000 people.

Excursions round the Prater

Coming from Praterstern, return along Praterstrasse for the town centre.

Just before Strauss's house, Dogenhof (No 70) is worth noting, a pastiche of the Ca'd'Oro on the Grand Canal in Venice. This neo-Gothic "Doge's palace" probably dates from the same era as the little Viennese Venice constructed in the 19C on the site of the Riesenrad during flow control projects on the Danube.

★**Strauss Haus** (**LP**) ⊙ – *Praterstrasse 54. 1st floor. Underground: Nestroyplatz (U1); bus: Praterstrasse (5A)*. It was in this apartment that Johann Strauss the Younger composed in 1867 *The Blue Danube*, an exceedingly famous waltz which seems to incarnate the long and eventful history of this type of music *(see Introduction, Music)*. The first public performance of this work took place on 15 February, in the Diana's Bath ballroom, before over a thousand spectators who had come to hear the "Waltz King"'s latest composition; as often happened, he was conducting elsewhere that night. It was an immediate success. Eight months later, during a concert in London, there was such applause for Waltz Opus 314 that Strauss had to play it four times in succession. A unique occurrence.

ROGER-VIOLLET

Theme from the Beautiful Blue Danube, signed by Johann Strauss the Younger

The museum – Numerous interesting objects and documents are on view here. Some attract attention more than others *(numbers in brackets correspond to the numbering of the exhibits)*: a xylograph depicting a masked ball at Diana's Bath where *The Blue Danube* was first performed *(9)*; several scores of this work *(22, 26, 27)*; the piece of furniture where the Strauss family kept their violins *(18)*; portraits of his parents, Maria Anna Strauss by J.H. Schramm (1835) *(42)* and Johann Strauss the Elder by J. Kriehuber (1835) *(43)*; the invitation to the ball on 15 October 1844 *(see The stormy early career of Johann Strauss the Younger, Hietzing)*; a letter from the son to his father, rejecting the latter's attempt at reconciliation following his liaison with a dressmaker *(51)*; his death mask by Kaspar von Zumbusch *(93)*. Finally, there are numerous portraits of Johann Strauss the Younger, including a copy signed by Maschnik of a bust by Tilgner *(81)*, or an oil painting by August Eisenmenger *(75)*. Also of interest are the caricatures and silhouettes on display in the room where one can hear musical excerpts *(earphones)*, particularly: *Schani*, on the first page of the Viennese newspaper *Der Floh* published on 21 February 1869 *(99)*, *Johann Strauss als Vogel* (Johann Strauss as a Bird, *102*) by Josef Beyer, or the famous silhouette of the composer by Hans Schliessmann *(121)*.

Return to Praterstern and turn left into Klang-Heinestrasse to enter the park by a small side entrance, in line with the street.

Augarten – *Main entrance: Obere Augartenstrasse. Tram: Heinestrasse (21, N), Obere Augartenstrasse (31, 32); bus: Obere Augartenstrasse (5A).* In 1650 trees covered this 52 hectare – 128 acre park. In 1712, the Frenchman Jean Tréhet, the creator of Schönbrunn Park, redesigned it and in 1775 Joseph II opened it to the public, as he had the Prater in 1766. The park lies at the north end of the district.

Porzellanmanufaktur Augarten – After closure in 1864, the famous **Augarten porcelain factory** reopened in 1923. The former imperial factory was founded in 1718 and its "beehive" monogram is famous among connoisseurs of porcelain throughout the world, especially for its Du Paquier, Prince Eugène or Maria Theresa services. Nowadays, the most popular items are admittedly more insipid than their predecessors: they represent Lippizaner horses from the celebrated Spanish Riding School. These figurines which are great favourites today draw inspiration from models dating back to the era of Maria Theresa. Since reopening, the factory has been under the administration of the city authorities and occupies Leopold I's Alte Favorita. The Turks destroyed this small 1654 palace. In 1705, during Joseph I's reign it was rebuilt as an orangery. There, Mozart, Beethoven and Johann Strauss the Elder performed concerts which were very popular with the city's music lovers.

Porcelain workshop in Augarten.

Augartenpalais – In the south corner of the park stands the garden palace. It was probably Johann Bernhard Fischer von Erlach who built it for a city councillor at the end of the 17C. Since 1948, this building has housed the *Wiener Sängerknaben* (Vienna Boys' Choir).

Strange concrete towers – On 9 September 1942, Hitler decreed that, like Berlin and Hamburg, Vienna should have some anti-aircraft towers. Six of them were built around the town centre, including two in Augarten park. Unfinished, they served only as air raid shelters, and could each accommodate up to 30,000 people. They had their own electricity and water supply, and the air was filtered. The upper platforms are all at the same height. It is easy to believe that these giant bunkers built in 1944 by Friedrich Tamms are indestructible. One of them contains a museum *(see Haus des Meeres)*, two are for the use of the army and three are empty.

The nearest sights are in the Fleischmarkt and Hoher Markt Districts, the town centre, and Alsergrund, Donaustadt and Landstrasse Districts (the latter appears in this guide under the heading of Belvedere area).

Join us in our constant task of keeping up-to-date.
Please send us your comments and suggestions.
Michelin Tyre PLC
Tourism Department
The Edward Hyde Building
38 Clarendon Road
WATFORD - Herts WD1 1SX
Tel: 01923 41 5000

SCHÖNBRUNN★★★

Hietzing – 13th District
Local map page 2, **AZ**
Underground: Schloss Schönbrunn (U4), Hietzing (U4)
Tram: Hietzing (58, from Westbahnhof)
By car: If there is no room near Am Platz, it is easiest to park south of the park
(Seckendorff-Gudent-weg, via Maxingstrasse then left to Elisabethallee)
and enter the park by Meiereitor.

Schloss Schönbrunn station is less than 200m/218yds from Hofpavillon, which is near the palace entrance.

Hofpavillon ⏱ – *Schönbrunner Schlossstrasse* – This former underground station spanning the present line was for the sole use of the imperial family and the Court. Otto Wagner designed the capital's overhead railway between 1893 and 1902 (stations and bridges); he built this pavilion in 1899 with the assistance of Leopold Bauer (his pupil) and Josef Maria Olbrich, the creator of the famous Secession pavilion near Karlsplatz.
This building underwent restoration between 1986 and 1989 and possesses a fine central octagonal room: the emperor's waiting room. The sober decoration combines the rigour of imperial protocol with the principles of the Secession (the carpet is a recent copy of the original).

★★★SCHLOSS SCHÖNBRUNN

Three centuries ago, immense forests covered Schönbrunn's present site, providing hunting grounds for the Habsburgs. The first building was Katterburg castle, destroyed by the Turks in 1529. Forty years later, Maximilian II bought the estate from a former mill with the surrounding wooded land and reconstructed the castle on it. Rudolf II then enlarged Katterburg; according to tradition, it was his brother Matthias who discovered, at the beginning of the 17C, the *"Schöner Brunnen"*, literally "the lovely fountain", the spring which has given its name to the area. From it, there is a fine view over the vine-clad hills and the Kahlenberg north of the town. Initially no more than a hunting lodge, Katterburg was enlarged once again by Eleonora Gonzaga, wife of Ferdinand II, who made it her summer residence. In 1683, the Turks totally destroyed the imposing hunting lodge for the second time. After the final victory over the Ottomans, there began a period of prosperity during which aristocrats built many magnificent palaces in Vienna. In 1695, Leopold I commissioned Johann **Bernhard Fischer von Erlach** to design a splendid summer residence for his son Josef. He wanted the palace to eclipse all other royal residences, including Versailles.

The facade overlooking the courtyard

Grandiose magnificence – Versailles was not yet in danger of being surpassed. The great architect's first plan was to place the imperial hunting lodge at the top of the hill where the Gloriette now stands. It would have been a huge palace (4 wings, 3 main courtyards) beyond a series of terraces embellished with cascades. After studying the proposal and consulting his Treasury, the emperor wisely turned down the artist's extravagant dream.

Plans were accepted for another palace at the foot of the hill. A less costly project, it would contain a mere 1,441 rooms. Instead of a panoramic view down over Vienna, it would have an extensive prospect of the gardens. Work started in 1696 during the reign of Josef I and stopped at his death. Karl VI was not particularly interested in Schönbrunn, preferring his "little Escorial" project *(see Neues Stiftgebäude, Klosterneuburg)*. He made it into a summer residence for his daughter Maria Theresa who had married in 1736. This is why work started again during her reign: she liked "her house". Wishing it to be more grandiose, she summoned **Nikolaus Pacassi** (from 1744 to 1749) to complete, modify and enlarge the residence on which she left her own mark, indicative of the brilliant, lively sovereign she became. The final result is a palace reminiscent of Versailles with its succession of major courtyards and its series of lavish state appartments. Architecturally, it was a huge success, a monumental edifice in classic Baroque style, although inside the Rococo style is dominant, representing a victory for French taste over the Italian taste prevalent until then. The decoration of the rooms dates from the reign of Maria Theresa who appreciated Rocaille style panelling, marquetry of rare hardwoods, floral embellishment and coloured chinoiserie, glowing damask and sinuous curlicues: an exuberantly decadent style typical of the Régence period in France.

A place steeped in history – Many historical memories are linked to the palace and the park. During Maria Theresa's reign, Schönbrunn was the summer residence of the Court. **Marie-Antoinette**, the future Queen of France, spent her childhood there. It was in the palace that Mozart played *(see Spiegelsaal or Hall of Mirrors and inset "The palace theatre")*, amazing the empress and her court with his precocious talent. Here too, in 1805 and 1809, Napoleon I set up his headquarters, some years before the famous Congress of Vienna. After the fall of the French empire, Schönbrunn served as a residence for Napoleon's son, the young King of Rome, placed under the guardianship of his grandfather, Emperor Franz who forbade him all contact with France *(see inset The King of Rome)*. It was in Schönbrunn that Emperor Franz-Josef was born and where he died. Here too, Karl I, last of the Habsburgs to reign, signed the Act of Abdication on 11 November 1918. In 1961, John F. Kennedy and Nikita S. Khruschev met here for the first time for a historical "summit conference".

The King of Rome

On 20 March 1811, Napoleon II was born in the Tuileries palace in Paris. He was the son of Napoleon I and Marie Louise, the daughter of Emperor Franz I. Napoleon François, an imperial prince, King of Rome from 1811 to 1814, left Paris with his mother on 29 March 1814 for Blois then Austria. He was acknowledged as Emperor of France by the Chamber of Deputies on 22 June 1815 and became Prince of Parma from 1815 to 1818, then Duke of Reichstadt on 18 July 1818. Reichstadt is a castle situated 65km/40 miles from Prague; this duchy enabled the child to rank at court just below the archdukes.

Although the King of Rome may have been known as *the Aiglon* ("the Eaglet") soon after his birth, it was Victor Hugo who revived the name in his poem *Napoleon II* written in 1852, some twenty years after the death of the child in a gilded prison. He was renamed Duke of Reichstadt to wipe out the nickname of "Ogre".

Finally, it was in Edmond Rostand's famous play starring Sarah Bernhardt in Paris in 1900 that the name was popularised.

His coffin lay in the Capuchin crypt before being transferred to Paris to the Invalides on 15 December 1940. His heart (Augustinerkirche) and his entrails (catacombs of St Stephen's Cathedral) are still in Vienna *(see Kaisergruft)*.

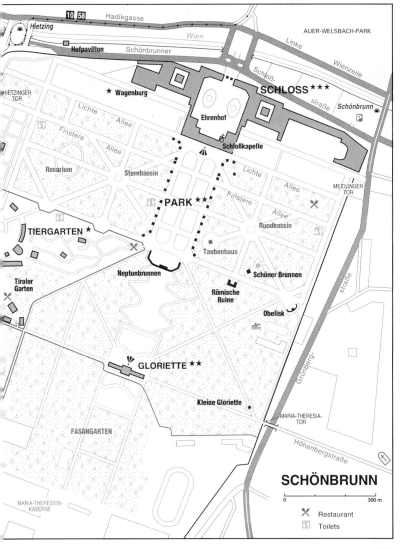

From Napoleon's Eagles to Maria-Theresa's Gloriette

Ehrenhof – The gateway to this huge courtyard (24,000sq m/28,703sq yds) is flanked by two obelisks surmounted, since 1809, by Napoleonic eagles *(concerning Napoleon in Vienna, see Introduction, the Habsburg Empire)*. These French military emblems were not removed after Napoleon's defeat, or at his death. Reportedly, Franz Josef remarked in Viennese dialect *Mi störts nit, und den Leuten g'fällts*: "They don't worry me and folk seem to like them". On the right is the sole remaining and oldest Baroque theatre in Vienna *(see inset)*. Ehrenhof, this immense courtyard, witnessed the parade of Napoleon's Grande Armée as well as the arrival of sovereign powers for the Congress of Vienna. It is bordered by the Cavalier wings and adorned by two fountains commissioned by Maria Theresa, allegories of rivers and kingdoms within the Austro-Hungarian empire.

The vast main body of the palace lies behind a façade with redans 180m/590 ft long. This lacks the fluidity characteristic of Viennese Baroque at its height, in the time of J.B. Fischer von Erlach. The green of the window frames emphasizes the yellow ochre colour of the buildings which brings harmony to the whole construction.

"Maria-Theresa yellow" – The yellow paint covering the exterior of the palace is also known as "Schönbrunn yellow". It became standard for all administrative buildings in Maria Theresa's reign. In Room VII of the Kunsthistorisches Museum *(see under this heading)*, there is a painting by the Venetian Canaletto, dated 1758-1761, showing a view of the pink walls and grey pilasters of the palace from the main courtyard.

★**Wagenburg** ◷ – The Carriage Museum has occupied the former winter riding school since 1922. It has a large display of coaches, carriages, sleighs and sedan chairs belonging to the imperial court, from 1690 to 1918.

In the first room is a collection of travelling coaches, barouches, funeral coaches and baby carriages. The chief exhibits are: Napoleon I's coach for the coronation of the King of Italy in Milan (1805); **the King of Rome's phaeton★**, a gift from Caroline Murat to her nephew, in which he was taken to the Tuileries (1811); Franz I's carriage (1815); Empress Elizabeth's two-seater state carriage (1855) and the barouche in which she drove to Geneva, where she was assassinated; the black funeral coach used to take the Habsburgs to their last resting place (1877); the coupé (1887) and state coach (1890) of Emperor Franz-Josef I.

The second room contains the most sumptuous exhibit in the collection, the **imperial carriage★★** built in 1765 for the coronation in Frankfurt of François-Étienne of Lorraine, Maria Theresa's husband. This richly decorated carriage was drawn by eight white horses from the Kladrub imperial stud farm; it served for weddings, coronations and religious festivals. The horses had red velvet harnesses embroidered in gold, which are on view on the mezzanine floor of the museum together with oriental saddles and Empress Elizabeth's riding whip; she had the reputation of being one of the best horsewomen of her time.

Schlosskapelle – *Enter through interior of palace; free.* Although the chapel was built in the late 17C, its architecture and decoration dates from Maria Theresa's reign. The high altar by Franz Kohl is surmounted by Paul Troger's painting of the

Schönbrunn - The Carriage Room

Trumler/ÖSTERREICH WERBUNG

Marriage of the Virgin to St Joseph. Paintings on the side altars are by the Venetian artist Giovanni Battista Pittoni.

The future Josef II married Isabella of Parma here, in 1760. When she died, he married Marie-Josephine of Bavaria, in 1765.

★★TOUR OF THE PALACE ⊙

Two tours are suggested: the "Imperial Tour" and the "Grand Tour". The first comprises 22 rooms: the state apartments of the imperial couple including reception rooms. The second comprises 40 rooms: the first tour plus the audience chambers of Maria Theresa and her husband François Étienne de Lorraine.

Schlosstheater

Maria Theresa wanted the palace to have a theatre, for her entertainment "in such a huge residence". The Schönbrunn palace theatre was built by N. Pacassi from 1741 to 1749 and decorated by F. Hetzendorf von Hohenberg about 20 years later.

Marie Antoinette danced and the King of Rome acted on the stage of the Hapsburgs' private theatre. It was also the setting for Haydn's marionette opera *Dido*, and the young prodigy Mozart conducted his opera *Der Schauspieldirektor (The Theatre Director)* there. In 1873, Chancellor Otto von Bismarck was sitting among the flower of the European nobility listening to the actress Amalia Heinzinger, when he exclaimed "By Jove, what a graceful little woman!" It marked a milestone in the theatre's history.

Nowadays, the theatre is the summer setting for performances from the Wiener Kammeroper.

Rich in historic memories, these appartments are a triumph of Rococo style, with their red, white and gold colour scheme, the delicate elegance of the stuccowork framing frescoes and ceilings with scrolled whorls, the crystal chandeliers, the faience stoves, tapestries and priceless furniture.

Imperial Tour – *About 1/2 hour. Tickets show the starting time for the tour. During busy periods, arrive at this time; there is no need to queue. "Audioguides" are available on request (free and in several languages) after entering.*

Emperor Franz-Josef's apartments – After the **guard room** (1) and its portraits comes the **Wartezimmer** (2) (antechamber) with its Biedermeier billiard table, the waiting room for those to whom the emperor had granted an audience. Since petitioners might have to wait five hours, they had plenty of time to appreciate the paintings depicting the foundation of the Maria Theresa military Order in 1758, and the banquet over which the emperor presided in the *grosse Galerie* (great gallery) for the centenary of the Order. The Rococo-style **Nusszimmer** (3) or audience chamber acquired its name because of its walnut panelling; it displays busts of emperor Franz-Josef, aged 23, and of his father Archduke Franz-Karl. This opens into the **study** (4) which is hung with portraits of the emperor at 33, his wife Elizabeth, the celebrated Sissi, and Crown Prince Rudolf. In a corner of the **emperor's bedroom** (5) is the iron bed in which Franz-Josef died on 21 November 1916. In front of it is his funerary portrait painted the day after his death. After visiting three small rooms, where a Louis XV desk inlaid with mother-of-pearl is noteworthy, one reaches the **imperial couple's bedchamber** (9) where the rosewood furniture contrasts with the blue Lyons silk covering the walls; this room was only used during the first years of the marriage.

Empress' Apartments – **Empress Elizabeth's salon** (10) displays the portraits of several of Maria Theresa's children; she had eleven girls and five boys. One of her daughters was Marie Antoinette who, at 15, married the dauphin of France, the future Louis XVI. After the **empress's grand drawing room** (11) and its portrait of Franz I, Napoleon's father-in-law, staring implacably at visitors, the tour reaches **Marie Antoinette's drawing room** (12). This contains a fine escritoire which belonged to the last queen of France, depicted above it. The bathroom on the left was designed in 1917 for the imperial couple, Karl and Zita. The charming **Frühstückzimmer** (13) (breakfast room) leading off one corner of the drawing room is decorated with 26 framed yellow silk medallions. Maria Theresa and her daughters embroidered the flowers on them. The **yellow drawing room** (14) contains a clock, a gift from Napoleon to his father-in-law.

Reception rooms – In 1762, at the age of 6, Mozart gave his first recital in the **Spiegelsaal** (16) (Hall of Mirrors), with its white wood and gold leaf panelling. The three **Rosa drawing rooms** (17 to 19) take their name from the Austrian painter Joseph Rosa who decorated them with Swiss and Italian landscapes from 1760 to 1769; the first panel on the left depicts the ruins of the Habsburg palace in the Aargau canton, between Basel and Zürich, which gave its name to the dynasty. The **Lanternzimmer** (20) (lantern room) serves as an antechamber to the 40m/131ft long

Grosse Galerie★★★ (21) (great gallery), a setting both in the past and the present for official banquets, balls and concerts (where from 1814 to 1815 delegates to the Congress of Vienna danced their time away; where John F. Kennedy and Nikita S. Khruschev met in 1961). The allegorical ceiling frescoes (1760) by the Italian artist Gregorio Guglielmi represent the hereditary territories of the empire together with the Austrian nation as a major power for War or Peace.

The **kleine Galerie** (22), a games or music room, has two superb **Chinese cabinets**★ or chambers (23 and 24, *visible through the glass doors*) on either side of it. The first of these, which is circular, is magnificently decorated with lacquered panels, porcelain, gold-plated bronze chandeliers and Chinese porcelain vases (the monkey sitting under the console table is noteworthy). Maria Theresa held meetings there with her chancellor, Count Kaunitz, who could reach it at any time via a secret staircase behind a concealed door; the room was equipped with a most ingenious device, a trap door in the centre through which a table of refreshments would appear; to emphasize the secret nature of this chamber, it bore the name of "conspiracy table".

The **Karusselzimmer** (25) (carousel room) was named after the painting of the Spanish riding school in the capital and opens into the **Zeremoniensaal** (26) (ceremonial hall) which displays Maria Theresa's famous portrait by the court painter Martin van Meytens; the painting on the left depicts the marriage of the future Josef II with Isabella of Parma in 1760; on the right of the portrait is a painting of a concert given in the **Redoutensaal** of the Hofburg; visitors can see *(using the magnifying glass)* a child said to be Mozart. The walls of the **Horse Room** (27, *visible through a glass door)* are decorated with hunting scenes painted on copper.

The Great Gallery

Grand tour – *about 50 mins (including the previous rooms).*

Maria Theresa rooms – The walls of the **blauer chinesischer Salon**★ (28) (blue Chinese salon) are covered with valuable rice paper. This is where the last Austrian emperor, Karl I, signed his abdication, bringing to an end the reign of the Habsburgs, on 11 November 1918; thereafter, Schönbrunn was no longer an imperial residence. Maria Theresa lived in the magnificent **Vieux-Laque-Zimmer**★ (29) (old-lacquer room) after her husband's death (posthumous portrait by Pompeo Battoni) in 1765; this room adorned by black Japanese lacquer framed in walnut served later as a study for Napoleon during the periods of French occupation (1805 and 1809). It was in **Napoleon's bedchamber** (30) that his son, the King of Rome or Duke of Reichstadt, died at the age of 21 on 22 July 1832; the Brussels tapestries date from the 18C. Maria Theresa used the **Porcelain room** (31), with walls decorated in blue and white in imitation of porcelain, for work and relaxation. After it is the **Millionenzimmer**★ (32) which bears the name of Million Room because it cost a million florins. It is covered in rosewood panelling displaying Indo-Persian miniatures (painted on parchment after 16C and 17C originals) set in gilt Rocaille frames. 18C Brussels tapestries decorate the **Gobelinssalon** (33) (tapestry drawing room); the seats and backs of the 6 armchairs feature Gobelins tapestries representing the months of the year. The **memorial room** (34) contains a memento of the *Aiglon*: a stuffed

Traumer/Schloß Schönbrunn K-u.BetriebsgesmbH / Archiv Schönbrunn

crested lark, his beloved companion during his lonely time at Schönbrunn. The portrait depicts him at the age of 5; the marble work by Franz Klein executed from his death mask shows him on his deathbed (copy, the original is in Paris). The **red drawing room** (35) is hung with the portraits of three emperors: Josef II, Leopold II and Franz-Josef (at the ages of 18 and 68).

Archduke's apartments – The **bedroom** (37) affords an opportunity for seeing one of the state beds – this one dates from 1736 – used for giving audience on rising and before retiring rather than for sleeping in; Franz-Josef was born in this room on 18 August 1830. **Archduke Franz-Karl's study** (38) contains an interesting family portrait by Meytens of François Étienne of Lorraine and his wife Maria Theresa: it is evident from the way in which they were represented which one exercised power and authority. To the left is a portrait of Countess Fuchs-Mollard, governess and confidante to Maria Theresa. The adjoining **drawing room** (39) is visible through a glass door.

★★ PARK ⊙

Designed by the Frenchman Jean Trehet (who was responsible for the Schwarzenberg palace gardens) about 1691, it was modified by Josef Hätzl and Adrian von Steckhoven from 1750 to 1780. From the façade of the palace facing the park there is a splendid **view★★** of the Gloriette.

These gardens, extending for nearly 2km²/0.76sq miles were already open to the public when Schönbrunn was an imperial residence, excepting the areas on either side of the palace, namely *Kronprinzengarten* and *Kammergarten*. Arbours, clusters of greenery and vast formal flowerbeds form a backdrop for graceful fountains and elegant groups of allegorical statues, most of them by Wilhelm Beyer von Gotha (about 1772). The park is one of the most popular tourist attractions in Austria (8 million visitors a year).

Neptunbrunnen – This fine, imposing Neptune fountain lies at the foot of the mound surmounted by the *Gloriette*. It is a white marble creation by Franz Anton Zauner (1780). The artist crowned the work with a scene from Greek mythology, depicting Thetis kneeling to Poseidon (Neptune) entreating him to protect her son Achilles on his journey to Troy. Her prayer was answered, but only as far as Troy, where the young hero died killed by an arrow which Paris aimed at the only vulnerable point of his body: his heel.

Schöner Brunnen – According to tradition, it was Emperor Matthias who discovered the "beautiful fountain", the spring whose water was said to preserve the beauty of anyone who drank it. Josef I always had it served at table.

Obelisk – Ferdinand Hetzendorf von Hohenberg designed this obelisk in 1777. It used to rest on top of four gilded turtles. Scenes carved on it trace the history of the Habsburgs until Maria Theresa's reign.

The Palmenhaus

Römische Ruine – *"These ruins are as fake as possible, but built by a pleasant archeologist and delightfully situated at the foot of a wooded hillside [...] Dotted around are fragments of low reliefs from the shafts of ivyclad columns and heads of decapitated marble statues..."* This is the setting for the 4th act of Edmond Rostand's play, *L'Aiglon*, a romantic backdrop typical of the late 18C.

The Roman ruins are a folly, conjuring up images of the destruction of Carthage by Rome, for instance. They, too, were the work of F. Hetzendorf von Hohenberg (1776). The slightly Mannerist style conveys a magical atmosphere.

Little Gloriette – East of the earlier *Gloriette* is this pavilion, decorated with frescoes, where Maria Theresa sometimes took her breaskfast.

★★Gloriette ⊘ – F. Hetzendorf von Hohenberg built this elegant gallery with arcades in 1775 to commemorate the Battle of Kolin in 1757, when Maria Theresa's troops defeated the armies of Frederick II of Prussia. Outlined against the sky on top of its mound, the monument suggests a classical triumphal arch. It also heralds the start of the colder Empire style. This belvedere provides a fine view extending as far as Kahlenberg and Leopoldsberg. Since 1996, the *Gloriette* has housed a café open during the summer months.

The Gloriette

★Palmenhaus ⊘ – This tropical glasshouse dates from 1882. Undoubtedly, its architect, F. von Segenschmidt, took as his inspiration the palm house in Kew Royal Botanical Gardens, built in 1848 in west London by Decimus Burton. It is the largest glass and iron greenhouse on the continent of Europe. Its three sections house a splendid variety of tropical plants together with wooden benches where it is pleasant to sit and muse. In one of them, a few birds fly around in comparative freedom.

★Tiergarten ⊘ – The zoo was founded in 1752 by François Étienne of Lorraine, Maria Theresa's husband, and is the oldest in Europe. It is also one of the best managed. It is very popular with the Viennese. On fine Sundays, swarms of children come here to see the elephants, giraffes, monkeys, bears and penguins.

Since May 1994, the park of the Tyrolean garden has given younger children an opportunity to approach farm animals.

In the centre of this garden, by the French architect Jean-Nicolas Jadot de Ville-Issey, stands the emperor's pavilion which displays paintings of animals on the panelling enhanced with gilt together with the inevitable portrait of Franz-Josef; it has been turned into a restaurant and café.

Tiroler Garten – To the west of the hill, Archduke Johann introduced an alpine note to Schönbrunn Park by rebuilding two Tyrolean chalets and an alpine garden towards 1800.

Botanischer Garten – Franz I, who was passionately interested in natural sciences, founded this botanic garden in 1845. Worldwide expeditions to remote countries helped to endow it with rare plants.

HIETZING

In the late 19C, the 13th District became fashionable and attracted many industrialists, artists and intellectuals, such as Egon Schiele and Gustav Klimt. The latter was born there and his last studio was in Feldmühlgasse. The Austrian television (O.R.F.) buildings overlook Hietzing. Once the abode of the aristocracy, it is now the smartest district in the capital. It is the residential area par excellence, bathed in a timeless atmosphere that is particularly discernible in the streets separating Lainzerstrasse from Maxingstrasse.

The stormy early career of Johann Strauss, the Younger – Johann Strauss, the Elder began his musical career in the Pramer orchestra and in the quartet conducted by the famous Josef Lanner. Rivalry soon developed between them and it was to prove of lasting benefit to Viennese music. In the 1830s, Lanner played at the *Redoutensaal*, Strauss at the *Sperl*. He was already internationally renowned, when he learned that his son, a mere twenty-year old, intended to form his own orchestra. Their rivalry came to a head with Johann Strauss the Younger defying his father's ban and performing his first concert on 15 October 1844 at Hietzing, at *Dommayer*'s. Its resounding success sealed the antagonism between father and son: in 1848, the year of the revolution, the father supported the Habsburgs and composed the immortal *Radetzky March*, while the son favoured the rebels and incorporated *La Marseillaise* in his works. *Dommayer* still exists, not far from Am Platz *(Dommayergasse 1)*.

Leave Schönbrunnpark by Hietzinger Tor.

Immediately on the right there is a post office (opposite Park Hotel) which was once the Kaiserstöckl (1770) or summer residence of Maria Theresa's Ministers of Foreign Affairs.

On Am Platz stands Pfarrkirche Maria Hietzing, better known as Maria Geburt, dating from the 13C. Refurbished in the 17C, the interior displays decoration in the Baroque style; the ceiling frescoes are by Georg Greiner, the stucco work by Dominicus Piazzol and the altars by Matthias Steindl. The square displays four other sights: a Plague column (1772); a statue of Maximilian, Emperor of Mexico (1871); the **Hietzinger Heimat Museum** which houses extensive documentation on the painter Egon Schiele and the last Viennese gas street lamp (on the right of the museum entrance).

Walk of architectural interest

West of Schönbrunnpark, the Hietzing District contains several residences in Secession or modern styles; while some are sumptuous and others are minimal, they all illustrate the best examples of the architecture of their time. The itinerary described below summarizes in many ways the history of Viennese residential architecture from 1900 to 1932. To avoid a long walk, the location of the nearest tram stop is given for houses furthest from Am Platz.

Walk down Altgasse where No 16 is a Heuriger from the Biedermeier era and bear left into Fasholdgasse. Turn right into Trauttmannsdorffgasse.

Trauttmannsdorffgasse – In this street are several Biedermeier houses which form an interesting group, typical of its period. Alban Berg lived at No 27 *(wall plaque)*.

Turn left into Gloriettegasse to No 9, home of the actress Katharina Schratt, friend and confidante of Emperor Franz-Josef. Retrace your steps and bear right into Wattmanngasse.

Lebkuchenhaus – *Wattmanngasse 29.* Built in 1914 by a pupil of Otto Wagner, the "gingerbread" *(Lebkuchen)* house displays a remarkable façade decorated with dark majolica at the level of the windows and the entablature.

Retrace your steps and turn right into Gloriettegasse.

Villa Primavesi – *Gloriettegasse 14-16. From Hietzing terminus, take tram 60 and alight at Gloriettegasse.* This building, by **Josef Hoffmann** (1913-1915), now houses the *Kulturamt der Stadt Wien* (Vienna council cultural department). Also known as the villa Skywa, it was built for Robert Primavesi, representative at the Diet of Moravia and Member of Parliament. The architect came from the region.

Turn left into Alois-Kraus Promenade. At the end bear left into Lainzerstrasse before taking the first street on the right, Veitingergasse. Walk up the street and turn right into Nothartgasse.

Hornerhaus (**AZ**) – *Nothartgasse 3. From Hietzing terminus, take tram 60 and alight at Jagdschlossgasse.* The barrel-shaped roof of the Horner house (1912) is somewhat startling. Forced by regulations not to build more than one storey on the street or garden side, **Adolf Loos** resorted to this shape to gain an extra storey. Partly modified, the house became a listed building in 1972.

Return to Veitingerstrasse. Walk up the street and turn left into Jagicgasse.

Werkbundsiedlung (**AZ**) – Lovers of 20C architecture will be interested by this modern (modernistic) housing development greatly ahead of its time. Founded in Germany in 1907, the *Werkbund* was an artistic movement embodying most of the principles of the English Arts and Crafts movement, except that it did not oppose mass production. The period of *Werkbundsiedlungen*, or Werkbund-cities, began in 1927 with the Stuttgart *Weissenhof*. This, under the direction of Mies van der Rohe, included prototypes of residential buildings incorporating research on new construction methods. There followed the Breslau *Wohnung und Werkraum*, in 1929, and the Vienna *Werkbundsiedlung*, in 1932. In this city, activity in the socialist town council had begun in 1922 with compact housing estates, among which was the famous Karl-Marx-Hof *(see under this heading)*. The team in this housing estate-Werkbund, working under the direction of Joseph Frank, showed a taste for innovation by developing a district with 70 Minimalist housing units.

The City of Vienna bought back most of the houses in this architectural "laboratory" between 1983 and 1985 and restored them. There were some famous names among the architects involved in the original project *(see map at the entrance to Jagicgasse)*: the Viennese Adolf Loos, Josef Hoffmann, Oscar Strnad; the Frenchmen André Lurçat and Gabriel Guévrékian (former pupil of Strnad); the Dutchman Gerrit Rietveld; the American Richard Neutra (former pupil of Loos); etc. There is a small museum ⊘ in the district, which is part of the Bezirksmuseum Hietzing *(Woinovichgasse 32)*.

Additional sights

Friedhof Hietzing ⊘ – *Maxingstrasse. From the Hietzing stop, take bus 56B or 58B and alight at Montecuccoliplatz. Numbers in italic in brackets specify the location (see plan at the entrance).* South of the Tiroler Garten (Tyrolean garden) at Schönbrunn is the cemetery of the 13th District of Vienna. Many famous people are buried here: the composer Alban Berg (1885-1935) *(group 49-tomb 24F)*; chancellor Engelbert Dollfuss (1892-1934) *(27-11/12)*, murdered during an attempted putsch in the chancelery; Franz Grillparzer (1791-1872) *(13-107)*, the greatest Austrian playwright; Gustav Klimt (1862-1918) *(5-194/195)*, "academic" painter; Koloman Moser (1868-1918) *(16-14)*, very active in the *Wiener Werkstätte;* Anton Schmerling *(5-47)*, statesman. Finally, Jean-Baptiste Hanet *(3-6)*, "faithful Cléry", Louis XVI's last servant, was buried here in 1809 after being valet to the guillotined King of France.

★ **Lainzer Tiergarten** (**AZ**) ⊘ – *From Hietzing terminus, take tram 60 and alight at Hermesstrasse. Take bus 60B to Lainzer Tor terminus. Enter through Lainzer Tor (car park outside, map of park at the entrance).* West of Hietzing is Maria Theresa's hunting ground covering 25km²/9sq miles, which was converted into a forest park. Most of the trees are oak or beech. In 1782, the empress decided to enclose the estate by a stone wall 24km/14 miles long with 6 gates: Gütenbachtor, Lainzer Tor, St Veiter Tor, Adolfstor, Nikolaitor and Pulverstampftor. Open to the public since 1921, this vast domain, with footpaths covering 80km/49 miles, affords excellent walks in the open air, if visitors tire of the city's museums.

Hermesvilla ⊘ – *1/4 hour by the main avenue.* Karl von Hasenauer built this residence as a retreat for the empress between 1882 and 1886 at the request of Franz-Josef. In it are temporary exhibitions organised by the Historisches Museum der Stadt Wien. These offer an opportunity of viewing the bedroom and scenes from *Midsummer Night's Dream* designed by Hans Makart and painted by his followers (including Georg and Gustav Klimt)

Sadness beneath the brilliance – The wayward and elusive **Sissi** conquered everyone by her charm, beauty and grace, magnificently translated on the silver screen by Romy Schneider. At the time of the construction of Hermesvilla, there was little doubt that the marriage of Elizabeth and Franz-Josef had failed. An attentive study of the interior will provide evidence of this. The scenes from Shakespeare are by H. Makart, a painter in the grand manner. Unintentionally, they convey the forlorn solitude of a sensuous yet ascetic empress, a woman who withdrew into herself after her son's tragic death at Mayerling in 1889.

Through the woods to the viewing point – There are numerous animals on the estate, some more visible (deer, mouflons, etc.) than others (grass snakes, vipers, asps, great spotted woodpeckers etc.). Since it covers a huge area, here is a short round trip on foot *(1 1/2 hours)*. Anyone arriving either from Lainzer Tor or the villa, should go towards "St Veiter Tor". After this gate (open Sundays and public holidays), follow the wall, turning left after 50m/54yds up a fairly steep path rising beneath the trees. Pass the animal enclosure, which is entered through a gate with wire netting (signpost: "Nikolai-Tor-über-Wienerblick), and climb the hill on the right. Go straight on and, from the top of the hill (alt. 434m/1,423ft) there is a fine **view** of west Vienna including Kirche am Steinhof (Otto Wagner's church) and further to the right the two towers of Votivkirche and the spire of Stephansdom. After a short pause, skirt the forest to the left towards "Rohrhaus" and its café with a children's play area. Follow the Hermesvilla signs to return to Lainzertor.

EXCURSIONS

Mode-Sammlungen (**AZ**) ⊘ – *Hetzendorferstrasse 79 in Meidling, 12th District. From Hietzing terminus, take tram 60 and alight at Hofwiesengasse. Take tram 62 and alight at Schloss Hetzendorf.* One of Maria Theresa's former palaces, Hetzendorf (late 17C, refurbished in the mid 18C) houses the fashion section from the Historisches Museum der Stadt Wien. It comprises about 18,000 costumes and accessories mainly from the 19C; few items are on permanent display. Of special interest are the temporary theme exhibitions which take place there regularly *(see the calendar of events available free from the Vienna tourist information centre).*

During the summer of 1876, Hugo Wolf, the great composer of *lieder*, lived at the corner of Schönbrunner Allee (No 53) and Hetzendorferstrasse, opposite the palace entrance.

From Schloss Schönbrunn and its immediate surroundings, the nearest sights are: the Mariahilf, Penzing and Liesing Districts.

Those travelling by car can easily follow the itinerary described in the Wienerwald section.

WÄHRING

18th District

Map pages 2-3, **ABXY**

Tram and bus: details next to the sights

Währing District lies between the Döbling and Hernals Districts, northwest of the city centre, beyond the Josefstadt and Alsergrund Districts. Währing is a quiet residential area dotted with delightful Jugendstil houses.

Schubertpark (**ET**) – *Währingerstrasse. Tram: Martinstrasse (40, 41).* A short distance from Volksoper *(see under this heading)* Schubert Park displays an unusual feature, visible to passers-by: several tombs and a cross, the remains of the former Währinger Friedhof (Währing cemetery). Franz Schubert and Ludwig van Beethoven were buried here, next to the east wall. Their coffins were transferred to the Central Cemetery *(see Zentralfriedhof)* in 1888.

Türkenschanzpark – *Tram: Türkenschanzplatz (41); bus: Türkenschanzplatz (10A).* This park takes its name of Turks' fortifications from the encampment which Suleyman the Magnificent's janissaries created on its site, when retrenching in the face of glorious resistance by Count Salm's army during the 1529 siege. In the 1880s, this land covering 15 hectares/37 acres became a public park and Gustav Sennholz laid it out with pools and avenues. With its pretty Jugendstil gate and lovely trees, the park was soon a focus of attraction for Viennese who enjoyed walking, notably Arthur Schnitzler who appreciated its small hills and dales.

South of the park, lovers of architecture may see three houses from the early 20C; the first two are by Robert Oerley and the third by Hubert and Franz Gessner: villa Paulick (1907, Türkenschanzstrasse 23), villa Schmutzer (1910, Sternwartestrasse 62/64), villa Gessner (1907, Sternwartestrasse).

Villa Moller – *Starkfriedgasse 19. Closed to the public. Tram: Gersthoferstrasse/Scheibenbergstrasse (41).* Loos built this house in 1928 for Hans and Anny Moler. It was a major landmark in his career and its pure, stark geometric style shocks some, attracts others and never fails to elicit a response.

Geymüller-Schlößl ⊘ – *Pötzleinsdorferstrasse 102.* The banker Heinrich Geymüller commissioned this manor house in 1808. It contains a collection of 17C to 19C antique watches and clocks, ranging from the Baroque to the Biedermeier style. Visitors should pay as much attention to the decoration, furniture and ornaments in the seven rooms on view, as to the collection, from the Österrreichisches Museum für Angewandte Kunst (Austrian Museum of Applied Arts).

The nearest sights are in the Alsergrund, Josefstadt and Grinzing Districts.

ZENTRALFRIEDHOF

According to one perhaps exaggerated view, Vienna is for many a city of the dead. The town and its suburbs comprise about fifty cemeteries, some of which have almost become tourist attractions, such as Hietzing, St Marxer Friedhof and to a lesser extent Grinzing. Kapuzinergruft *(see Kaisergruft)* where 138 members of the imperial family are buried is a standard part of any tour programme for visitors to Vienna. Several burial grounds such as the Michaelerkirche crypt or the Stephansdom catacombs *(see under these headings)* appeal to tourists because of their special atmosphere. So it is not so strange to see the Viennese adorning with flowers, on the first Sunday after All Saints' Day, the numerous tombs of the *Friedhof der Namenlosen* (cemetery of the nameless ones). This lies in Simmering on the banks of the Danube, and contains the remains of those washed up on the river bank.

Zentralfriedhof is colossal yet less romantic than Père Lachaise in Paris. It forms part of the traditional attractions of Vienna, because it contains the tombs of most Austrian celebrities from the political and artistic worlds.

Today, people rarely visit and may have perhaps forgotten some sections, which illustrate the cosmopolitan character of this Viennese cemetery. Few now remember the members of the Czech resistance (group 42), the soldiers of the Soviet army (44B) or the French soldiers killed in 1809 (88).

An immense cemetery ☺ – *A map of the cemetery is available at the main gate.* Zentralfriedhof was created in 1874 and contains nearly half a million tombs and monuments. It is the largest cemetery in Austria. The area covers 3.1km²/1sq mile (including the crematorium) and its boundary wall is 8km/5miles long, which is why some people drive through it by car.

The impressive main gate (1905) is the work of Max Hegele who also built the church *(see below)*.

Dr-Karl-Lueger-Kirche ☺ – This impressive Jugendstil church is dedicated to St Charles Borromeo and was named after the founder of the Christian-Socialist party, former mayor of Vienna. Max Hegele completed it in 1910. Built on the same scale as the cemetery, it occupies an area of 2,000m²/2,392sq yds and the cross above the dome is about 60m/200ft high.

V.I.P.'s – The list is almost endless. Our selection is therefore based on personal choice; it features brief biographical notes. Foreign visitors to this cemetery will soon realize the extent to which Vienna attracted creative artists, particularly in the world of music. Most of the artists mentioned in this guide are buried here.

Group 32A – No **5**: **Eduard van der Null**. Born in Vienna in 1812, died in Vienna in 1868. Architect of the Staatsoper *(see Staatsoper)* and Karltheater. No **6**: **Johann Nestroy**. Born in Vienna in 1801, died in Graz in 1862. Comedian, satirist, moralist and theatre director. No **10**: **Hugo Wolf**. Born in Windischgrätz in 1860, died in Vienna in 1903. Composer of lieder, Kapellmeister (director of music) in Salzburg and music critic on the *Wiener Salonblatt* from 1884 to 1887. No **15**: **Johann Strauss the Elder**. Born in Vienna in 1804, died in Vienna in 1849. Composer and conductor who, with J. Lanner, contributed to the world-wide triumph of

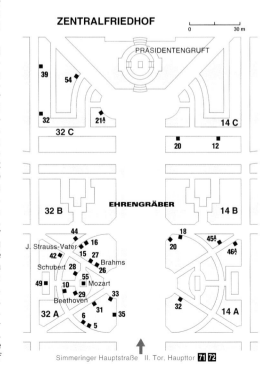

ZENTRALFRIEDHOF

the Viennese waltz. No **16**: **Josef Lanner**. Born in Vienna in 1801, died in Vienna in 1843. Composer *(see above)*. No **26**: **Johannes Brahms**. Born in Hamburg in 1833, died in Vienna in 1897. Composer who settled in the Austrian capital in 1862 where he wrote his five symphonies and the famous *Deutsches Requiem*. No **27**: **Johann Strauss the Younger**. Born in Vienna in 1825, died in Vienna in 1899. Composer who gave the waltz a symphonic structure and then wrote operettas; the graceful nymph on the tomb recalls *The Blue Danube*, while the bat alludes to the famous operetta. No **28**: **Franz Schubert**. Born in Vienna in 1797, died in Vienna in 1828. Composer, master of lieder, composer of nine symphonies. Tomb by Theophil von Hansen. No **29**: **Ludwig van Beethoven**. Born in Bonn in 1770, died in Vienna in 1827. This

B. Kaufmann

Music Mourning, in the central cemetery

world-renowned composer wrote most of his works in Vienna; his tomb was moved from Währing to Vienna in 1888. No **31**: **Franz von Suppé**. Born in Split in 1819, died in Vienna in 1895. Composer, conductor in the Theater An der Wien, composer of operettas which have become classics. No **33**: **Karl Hasenauer**. Born in Vienna in 1833, died in Vienna in 1894. Architect who built jointly with Gottfried Semper the Burgtheater and Neue Burg. The allegorical statue on his tomb represents Architecture. No **35**: **Carl Millöcker**. Born in Vienna in 1842, died in Baden in 1899. Composer of operettas. No **42**: **Eduard Strauss**. Born in Vienna in 1835, died in Vienna in 1916. Composer, brother of Johann and Joseph Strauss, whom he replaced as conductor of the Strauss orchestra. No **44**: **Josef Strauss**. Born in Vienna in 1827, died in Vienna in 1870. Composer, kapellmeister, brother of Johann and Eduard, composer of melancholy waltzes. No **49**: **Christoph Willibald Glück**. Born in Erasbach in 1714, died in Vienna in 1787. Composer of operas, imperial kapellmeister. No **55**: **Wolfgang Amadeus Mozart**. Born in Salzburg in 1756, died in Vienna in 1791. Music's child prodigy was buried in a mass grave in St Marxer Friedhof. The monument is therefore a cenotaph and the statue holds the score of the *Requiem* in its right hand.

Group 32C – No **21A**: **Arnold Schönberg**. Born in Vienna in 1874, died in Los Angeles in 1951. Composer, inventor of atonal composition leading to serial music. Monument by F. Wotruba. No **32**: **Fritz Wotruba**. Born in Vienna in 1907, died in Vienna in 1975. Sculptor, pupil of Anton Hanak, creator of the Dreifaltigkeitskirche (Church of the Holy Trinity) in Liesing. No **39**: **Franz Werfel**. Born in Prague in 1890, died in Beverley Hills in 1945. Poet and man of letters who married Alma Mahler in 1929 and emigrated in 1938 to the United States via France. No **54**: **Kurt Jürgens**. Born in Munich in 1915, died in Vienna in 1982. Theatre actor and film star who became famous in the Burgtheater from 1941 to 1953 then in numerous films.

Präsidentergruft – This crypt contains the graves of the presidents of the Austrian Republic. **Karl Renner**. Born in Untertannowitz in 1870, died in Vienna in 1950. President from 1945 to 1950. **Theodor Körner**. Born in Uj Szönyi in 1873, died in Vienna in 1957. President from 1951 to 1957. **Adolf Schärf**. Born in Nikolsburg in 1890, died in Vienna in 1965. Prsident from 1957 to 1965. **Franz Jonas**. Born in Vienna in 1899, died in Vienna in 1974. President from 1965 to 1974.

Group 14C – No **12**: **Walter Nowotny**. Born in Gmünd in 1920, died in Osnabrück in 1944. Flying ace in the *Deutsche Luftwaffe*; 258 victories, shot down on 8/11/1944. No **20**: **Josef Hoffmann**. Born in Pirnitz in 1870, died in Vienna in 1956. Architect, pupil of Otto Wagner, co-founder of *Wiener Werkstätte*, founder of Austrian Werkbund.

ZENTRALFRIEDHOF

Group 14A – No **18**: **Anton Dominik Fernkorn**. Born in Erfurt in 1813, died in Vienna in 1878. Sculptor, creator of the Aspern Lion and the equestrian statues on Heldenplatz. No **20**: **Theophil von Hansen**. Born in Copenhagen in 1813, died in Vienna in 1891. Architect of several official buildings, including the Parliament. No **32**: **Hans Makart**. Born in Salzburg in 1840, died in Vienna in 1884. Painter of historical scenes and portraits, some of which are on view at the oberes Belvedere (upper Belvedere). No **45A**: **Joseph Kornhäusel**. Born in Vienna in 1782, died in Vienna in 1860. Biedermeier architect, some of whose works are in Baden. No **46A**: **Pietro Nobile**. Born in Campestra in 1774, died in Vienna in 1854. Architect, director of the Academy of architecture, designer of the Äusseres Burgtor in the Hofburg.

Group 0 – No **54**: **Antonio Salieri**. Born in Legnano in 1750, died in Vienna in 1825. Composer who influenced Beethoven, Schubert and Meyerbeer, a rival of Mozart, imperial kapellmeister from 1788 to 1790. No **84**: **Peter Altenberg**. Born in Vienna in 1859, died in Vienna in 1919. Poet, author, journalist, brilliant writer of aphorisms. Cross by Adolf Loos. No **112**: Count **Theodor Baillet-Latour**. Born in Linz in 1780, died in Vienna in 1848. The mob hanged this Minister of War during the 1848 revolution. No **195**: **Adolf Loos**. Born in Brünn in 1870, died in Kalksburg in 1933. A great architect and pioneer notable for his functional style, active in Vienna and Paris.

Group 5A – No **R 1/33**: **Karl Kraus**. Born in Jičin in 1874, died in Vienna in 1936. Linguist, literary and theatre critic, journalist, satirist.

Group 24 – **R3**: corner crypt: **Victor Adler**. Born in Prague in 1852, died in Vienna in 1918. Doctor and politician, unifier of Social Democracy in Austria. **Otto Bauer**. Born in Vienna in 1881, died in Paris in 1938. Politician, leader of the Austro-Marxist movement in Austria during the 1920s.

Jewish section – *1. Tor*. Group 19, row 58: **Arthur Schnitzler**. Born in Vienna in 1862, died in Vienna in 1931. Doctor, author, and psychoanalytical poet. He is said to have asked to be stabbed in the heart to ensure he would not be buried alive... On the other side of Simmeringer Hauptstrasse is the crematorium, which Clemens Holzmeister built in 1922 *(Simmeringer Hauptstrasse 337)*.

Zentralfriedhof is not far from the sights in the Favoriten and Landstrasse Districts (Belvedere quarter)

People travelling by car can easily go to Petronell-Carnuntum or Neusiedler-See.

Animals – would enjoy the Tiergarten in the park at Schloss Schönbrunn, or Lainzer Tiergarten (Hietzing) and the Naturhistorisches Museum (Burgring) which has a remarkable collection of stuffed animals.

Otto Wagner's Architecture – would enjoy Postsparkasse (opposite Stubenring), the Wagner-Pavillons (Karlsplatz), Linke Wienzeile (near Karlsplatz), or Wagnerhaus (Neubau), Kirche am Steinhof (Penzing) and Wagner's two villas in Penzing.

Splendid Baroque churches – would enjoy Jesuitenkirche (near Fleischmarkt), Peterskirche (near the Graben), Servitenkirche (Alsergrund), Piaristenkirche Basilika Maria Treu (Josefstadt) and naturally Karlskirche (Karlsplatz).

Reminders of Sissi – would enjoy the Kaiserappartements in the Hofburg, Schloss Schönbrunn and its apartments, and also the Volksgarten, Peterskirche and Mayerling where her son Rudolf committed suicide.

Furniture – would enjoy the Österreichisches Museum für Angewandte Kunst (Stubenring), Schloss Schönbrunn and its apartments, Bundessammlung Alter Stilmöbel (Neubau).

The paintings of Klimt and Schiele – would enjoy the Österreichische Galerie des 19. und 20. Jahrhunderts (Oberes Belvedere), Burgtheater (Dr.-Karl-Lueger-Ring), the stairwell of the Kunsthistorisches Museum (Burgring), Historisches Museum der Stadt Wien (Karlsplatz), Secessiongebäude (near Karlsplatz), Graphische Sammlung Albertina once it has reopened (Hofburg), Hietzinger Heimat Museum (Hietzing, near Schönbrunn).

Sculptured fountains – would enjoy some fine examples in Vienna, such as Michaelertrakt (Hofburg, Michaelerplatz), Austria-Brunnen (Freyung), Donaunixenbrunnen (Palais Ferstel), Vermählungsbrunnen (Hoher Markt), Andromeda-Brunnen (Neuer Markt and Österreichisches Barockmuseum), Pallas-Athene-Brunnen (Parlament), Mosesbrunnen (Franziskanerplatz).

Classical composers – would enjoy Pasqualatihaus (near Freyung), Beethovenhaus (Heiligenstadt), Eroicahaus (Oberdöbling), Beethoven-Schauräume (Baden) where Beethoven stayed, the Haydn-Museums (Mariahilf and Eisenstadt) occupying houses where Haydn lived, Schloss Esterházy (Eisenstadt) where he worked and Rohrau his birthplace, Liszts Geburtshaus (Raiding) Liszt's birthplace, Deutschordenhaus and Figarohaus (near Stephansdom) where Mozart lived, the Schubert-Museum and Schubert-Sterbewohnung where Schubert was born and died, Strausshaus (near the Prater) where Johann Strauss lived, without forgetting the Musiksammlung des Nationalbibliothek, the Sammlung alter Musikinstrumente (Hofburg) and Staatsoper (Opernring).

Reminders of Sigmund Freud – would enjoy visiting the Sigmund-Freud-Museum (Alsergrund), the house where he used to live and work; he was a professor at the University (Dr.-Karl-Lueger-Ring) and was an habitué of Café Landtmann (Dr.-Karl-Lueger-Ring). The Museum für Geschichte der Medizin (Josephinum) has exhibits relating to the great physician.

Roman remains – would enjoy the Römische Baureste (Am Hof), Römische Ruinen (Hoher Markt), Archäologischer Park and the Archäologisches Museum in Petronell-Carnuntum, as well as the Ephesos-Museum collection (Hofburg).

Red Vienna and its architecture – would enjoy a visit to Karl-Marx-Hof (Heiligenstadt), George-Washington-Hof (Favoriten) and Reumannhof (near Reumannplatz, Favoriten), not included in this guide.

Houses on piles in Neusiedler See

Further afield

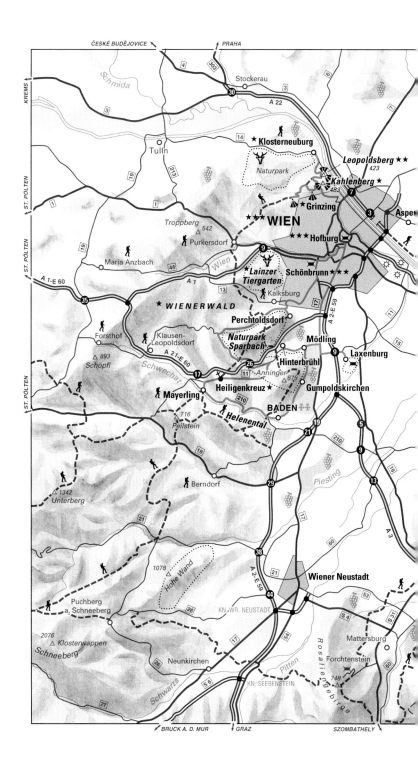

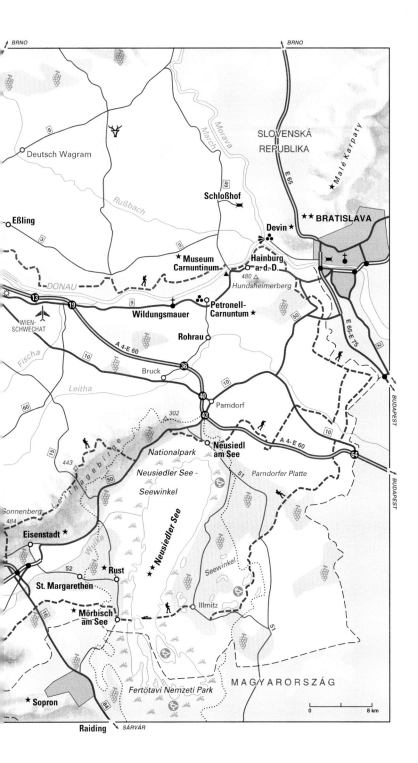

The chapter on art and architecture in this guide
gives an outline of artistic creation in the region,
providing the context of the buildings and works of art
described in the Sights section.
This chapter may also provide ideas for touring.
It is advisable to read it at leisure.

BADEN ✝✝

Near Vienna at the end of the Helenen Valley is the celebrated spa town of Baden, dreamy and romantic. Lying on the edge of the Vienna Woods, it is surrounded by meadows and vineyards yielding excellent wines such as *Bockfuss* or *Bärenschwanzl*. With its splendid Biedermeier architecture and magnificent houses, it deserves its reputation as a delightful resort offering a wide variety of entertainments culminating in the *Operettensommer*, the summer festival.

The resort – The beneficial effects of its sulphur springs were already known to the Romans and the emperor Marcus Aurelius mentions the *Aquae Pannoniae* situated "18,000 double paces south of Vindobona" (Vienna). Today the 15 springs yield over

B. Kaufmann

Holy Trinity Column

4 million litres/880,000 gallons of water daily with a natural temperature of 36°. The mineral waters are prescribed for the treatment of rheumatism and for strengthening the metabolism, the tissues of the joints and the vascular system. The spa had its golden age during the Biedermeier era and Emperor Franz I was a frequent summer visitor between 1803 and 1834; it regained popularity with the opening of the southern railway.

Famous guests – This idyllic setting attracted mainly musicians: Wolfgang Amadeus Mozart wrote his *Ave Verum* here, Franz Schubert stayed here as well as Ludwig van Beethoven who made five visits and finished his *Ninth Symphony* here during the winter of 1823-1824. The writer Franz Grillparzer and the painter Moritz von Schwind were also visitors. Later, the town welcomed the kings of the waltz and the operetta: Johann Strauss, Joseph Lanner, Karl Millöcker, and Karl Zeller. From 1805, the guest list of people taking the waters reads like a *Who's Who* of European nobility. The Emperor Napoleon, fascinated by the picturesque **Helenental** *(see Wienerwald)* west of the city, stayed here with his wife Marie-Louise.

SIGHTS

If going to Baden by tram, alight at Josefsplatz and take the Frauengasse to reach the Hauptplatz. If arriving by car, it is easiest to park near the Casino.

A visit of the town reveals houses in the Classical or Biedermeier style, particularly on Kaiser-Franz-Ring (near the Casino), Rainer-Ring (between the Casino and Josefplatz) and Breyerstrasse (between Josefplatz and Wassergasse).

Hauptplatz – This pedestrianised square in the centre of town is recognizable by its *Dreifaltigkeitssäule*, a **Trinity Column** built in 1718 by Giovanni Stanetti (from a drawing by Martino Altomonte who was in the service of the Imperial family) after the city had survived an outbreak of plague; the small fountain adjacent to it was added in 1833. The town hall *(Hauptplatz 1)* was designed in 1815 by Josef Kornhäusel who created a wealth of remarkable buildings for the city. The central entablature is adorned by 4 Ionic columns and a triangular gable; the 3 lunettes contain allegories of Intelligence and Justice.

The Kaiserhaus *(Hauptplatz 17)*, built in 1792, was for thirty years the summer residence of Emperor Franz I; the last Kaiser, Charles I, also stayed there in 1916-1918.

North of Hauptplatz, turn right into Pfarrgasse. On the left is the Jubiläumsstadttheater.

A long theatrical tradition – For the past three centuries, Baden has been enlivened all year round by plays, classical music concerts and operettas, performed at the Jubiläumsstadttheater (700 seats) from October to March and at the Stadtische Arena *(see Kurpark)* in summer.

Stadtpkarrkirche Hl. Stephan – Nothing remains of the ancient Romanesque edifice of 1312 except two truncated towers between which a Gothic belltower with an onion dome was added in 1697. Inside, the most interesting work is a *Stoning of St Stephen* by Paul Troger *(south wall of the chancel)*. Above the door leading to the organ *(facing the entrance)*, a plaque states that Wolfgang Amadeus Mozart wrote his *Ave Verum* in 1791 for his friend Anton Stoll who conducted the church choir. The fine organ designed in 1744 by Johann Genckl for the Dorotheerkirche *(see Dorotheum in Vienna)* was moved here in 1787.

Go along the west face of the church and turn left into Kaiser-Franz-Ring to enter the Kurpark.

★**Kurpark** – The spa park is a splendid place for a stroll. It runs up to the edge of the Vienna Woods *(there are two waymarked footpaths, see map at the park entrance)*. On the left stands the magnificent **Casino** (and conference centre), a dazzling sight since its recent restoration. This building occupies an historic site, since from the Roman well *(Römerquelle)* beneath its walls arose the oldest thermal spring. Just above, the **Stadtische Arena** (1906), a theatre, which is a blend of Art Nouveau and Art Deco, forms a prestigious setting for the *Operettensommer*, thanks to its sliding glass roof which allows open-air performances.

Beyond the bandstand, where afternoon concerts are much appreciated by people taking the waters, the park is adorned by several memorials to famous musicians who visited the town: Lanner and Strauss, Mozart, Beethoven. The small oval pavilion dedicated to Beethoven is dominated by a circular viewing platform aptly named "Bellevue".

It is worth making the effort to climb a little further up the steep slope of the park to the Viennese forest, past enclosures where animals such as stags, deer, does, ponies, goats, etc. peacefully graze.

Bear right after leaving the park, go along Kaiser-Franz-Ring and turn left opposite the Casino into Erzherzog-Rainer-Ring. Turn right for Brusattiplatz.

★**Thermen** – During the first half of the nineteenth century, innumerable mock classical temples were constructed. Some of them are still existant, even if most are put to a different use. The **Leopoldsbad** *(Brusattiplatz)*, built in 1812, which now houses the tourist information centre, was the dispatch point for mineral water; it was named after Margrave Leopold the Pious. To the right, partly concealed by a cluster of trees, is the **Mineral-Schwimmbad** *(Marchetstrasse 13)*, a thermal establishment with warm water baths from 26° to 34°; it was built in 1847 by Eduard van der Nüll and August Siccard von Siccardsburg, the architects of Vienna's Staatsoper. On Josefsplatz nearby, the **Josefsbad** (1804) is a small rotunda reminiscent of a temple to Vesta. It is now used as an exhibition centre. The **Frauenbad** (1821) by Charles de Moreau now houses an art gallery. On the other bank of the Schwechat stands J. Kornhäusel's **Sauerhof** *(Weilburgstasse 11-13)*, now converted into a high class restaurant.

Go down Frauengasse beside the Frauenbad.

View of the Spa Spring in Theresienbad by Johann Ziegler

Fotostudio Otto/Museen der Stadt, Wien

Frauengasse – At No 10 is the Magdalenenhof, a Biedermeier house that accommodated Beethoven (autumn 1822) and Franz Grillparzer (summers 1848 to 1850 and 1860). At No 5 is the Florastöckl, a building attributed to J. Kornhäusel adorned above the cornice of its façade by a statue of the goddess Flora (Joseph Klieber); the Duke of Reichstadt, the son of Napoleon Bonaparte and Empress Marie-Louise, stayed here with his mother between 1818 and 1834. The Frauenkirche just before Hauptplatz was constructed in 1825 on the site of a church built towards 1260. Both churches were dedicated to the Virgin Mary.

Hauptplatz, turn left into Rathausgasse.

Beethoven-Gedenstätte ⊘ – *Rathausgasse 10.* It was here that the great composer stayed from 1821 to 1823 and wrote part of the *Missa Solemnis* and the *Ninth Symphony*. The house commemorates his visits to Baden and the surrounding area between 1804 and 1825.

A room is devoted to the most famous of Baden's sons, such as the actor Max Reinhardt *(see Gedenkräume des Österreichischen Theatermuseums in Vienna)* or the pianist Erik Werba (1918-1992).

Return to Josefsplatz and turn right into Pergerstrasse. Continue straight on to Pelzgasse and enter the park opposite.

Doblhoffpark – The most interesting sight in this park is its *Rosarium*, an extremely well-maintained **rose garden**★ of 9ha/22 acres created in 1969. Rose enthusiasts will enjoy the wide range of specimens (25,000 roses, 600 varieties), such as the glowing red *Ruth Leuwerik* (1960), orange-tinted *Gloire de Dijon* (1853) or *Ave Maria* (1972), dazzling white *John F. Kennedy* (1965), pink *Else Poulsen* (1924), etc. In June, the *Badener Rosentage* festival attracts numerous connoisseurs of this flower which has always been an important symbol in western Christianity.

Leave the park by the south and bear right into Helenenstrasse.

Thermalstrandbad – *Helenenstrasse 19. See Practical Information.* This public swimming pool was built in 1926 in the Art Deco style, which, despite being rare in Austria, does not jar in the birthplace of the Jugendstil and the Secession.

There are in fact several open-air swimming pools (5,000m²/5,980sq yds) and a sandy beach; the architects hoped visitors would feel transported to the blue-tinged shores of the Adriatic.

EXCURSION

Wienerwald – *See under this heading.*

BRATISLAVA★★

Slovakia

Michelin map 426 fold 13 – 53km/32 miles east of Vienna

On 1 January 1993, Bratislava became the capital of the Republic of Slovakia, a country with immense untapped potential for tourism. The former Pressburg lies on the banks of the Danube, at the western tip of the country, near the Austrian and Hungarian frontiers, between the Carpathians, the Danubian plain and Moravia. Owing to its strategic position, it became the capital of Hungary in the 16C under the name of Pozsony (until the 19C). It was the setting for the coronation of many Hungarian kings. In 1920, the city became part of Czechoslovakia following the division of the Austro-Hungarian Empire. With a population of about 450,000, it is now a capital boasting numerous national political and cultural institutions and a famous university.

A major road and railway junction, Bratislava is a busy industrial city (chemical, electrical and engineering plants). Visitors arriving by car cannot fail to notice this. In particular, they will see a major oil terminal at Slovnaff which, since 1973, has connected with a pipeline carrying Russian oil. There is a programme of waterway links to the Oder via the rivers Morava and Elbe, which includes the impressive Gabcikovo dam, completed in 1992 south of the city. It enables Slovakia to meet almost one-fifth of its energy needs, as well as canalising a stretch of the river.

A DAY IN BRATISLAVA

EU Members will need passports to cross the border..

By car – *Head eastwards out of Vienna, on the A 4-E60 motorway signposted Budapest. Leaving the motorway at exit No 19 (Fischamend), take road E58 to Bratislava.*

After an early start, it is possible to combine a day in Bratislava with a visit to the Roman excavations at Petronell-Carnuntum (see under this heading).

By boat – *Hydrofoils link Vienna to Bratislava in about 2 1/2 hours. Besides providing the opportunity to see the banks of the Danube and the spectacular* Fredenau lock, *this excursion includes a day in the capital of the new Republic of Slovakia (see Practical information).*

TOUR OF THE CITY

There are three striking landmarks in the city: the **castle** with its four towers perched on a rock, the futurist **bridge of the Slovak National Uprising** (most SNP) soaring from its single leaning tower, and **St Martin's Cathedral** on the outskirts of the old town. Along the ancient fortifications, there are a series of bustling squares surrounding the historic heart of Bratislava. It seems small in comparison with the impressive but soulless suburbs and industrial areas which are now overrunning the banks of the Danube. Bratislava's charm lies in its old town, which can easily be explored on foot. It is an interesting panorama of splendid Baroque palaces, churches with large congregations and attractive squares.

★★**Hrad** – The **castle** stands on the summit of the last promontory of the Carpathians, overlooking the Danube, which is wider than in Vienna. Although it underwent several reconstructions, its rectangular structure dates from the Middle Ages. Empress Maria-Theresa commissioned the baroque decoration in the second half of the 18C. In 1811, a fire destroyed it and it was restored just a few years ago. It houses the historical collections of the **National Museum**.

From the castle ramparts as well as the terraces and gardens around **Parliament** nearby, there are unimpeded **views**★★ over the city, the Danube, the plains to the horizon. The view also embraces the SNP bridge, which seems to be out of science fiction, and the sprawling Petrzalka suburbs on the right bank of the river.

★★**Hlavné námestie and surroundings** – This former market square was the centre of medieval Bratislava and features the Renaissance-style Roland fountain. At present, it has a strong 18C and 19C atmosphere. The café at No 5 is a masterpiece of Art Deco architecture, but the most impressive building is the old Town Hall (Stará Radnica) with its large tower. It is in a variety of styles from different periods, which all provide evidence of the city's long history.

Opposite the town hall, the French embassy and cultural centre occupy the Rococo style **Kutcherfeld palace**.

Franciscan square (Františkánske námestie) lies to the north, its trees forming an almost rustic setting for the Jesuit church. Further away is the Rococo **Mirbach palace★**, one of the finest of its type. Near it are the Franciscan church and monastery. In the palace, two **rooms★** are curiously decorated with over 200 coloured 17C and 18C engravings, set into the wood panelling. Along the municipal museum (Metské), a narrow road links Hlavné square to Primacialné square. The **Primatial palace** displays a delightful **façade★**, even lovelier when illuminated at night; it is notable for being the place where Napoléon and Emperor Franz I of Austria signed the Treaty of Pressburg in December 1805 after the battle of Austerlitz.

★**Michalská brána** – St Michael's is the only remaining gate in the city's medieval walls. After expansion, its Gothic tower underwent refurbishments in its present Baroque style. **St Michael's statue** surmounts it, soaring 51m/167ft above the ground. A fascinating pharmaceutical Museum is nearby. The road to the south (Michalská extending into Venturská) is lined with ravishing houses and palaces from the Baroque and Renaissance periods, encircling the tiny Gothic St Catherine's chapel.

★**Dom sv. Martina** – The Gothic cathedral of St Martin stands on the southwest corner of old Bratislava. The road to SNP bridge (most SNP) separates it from the hill with its castle. The architects of St Stephen's cathedral (Stephansdom) in Vienna took part in the construction of St Martin's cathedral. Until 1830, it witnessed the coronations of Hungarian monarchs.

★**U Dobrého Pastiera** – This delightful Rococo house of **"The Good Shepherd"** now contains the Múzeum Bratislavskych Historickych Hodín (Museum of historical clocks), at the foot of the steep slope leading up to the castle. It evokes the charm of the old Jewish quarter which once stood there. The picturesque Jewish quarter extended between the castle and the cathedral. It had become insalubrious and the authorities tore it down to build the dual carriageway.

Hviezdoslavovo námestie – Many of the city's cultural institutions lie between the ramparts of the former town and the Danube. The 1886 National Theatre stands at the eastern end of the tree-lined **Hviezdoslav square**. It is one of the numerous edifices dating from the days of the Austro-Hungarian empire by the Viennese architects, Fellner and Helmer. Near the river, the **Reduta** rises into view, a Neoclassical building dating from 1919 which houses the Slovakian philharmonic orchestra. On the Danube

The Primate's Palace

Y. Travert/DIAF

waterfront itself is **Slovenské Narodná Galéria**★★, the Slovak National Gallery. The most interesting works are those dating from the late Middle Ages and the interwar period of the first Czechoslovakian Republic. The boldly coloured paintings of Lucovit Fulla and Martin Benka depict scenes from traditional peasant life.

EXCURSIONS

★ **Devin** – *11km/6 miles to the west*. From its rock, the old fortress of Devin overlooks the spot where the Morava meets the Danube. This medieval fortress is even more impressive than Bratislava castle. It forms part of a series of Celtic, Roman and Moravian strongholds and has been little more than a romantic ruin since Napoleon's troops passed this way in 1809.

★ **Malé Karpaty** – Vineyards spread to the foothills of the Little Carpathians from the gates of Bratislava. To the northeast there lies a string of wine-growing villages and small towns, including **Sv. Jur** with its famous early Renaissance **altar piece**, **Pezinok** with its charming Little Carpathians museum, and **Modrá** famous for its pottery and its wines.

EISENSTADT★

Burgenland

Michelin map 426 fold 25 – 51km/31 miles south of Vienna

Eisenstadt has developed on the south slope of the Leithagebirge, forested like a huge park, the last outpost of the crystalline massifs of the eastern Alps. This marks the start of the great Central European plain. The mild climate makes it possible to grow vines, peaches, apricots and almonds.

The proximity of Vienna has checked the economic expansion of the town which, though small, is nevertheless the largest wine-trading community in the region. Since 1925, when Eisenstadt became the capital of Burgenland, its political and administrative role has lent new life to the city. It is well situated about 15km/9 miles – from the shores of Lake Neusiedl, a major local tourist attraction.

The Austrian fief of the Esterházys – The Esterházys belong to one of the oldest noble Hungarian families. Good Catholics and loyal to the Habsburgs – which in Hungary was exceptional – they owned in the mid 17C the Eisenstadt and Forchtenstein domains, as well as present-day Fertöd (formerly known as Esterháza) southeast of Lake Neusiedl, in Hungary. In 1919, on the eve of the Treaty of St Germain-en-Laye, the family possessed a large part of Burgenland. Today, Princess Esterházy, Marchioness of Carabas and widow of the last duke Paul IV, still owns a great deal of land in the province and is said to be one of the richest women in the country.

Eisenstadt was the winter residence of this great family who made a major contribution to the establishment of Habsburg rule in Hungary. **Nicholas I** (1582-1645) ruled as Palatine and was made a Count by Ferdinand II; his son **Paul I** (1635-1713), also a Palatine, fought on the side of Leopold I who, in gratitude for his help during the Siege of Vienna by the Turks in 1683, made him a prince in 1697; despite this, Paul later opposed the Emperor by refusing to tax the Hungarian aristocracy; **Nicholas I the Magnificent** (1762-1790) employed Haydn as musical director at Eisenstadt.

Haydn's Town – Everything here calls to mind the brilliant composer who created the classical symphony and string quartet. For thirty years Joseph Haydn (1732-1809), born in Rohrau *(see under this heading)* divided his time between Eisenstadt and the Esterházy Palace, nicknamed the "Hungarian Versailles", in the service of Prince Nicholas where he was the Court conductor and composer. Haydn's situation resembled that of a high-class prisoner in a golden cage, since he was not free and even had to don blue and gold livery before appearing before his patron and receiving his orders. Having an orchestra and a theatre at his disposal, Haydn worked without respite and achieved ever growing fame. His considerable number of works makes him one of the greatest names in music.

Nicholas I the Magnificent

Schloss Esterházy/AKG PARIS

SIGHTS

★**Schloss Esterházy** – *Esterházyplatz. Guided tours only (in German).*
Prince Paul Esterházy commissioned the Italian architect C.M. Carlone to build him a palace appropriate to his rank. On the site of a medieval fortress built in the late 14C for the Kaniszai family, Carlone built a great quadrilateral structure between 1663 and 1672 around a main courtyard. At the time, each of the four corner towers was crowned by an onion dome.
From 1797 to 1805, the French architect Charles de Moreau updated the building in line with contemporary taste. The façade opposite the park acquired a Neoclassical portico with Corinthian columns, and a terrace supported by Tuscan columns was built above the entrance gateway in the main façade. Terra-cotta busts portraying the ancestors of the Esterházy family and several Kings of Hungary adorn this façade topped with a belltower and bulbous dome.
On the far side of the courtyard are the former royal stables, built in 1743.

Interior ◷ – Visitors to the Esterházy museum will see several rooms devoted to the family (paintings, silver, furniture, library, etc.) The high point of the visit is undoubtedly the **Haydn Room**★, former ballroom and banqueting hall of the Esterházy princes; its marble floor was replaced by a wooden one in the 18C to improve the acoustics *(for concerts, see Practical Information)*. In the noble setting of this huge hall decorated in the late 17C with stucco, grisaille (Kings of Hungary) and frescoes by Carpoforo Tencala (scenes from Greek mythology), Joseph Haydn conducted the orchestra of the princely court nearly every evening, often performing his own works.

Haydn-Haus ◷ – *Haydngasse 21.* A covered passage leads to the modest house where the composer lived from 1766 to 1778. It now contains a small museum that will delight his

ROGER-VIOLLET

Josef Haydn

EISENSTADT

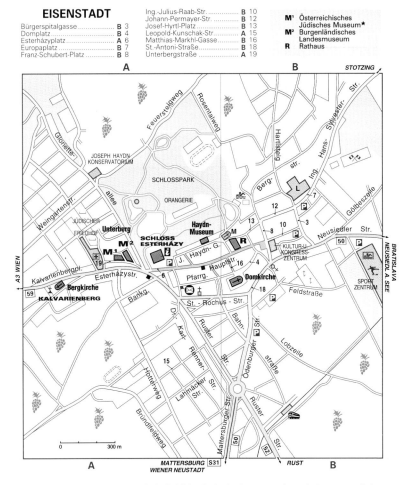

admirers (scores and portraits). Exhibits include the manuals and the stops of the old organ from the Bergkirche on which Haydn and Beethoven played.

At Franziskanerkirche, turn right and into Hauptstrasse leading to the Town Hall.

Rathaus (**R**) – The Renaissance Town Hall dates from the mid-17C. Its façade has a number of highly unusual features – pediments with cymas in counter-curves, three oriel windows, a semicircular gateway adorned by a boss with nail-head ornamentation, and frescoes alternating with windows.

Return towards Matthias-Markhlgasse, on the left to reach Domplatz.

Domkirche – This cathedral in late-Gothic style was built in the 15C and 16C. It is dedicated to St Martin, patron saint of Burgenland. Of its late Baroque interior, there remains only a splendid pulpit, the chancel and the organ. There is a fine relief of the Mount of Olives (pre-1500).

Go down Pfarrgasse and return to Esterházyplatz then turn left opposite the palace.

Unterberg: the old Jewish quarter – Records state that there have been Jews in Eisenstadt since 1296. After Kaiser Leopold I had driven them from Vienna in 1671, many of them sought

---

"Court Jews"

Since medieval decrees forbidding Christians to practise usury, a few Jews played a major role in German and Austrian finances over the 17C and 18C. The Hapsburgs appointed "Court Jews" who found themselves in a privileged position and who were given absolute freedom to trade as they wished. Among them was Samuel Oppenheimer, a banker from Speyer, who funded Prince Eugène of Savoy's campaigns against the Turks after being brought to Vienna by Charles of Lorraine. Another was Oppenheimer's son-in-law, Samson Wertheimer, who worked for Leopold, Josef I and Karl VI. Although a number of Jews enjoyed commercial freedom, insecurity and oppression was more often the daily lot of the community as a whole.

refuge in the Unterberg District, bounded by Museumsgasse, Wolfgasse, Unterbergstrasse and Wertheimergasse, which is still very well preserved. The old ghetto still has the chain used to close the area off in order to maintain the peace of the Sabbath. It was once famous throughout the Empire for its Rabbinical School. From it emerged two outstanding personalities: Samson Wertheimer, assistant to Leopold I, and Sandor Wolf, collector and patron of the arts.

★**Österreichisches Jüdisches Museum** (**M**¹) ⊙ – *Unterbergstrasse 6*. The Austrian Jewish Museum is housed in Samson Wertheimer's charming old residence. It includes a fine **synagogue**, which escaped destruction by the Nazis and where in 1979 the scrolls of the Torah were found. This richly documented museum traces the daily life of the community; numerous temporary exhibitions are held here. Nearby is the Jewish cemetery *(at the end of Wertheimergasse)* with 17C and 18C tombstones.

Burgenländische Landesmuseum (**M**²) ⊙ – *Museumsgasse 5*. The Burgenland Regional Museum set out in two old interconnecting houses is devoted to popular arts, crafts and traditions, including those of various ethnic minorities still living in the area. One room commemorates **Franz Liszt**, another musical genius, born on 22 October 1811 in Raiding (south of the province) where his father was bailiff to the Esterházy sheep-rearing estates.

Return to Esterházystrasse and continue westwards to Kalvarienbergplatz.

★**Kalvarienberg and Bergkirche** – "Calvary Hill" was artificially created in the 18C to accommodate the **Way of the Cross**★. In a Baroque style, its 24 Stations of the Cross, consisting of 260 traditional wood statues and 60 stone statues, describe the Passion with great realism and drama. The platform at the top gives a fine view of the town.

The **Bergkirche** ⊙ is a baroque edifice with a marble chapel (1722) containing the **Haydn Mausoleum**. The composer's remains were transferred here in 1820 by Nicholas Esterházy; Haydn died in Vienna in 1809.

GUMPOLDSKIRCHEN
Lower Austria
Michelin map 426 fold 25 – 18km/11 miles southwest of Vienna
Local map Wienerwald

Amid the vineyards at the foot of the Anniger (alt. 675m/2,217ft), this attractive village dating from the Middle Ages is famous for its white wines, which can be savoured in several *Heurigen*. Some of these taverns are in 16C houses. At the end of June and August, the streets of Gumpoldskirchen are transformed into open-air cafés celebrating the wine festival. Lovers of water should bypass the village and go straight to Baden, the spa town 7km/4 miles away, unless they are interested in the Renaissance Town Hall or wish to sample the delicious grape juice served in September and October by some wine growers.

The village – Surrounded by vines, most of it stretches along Wienerstrasse. To appreciate its charm, go along the small Kirchengasse, signposted near the Town Hall (mid 16C).

At the top of the street beyond a pretty stone bridge is the "Gumpoldskirche", a hall-church (15C) dedicated to St Michael; its interior door is stamped with the cross of the Order of the Teutonic Knights *(see Singerstrasse, Around the Stephansdom)* who had lived in the village since the mid-13C. Wine is produced in the castle of the Order (note the Cross used as a weathervane) opposite the church.

A walk through the vineyards – *From Kirchenplatz, go along Kurzegasse below the castle.* The path wanders through the vineyards and at regular intervals there are information panels *(in German)* about the origins and areas of cultivation of the various vines grown on this slope: Welschriesling (Austria, Hungary, Yugoslavia and Italy); Rheinriesling (Rhine Valley); Neuburger (Wachau, Burgenland and Thermenregion); Weisserburgunder (Burgundy); Rotgipfler (Gumpoldskirchen and the surrounding area); Zierfandler or *Spätrot* (Gumpoldskirchen and the surrounding area); Blauer-burgunder (throughout the world); Blauerportugieser (Portugal and Austria).

At the top of Kalvarienberg is a chapel. From its terrace *(Kreuzwegstationen)* there is a fine view of the plain.

Every year
the **Michelin Red Guide Europe**
*presents a wealth of up-to-date information in a compact
form; it is the ideal companion for a holiday or a business trip.*

HEILIGENKREUZ ★

Around 1130, the Abbey of Heiligenkreuz was founded by Leopold III the Pious of Babenberg who had built Klosterneuburg Abbey north of Vienna. It was to house a piece of the true Cross brought back from Jerusalem by his grandson Leopold V in 1182. In 1133 twelve monks from Morimond in France, one of the four daughter establishments of Cîteaux, were installed there. Leopold may have wanted both to create a burial place for his dynasty and at the same time establish a monastic order in the border province of which he was Margrave. Nevertheless he was not indifferent to the fact that one of his sons, Otto, joined the Cistercian order at Morimond in 1132.

The Cistercian order – After the strife during the decline of the Carolingian Empire, there was a revival of monastic life throughout western Europe. The successful establishment of St Benedict of Nursia's Rule in Italy, Gaul and Germany at the beginning of the 10C was due to its flexibility. For two or three generations, Cluny, in Burgundy, was the heart of an empire, enjoying near absolute autonomy owing to its distance from the seat of papal power. The growth of the Cluniac order was impressive: at the start of the 12C, it had 1,450 establishments with 10,000 monks, throughout France, Germany, Spain, Italy, and Great Britain.

St Bernard protested against the luxury and slackness of the Cluniac monks, typified by the splendid abbey church in Cluny built between 1088 and 1130 by the abbots St Hugh and Peter the Venerable. Bernard, a Burgundian by birth, seemed to many the strongest and most influential personality in the western world. A young nobleman of 21, he arrived in 1112 with 32 companions at the monastery of Cîteaux founded in 1098. *Cistercium* was its Latin name. The Cistercians were therefore Benedictines conforming to the rule of the monastery of Cîteaux. The Baden door in the abbey of Heiligenkreuz bears the motto of the order: *Cistercium mater nostra.*

In 1115, he left Cîteaux while it was flourishing for the borders of Burgundy and Champagne in a poor area. On his death in 1153, Cîteaux had 700 monks and was exceedingly prosperous.

The Cistercian Rule – St Bernard redefined the Benedictine Rule, following it strictly to the letter. He forbade the levy of tithes, the acceptance or purchase of land and imposed on his monks of Clairvaux – and thus by extension to all other Cistercian monks – harsh living conditions: for example, a frugal diet and a 7-hour period of sleep in a communal dormitory. The daily routine was regulated with draconian precision: after waking between 1 and 2am., the monks sang matins, then laudes, celebrated private Mass, recited the canonical hours (prime, tierce, sext, nones, vespers, compline) and attended monastic Mass. Religious services accounted for 6 to 7 hours and the rest of the time was divided between manual labour, intellectual work and reading religious texts.

The abbot, head of the community, was elected for life and lived with his monks, sharing their meals, presiding over services, the chapter, and meetings. He was assisted by a prior who deputised for him in his absence.

The Cistercian order in the 20C – The organisation of the order is based on the "charter of charity" established in about 1115, linking the various abbeys, which are all equal. At present, 3,000 reformed or trappist Cistercians, directed by a general abbot resident in Rome, are dispersed throughout the world in 92 abbeys or priories. The abbots of the order meet periodically at a general chapter. The Heiligenkreuz community now has 60 members.

THE ABBEY ⏱

Although the abbey was founded in the 12C, most of the buildings date from the 17C, except the church (12C) and the cloister and adjoining buildings (13C). In the courtyard facing the church stands a **Trinity Pillar** by the Venetian artist Giovanni Giuliani (1663-1744) who was highly influential in Vienna and is buried in the church.

★**Church** – The west face is Romanesque. Its sober design, highly unusual in Austria, is due to the Burgundian origin of the monks who built it. The three central windows and the absence of a tower on the façade are typically Cistercian; the doors were built later (the churches of the order, built at the heart of remote enclaves, had no need to open their doors to a congregation of lay worshippers). The interior displays a Romanesque nave and transept (1187) possessing austerity as well as vastness and great unity, and a Gothic chancel (1295). The decoration is baroque: fine stalls by G. Giuliani topped by carved saints of the order; *Descent from the Cross* and *Vision of St Bernard* by Johann Michael Rottmayr. The high altar in the chancel is a neo-Gothic construction with the ciborium placed without regard to the windows of the chevet. Behind the high altar, the tabernacle of the altar of the Cross contains the relic which gave the abbey its name (Holy Cross).

Cloisters – The cloisters, on the south side of the sanctuary, date from the 13C. Their evolution may be traced by observing the Romanesque arches of the north wing and the Gothic arches of the south wing. The cloisters contain *The Washing of Feet* and *The Sinner Tending the Feet of Christ* by G. Giuliani and the tombstones of aristocratic patrons. In front of the south wing is the **lavabo**, a small building (late 13C) containing a Renaissance fountain for washing which is both elegant and functional (the silicate deposits form part of the decor of the fountain).

St Anne's Chapel – This former library is now a chapel with an austere baroque interior.

Chapterhouse – The building where the abbot is elected and where novices take holy orders houses the tombs of the Babenbergs with mural paintings depicting each member of the family. In accordance with the founder's wishes, the

The abbey courtyard

R. Dechamps/MICHELIN

community celebrates their memory by a daily procession through the cloister. The most ornate tomb is that of Frederick II the Warlike, the last of his line. It was under Babenberg rule that Christianity took root in Austria; Leopold, the first member of the dynasty, was a bishop.

Chapel of the dead – The coffins of the monks are displayed here before burial. The decoration of the chapel is by G. Giuliani. Some visitors may be taken aback by the exaggerated Mannerist gestures of the four macabre sculptures surrounding the catafalque, but it must be remembered that the Baroque style embraces life and death with the same zest.

Monks' room – The mural decoration of this workroom simulates freestone. Its most interesting characteristic is, however, the unusual type of monolithic columns in the room: the load of the vault does not lie on the capitals but falls directly on to mouldings shaped like Romanesque gadroons.

Sacristy – The annexe to the church contains cupboards with fine trompe-l'oeil marquetry made in the early 19C by lay brothers.

In the little churchyard in the village lies the tomb of Maria Vetsera *(see Mayerling)*, with the words: *"Like a flower, man blossoms only to be cut down."* As suicide was mentioned in the death certificate, the abbot of the abbey had to be persuaded to grant a Christian burial.

KLOSTERNEUBURG★

Lower Austria

Michelin map 426 fold 12 – 13km/8 miles north of Vienna

Train: Klosterneuburg-Kierling (S40) from Franz-Josefs-Bahnhof

Bus: 239, 341, from Heiligenstadt

Once upon a time, Agnes von Babenberg was admiring the view from the top of her castle on Leopoldsberg, when the wind snatched her veil away. A search for it was unsuccessful. Several years later, the precious cloth reappeared undamaged on top of a tree, in a place called Neuenburg. Agnes' husband, Leopold III, who was to be canonised in later years, took this to be a sign from God and decided to build a great sanctuary on the site of what was obviously a miracle. Following this divine inspiration, Klosterneuburg Abbey was created in 1114. After his marriage to Agnes, daughter of Emperor Henry IV, the Babenberg Margrave Leopold III transferred his residence from Melk to the heights of Neuenburg, probably a Roman settlement. Later, in 1156, when Henry II Jasomirgott acquired from Emperor Frederick Barbarossa the status of hereditary duchy for the Marche, he chose Vienna as his ducal capital and left Klosterneuburg.

Pleasantly situated on the right bank of the Danube, Klosterneuburg stands on the northeast edge of the Wienerwald (Vienna Woods). In 1296, it acquired the status of a city. It prospered and gradually grew into the small modern bustling town of today.

STIFT KLOSTERNEUBURG ⊙

Conducted tour of the abbey in German only (about 1 hour) comprising: the square, church, cloisters, imperial apartments. There is a separate tour of the Stiftsmuseum which is not guided.

Augustinian Canons – Under the influence of the Crusades and the Counter-Reformation, monastic architecture flourished in Lower and Upper Austria. Three orders occupied the abbeys: Benedictines (Melk), Cistercians (Heiligenkreuz) and regular Augustinian Canons. The pomp of Baroque architecture suited this order, which settled at Klosterneuburg. Hence despite its great age, this abbey, which once dominated a branch of the Danube, now filled in, contains few medieval remains. At present, it accommodates about forty priests.

Stiftsplatz – This square gives access to the abbey and the palace. In the middle stands a Gothic Lichtsäule (lantern column) of 1381 featuring scenes from the Passion. Opposite the side entrance of the abbey church is Sebastianskapelle (St Sebastian's chapel) *(closed to the public)* containing Albert II's altarpiece (1438), one of its panels showing the oldest view of Vienna cathedral. To the right is the chapter-house, and on the right again is the Stiftsbinderei (cooper's shop) housing the famous *Tausendeimerfass* (thousand-bucket barrel) made in 1704 with a capacity of 56,000 litres/12,318 gallons. The Klosterneuburg vines are famous; every year on 15 November, St Leopold's Day, a barrel-rolling competition takes place in the abbey precinct.

Stiftskirche – *For those not taking part in the guided tour, the interior is visible through the railings.* The three-aisled Romanesque abbey church was begun in 1114 and completed a few days before Leopold III's death in 1136. Over the

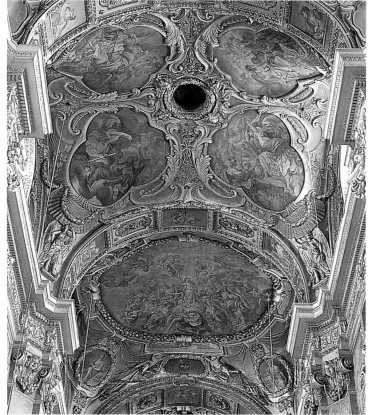

Vaulting in the minster

centuries it underwent many alterations. Between 1634 and 1645, the Genoese architect Giovanni Battista Carlone and Andrea de Retti refurbished it in the Baroque style. In 1879, Friedrich von Schmidt, architect of Vienna's Town Hall, restored its medieval appearance; both towers are now in the neo-Gothic style. The **interior**★ of the church is almost entirely Baroque (1680-1702 and 1723-1730). It conveys harmony and grandeur owing to the excellence of the artists involved. Georg Greiner painted the **frescoes** on the vault about 1689. They depict the Turks before Klosterneuburg, the Fathers of the Church, the Coronation of the Virgin Mary, and scenes from the life of the Virgin Mary; portrayals of the Assumption (chancel and apse) are by Johann Michael Rottmayr. The Späz brothers carved the decoration on the 6 side altars (early 18C). Matthias Steindl made the high altar *(Birth of the Virgin* by Johann Georg Schmidt), the copper sounding board above the marble pulpit and the magnificent **choirstalls** (1723) bearing 24 Habsburg coats of arms. The great Baroque organ dating from 1636 is famous for its superb sound quality. Anton Bruckner enjoyed playing it.

Kloster – The cloisters stand north of the church. A fine example of early Gothic architecture with Burgundian influences, dating from the 13C and 14C.

Leopoldskapelle – This former chapterhouse, now St Leopold's chapel, contains the tomb of Leopold III who was canonised in 1485; his relics rest in a reliquary (1936) which is somewhat unfortunately placed above the famous Verduner Altar (Verdun altarpiece) *(see below)*. The glowing colours of the 14C **stained-glass windows**★ are magnificent.

Leopoldsbrunnen – This old fountain stands in the centre of Leopoldshof (St Leopold's courtyard).

Freisingerkapelle – This nine-sided chapel contains a seven-branch bronze **candelabra**, a 12C work from Verona shaped like the Tree of Jesse. It also houses the recumbent figure of Berthold von Wehingen, Bishop of Freising who died in 1410.

Nicolas of Verdun – Nicolas was a goldsmith and enameller from Lorraine. This is virtually all that is known about him. The long sides of the reliquary of the Three Wise Men in Cologne cathedral are attributed to him. However, his name only appears on two objects: St Mary's reliquary in Tournai Cathedral and this masterpiece in Klosterneuburg, which ranks among the finest achievements of medieval art.

★★**Verduner Altar** – *The guided tour unfortunately pauses for too short a time before this unique work of art*. In 1181, Prior Wernher commissioned Nikolaus to enamel the abbey lectern. The artist made 46 panels of gilded metal using the champlevé technique. In 1331 after a fire, the provost had the work turned into an altarpiece, by the addition of 6 plaques and 4 painted panels *(see Stiftsmuseum)*. The altarpiece comprises three levels depicting scenes from the Old Testament *(upper and lower levels)* and the New Testament *(middle level)*, an intriguing typological arrangement summarizing three centuries of the Bible. Scenes from the New Testament are clarified by those occurring before the Mosaic Law *(above)* and during its dominance *(below)*. To the left of the central panel, for instance, one sees from the top downwards, *The Crossing of the Red Sea* (parable of baptism), *The Baptism of Christ, The Sea on the Back of 12 Oxen* (pool in King Solomon's temple). In the centre of the middle panel is *The Crucifixion*, the climax of the Passion of Christ and the cornerstone of Christianity.

From an artistic point of view, the gilded figures stand out from a predominantly blue polychrome enamelled background; this is typical of Rhenish art rather than of the Moselle country to which Nicolas belonged. Influenced by the School of Rheims, the illuminations and ivories in his region and late 11C Byzantine art, the most celebrated goldsmith of the 12C was the founder of original and expressive aesthetic principles.

★**Neues Stiftsgebäude or "Small Escorial"** – After the loss of Spain under the Treaty of Utrecht (1713), Charles VI, Maria-Theresa's father, concentrated upon Vienna, where much building was taking place. In 17C and 18C central Europe, when the middle classes had not yet succeeded in making their presence felt as an autonomous social class, display as an ideal was at its peak. In 1720, there were about 200 castles, palaces and belvederes on the outskirts of Vienna, and twice as many twenty years later! To represent the power of a centralising empire, Charles VI decided to turn the abbey into no less than an Austrian Escorial.

This edifice would naturally symbolize temporal power as opposed to the abbey church embodying spiritual power; the dual nature of the architecture would express the alliance of the two powers, as in the Spanish *Escorial*. Josef Emmanuel Fischer von Erlach was in charge of the project. It was grandiose and included several wings surmounted by nine domes. However, the son of the great J.B. Fischer von Erlach was working on other large-scale enterprises (the Hofburg winter riding school and the National Library among others). The Milanese architect Donato Felice d'Allio was summoned and had to face numerous obstacles,

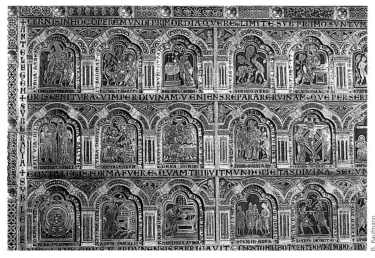

Verdun altarpiece (close-up)

mainly of a financial nature. The last difficulty, however, proved insurmountable: the emperor's death in 1740. Work was interrupted, and Maria-Theresa disliked the huge unfinished palace-monastery. In fact, it represents only a quarter of the original plan: a Baroque building with one courtyard and two domes to which the architect Josef Kornhäusel added a wing around 1840 to close off the courtyard.

Kaiserzimmer – One reaches the imperial apartments through the extraordinary Kaiserstiege (imperial staircase, 1723) left undecorated, apart from 4 angels playing music on the upper landing. Two of the rooms are especially noteworthy: the Brussels Tapestry Room (18C, when Brussels was under Austrian rule, a time marking the decline of this art in the capital of Brabant) and the Marble Hall with frescoes by Daniel Gran representing the Glory of the House of Austria on the cupola.

Bibliothek – Austria's largest private library possesses 200,000 books, 1,250 manuscripts and 850 incunabula.

★**Stiftsmuseum** ⊘ – The abbey museum is above the imperial apartments and displays some remarkable objects such as the **Archducal Crown** (1616, Augsburg ?) and the **4 panels★** of the wings and the reverse side of the Verdun Altar (1331), a work marking the start of Austrian painting: *Crucifixion, Christ with the Holy Women, Death and Coronation of the Virgin Mary*. Also noteworthy are the Babenberg family tree by Hans Part (1492), the Klosterneuburg Virgin (14C), some Byzantine (late 10C) and German ivories (*Coronation of the Virgin*, about 1630, and *Daniel in the Lions' Den* by Simon Troger), and the impressive and complex *Fall of the Angels* by the very patient Jakob Auer.

ADDITIONAL SIGHTS

Martinstrasse – North of Stadtplatz opposite the station, this narrow rising street presents a picture of idyllic calm. It is lined by fine residential houses, such as Kremsmünsterer Hof (No 12) and Martinschloss (No 34) and leads to **Martinskirche**, a church containing fine Baroque decoration.

Kierling – This village, west of Stadtplatz via Kierlingerstrasse, is famous for its former sanatorium where Franz Kafka died of tuberculosis. A small museum displays mementoes of the great writer.

If arriving by car, it is possible and pleasant to return to Vienna via Leopoldsberg and Kahlenberg (see Grinzing).

*An important selection of hotels and restaurants is included in the chapter on Vienna in the **Michelin Red Guide** to **Europe**.*

This guide offers up-to-date information in compact form. An ideal companion on holidays, business trips and weekends away. You won't regret buying the latest edition.

LAXENBURG

A former imperial summer residence, Laxenburg estate lies near the Wienerwald hills, at the heart of the Habsburg hunting grounds, where Maximilian I hunted herons with a hawk. Initially, Albert II the Lame acquired the land in 1340. There, his son, Albert III, built a fortress, surrounded by water, where his wife, the beautiful Beatrix, liked to stay. Later, Laxenburg greatly appealed to Karl VI and court festivities soon replaced the delights of hunting. Today, the estate comprises three palaces and an immense park with trees hundreds of years old, where many Viennese families enjoy walking on Sundays.

Blauer Hof – *Schlossplatz*. The "blue palace" has yellow ochre roughcast walls, a colour known as "Maria Theresa yellow". It probably takes its name from its first architect, the Dutchman Sebastiaan Bloe. The architect Nikolaus Pacassi altered it, adding the main courtyard and a small theatre. The palace had its hey-day in Maria Theresa's reign and Crown Prince Rudolf was born there on 21 August 1858. The back opens on to the park.

Pfarrkirche Laxenburg – *Schlossplatz*. Between 1693 and 1699, Christian Alexander Oedtl was commissioned by Leopold I to build this church on the site of an earlier sanctuary that had been destroyed by the Turks in 1683. Its towers date from 1722. Inside, there is a fine Baroque **pulpit** of gilded wood (1732) by Johann Baptist Strauss, an artist from Munich. The frescoes on the dome are probably after a drawing by Johann Michael Rottmayr; they depict Jerusalem the Celestial City.

Park ⓥ – *Entrance through Hofstrasse*. Car park opposite the entrance. During a visit to his sister, Marie Antoinette, the future Joseph II went to Ermenonville park. On his return from France, he had the 250 hectare – 617 acre park laid out in the English style. Franz I added a large lake, where now a few courageous oarsmen row their boats.

Bearing right after the entrance, one reaches **Altes Schloss**, the old palace, where in 1713 Karl VI issued the Pragmatic Sanction which enabled his daughter Maria Theresa to succeed to the throne. It now houses the Austrian film archives.

On the island *(passage: 5,-ATS)* on the Grosser Teich or large lake stands the **Franzensburg**, an early 19C neo-Gothic fortress by Michael Riedl. Its romantic appeal has decreased since the opening of a café with a terrace displaying multicoloured sunshades which seem somewhat incongrous beneath a crenellated façade. In the interior courtyard are niches housing 37 Habsburg busts.

MAYERLING

The tragic story of Mayerling – In 19C Vienna, a single word summed up all the disasters that could befall a nation – the name of a quiet village situated on the Schwechat, in the Vienna Woods.

On 30 January 1889, Count Josef Hoyos rushed to the Hofburg, bearing the horrific news of the death of the Archduke Rudolf. He told the Empress Elizabeth, who in turn informed her husband in his study of the death of their only son. From 31 January, the Imperial court surrounded the affair with secrecy and a tissue of lies which gave rise to the most fanciful and contradictory rumours. Today the truth is scarcely in doubt: Prince Rudolf, heir to the throne of Austria-Hungary, shot himself six hours after having killed his mistress, Maria von Vetsera, who was only 17.

Why? – Why should the heir to the throne of a great power commit suicide? Although the reason is undoubtedly complex, certain arguments may be advanced to explain the circumstances if not the motive for his action.

First – and this is probably at the heart of the tragedy – the attitude of Franz-Josef towards Rudolf springs to mind. The Emperor, who from the outset of his reign was dominated by his mother, fulfilled his role as monarch firmly to the point of becoming inflexible. He showed little affection to his son, demanding that he behave like a subject and excluding him from politics. This was a serious mistake since the prince, whose interest in history had been stimulated by his tutor Count Latour (chosen by Elizabeth), wanted to make use of his knowledge of his country's affairs. Since his opinions were never sought, he resorted to sending anonymous articles to the liberal press, some of which were openly hostile to the aristocracy.

The venereal disease he contracted in 1886 must also be taken into account, since it was then considered incurable. Because of this disease, he feared for his sanity, thinking perhaps of his cousin Ludwig II of Bavaria. Finally, his marriage to the Belgian princess Stephanie was a failure. She had warned her father-in-law about her husband's depression, but to no avail.

The circumstances – The prince's last mistress was the young Baroness Maria von Vetsera, whom he met at a ball at the German Embassy. Rudolf fell in love with her and his love was returned. Hearing of this liaison, the Emperor decided to put an end to the scandal. On 28 January 1889, he had a stormy interview with his son during which he told him of Pope Leo XIII's refusal to annul the marriage and of his own continuing opposition to a divorce. He also demanded that his son reveal the names of the Hungarian conspirators who were part of a plot headed by Count Samuel Teleky.

The following day, Rudolph did not appear at dinner at the Hofburg, but took refuge with Maria von Vetsera in the hunting lodge at Mayerling. Refusing to betray his friends

Archduke Rudolf

ROGER-VIOLLET

and weary of a situation full of insoluble problems, Rudolf decided to commit suicide, taking with him a young girl, blinded by love. Before shooting himself, he wrote to his mother – *"I know full well that I was unworthy of being your son"* – to his wife – *"I choose death voluntarily, since death alone can save my reputation"* and to an old friend, the beautiful and dashing Maria Casper (Mizzi).

An unfortunate "cover-up" – As soon as Franz-Josef learned from his doctor that his son had not been murdered but had committed suicide after taking another's life, he constructed an elaborate cover-up which became the source of a multitude of hypotheses to explain this tragedy.

Maria von Vetsera, whose presence at Mayerling he wished to conceal, was immediately buried secretly in the abbey of Heiligenkreuz *(see under this heading)*. To stifle all rumours and hush up the murder, newspapers were confiscated – one of them conjectured that the prince had been murdered by a drinking companion. Several days later a Munich newspaper advanced the theory of a double murder, and the police tried to prevent the postal circulation of the paper. The endless series of embellishments surrounding the tragedy at Mayerling was only just beginning.

In Vienna, there was a revival of the censorship which had stifled the city from the Congress of Vienna to the 1848 revolution. Vienna, which had just learned of Rudolf's death, suffered from a malaise identical to that afflicting the Empire. By a strange twist of fate, Rudolf, who was fiercely opposed to Wilhelm II's Prussia and considered by some as a possible saviour of the Empire, died in the same year which saw the birth in Braunau-am-Inn, in Upper Austria, of the son of Klara Pölzl and Aloïs Hitler.

A century of reinterpretations – When in 1982 the former Empress Zita "revealed" to the *Neue Kronen Zeitung* that Rudolf had been assassinated for political reasons, people understood that this event had become an inexhaustible source of rumours and reinterpretations. Indeed, there was no lack of scenarios: Rudolf and Maria committed suicide out of love; Rudolf killed Maria who had just emasculated him then shot himself; Rudolf was executed by Austrian loyalists; Rudolf saved his honour after plotting against his father; Rudolf could not bear the news that Maria was his half-sister; Rudolf and Maria killed themselves because she was pregnant; Rudolf died in an American-style shoot-out with prince Auersperg, etc.

Then in 1992, a Linz businessman confessed that he had desecrated Maria's coffin 4 years earlier. He revealed its place of concealment and the remains were taken to be examined at the Vienna mortuary. The story was resurrected and there were further enquiries, such as for example the one concerning the contents of the second dispatch addressed to Leo XIII by Franz-Josef, which were never published, but prompted the pope to authorise a religious burial for the suicide mentioned in the first dispatch. An affair worth following by anyone who enjoys a good mystery.

Kronprinz Gedenkstätte ⏱ – *Coming from Heiligenkreuz, park on the right at the bottom of the descent at the crossroads before entering the village*. At the edge of the Vienna Woods, a Carmelite convent, constructed by the Emperor Franz-Josef, marks the site of the hunting lodge which was the scene of this world-shaking tragedy. The lodge was originally a farm with a chapel added by Heiligenkreuz abbey. In 1886, the *Kronprinz* Rudolf inherited it and converted it. A neo-Gothic church was erected on the spot where the two bodies were discovered. The fresco on the altar represents St Joseph, patron saint of the imperial family, St Rudolf the martyr, patron saint of the royal prince, St Elizabeth and St Leopold, patron saints of Austria. In the chapel, the altar from the Empress' palace at Corfu, the Emperor's prie-dieu and a *Mater Dolorosa* may be seen. The door into the dining room of the lodge is on the south side. The room contains some of the original furniture together with mementoes such as a fragment of carpet from the Crown Prince's room.

MÖDLING

Lower Austria
Michelin map 426 fold 25 – 12km/7 miles southwest of Vienna
Local map Wienerwald
Train: S1, S2, (Schnellbahn), R10 (Regionalbahn) from Südbahnhof
By car: from Vienna town centre take route 12, Breitenfurterstrasse, past Perchtoldsdorf and take Enzersdorferstrasse to the town centre
(see also local map of the Wienerwald tour).

Mödling was founded in the 10C. After suffering fire damage from the Turks in 1529 and war damage during World War Two, Mödling is now a small town, pleasantly restored. Three composers lived here and enjoyed its quiet ambiance: Ludwig van Beethoven *(Hauptstrasse 79, in 1818 and 1819; Achsenaugasse 6, in 1820)*, who worked there on the first pages of his *Missa Solemnis*, Arnold Schönberg *(Bernhardgasse 6)* and Anton von Webern *(Neusiedlerstrasse 58)*.

In addition to a traditional Pestsäule (Plague column, *Freiheitsplatz*) in the form of a wreathed column, Mödling possesses a charming pedestrian precinct *(Fleischgasse and Elisabethstrasse)* which is a mixture of several architectural styles. The town contains some historic monuments such as the ruins of an 11C castle *(Brühlerstrasse)*, two 15C churches (St Othmar and St Aegyd) and a 16C town hall *(Schrannenplatz)*.

From Hauptstrasse, take Herzoggasse which extends into Pfarrgasse.

Pfarrkirche St Othmar – Building began on this late Gothic style hall-church in 1454 and was completed in 1523. The church stands on a small hill overlooking the town. Until 1556, the parish depended on Melk Abbey, also in Lower Austria. After suffering damage by the Turks in 1529 and 1683, the building acquired 12 columns to support its vault, symbolising the number of the apostles. On the left is the St Nepomucene altar with a painting by Brandl (1725).

Outside, St Pantaleon's chapel dates from the second half of the 12C. This small Romanesque chapel has a charming portal and a crypt with 12C frescoes. Originally, the chapel was a charnel-house.

NEUSIEDLER SEE★★

Burgenland
Michelin map 426 fold 26 – 50km/31 miles southeast of Vienna

Neusiedler Lake (alt. 113m/370ft) is the only example in Central Europe of a steppe lake and is one of the most interesting sights in Burgenland. The word "steppe" has a strange ring in a region so near Vienna. Yet the Hungarian puszta starts here, at the edge of the first foothills of the Alpine chain, rising to the Leithagebirge which reaches an altitude of 300m/984ft above the water.

For some, the lake is steeped in melancholy, perhaps because it has remained Austro-Hungarian. The area it covers, 320km²/121sq miles, belongs mostly to Austria, while Hungary owns the southern basin (about 1/5th of the total area).

A capricious lake – A girdle of reeds up to 5km/3 miles wide surrounds Neusiedler See. Its waters are shallow, cloudy, relatively warm and slightly salty. Its depth varies from 1m/3.28ft to 1.5m/5ft, never exceeding 2m/6.5ft. Storms, although they are rare, are therefore highly dangerous since boats may easily run aground; these storms usually occur in spring. The lake has no permanent outflow; its only tributary, the Wulka, is of negligible importance as the volume of evaporation is four times the quantity of water that flows in. Thus, it is fed mainly by rain, the melting of copious winter snow and underground water tables. When a strong wind blows for some time in the same direction, the water level on the lee shore drops perceptibly; when the wind abates, the lake returns to its former level and appearance.

Very occasionally (the last time was 1868 to 1872), the lake dries up completely only to reappear later as mysteriously as it vanished.

Geography and landscape – Although Neusiedler Lake is reminiscent of the Camargue or the Danube Delta, its shores are quite distinctive. On the eastern side is a plateau, Parndorfer Platte, and a steppe plain strewn with small lakes, the Seewinkel, which is gradually being taken over by orchards and crops, while to the west are two mountain chains, the Leithagebirge visible behind Donnerskirchen and Purbach, and the slopes of Ruster Höhenzug overlooking Rust and Oggau. At the foot of these uplands, vines, maize, fruit trees (even almonds), and market gardens flourish in the rich ochre soil and gentle climate.

A national park – Dating from 1992, the Neusiedler See-Seewinkel National Park straddles the border and is jointly administered by Austria and Hungary. It aims to preserve the fauna and flora typical of the transition zone between the Alpine and Eurasian areas. At Illmitz, the National Park office organises excursions on the lake and in the surrounding area. These trips are of particular interest to keen ornithologists (some of the tour guides speak English). In Parndorf, to the north of Neusiedl, there is a bird sanctuary specialising in storks.

An eldorado for botanists – With the first warmth of spring, myriads of flowers start to open in this ancient, apparently arid Roman land of Pannonia. First to appear, towards February-March, is the spring-like yellow pheasant's-eye *(Adonis vernalis)* with its finely cut golden foliage. In season, there are displays of elegant dwarf irises *(Iris pumila)* no higher than 15cm/6ins, hybrid lilies *(Iris spuria)* with their sword-shaped corolla, a tall mauve-tinted variety of clary *(Salvia nemorosa)*, slender purple mullein known as Violette Königskerze (king's candle) *(Verbascum phoenicium)*, luminous blue Austrian flax *(Linum ostriaca)*, superb salmon asters *(Aster canus)* indigenous to this region, and thousands of rosy stars *(Aster tripolium)* which in autumn carpet the sandy soil. Volumes would not suffice to list all the plant life on the lake shores.

A paradise for birds – In the dense thickets of reeds around Neusiedler See and the lakes at Seewinkel, there is an extraordinary variety of aquatic fauna ranging from Aesculapius' wild grass snake to the southern Russian tarentula. This almost invisible environment can only be examined with the patience of an entomologist. The region provides an exceptional natural habitat and breeding ground for migrating birds. The only breaks on this otherwise flat horizon are the observation posts for ornithologists watching for 250 species of birds. Thus, there is some chance of seing a purple heron, concealed in the midst of aquatic plants, a bee-eater, perched in a hieratic stance, a little ringed plover, nesting on the ground, an elegant avocet, its beak slashing into the water as it looks for food, a little bluethroat, a bird that hops and sings tunefully, and even a great bustard moving in groups with its head up. *(see double page illustration)*.

Famous vineyards – The vineyards are terraced on the slopes or lie scattered throughout the plain. They enjoy plenty of sunshine and produce much-acclaimed vintages, the wines of Rust, Mörbisch, Gols and Illmitz being the most famous for their bouquet. This is why, in 1524, the winegrowers of Rust received royal recognition for the quality of their wine. By virtue of the royal warrant, they are entitled to display the arms of the town on the enormous vats in their vaulted cellars.

In all the villages around the Austrian side of the lake, that is from Mörbisch to

> **Between Austria and Hungary**
>
> Following the treaty of Saint-Germain-en-Laye in September 1919, Austria recognized Hungarian independence. Magyar influence is still strong in Burgenland, which had been part of the kingdom of Hungary. In Siegendorf, Trausdorf an der Wulka and Apetlon for instance, there are still *tamburizza* orchestras. In fact, Burgenland still displays a mosaic of ethnic minorities: Rom and Sinté gypsies, German-speaking incomers, Croat refugees fleeing from the Turks, Hungarians who have become Austrian. These minorities settled in Burgenland, particularly around the lake, because the region formed part of a defensive belt deliberately depopulated by Hungarian sovereigns who had bordered their kingdom by a no-man's-land known as *gyepü*. As everyone knows, abandoned territory has always attracted refugees.

Apetlon, there are *Buschenschenken*. These are open-air cafés, embellished by lilacs in spring, where one may enjoy a fruity white wine that loosens the tongues of even the most taciturn.

Vienna's "Seaside" – Excepting Podersdorf which is directly on the water, nearly every village by the lake has a small bathing beach, reached by a causeway through the rushes.

Owing to its proximity to Vienna (50km/31 miles), it attracts in summer all those who care for water sports (sailing, windsurfing, rowing, swimming) and in winter those keen on ice sports, particularly windskating. Today, leisure boats have replaced fishing craft and the boats of reed cutters. Yet anglers and wildfowlers still use flat-bottomed boats to make their way along the network of canals among the reed-beds. Unfortunately, there is a surfeit of campsites and hotels around the lake; this constitutes a danger for this fragile environment, which some years ago was threatened by a a bridge-building project. Environmental protection associations from the whole of Europe came to its rescue.

FROM NEUSIEDL TO EISENSTADT

Go to Neusiedl by the A 4-E60 motorway and leave by exit 43.

Neusiedl am See – The little town which gave its name to the lake has some interesting sights: a ruined 13C fortress, a 15C church near the town hall, and the **Pannonisches Heimatmuseum** ⊙ *(Kalvarienbergstrasse 40)*. This Pannonian Museum displays objects relating to the region's popular crafts and traditions.

Leave Neusiedl northwestwards on the Eisenstadt road. Bear left 2.4km/1 1/2 miles after Donnerskirchen for Rust.

Nightingale

Bee-eater

Whinchat

Little ringed plover

Waterfowl

Grey partridge

Coot

Black-tailed godwit

Great white heron

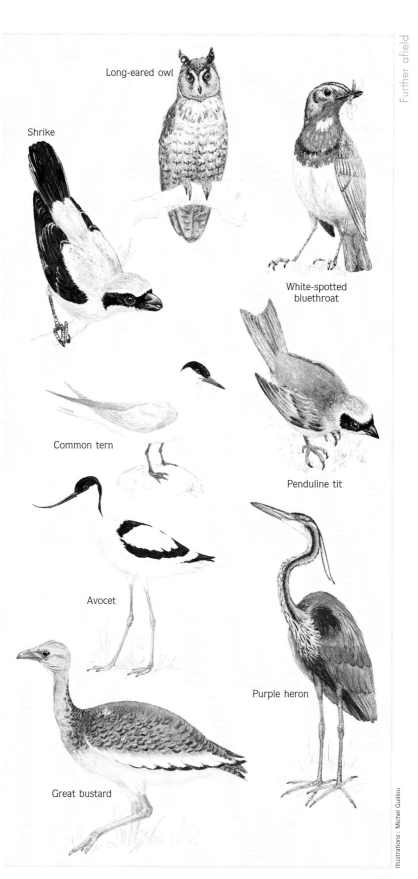

Long-eared owl

Shrike

White-spotted
bluethroat

Common tern

Penduline tit

Avocet

Purple heron

Great bustard

241

Seefestspiele Mörbisch

Summer Festival in Mörbisch

★ **Rust** – This affluent and attractive town is famous for its storks' nests to which the birds return every year. Rust bought borough status from Leopold I in 1681; it cost 30,000 litres of wine and 60,000 gold florins. The town has many scenic sights: delightful Renaissance and Rococo façades with corbelling and impressive carved doorways, pleasantly arcaded inner courtyards and partly preserved fortifications. Because of its considerable architectural heritage, the old town is classed as a historic monument. The slanting eyes of the winegrowing inhabitants may remind visitors that they are in the land from which Attila's raging hordes set out to conquer the world in 450.

Fischerkirche – *West side of Rathausplatz.* A wall surrounds the fortified Fishermen's Church. It is is an irregular building with remarkable 14C and 15C **frescoes★**. In the aisle, the three statues on the Magi Altar (late Gothic style) is a major work. There is a fine 1705 organ.
From this quiet and welcoming town, named *Ceel* (city of elms) by the Hungarians, a causeway leads through the reeds to the **bathing resort** *(see Practical information)* and the curious lakeside dwellings. These *Pfahlbauten* are amazing wooden houses resting on piles, linked by pontoons. Tucked away in the reeds, their thatched roofs are not visible from a distance.

★ **Mörbisch am See** – This is the last village on the western shore of the lake before the Hungarian border. It has great charm with its colourful and picturesque alleys running at right angles off the main street. The houses are whitewashed and nearly all have an outdoor staircase with a porch above it. They form a delightful and cheerful scene, with their brightly painted doors and shutters, bunches of maize hanging along the walls, flower-decked balconies and windows.
East of the village, the Seestrasse leads across marshes and reed-beds to a pier and a bathing resort on the lake, as well as to the site of the summer festival, with its floating stage *(see Practical information)*. It is the setting for performances of Viennese and Hungarian operettas and folk music is played.
By renting a bicycle and provided one has a passport, it is possible to visit the Hungarian side, in Nemzeti Park, by crossing the border at Fertörakos *(see Practical information)*. It is also an excellent opportunity for visiting Sopron (formerly Ödenburg), a small Magyar community with a town centre dating from the 15C.
Return to Rust and bear left for St Margarethen.

St Margarethen – In summer, the old Roman quarries in this area are the setting for an open-air Passion Play *(see Practical information)* featuring hundreds of amateur performers. St Margarethen's famous sandstone was used for the construction of renowned Viennese buildings: the cathedral as well as the Burgtheater, Parliament and Votivkirche.
Continue to Eisenstadt.

Eisenstadt – *See under this heading.*

*Information in this Guide is based on data
provided at the time of going to press;
improved facilities and changes in the cost of living
make subsequent alterations inevitable.*

PERCHTOLDSDORF

Lower Austria
Michelin map 426 fold 25 – 8km/5 miles southwest of Vienna
Local map Wienerwald
Train: S1, S2 (Schnellbahn), R10 (Regionalbahn) from Südbahnhof
By car: from Vienna town centre, take road 12, Breitenfurterstrasse, to the town centre
(local map of Wienerwald tour)

Further afield

The Marktplatz is worth discovering in the muffled silence of falling snow while drinking a warming *Glühwein* from one of the miniature chalets open during the Advent and Christmas season. It is a typically Viennese winter scene. Hugo Wolf lived in this winegrowing village *(Brunnengasse 26)* and its centre has much to offer throughout the year.

Marktplatz – At the centre of the square stands a fine **Pestsäule★** (1713) (plague pillar) with 8 scupltures by Johann Bernhard Fischer von Erlach. These pillars, so numerous in the area, are a reminder that the plague once destroyed a major part of the European population. Vienna and its surroundings suffered four particularly disastrous epidemics in 1348, 1629, 1679 and 1714, causing over 30,000 deaths each time. People erected plague pillars as votive monuments to thank God for having brought the plague to an end; the most famous of these is the votive Dreifaltigkeitsäule (Trinity Column) in the Graben. J.B. Fischer von Erlach built part of it. He had studied in Rome and greatly admired Francesco Borromini's work *(see tour around Stephansdom, in Vienna)*.

The town hall *(Marktplatz 10)* is in a late Gothic style (end of 15C) and houses the **Türkenmuseum** ⊘, a small museum tracing the Ottoman invasions of Lower Austria. On the north side, Marktplatz is closed off by St Augustine's church and Perchtoldsdorfer Turm. This massive square tower, dating from between 1450 and 1520, has sides measuring about 13m/42ft and rises 59.5m/195ft from the ground.

Pfarrkirche zum Hl. Augustinus – St Augustine's hall-church, begun in 1435, contains some interesting works. The entrance is through the south porch, which displays *Fear* (1511 polychrome relief). In the porch is **The Death of the Virgin★** (1449 polychrome relief). This work is noteworthy, because the Virgin is lying down, a typically Byzantine concept. Western art usually depicts the Virgin as dying with a candle in Her hand. A monumental Baroque high altar (about 1740) dominates the interior. On either side of the altar-piece, there are 4 statues of the patron saints of the imperial *Länder*, from left to right: Joseph (Styria), Domitian (Carinthia), Florian (Upper Austria) and Leopold (Lower Austria). To the left of the high altar, the piscina dates from the 15C.

Outside, to the west, the remains of the Herzogsburg (dukes' palace) are visible. It dates from the 11C to the 15C and now houses a cultural centre. To the south is Martinikapelle, built between 1512 and 1520.

Almost opposite the church is Wienergasse.

Spitalskirche – *Wienergasse.* Duchess Beatrix von Zollern founded this church between 1406 and 1419.

Close-up of the Plague Column

H. A. Jahn/VIENNASLIDE

PETRONELL-CARNUNTUM★

Lower Austria
Michelin map 426 fold 26 – 35km/22 miles east of Vienna
Train: Petronell (S7) from Wien Nord

On the site of this and the neighbouring town of **Bad Deutsch-Altenburg**, excavations have led to the discovery of numerous interesting remains from the garrison which the Roman established on the Danube during the 1C. At the beginning of the following century, this garrison became the seat of the governor of Upper Pannonia.

Origins – From a map of the Roman empire, it is immediately apparent that the Rhine and the Danube form a northeast frontier along which the Romans built several settlements: Cologne and Mainz on the Rhine, Carnuntum and Aquincum (Buda, of the present Budapest) on the Danube. The ancient Illyrian-Celtic town of Carnuntum was built on the banks during the 1C and was also on the amber route linking Italy to the Baltic. There is little doubt about the exact date of the Roman settlement on this site. The garrison is thought to date from the year 15, when the Emperor Tiberius (14-37) decided to send to the Danube his dreaded 15th *Apollinaris* legion to quell the Marcomani.

The capital of Upper Pannonia – Pannonia corresponded approximately to present-day Hungary. Augustus conquered it after the rebellion of 16 BC. It became a Roman province after 9 BC. It was an Illyrian garrison town on the Roman *limes* near *Vindobona* (Vienna), *Ala nova* (probably Schwechat), *Castra Regina* (Bratislava) and *Scarbantia* (Sopron). The camp quickly grew in size owing to the establishment of numerous veterans, who brought their families and attracted shopkeepers and traders. During the first decade of the 2C, Carnuntum became the capital of Upper Pannonia, the military, political and economic centre of the province. During the reign of Emperor Hadrian (117-138), it acquired the status of *municipium*, which meant that all its inhabitants became Roman citizens.

In 171, Emperor Marcus Aurelius came to Carnuntum in person – according to tradition, this is where he wrote his *Meditations* – to drive back the Marcomani and the Quades, whom he eventually defeated in 174. After suffering damage from these battles, the town was rebuilt and enjoyed a new period of prosperity. Marcus Aurelius returned to *Vindobona* camp to face further threats from the Barbarians and died there on 17 March 180, from an epidemic that decimated his troops. After the murder of his son Commodus (180-192), Septimius Severus was elected emperor. He was then commander-in-chief of Upper Pannonia, which is why Carnuntum immediately acquired the status of *colonia*. In 261, during a phase of complete military anarchy, the city, in a spirit of independence, even elected its commander as emperor, a man by the name of Caius Publius Regalianus. His soldiers killed him a short time later. Diocletian (284-305) re-established the empire by creating two sections (western and eastern); one emperor (augustus) would reign over each, with the assistance of a successor (caesar). On 11 November 308, after Diocletian's abdication, the imperial conference for the preservation of the empire took place in Carnuntum. Licinius became augustus of the western section, while Galerius remained at the head of the eastern section.

In 375, Emperor Valentinius I died. This marked the start of the great invasions. In his *Rerum gestarum Libri*, the historian Ammienus Marcellinus describes Carnuntum as a "dirty and derelict village". The Goths – the Quades to be precise – then the Huns finally destroyed (407) the city "at the foot of the rock".

★**Archäologischer Park Carnuntum** ⊙ – *Hauptstrasse 296* – In this archeological park, the Roman excavations extend over nearly 8km/5 miles, just like an open-air museum. They began in 1885, although the idea originated with Wolfgang Lazius who visited the area in the 16C. He was the author of the chronicle *Vienna Austriae* and had come to make an inventory of votive altars. These excavations brought to light the **military camp** (and its hospital) of the 15th legion which consisted of 10 cohorts, a total of about 5,000 soldiers. Two **amphitheatres** are on view: I, an elliptical arena measuring 72m by 44m/78yds by 47yds – with seating for 6,000 to 8,000 (in the centre there is a rectangular basin to which a canal supplies water for cleaning the track); and II, which could accommodate 13,000 spectators, and is also an elliptical building with two gateways. The southern gateway possesses a basin which is probably an early

---

What is a limes ?

In Latin, the word *limes* signifies a strip of land between two fields. It is a demarcation line. In the Roman empire, the word was used to describe the fortification system at the frontiers, often consisting of a series of military camps interlinked by a communications line with a palissade. There were several *limes*, of which the most famous is probably Hadrian's Wall built in Great Britain in 122. However, since a *limes* is mainly a boundary, it could easily consist of a river or just a fortified ditch.

Christian baptistry. The **thermal baths**, designed for idle relaxation, are in the civilian settlement, or more precisely in Septimus Severus' colony, which numbered about 50,000 inhabitants. They also bear the name of "palace ruins" and are one of the most extensive (250m/272yds) ancient remains north of the Alps. These baths underwent alterations to accommodate the imperial conference in 308. Visitors see the changing-room, the rest room and its grotto, small and large basins and the hot water system. Nearby is a reconstructed **temple of Diana**, and, further to the south, **Heidentor** (pagans' gate), one of the four city gates; it is 20m/65ft high.

The park also displays remains of the cavalry camp, the cemetery, the temple of Jupiter and the foundations of Pannonian houses.

Rundkapelle ⊘ – *By No 73 Hauptstrasse. Entrance through the car park of Marcus Aurelius Hotel.* This circular chapel stands on the right of the road and is unusual for its pointed roof and semicircular chancel grafted on its east end. Outside, the building has a sober display of columns and arcades resting on ornamental brackets. The small carved **tympanum★** above the entrance represents the Baptism of Christ; this is perhaps an indication that the chapel was originally a baptistry. On the left, there is John the Baptist in his sheepskin; in the centre, Christ in a loincloth is surmounted by the dove of the Holy Ghost, the embodiment of divinity; on the right a winged Angel holds the chrismal cloth for covering the anointed part. Artists often depicted the Jordan as a person, but here it appears in the form of semicircular incisions; in accordance with the iconography of Christian art, it is almost dried up. This carved scene is delightful.

Pfarrkirche der Hl. Petronilla – This church stands in the centre of the village, in the middle of the cemetery. Bishop Altmann of Passau founded it in 1078. Although the Turks damaged it in 1529, it still retains an attractive Romanesque chevet.

Go to Bad Deutsch-Altenburg; turn left just before the junction with road No 9. Leave the car beside the park bordering the Danube.

★Archäologisches Museum Carnuntinum ⊘ – *Badgasse 40-46.* In 1904, Emperor Franz-Josef opened this building and his statue stands facing the park. Magnificent restoration work took place there between 1988 and 1992.

During a visit to this museum, one should bear in mind that it displays only 5% of the remarkable collection of remains and objects from the excavation of the Roman city. The items belong in various categories (weapons, jewelry, brick-coloured sigillated pottery, intaglios and cameos, oil lamps, gold and silver coins, religious objects, tombstones and votive altars, military uniforms, glass, etc.). Statuary dominates this magnificent ensemble. The most outstanding exhibit is the superb *Dancing maenad of Carnuntum★* (2C) *(No 17)*, a fine white marble imported sculpture, which conveys the spell-binding enthusiasm of the priestesses of Bacchus, god of wine. Other items of particular interest include a statue of Hercules (late 2C) *(No 18)* famous for his strength and his 12 labours; the head of a statue of Minerva (3C) *(No 14)*, goddess of wisdom and intelligence; a head of Aesculapius *(No 4)*, god of medicine, and a head of Diana *(No 5)*, goddess of hunting; the bronze head of Athena Parthenos *(No 5)*, a warlike goddess who protected heroes; a statuette of Hermes *(No 16)*, god of trade and source of inspiration for poets and a small sculpture of a phallic buffoon *(No 36)*, symbolizing the fecundity of nature.

A huge map of the Roman site made of strips of wood adorns the staircase. Most

Carnuntinum Museum

The *Maenad Dancing*

of the items on the ground floor relate to the **cult of Mithra** and come from the mithraeum, a subterranean sanctuary found on the site. Mithra was an Iranian divinity, to which Roman soldiers paid great homage after the 2C. They associated the god with the sun, and therefore with fire. Mithraic ceremonies and mysteries often entailed human sacrifice. Hadrian abolished this religion, but Commodus restored it.

EXCURSIONS

Wildungsmauer – For anyone arriving from Vienna, this large village lies 5km/ 3 miles before Petronell. Despite restorations and additions (including a 19C porch and tower), the little church of St Nicholas has kept its essentially Romanesque character. This single-naved church originated from alterations to a fortified building, which took place before 1300.

Rohrau – The beautiful 16C castle houses the **Harrach gallery**★★ ☉ created in 1668 and preserved until 1970 in the Harrach palace *(see Freyung district, in Vienna)*, the collection was brought together by the Counts of Harrach, an illustrious and influential family which included among its number a viceroy of Naples, an ambassador to Madrid and several archbishops. This art collection includes works by 17C and 18C Spanish, Neapolitan and Roman masters. Neapolitan, and Roman masters, and also by 16C and 17C Flemish and Dutch masters (Brueghel, Jordaens, Rubens, Ruysdael, Van Dyck). *The Concert* is a graceful painting of half-length figures supposedly by a Dutch master, which enjoys special renown.

Haydn's birthplace ☉ is on the road through the village. The composer was born there on 31 March 1732. His mother was cook at the castle and his father was a wheelwright. On view are copies of the birth certificates of the Haydn brothers, Joseph and Michael, facsimiles of scores and some engravings. There is also a watercolour by Balthasar Wigand showing the concert of *The Creation* at Alte Universität *(see Akademie der Wissenschaften)*. The piano (1809) is from Érard Frères, Paris.

Return towards Petronell-Carnuntum and Bad Deutsch-Altenburg. Cross the Danube and head towards Marchegg. After 9km/5 miles, bear right to Schlosshof.

An embankment 2km/1 mile long carries the road across the floodplain of the Danube. The road crosses the river itself by means of a bold piece of engineering in the form of a suspension bridge with cables hung from a single central tower. Here and there, squat, single-storied houses break up the monotony of the endless flat arable fields. This architectural style is characteristic of central Europe.

Schlosshof ☉ – In the 18C, this vast Baroque palace became famous as the residence of the Imperial Court. Prince **Eugène of Savoy** reconstructed the castle from 1725 to 1729. He was a great prince, whom Louis XIV slighted *(see also Belvedere, in Vienna)* and who later became the Emperor of Austria's general-in-chief. He employed the architect Lukas von Hildebrand and a workforce of 800, including 300 gardeners. They created a magnificent landscape in the French style. With its sculptures, fountains, terraces, wrought-iron gates, the garden was the envy of the prince's contemporaries. Empress Maria-Theresa bought the castle in 1760, added a storey and decorated the interior sumptuously. Today, most of the castle has been restored and is the setting for a large annual exhibition.

Between Bad Deutsch-Altenburg and Hainburg, a range of hills comes into view, overlooking the Slovakian bank of the Morava and its confluence with the Danube; these are the Little Carpathians, the foothills of the great mountain chain of central Europe encircling the Hungarian plain to the north.

Hainburg – In the Middle Ages, this town played a strategic role. Below the remains of its castle, it still retains its ring of walls and fortified gateways.

If there is time to spare before returning to Vienna, Bratislava (see under this heading), capital of Slovakia, is about 10km/6 miles away from Hainburg.

SOPRON★★

Hungary

Michelin map 426 fold 25 – 63km/39 miles southeast of Vienna

EU nationals should take their passports to cross the border.

Formerly Ödenburg in the Austro-Hungarian empire, the small town of Sopron lies only 7km/4 miles from the frontier. It attracts numerous Austrians from Vienna, Lower Austria or Burgenland who come to shop for bargains (mainly cigarettes and clothes) or gamble at the casino. However, this small but dynamic town also has other amenities such as its delightful town centre and its medieval walls built over Roman foundations.

Historical sketch – During the first century, the Romans settled a garrison on the Danube. At the beginning of the following century, it became the seat of the governor of the province of Pannonia *(see Petronell-Carnuntum)*. Not far from there, they established camps, including *Vindobona*, the future Vienna, and *Scarbantia*, the future

Sopron. Both soon acquired the status of *municipium*, a town whose people were granted Roman citizenship. Sopron owes its existence to its location on the amber route linking the Baltic to Italy. Pliny the Elder (23-79) refers to it in his *Natural History* as *oppidum Scarbantia Iulia*. Anticipating the great invasions, Emperor Valentinus reinforced the city (about 370) which acquired a defensive aspect. Nevertheless, the Quades and Sarmates soon destroyed the Roman settlement.

After the Avars, who settled in the region about 570, came the Bavarians, attracted by the iron deposits. In 907, they were defeated in Pozsony by the Hungarians, whose name of Turkish origin signifies "ten tribes of archers". King Stefan I (997-1038) had the city walls rebuilt (5m/16ft wide and 15m/49ft high), enabling the inhabitants to resist the adventurers. Peter the Hermit took them with him to Jerusalem in 1096. In 1277, Sopron acquired the status of royal borough; in less than a century, its ramparts, on their Roman foundations, were bristling with 34 strongholds. At the time, the town had 20,000 inhabitants.

"Civitas fidelissima"

On 11 November 1918, Karl I, the last Hapsburg ruler, signed an act of Abdication. The Hungarian Republic was proclaimed on 16 November 1918, with Count Mihály Károlyi as president. He resigned on 21 March 1919, when the Communist and Socialist parties set up the Soviet Hungarian Republic under Béla Kun. The National Assembly appointed Rear-Admiral Miklós Horthy as regent. Having fought on the side of Germany during the war, the Hungarians lost the right to self-determination. On 4 June 1920, the treaty of Trianon confirmed the dismembering of the country: the loss of Slovakia, Transylvania, sub-Carpathian Ukraine, Croatia, as well as Sopron and its surrounding area which had to become part of Austria.

Proud of being Magyars, the inhabitants opted for self-determination. In December 1921, the government instituted a plebiscite which requested this. Agreement was reached and they remained Hungarian. Since then, Sopron has been known as "the most faithful city".

Tour of the centre

The town centre is 400m/436yds long and 250m -272yds wide and contains only a few streets with delightful buildings dating mostly from the 15C.

★ **Belfry** – The defensive Roman walls featured a single gate opening onto the *Carnuntum* road. Towards the end of the 13C, the gate, now called *Elökapu*, acquired a belfry, which is the cylindrical section (note certain Gothic openings). The belfry, damaged by fire in 1676, was rebuilt two years later and now soars above the city walls for 58m/190ft. Its most striking feature is the circular gallery with Renaissance arcades. The slender Tuscan columns of the arcades rest on an elegant balustrade from which there is a fine **view** of the town.

On the side of the gate facing the town centre, there is a group by the sculptor Zsigmond Kisfaludy-Strobl, an allegory of Hungary gathering together the faithful citizens of Sopron *(see inset)*.

Fö square – The belfry *(see above)* acts as a landmark. Like many squares in neighbouring Austria, this one has a plague column (1701) in the centre.

Opposite the town hall is Storno House, a fine aristocratic palace dating from the 14C and housing the largest collection from Sopron museum.

Soproni Múzeum – *Fö tér 8*. This archeological exhibition, located behind the palace, displays the results of excavations in and around Sopron, dating from the Stone Age to the 16C. Among the most interesting items are the **Hasfalva bronze disk**★ (Hallstatt period, 1000-500 BC), fragments of marble statues from the triad in the Capitol (2C), the Veskény bronze harness plates (6C), and an engraved bronze chalice by the Bavarian goldsmith Cundpald (late 8C), which provides evidence that the Carolingians had converted the area to Christianity.

Storno House contains another permanent exhibition (from the 17C to the 20C): furniture, artefacts and traditional crafts. Exhibits of special interest are the chest by the Sopron cabinet-makers (late 17C) and the clock bearing Ferenc Zoller's signature (1773).

Walk along Új Street.

Near No 22 "New" Street, the **old synagogue** (mid 14C) has retained a fine multifoiled tympanum (entrance) and the niche for the scrolls of the Torah. This niche is gracefully decorated with bunches of grapes and vineleaves carved in stone. The hexagonal pulpit is a reconstruction. King Louis I the Great drove the Jews out in the mid 14C; they had all left by 1526.

The street opens into Orsolya square. Turn left into Szent-György Street.

At the corner of Hátsókapu Street is the elegant Caesar House (No 2).

J. Gabanou/DIAF

The belfry

Museums – Soproni Múzeum dates from 1963 and occupies ten buildings, most of which are in the town centre. It is possible to visit Fabricius House (6 Fö Square) which concentrates on the Roman period, the chapterhouse (1 Templom Street) or the "arcaded" house (5 Orsolya Square) which holds temporary exhibitions.

Franz Liszt in Sopron – Franz (Ferenc) Liszt was born in Doborján, the present Raiding *(see below)*, a few kilometres away from Sopron, both localities being in the same Hungarian province. In 1820, at the age of only 9, he went to Sopron to give a recital, and frequently returned there to perform his works. Sopron recalls the composer of the *Hungarian Rhapsodies* with affection, since he always donated the earnings from his concerts to the charitable organisations in the town.

Excursions

Raiding – *Leave Sopron by Road 84 (to Balaton) and turn right towards Deutschkreuz to return to Austria. At Horitschon, turn left for Raiding.*

Liszts Geburtshaus ⊙ – The **Franz Liszt Museum** occupies part of the residence that went with his post as steward in charge of the Esterházy sheep farms at Raiding, where the composer was born on 22 October 1811. There are various family mementoes, photographs and documents tracing the career of the young prodigy. The small organ of the former church, on which he played, has been moved here.

Michelin Maps, Red Guides and Green Guides are complementary publications – to be used together.

As its name implies, this "new town" was created out of nothing in 1194 by Leopold V of Babenberg. Aware of threats from the east, the duke wanted to protect the new duchy of Styria which he had acquired in 1192. The town acted as a frontier fortress against Magyar incursions from Hungary.

Richard the Lionheart's ransom – According to tradition, during the Third Crusade, the King of England, Richard the Lionheart, quarrelled violently with the Duke of Austria, Leopold V. The Englishman had torn down the banner which the duke had just placed at the top of a tower during an attack on Acre. To regain his honour, Leopold of Babenberg took the naïve Richard, returning from the Holy Land via his rival's territory, arrested in 1192 at Erdberg, now part of Vienna's 11th District. He had him imprisoned at Dürnstein in Lower Austria, then in the imperial castle of Trifels, in the Rhineland Palatinate.

Part of Richard the Lionheart's huge ransom paid for the construction of *nova civita*, later called *Niwenstat* then *Neustadt*: a quadrangular precinct with thick outer walls, strategically placed between the Leithagebirge and Höhe Wand mountains.

Imperial residence – After withstanding many attacks by the Mongols, the town became an imperial residence between 1440 and 1493, during the reign of Frederick III. He allowed the city to incorporate the double-headed eagle in its coat-of-arms. The Emperor Maximilian was born there and buried there (although he died at Wels) far from his magnificent mausoleum in Innsbruck, a major legacy of German Renaissance sculpture. The town achieved new splendour in Maria-Theresa's reign, and this continued until the 19C. The old town is now an elegant pedestrian precinct, which still displays the regular layout of the medieval streets.

SIGHTS

Burg – The central part of the former fortress dates from the 13C, but it has seen a series of extensions and alterations. In 1751, Maria Theresa established there a military academy for the training of elite officers; it is now considered the oldest in the world. General Erwin Rommel was its director when the Germans annexed it in 1938 (it reopened in 1958, having been closed after the Second World War).

St. Georgskapelle ⊘ – The east façade overlooking the interior courtyard owes its name "Wappenwand" (heraldic wall) to the 107 carved coats of arms (15C) around the central window and Fredrick III's statue; some of the coats of arms are from the House of Habsburg, while others may be imaginary. Peter von Pusika built this church, then known as the Virgin's chapel, during Frederick III's reign. It was reconstructed after the Second World War. The Gothic hall-church houses a *Virgin with Cherries* (south altar); some stained-glass fragments (escutcheons) are the most outstanding remains of the original furnishings. Maximilian's mortal remains rest beneath the steps of the high altar, in a **red marble sarcophagus** in the Apostles' chancel.

Neuklosterkirche – *Ungargasse, near Hauptplatz*. This Gothic building, in which the chancel (first half of the 14C) is higher than the nave, has Baroque furnishings and decoration.

In the apse, behind the high altar, there is the splendid **tombstone★** of Empress Eleanor of Portugal, wife of Frederick III, carved in 1467 by Nikolaus of Leyden. His real name was Nikolaus Gerhaert. He was a German sculptor of Flemish origin (hence his nickname) who died in Vienna in 1473. He also designed Frederick III's tomb *(see Stephansdom)*.

Hauptplatz – The Rathaus (town hall), built in 1488, stands south of this square, most of which is closed to traffic. In the 16C it acquired a rusticated stone tower, and, in 1834, was refurbished in neo-Classical style. The *Mariensäule* dates from 1678. The fine houses to the north of the square are Gothic.

Go to Domplatz via Böheimgasse.

Stadtpfarrkirche – *Domplatz*. This late Romanesque basilica acquired a Gothic transverse nave and chancel in the 14C. The **Brauttor★** (bride's doorway), on the south side, is earlier than 1246 and displays diamond and zigzag patterns. Inside, the high ceiling is evidence of the interest Frederick III took in this church. The gallery in the courtyard bears his motto: "A.E.I.O.U." *(see inset, Hofburg, in Vienna)*. He probably donated the *Apostelchor*, 12 larger than life-sized statues of the apostles attached to the pillars by the sculptor Lorenz Luchsperger. The **high altar** with its six Corinthian columns of red marble is sumptuous. Above the **pulpit** (1609) by Johann Baptist Zelpi are statues of the Doctors of the Church: St Augustine, St Ambrose, St Gregory and St Jerome.

Propsthof housed the bishop's palace from 1469 to 1785 and lies north of Domplatz. It has a finely carved Baroque doorway bearing the arms of Bishop Franz Anton, Count Puchheim.

WIENERWALD★

The Vienna woods might well be called the Vienna hills, since they form the eastern foothills of the Alps. This vast green belt stretches westward from the boundaries of the city, providing the heart of the city with a rural charm and a breath of fresh air. Vienna is one of the few major capitals which within its walls has managed to retain the attractions of the villages of bygone times. Elsewhere, these villages have disappeared in the course of centuries, giving way to industrial cities full of iron and concrete. In Vienna, the forest is a setting for vineyards and walks in the coolness of the woods during hot summers. However, it is more than this. The Wienerwald is also a tune on a zither emerging from a lonely inn, a scene evoked by Beethoven's *6th Symphony*, "the Pastorale", or the strains of a Strauss waltz floating over the waters of the Danube. This secluded landscape has nothing in common with the wild forests of Arthurian legend; it is a vast and leafy rural area with famous abbeys and attractive footpaths where people greet one another as they pass by.

For those coming from Vienna by car, or intending to rent a vehicle, there is a suggested programme of excursions from Perchtoldsdorf to Baden through the part of the forest which Schubert and his friends enjoyed visiting for their joyous bucolic escapades.

Leave Vienna by road 12 and follow the "Perchtoldsdorf Zentrum" sign. At the end of Mühlgasse, turn right then immediately left. Turn left again at the stop sign on Plättenstrasse. Follow the "Zentrum" sign.

Perchtoldsdorf *– See under this heading.*

From Perchtoldsdorf, take road 13 at the corner of Spitalskirche (Donauwörtherstrasse then Hochstrasse) for Vienna. After 1.3km/0.8 miles, turn left into Kaltenleutgebnerstrasse which becomes Hauptstrasse. After 11km/6 miles, turn left for Sulz in Wienerwald. Cross Sittendorf and follow the sign for Sparbach Naturpark just before the motorway.

Naturpark Sparbach ☺ *– If coming directly from Vienna by E60/A 21 motorway, take exit 26 and turn right. Turn right again and carry on for 600m/654m, following the signs. Large car park opposite the entrance.* This natural park is also a zoo: several paths lead to enclosures with boars, does, mouflons, etc. It also has several ruins, the most noteworthy being Burg Johannstein and Köhlerhaus (alt 567m/1,859ft). There is a charge for admission to the park. It is pleasantly cool during the Viennese summer, and will appeal to keen walkers, who should, however, take care when approaching the boars' enclosure: it was not properly shut during our visit!

Pass over the E60/A 21 motorway and turn right into road 11 which runs through woods and vales to Gaaden and Heiligenkreuz Abbey.

★**Heiligenkreuz** *– See under this heading.*

Continue along road 11 towards Alland. After 4km/2 1/2 miles, turn left for Mayerling.

Mayerling *– See under this heading.*

Turn left into road 210 for Baden.

Helenental – The river Schwechat flows through this scenic valley lying between Mayerling and Baden. The valley includes 60km/37 miles of signposted paths, enabling visitors to explore the valley on foot, which is particularly pleasurable in autumn. Just before Baden are the ruins of two once great castles: Rauhenstein (12C) on the left and Rauheneck (11C) on the right.

‡‡**Baden** *– See under this heading.*

Leave from Baden town centre to take the wine road ("Weinstrasse") to Gumpoldskirchen and Mödling: take Kaiser-Franz-Joseph-Ring signposted to Gumpoldskirchen and Pfaffstätten. Continue under the railway bridge and turn left immediately beyond it (road 212). Pass under the railway bridge again and follow the Gumpoldskirchen road. Turn right at the stop sign, then immediately left for Gumpoldskirchen.

Gumpoldskirchen *– See under this heading.*

The road rises through vineyards then winds down to Mödling. The bends in the road provide fine views of the town (as far as Kahlenberg on a clear day).

Mödling *– See under this heading.*

Go in the direction of Seegrotte to the west (signposted E60/A 21) by Spitalmühlgasse which soon becomes Brühlerstrasse. After the football stadium, turn right into Hauptstrasse, following the signs. After the bridge, turn right again and park.

Hinterbrühl – Lying west of Mödling, Hinterbrühl boasts a fascinating tourist attraction, which is very popular and possibly too commercial: **Seegrotte**★ ☺. It is the largest underground lake in Europe, covering over 6 hectares/14 acres. Visitors explore it by motorboat. The lake was formed in 1912, when some 20,000,000 litres/4,399,380 gallons of water rushed into the lower gallery of this former mine.

Return to Mödling by road 11. Cross the town and rejoin road 11 via Triester-strasse, towards Schwechat. The road passes over the E59/A 2 motorway. Follow the signs to Laxenburg.

Laxenburg – *See under this heading.*

Return to Vienna by the E59/A 2 motorway or by Triesterstrasse.

Suggested walks – Wienerwald extends far beyond the tour described above. For the benefit of keen walkers, we have listed a few signposted footpaths, which are among the most attractive in the Vienna woods. These are only suggestions. Anyone sufficiently interested should buy a detailed map. Maps of every kind are available at Freytag & Berndt, 9 Kohlmarkt, 1st District.

Klosterneuburg – **Weidling** – North of Vienna. Departure from Klosterneuburg station for Weidling via Leopoldsberg (alt 423m/1,387ft) (2 3/4 hours).

Maria Anzbach - **Maria Anzbach** – Between Vienna and St Pölten. Round trip via Kohl-reitberg (alt 516m/1,692ft) (2 hours).

Böheimkirchen - **Pottenbrunn** – East of St Pölten. Departure from Böheimkirchen station for Pottenbrunn station, via Schildberg (alt 393m/1,289ft) (1 1/4 hours).

A walk in the Vienna Woods

Purkersdorf – On the western edge of Vienna. Round trip, departure from Unterpurkersdorf station (2 hours).

Kalksburg - **Breitenfurt** – West of Vienna. Departure from Kalksberg for Breitenfurt via Laabersteigberg (alt 530m/1,738ft) (4 1/2 hours).

Klausen-Leopoldsdorf - **Alland** – Northwest of Mayerling. Departure from Klausen-Leopoldsdorf for Alland (3 hours).

Le Schöpfl – West of Mayerling. Round trip, departure from Forsthof. Climb and descent of the Schöpfl (alt 893m/2,929ft) (2 hours).

Mayerling - **Bad Vöslau** – This long and very pleasant tour leads to Bad Vöslau station (6 hours).

Berndorf - **Pottenstein** – Southwest of Baden. Departure from Berndorf station for Pottenstein station on the same line (4 hours).

Sacher Torte

Frau Sacher, a leading personality in late 19C Vienna, fed the impoverished Austrian nobility in her famous restaurant long after they had ceased to pay. She was less generous with the recipe for her celebrated torte, but many have tried to equal her pastry prowess.

Preheat the oven to 165°C/325°F (thermostat 3)

Grate 180g/5-6oz semi sweet chocolate.

Cream together until smooth 100g/ 1/2 cup sugar and 115g/ 1/2 cup butter.
Beat in 6 yolks, one at a time, until the mixture is light and fluffy.
Add the chocolate and 115g/ 3/4 cup dry bread crumbs,
30g 1/4 cup finely ground blanched almonds, a pinch of salt.
Beat the egg whites until stiff but not dry, fold them in gently.
Pour the mixture into an ungreased tin with a removable rim.
Bake 50 min to 1 hour.
When the torte is cool, slice it horizontally through the middle
(you may turn the top layer over so that the finished cake is flat on the top).
Spread 225g/1 cup apricot jam or preserves between the layers.
Cover with chocolate glaze.
For the genuine Viennese touch, heap on the *schlag!*

Practical
Information

Pratt-Pries/DIAF

General Information

TOURIST INFORMATION

Austrian National Tourist Offices
- Vienna, Kärntnerstrasse 38, open daily 9am to 7pm.
- Vienna, Rathaus, Friedrich-Schmidt-Platz, daily 9am to 7pm.
- Australia: 1st Floor, 36 Carrington Street, Sydney, NSW 2000. ☏ (2) 92 99 36 21. Fax (2) 92 99 38 08.
- Canada: 1010 Ouest rue Sherbrooke, Suite 1410, Montréal, Québec H3A 2R7. ☏ (514) 849 37 08. Fax (514) 849 95 77.
- Canada: 2 Bloor Street East, Suite 3330, Toronto, Ontario M4W 1A 8. ☏ (416) 967 33 81. Fax (416) 967 41 01.
- UK: 30 St. George Street, London W1R 0AL. ☏ (171) 629 04 61. Fax (171) 499 60 38
- USA: 11601 Wilshire Blvd, Suite 2480, Los Angeles, California 90025. ☏ (310) 477 33 32. Fax (310) 477 5141.
- USA: 500 Fifth Avenue, Suite 800, New York, N.Y. 10110. ☏ (212) 944 68 85. Fax (212) 730 45 68.

Tourist Offices of the *Länder* (Austrian Provinces) covered by this guide:
- **Vienna**: Wiener Tourismusverband, Obere Augartenstrasse 40, A - 1025 Wien. ☏ (01) 21 11 40; fax (01) 246 84 92.
- **Lower Austria**: Niederösterreich-Information, Heidenschuss 2, A - 1014 Wien. Request for brochures, ☏ (01) 531 10 62 00 (round-the-clock service). Advice on public holidays, ☏ (01) 533 31 14 34; fax (01) 531 10 60 60.
- **Burgenland**: Burgenland Tourismus, Schloss Esterházy, A - 7000 Eisenstadt, ☏ (02682) 633 84 20. Fax (02682) 633 84 20.

Local Tourist Information Centres:
These are shown by the symbol *i* on the town plans in this guide.
- Baden, Brusattiplatz 3, A - 2500 Baden, ☏ (02252) 445 31 59.
- Eisenstadt, Rathaus, A - 7000 Eisenstadt, ☏ (02682) 33 84.
- Klosterneuburg, Am Niedermarkt, A - 3400 Klosterneuburg, ☏ (02243) 20 38.
- Mörbisch, Hauptstrasse 28, A - 7072 Mörbisch, ☏ (02685) 84 30 or 82 01.
- Petronell-Carnuntum: Tourismusregion March-Donauland, A - 2405 Bad Deutsch-Altenburg, Hauptplatz 4, ☏ (02165) 64 820.
- Rust, Rathaus, A - 7071 Rust, ☏ (02685) 2 02 18 or 5 02.
- Wiener Neustadt, Herzog-Leopoldstrasse 17, A - 2700 Wiener Neustadt, ☏ (02622) 23 53 14 68.

Postal or fax enquiries:
- City of Vienna Tourist Information Office, 1 - 1025 Wien; fax 00-43-1-216 84 92.

Internet: http://www.magwien.gv.at/wtv

EMBASSIES

- Australia, 2 - 4 Mattiellistrasse, Vienna. ☏ (1) 51 28 58 00
- Canada, 2 Laurenzerbergasse, Vienna. ☏ (1) 5 31 38
- USA, 16 Boltzmanngasse, Vienna. ☏ (1) 31 33 90 (embassy)
- USA, 2 Gartenbaupromenade, Vienna. ☏ (1) 31 33 90 (consulate)

TRAVELLING TO VIENNA

By air – Major national airlines fly to Vienna's Wien-Schwechat Airport.

AUSTRIAN AIRLINES –
- 10 Wardow Street, London WIV 4BQ (0171) 434 7300.
- 3391 Peach Tree Rd, Suite 230 Atlanta (404) 814 6330.
Vienna: Kärntner Ring 18, 1010 Wien. ☏ 505 57 57; fax 505 14 34.

BRITISH AIRWAYS – Office in Vienna, Kärntner Ring 10. ☏ 5057691.
General Reservations within the U.K. (open 24 hours a day): ☏ 0395 222 111; within the U.S.A.: 530 Firth Avenue, F° 1 - 800 - AIRWAYS.

Wien-Schwechat airport – In the arrival hall, the Airport Travel Service (open Mondays to Fridays, 9am to 6pm) will make hotel reservations in Vienna. A bus stop and a taxi rank are opposite the arrival hall; the station is located under the arrival hall. A regular fast suburban train service (Schnellbahn S7, 34 ATS) connects the airport to the City Air Terminal under the Hilton Hotel, opposite the underground station *Landstrasse/Wien Mitte* (U2, U3).
☏ (0222) 2231 (general information); (0222) 2184 (departures); (0222) 2197 (departures).

Franz-Josefs-Bahnhof

BORDER CONTROLS

Formalities – Western European nationals require a national identity card or a valid passport or a passport which has expired in the previous five years. Minors travelling alone must have a document of authorisation from their parents issued by the police. Canadian nationals require identity cards or valid passports.
Pets (dogs, cats: maximum two per person) may be brought into Austria subject to the presentation of a rabies vaccination certificate together with a certified translation (forms available from the Austrian National Tourist Office).

Motorists – Drivers require a valid driving licence in 3 sections (E.U. type) or an international insurance certificate ("Green Card").

Health – Before departure, it is advisable to obtain a certificate of entitlement to the reimbursement of medical treatment (Form E 111) from the Department of Social Security, or Post Office.

Customs – Austria applies the E.U.'s internal regulations. Further information is available from the Austrian Customs in Vienna, ☎ (01) 79 49 09.

MOTORING

On the road – The wearing of seat belts is compulsory. In Austria, the speed limit is 130kph - 80mph on motorways and 100kph - 62mph on other roads. When driving with studded tyres, the limits decrease to 100kph - 62mph and 80kph - 50mph respectively; the same applies to cars towing loads of more than 750kg.
The speed limit in built-up areas is 50kph - 31mph.
The 1:400 000 scale Michelin map 426 gives details of likely road closures due to snow. The 1:100 000 scale Freytag und Berndt maps offer further valuable information.

Motorways – To drive on motorways in Austria, you need to display on your windscreen a sticker which can be bought at the Customs when entering the country by car.

Driving in snow – Studded tyres should be fitted or chains in exceptionally severe conditions. Studded tyres are allowed from 15 November to 7 April. If used, all 4 tyres must be studded.

Traffic information – At rush hours, on channel 03 after the news bulletin, and on *Radio Blue Danube* (102.5 Mhz), or by telephoning (01) 15 00. Information on road conditions from OAMTC, ☎ (01) 15 90.

Breakdown Service – This is provided by the two Austrian automobile clubs:
– **O.A.M.T.C.** (Österreichischer Automobil-, Motorrad- und Touring Club), ☎ 120.
– **A.R.B.O.** (Auto-, Motor-, und Radfahrerbund Österreich), ☎ 123.

257

Vienna

Austria offers a great variety of hotel accommodation. Lists of hotels and bed and breakfast accommodation are available from the Austrian National Tourist office and local tourist information centres.

The **Michelin Red Guides Main Cities Europe** are revised annually and give a choice of hotels and restaurants based on inspectors' reports.

Reservations of rooms at hotels or guest houses – From the Austrian National Tourist Office, Kärntnerstrasse 38, 1010 Vienna, open daily 9am to 7pm. Or from local travel agents. Summer season, from 1 April to 31 October; winter season, from 1 November to 31 March.

Reservation of rooms in private guest houses, or of apartments:
– Reisebüro Hippesroither, Zschokkegasse 91, Passage 1, 1220 Wien, ☎ 283 65 51; fax 283 65 451 99.
– Österreichisches Verkehrsbüro, Friedrichstrasse 7, 1043 Wien, ☎ 58 800-171; fax 586 85 33.

Bed and breakfast – Indicated by the sign *"Zimmer frei"*.

Youth hostels – Normally, a membership card of the Youth Hostel Association of one's home country is required. Jugendgästehaus Hütteldorf, Schlossberggasse 8, 1130 Wien, ☎ 87 70 263 (open throughout the year). Jugendgästehaus Brigittenau, Friedrich-Engels-Platz 24, 1200 Wien, ☎ 332 82 940 (open throughout the year). Information is available from Österreichischer Jugendherbergsverband, Schottenring 28, 1010 Wien, ☎ 533 53 3; fax 353 08 61.

Camping and caravaning – The Austrian National Tourist Office and local tourist information centres have lists of fully-equipped sites. There are four campsites in Vienna:
– Campingplatz Wien-West I, Hüttelbergstrasse 40, 1140 Wien, open from mid July to the end of August; no advanced booking. ☎ 914 23 14.
– Campingplatz Wien-West II, Hüttelbergstrasse 80, 1140 Wien, open from the beginning of March to the end of January; no advanced booking. ☎ 911 35 94.
– Campingplatz Wien-Süd, Breitenfursterstrasse 269, 1230 Wien, open in August; no advanced booking. ☎ 865 92 18.
– Campingplatz Wien-Süd, Rodaun, An der Au 2, 1236 Wien, open from the end of March to mid November; no advanced booking. ☎ 88 41 54.
– Campingplatz Schlosspark Laxenburg, Münchendorferstrasse, 2361 Laxenburg, open from mid April to the end of October; no advanced booking. ☎ (02236) 713 33.
Camping outside these sites requires the owner's permission. In Vienna, it is illegal to spend the night in a motor van on unauthorised sites and this may attract a fine.

Exchange bureaux, banks – The unit of currency in Austria is the Schilling (ATS), subdivided into 100 Groschen. Coins: 2, 45, 10, 50 Groschen; 1, 5, 10, 20 Schilling. Notes 20, 50, 100, 500, 1,000, 5,000 Schilling.
At the beginning of 1997, there were 19.5 ATS to £1.00.
Credit cards are usually accepted everywhere in Austria. To make a payment or obtain cash, "American Express", "Eurocard" and "Visa" cards are the most widely used. However, some restaurants still decline to take them. Similarly, not all petrol stations accept them, particularly outside the capital. It is therefore advisable to carry cash. Banks are open daily, excepting weekends and public holidays, from 8am till 12.30pm and from 2.30pm to 4.30pm (5.30pm on Thursdays).

Post Offices – Post offices are open 8am to noon and 2pm to 6pm, Mondays to Fridays. Money can be withdrawn there and the counters close at 5pm. In Vienna, main branches are always open, sometimes even on Saturday. At No 19 Fleischmarkt, the Minipostamt Nachtschalter has facilities for telephoning or posting at all hours of the day or night.

Telephones – Off-peak rates apply daily between 6pm and 8am, and at weekends from 6pm Fridays to 8am Mondays. In Vienna, telephone boxes often stand in pairs, one operating with telephone cards and the other with coins. In the preparation of this guide, we noticed that card-operated boxes were not always reliable (rejected cards or incorrect number of units debited). Telephone cards are on sale in post offices or tobacconists.

Public Holidays – 1 *(Neujahr)* and 6 January *(Dreikönigsfest)*, Good Friday (Protestants), Easter Monday *(Ostermontag)*, 1 May *(Tag der Arbeit)*, Ascension Day *(Christi Himmelfahrt)*, Whit Mondays, Corpus Christi, 15 August *(Maria Himmelfahrt)*, 26 October (National Holiday, *Staatsfeiertag*), 1 November *(Allerheiligen)*, 8 *(Maria Empfängnis)*, 25 *(Christtag)* and 26 December *(Stefanitag)*.

Underground, tram, bus and train – *See Introduction, On the town.*

Hiring a car and taxis – *See Introduction, On the town.*

"WIEN-KARTE"

The Wien-Karte is a 72-hour travel pass costing 180 ATS. It covers journeys on all public transport in zone 100 and must be stamped in a machine (at underground stations, or on trams and buses) when first used; it must also be filled in (name and date).

The Wien-Karte is a special offer from the Vienna Tourist Office and has advantages: reduced admission prices for many museums and temporary exhibitions (10 to 50%); reduced tickets for some concerts, walks and lectures (consult the leaflet that comes with the pass); reductions upon presentation of the pass in shops and restaurants displaying the pass initials.

It is available from many hotels, the city's tourist offices (e.g. No. 38 Kärntnerstrasse), several travel agents and the main public transport stations including: Westbahnhof, Stephansplatz, Karlsplatz, Landstrasse/Wien Mitte. Holders of a credit card may obtain the Wien-Karte in advance by telephoning 00-43-1-798 44 00-28.

TICKETS FOR THE STAATSOPER

Tickets are on sale one month before the performance: Österreichischer Bundestheaterverband, Hanuchgasse 3, 1010 Wien, 8am to 6pm Mondays to Fridays, 10am to noon at weekends; there is also a sales office under the right gallery of the Opera House, Kärntnerstrasse 40, 10am until one hour before the performance. It is possible to make phone bookings from abroad (with a credit card): 00-43-1-513 15 13, 10am to 6pm Mondays to Fridays, 10am till noon at weekends. Programme information: 00-43-1-514 44 29 60.

As performances are always heavily booked, tourists or casual visitors may well not be able to buy tickets. In this case, they should apply to an agency *(see list below)*. The agency will take a commission (performances for which tickets are available are posted in the window).

TICKETS FOR THE KAMMEROPER

Available from Österreichischer Bundestheaterverband, Hanuchgasse 3, 1010 Wien, 8am to 6pm Mondays to Fridays, 10am to noon at weekends. It is possible to make phone bookings from abroad: 00-43-1-513 60 72, noon to 6pm Mondays to Fridays, noon to 4pm on Saturdays.

TICKETS FOR THE VOLKSOPER

From the theatre: Währingerstrasse 78, 1090 Wien. From abroad, the telephone number is the same as for the Staatsoper. Programme information: 00-43-1-514 44 29 60.

A carriage ride

TICKETS FOR THE MUSIKVEREIN

Tickets are on sale at the Friends of Music building (Dumbastrasse 3) one month before the concert, 9am to noon Mondays to Fridays, 9am to 6pm on Saturday. Programme information: 00-43-1-505 13 63 (in German). It is possible to make phone bookings from abroad: 00-43-1-505 81 90, 9am to 6pm Mondays to Fridays, 9am to noon Saturdays; or by fax: 00-43-1-505 94 09. It is advisable to book 3 weeks before the concert.

To try one's luck for seats at the New Year concert, one should write before 2 January to: Wiener Philharmoniker, Bösendorferstrasse 12, A - 1010 Wien.

THEATRE RESERVATIONS

From Österreichischer Bundestheaterverband, Hanuchgasse 3, 1010 Wien, open 8am to 6pm Mondays to Fridays, 10am to noon at weekends.

TICKETS FOR THE SPANISH RIDING SCHOOL

Performances – Tickets are available from: Spanische Reitschule, Hofburg, A - 1010 Wien or from an agency *(see below)* which will charge a commission.

Rehearsals with music – Tickets are available from an agency *(see list below)*.

Rehearsals without music – Tickets are on sale at the entrance of the inner courtyard of the Hofburg. 100 ATS, children: 20 ATS. Information on dates and times is available from the Tourist Office at Kärntnerstrasse 38.

VIENNA BOYS' CHOIR

On Sundays and religious festivals, the Chapel Orchestra and the Vienna Boys' Choir (*Wiener Sängerknaben*) accompany Mass in the Hofmusikkapelle: from the beginning of January till the end of June and from mid-September till the end of December. The service starts at 9.15am. Seats: from 60 to 280 ATS. Standing room is free.

Reservations are available at least 8 weeks in advance from Hofmusikkapelle, Hofburg, A - 1010 Wien. Reservations must be collected and paid for 10am to 1pm Fridays or 8.30am to 9am Sundays at Hofburgkapelle.

It is also possible to obtain tickets for the following Sunday (maximum 2 tickets per person) at the ticket office in the Hofburgkapelle, 4pm to 6pm on Fridays.

TICKETS FOR THE EMPEROR'S BALL

Address: Hofburg-Heldenplatz, A - 1010 Wien. ☎587 36 66; fax 587 55 71 249 (tickets for the *Kaiserball* start at 1,500 ATS).

Stadtpark: Strauss monument

WHERE TO BUY SEATS FOR SHOWS AND CONCERTS

– *American Express*, Kärntnerstrasse 21-23, 1010 Wien, ☎ 515 40-(7)56, fax 515 40-(7)70.
– *ATT-Reisebüro*, Josefsplatz 6, 1010 Wien, ☎ 512 44 66, fax 215 33 55.
– *Austria Reiseservice*, Schottenring 3, 1010 Wien, ☎ 319 78 40, fax 3410 80 71.
– *Austrobus*, Opernpassage, 1010 Wien, ☎ 586 434 12, fax 587 20 16.
– *Flamm*, Kärntner Ring 3, 1010 Wien, ☎ 512 42 25, fax 513 99 62.
– *Intropa*, Kärntnerstrasse 38, 1010 Wien, ☎ 515 14-250, fax 4512 42 26.
– *Primus*, Rotenturmstrasse 10, 1010 Wien, ☎ 514 20-245, fax 512 72 46.

AUCTIONS

Dorotheum – *Dorotheergasse 17*, ☎ 515 60-212. Auction sales 2pm Mondays to Fridays, 10am Saturdays. Unrestricted sales 10am to 6pm Mondays to Fridays, 8.30am to noon Saturdays. Specialist auctions take place on Mondays (silver, table silver), Wednesdays (furniture and carpets), Thursdays (valuable jewellery) and Saturdays (curios). There is a branch at 88a Mariahilferstrasse (7th District).

VARIOUS SIGHTSEEING PROGRAMMES

Guided tours – The City of Vienna organises special interest tours with a German-speaking guide. Tours are also available in English, French and Italian. The monthly brochure *"Wiener Spaziergänge – Walks in Vienna"* gives details and a programme of tours in each language. It can be obtained from the Tourist Office (No. 38 Kärntner-strasse).
Guides are also available for individual visits not included in the programme. Details in the brochure mentioned above.

Organised tours – Several companies provide sightseeing tours of this kind:
– *Vienna Sightseeing Tours*, ☎ 712 46 83-0.
– *Cityrama*, ☎ 534 13-0.
– *City-Touring*, ☎ 894 14 17.
– *Alternative Stadtrundfahrten*, ☎ 317 33 84.

Exploring Vienna in a vintage tram – From the beginning of May to the beginning of October, 11.30am and 1.30pm weekends and public holidays, 9.30am, 11.30am and 1.30pm Sundays and public holidays. Departure from Karlsplatz. Tickets are available from the "Wiener Linien" information office at Karlsplatz underground station. ☎ 7909-44 026.

Cycling in Vienna – The Vienna Bike association organises bicycle tours in the city (with a commentary in English or German), ☎ 319 12 58. It is possible to hire bikes on Franz-Josefs-Kai, near Salztorbrücke, and at the Prater roundabout, near the cycle track. There are many cycle rental firms on Danube island (Donauinsel).

THE DANUBE BY BOAT

From the beginning of April to the end of October, the DDSG Blue Danube Schiffahrt GmbH organises boat trips, ☎ (0222) 72750-0; fax 72750-440. It is possible to sail to Passau or Budapest (via Bratislava), or cruise down the river for shorter distances. One day cruise: for example Vienna-Dürnstein-Vienna: departure 9am, arrival 2.45pm, return 4.15pm, arrival 8.15pm. Four day cruise: for example Vienna-Passau-Vienna through the Wachau valley stopping at Melk, Grein and Dürnstein.
Embarkation from Handelskai 2645, A - 1021 Wien.

Calendar of events

31 December to February – Fasching (pre-Lenten carnival) season.

1 January – New Year concert by the Vienna Philharmonic Orchestra (Musikverein).

March – Spring International Trade Fair (Prater exhibition ground). Vienna Film Festival (in the Urania building).

April – Flower show (Hofburg gardens).

Beginning of May to mid-June – Vienna Festival (music, opera): Wiener Festwochen (information on programmes and reservation: ☎ 589 22 22).

June – Public festivities on Danube island (Donauinsel).

June – 15 September – Major music festivals (200 concerts): Musik Sommer (information on programmes and reservations: ☎ 40 00 84 10; fax 48 83 48).

July – "Spectaculum": Baroque religious opera in the University church (information on programmes and reservations: ☎ 34 06 99).

Mid-July to end of August – Mörbisch: Operetta festival on Neusiedlersee (Neusiedler Lake). ☎ (02685) 6 62 10-0.

September – Autumn International Trade Fair. Austrian Film Days.

2nd week in September – Eisenstadt: International Josef Haydn Festival in the Esterházy Schloss. ☎ (06282) 91 86 60.

November – Schubert Days.

December – Christmas markets *(see Introduction, On the town)*.

USEFUL TELEPHONE NUMBERS

Police: 133

Fire brigade: 122

Ambulance: 144

Emergency medical service: 141

Lost property: 31 34 40

Dentists on call: 52 95 04 or 55 46 46

International Chemist – Kärntner Ring 17, 1010 Wien.

B. Kaufmann

Close-up of the roof of the cathedral (Stephansdom) in Vienna

Vocabulary

Hotel terms are underlined in red

Abendessen .... dinner
Abteilung .... collection
Ansichtskarte .... postcard
Ausfahr, Ausgang exit
Ausflug .... excursion
Auskunft .... information
Bahnhof .... station
Bauernmarkt .... market specialising in farm produce
Brücke .... bridge
Brunnen .... fountain,well
Burg .... fortress
Café .... tearoom
Denkmal .... monument
Dom .... cathedral
Einfahrt, Eingang entrance
Essen .... to eat
Fähre .... ferry
Fahrweg .... suitable for vehicular traffic
(Wasser) **Fall** .... (water)fall, cascade
Festung .... fortress, fortified town
Flohmarkt .... flea market
Forsthaus .... forestry commission house
Fremdenheim .... B&B
Frühstück .... breakfast
-"-pension .... see Fremdenheim
Garten .... garden
Gasse .... street,alley
Gasthaus .... café, inn
Gasthof .... inn
Gaststätte .... restaurant, buffet
Gebühr .... tax,tip,toll
Geburtshaus .... birthplace
Geradeaus .... straight ahead
Geschlossen .... closed
Gesperrt .... barred,closed
Gipfel .... peak
Gletscher .... glacier
Gobelins .... tapestry (in general)
Grüss Gott .... "God bless", traditional greeting
Guten Tag .... Good morning/day
Haus .... house
Hof .... courtyard, hotel, farm
Höhe. .... altitude
Höhenweg .... hilltop route
Höhle .... cave
Hütte .... mountain shelter, factory
Jause .... snack
Kanzel .... pulpit, belvedere
(Musik) **Kapelle** .... orchestra, brass or silver band
Kar .... limestone cirque or corrie
Karner .... ossuary
Kirche .... church
Klamm .... gorge, ravine

Kloster .... abbey, cloisters
Koge .... rounded hilltop
Krankenhaus .... hospital
Kreuzgang .... cloisters
Kur .... spa town, medical treatment
Landhaus .... seat of provincial government
Landungsstelle ..... landing-stage
Links .... left
Markt .... market square, market town
Maut .... toll (road, bridge)
Messner .... sacristan
Mittagessen .... lunch
Münster .... cathedral
Offen .... open
Pfarrkirche .... parish church
Postlagernd .... poste restante
Quelle .... spring, fountain
Rathaus .... Town Hall
Rechts .... right
Schloss .... château, castle
Schlucht .... gorge
Schlüssel .... key
Schwimmbad .... swimming pool
See .... lake
Speicher .... reservoir
Speisesaal .... restaurant or dining room in a hotel
Spielbank .... casino
Stadtturm .... belfry
Stausee .... artificial lake formed by a dam
Stift .... abbey, monastery
Strandbad .... beach
Strasse .... road, street
Stube, Stüberl ..... small dining room decorated in the local style
Tal .... valley
Talsperre .... dam
Tor .... gate, town gateway
Treppe .... steps, stairs
Verboten .... forbidden
Wald .... forest
Wechsel .... foresign exchange
Wildfütterung .... winter forage point for wild animals, affording at certain times sighting of deer, does, roebuck, etc
Zahnradbahn .... rack-railway
Zimmer frei .... rooms to let (sign usually displayed on private houses)
Zimmer nachweis. accomodation (see tourist offices and agencies in main-line stations)

Major Road Signs

Anfang	Start		*LKW*	Heavy lorries
Aussicht	Viewpoint		*PKW*	Private car
Bauarbeiten	Road works		*Rechts, links einbiegen*	Turn right or left
Baustelle	Works		*Rollsplitt*	Loose chippings
Einbahnstrasse	One-way street		*Sackgasse*	Cul-de-sac
Ende	End of		*Schlechte Fahrbahn*	Uneven surface
Freie Fahrt	No restrictions		*Schlechte Wegstrecke*	Uneven surface
Frostaufbrüche	Damage caused by severe frost		*Steinschlag*	Falling stones
Frostschäden	Damage caused by severe frost		*Umleitung*	Detour
Fussgängerzone	Pedestrians		*Verengte Fahrbahn*	Road narrows
Gefährlich	Dangerous		*Vorrang*	Priority
Glatteis	Black ice		*Vorsicht*	Caution
Kurzparkzone	Restricted parking – disk or parking voucher compulsory			

Design for a mosaic by Gustav Klimt

Admission times and charges

The opening times of the sights described in the main section of the guide and indicated by the symbol ⊙ are listed below, arranged in alphabetical order by place names or proper names. Within the alphabetical sequence of place names, attractions are listed in the order in which they appear in the main section of the guide.

As admission charges and opening times are liable to alteration, the information below is given for guidance only. The prices apply to individual adults (without reduction).

 denotes facilities for the disabled.

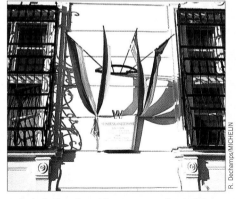

An indication of a public museum or other building

A

Albertina im Akademiehof – Open tuesdays to sundays 10am to 5pm. Closed: monday and public hollidays. 45 ATS/children 20 ATS. ☏ 01/5 81 30 60/21

Alpengarten – Open from April to July. Closed in wet or blustery weather. 40 ATS. ☏ 01/7 98 31 49

Alte Backstube – Café open Tuesdays to Saturdays 10am to midnight, Sundays 4pm to midnight. No charge for admission. ☏ 01/4 06 11 01

Alte Schmiede – Open Mondays to Fridays 10am to 3pm. No charge for admission. ☏ 01/5 12 83 29

Ausstellung der Österreichischen Freiheitskämpfe – Open Mondays and Wednesdays to Fridays 9am to 5pm. No charge for admission. ☏ 02 22/53 43 60 17 79

B

Beethovenhaus "Haus der Neunten" – Open March to December, Tuesdays, Thursdays, Saturdays and Sundays 10am to noon and 1pm to 4.30pm. Closed 1 May, 25 December. 15 ATS. ☏ 01/3 18 86 08

Belvedere

Museum mittelalterlicher österreichischer Kunst – Open Tuesdays to Sundays 10am to 5pm. Closed 1 January, on the Tuesdays after Easter and Whitsun, 1 May, 1 November, 24, 25 and 31 December. 100 ATS. (No charge for admission on 26 October and 23 December). ☏ 01/79 55 71 34

Barockmuseum – Open Tuesdays to Sundays 10am to 5pm. Closed 1 January, on the Tuesdays after Easter and Whitsun, 1 May, 1 November, 24 and 25 December, from 1pm on 31 December. 60 ATS. (No charge for admission on 26 October and 23 December). ☏ 01/79 55 71 34

Bundesgarten Belvedere – Open April to July from 6am till nightfall. 40 ATS. ☏ 01/7 98 31 49

Österreichische Galerie Belvedere – Open Tuesdays to Sundays 10am to 5pm (7pm on Thursdays). Closed 1 January, on the Tuesdays after Easter and Whitsun, 1 May, 1 November, 24, 25 December (afternoon only on 31 December). 60 ATS. (No charge for admission on 26 October and 23 December). ☏ 01/79 55 71 34

Bezirksmuseum Alsergrund – Open Wednesdays 9am to 11am, Sundays 10am to noon. Closed on public holidays and in school holidays. No charge for admission. ☏ 01/40 03 40 91 27

Bezirksmuseum Hietzing – The Bezirksmuseum is closed for renovation, and is expected to remain so until the end of 1999.

Burgtheater – Guided tours, contact the theatre for timings. 60 ATS. ☏ 01/5 14 44 26 13

D

Dom- und Diözesanmuseum – Open Tuesdays to Saturdays 10am to 5pm. Closed 1 January, 24, 25, 26 and 31 December. 50 ATS. ☏ 01/5 15 52 36 89

Dreifaltigkeitskirche – Alsterstraße 17. Open Mondays to Saturdays 7.30am to noon, Sundays 7.30am to 12.15pm. ☏ 01/4 05 72 25. Entrance through Schlösselgasse for services.

E

Ephesos-Museum – Same opening times as for the Hofjagd- und Rüstkammer. 50 ATS (No charge for admission on International Museum Day and 26 October). ☏ 01/52 52 44 84

Eroicahaus – Open Tuesdays to Sundays 9am to 12.15pm and 1pm to 4.30pm. Closed 1 January, 1 May and 25 December.

Esperanto-Museum – Open Mondays to Fridays 10am to 4pm, Wednesdays 10am to 6pm. Closed in September and on all public holidys. No charge for admission. ☏ 01/5 35 51 45

F

Feuerwehrmuseum – Open Sundays and public holidays 9am to noon. No charge for admission. ☏ 01/53 19 95 14 44

Franz-Schubert-Gedenkstätte "Geburtshaus" – Open Tuesdays to Sundays 9am to 12.15pm and 1pm to 4.30pm. Closed 1 January, 1 May, 25 December. 25 ATS (No charge for admission on Friday mornings). ☏ 01/3 17 36 01

Friedhof Hietzing – Open November to February, 8am to 5pm; March, April, September and October 7am to 6pm; May to August 7am to 7pm. ☏ 01/8 77 31 07

Fußball-Museum – Likely to remain closed until the beginning of the year 2000.

G

Gedenkräume des Österreichischen Theatermuseums – Open Tuesdays 10am to noon and 1pm to 4pm, Wednesdays to Sundays 1pm to 4pm. Closed 1 January, 1 May, 1 November, 25, 26 and 31 December. 40 ATS (No charge for admission on 26 October). ☏ 01/5 12 24 27

Gemäldegalerie der Akademie der bildenden Künste – Open Tuesdays to Sundays 10am to 4pm. 50 ATS. ☏ 01/58 81 62 25

Geymüller-Schlössel – Open March to November, Thursdays to Sundays 10am to 5pm. 30 ATS. ☏ 01/4 79 31 39

Globenmuseum der Österreichischen Nationalbibliothek – Open Mondays to Wednesdays and Fridays 11am to noon, Thursdays 2pm to 3pm. 20 ATS. (No charge for admission on 26 October). ☏ 01/53 41 02 97

Griechische Kirche zur Hl. Dreifaltigkeit – Open Mondays to Fridays 10am to 3pm. No charge for admission. ☏ 01/5 33 29 65

H

Haus des Meeres – Open 9am to 6pm. 85 ATS. ☏ 01/5 87 14 17

Haus Wittgenstein – Open Mondays to Fridays 9am to 5pm. 20 ATS. ☏ 01/7 13 31 64

Haydn-Haus – Open Tuesdays to Sundays 9am to 12.15pm and 1pm to 4.30pm. ☏ 01/5 96 13 07

Heeresgeschichtliches Museum – ♿ Open daily except Fridays 9am to 5pm. Closed 1 January, Easter Sunday, 1 May, 1 November, 24, 25 and 31 December. 70 ATS. ☏ 01/79 56 16 00 02

Hermesvilla – Open April to September, Tuesdays to Sundays 10am to 6pm; October to March, Tuesdays to Sundays 9am to 4.30pm. 50 ATS. ☏ 01/8 04 13 24

Historisches Museum der Stadt Wien – ♿ Open Tuesdays to Sundays 9am to 6pm. Closed 1 January, 1 May, 25 December. 50 ATS (No charge for admission on Friday mornings). ☎ 01/5 05 87 47

Hofburgkapelle – Open Tuesdays to Thursdays 11am to 3pm, Fridays 11am to noon. Closed July and August. 20 ATS. ☎ 01/5 33 99 27

Hofjagd- und Rüstkammer – ♿ Open daily except Tuesdays 10am to 6pm. Closed 1 Jan, 1 and 2 November, 24, 25 and 26 December. 50 ATS (No charge for admission on International Museum Day and 26 October). ☎ 01/52 52 44 84

Hofpavillon Hietzing – Open Tuesdays to Sundays 1.30pm to 4.30pm. Closed 1 January, 1 May and 25 December. 25 ATS. ☎ 01/8 77 15 71

Hofsilber- und Tafelkammer – ♿ Open 9am to 5pm. 80 ATS. ☎ 01/5 33 75 70

J

Jesuitenkirche – Open Mondays to Saturdays 7am to 7pm, Sundays and public holidays 8am to 8pm. ☎ 01/51 25 23 20

Jüdisches Museum – ♿ Open Mondays to Fridays 10am to 6pm (Thursdays to 8pm). Closed on Jom Kippur and Rosch ha-Schana. 70 ATS. ☎ 01/5 35 04 31

K

Kaiserappartements – ♿ Open 9am to 4.30pm. 80 ATS. ☎ 01/5 33 75 70

Kaisergruft – Open daily 9.30am to 3.40pm. ☎ 01/5 12 68 53

Kaiserliches Hofmobiliendepot – Open daily 9am to 17pm.

Kirche am Steinhof – Guided tours (45 minutes): Saturdays at 3pm. 40 ATS. ☎ 01/91 06 02 00 31

Kunstforum – ♿ Open 10am to 6pm (Wednesdays to 9pm). Closed 24 December, afternoon only on 31 December, morning only on 1 January. 95 ATS. ☎ 01/71 19 15 57 37

Kunsthalle – Only temporary exhibitions. Varying opening times. 100 ATS. Closed 24 and 31 December. Kunsthalle am Karlsplatz ☎ 01/5 21 89-0

Kunsthalle im Museumsquartier – ☎ 01/5 21 89-0

KunstHaus Wien – ♿ Open 10am to 7pm. 90 ATS. ☎ 01/7 12 04 95

Kunsthistorisches Museum – ♿ Open Tuesdays to Sundays 10am to 6pm (Thursdays to 9pm). 100 ATS (No charge for admission on International Museum Day and 26 October). ☎ 01/52 52 40

Kurzentrum Oberlaa – Open daily to 3pm. Wellnesspark one day admission 390 ATS. ☎ 01/6 80 09 97 70

Jesuitenkirche: *trompe-l'œil* dome

Leopold I. by Paul Strudel

L

Lainzer Tiergarten – Open mid February to mid November daily from 9am. No charge for admission. ☏ 01/8 04 13 15

M

Mariahilferkirche – Open Mondays to Saturdays 7.45am to 7pm, Sundays 8.15am to 7pm. ☏ 01/5 87 87 53

Michaelerkirche – The church is open daily 6.30am to 6.30pm (Sundays from 7.30pm). Crypt (guided tour 30 minutes)is open Mondays to Fridays at 11am and 3pm. Closed Saturdays, Sundays and public holidays. ☏ 01/5 33 80 00

Minoritenkirche – ♿ Open April to September 8am to 6pm, October to March 9am to 1pm and 3pm to 5pm. No charge for admission. ☏ 01/5 33 41 62

Mode-Sammlungen – Showroom open Tuesdays to Fridays 9am to noon. Library open Mondays to Fridays 8am to 4pm. Closed 1 January, 1 May, 25 December. 25 ATS (No charge for admission on Friday mornings). ☏ 01/ 8 04 04 68

Mozart-Gedenkstätte "Figarohaus" – Open Tuesdays to Sundays 9am to 6pm. Closed 1 January, 1 May, 25 December. 25 ATS (No charge for admission on Friday mornings). ☏ 01/5 13 62 94

Museum der Gold- und Silberschmiede – Guided tours (1 hour): Wednesdays 3pm to 6pm. Closed July and August. ☏ 01/5 23 33 88

Museum des 20. Jahrhunderts – Open Tuesdays to Sundays 10am to 6pm. Closed 1. January, 1 May, 1 November, 24, 25 December (afternoon only on 31 December). 45 ATS (No charge for admission on International Museum Day and 26 October). ☏ 01/7 99 69 00

Museum des Institutes für Geschichte der Medizin – Open Mondays to Fridays 9am to 3pm. Closed on all public holidays. 10 ATS. ☏ 01/4 27 76 34 01

Museum für Völkerkunde – Open daily except Tuesdays 10am to 4pm; January to March 10am to 6pm. Closed 1 January, Good Friday, 1 May, 1 November, 25 December. 80 ATS (No charge for admission on International Museum Day, 26 October, 10 and 24 December). ☏ 01/5 34 30

Museum im Schottenstift – Open Thursdays to Saturdays 10am to 5pm, Sundays noon to 5pm. 50 ATS. ☏ 01/53 49 86 00

Museum moderner Kunst – Stiftung Ludwig – ♿ Open Tuesdays to Sundays 10am to 6pm. Closed 1 January, 1 May, 1 November, 24, 25 and 31 December. 45 ATS (No charge for admission on 26 October). ☎ 01/3 17 69 00 25

Musiksammlung der Nationalbibliothek – The music collection is a department within the Nationalbibliothek. Guided tours only by arrangement and provided library staff are available. ☎ 01/53 41 03 07

Naturhistorisches Museum – ♿ Open daily except Tuesdays 9am to 6.30pm (Wednesdays to 9pm). Closed 1 January, 1 May, 1 November, 25 December. 30 ATS (No charge for admission on 26 October and 24 December). ☎ 01/52 17 70

Neidhart-Fresken – Open daily except Mondays 9am to noon. 25 ATS. ☎ 01/5 35 90 65

Neues Rathaus – Guided tours (30 minutes): Mondays, Wednesdays and Fridays at 1pm (except when the council is sitting). Closed on all public holidays. No charge for admission. ☎ 01/5 25 50

Österreichische Nationalbibliothek – Open May to October, Mondays to Wednesdays, Fridays and Saturdays 10am to 4pm, Thursdays 10am to 7pm, Sundays 10am to 2pm; November to April Mondays to Saturdays 10am to 2pm. 60 ATS (No charge for admission on 26 October). ☎ 01/53 41 04 64

Österreichisches Museum für angewandte Kunst – Open Tuesdays to Sundays 10am to 6pm (Thursdays to 9pm). Closed 1 January, 1 May, 1 November, 25 December. 30 ATS (No charge for admission on 26 October, 4 November and 24 December). ☎ 01/71 13 62 33

Österreichisches Museum für Volkskunde – ♿ Open Tuesdays to Fridays 9am to 5pm, Saturdays 9am to noon, Sundays 9am to 1pm. Closed 1 January, Easter Sunday, 1 May, 1 November, 25 December. 45 ATS (No charge on 26 October and 26 December). ☎ 01/4 06 89 05 16

Österreichisches Theatermuseum – Open Tuesdays to Sundays 10am to 5pm. Closed 1 May, 1 November, 31 December. Ticket 40 ATS. ☎ 01/5 12 88 00 10. The ticket includes entry to the commemorative rooms (see entry).

P

Palais Harrach – The Arts Center organises temporary exhibitions here. Open 10am to 6pm. 100 ATS (No charge for admission on International Museum Day and 26 October). ☎ 01/52 52 44 04

Papyrussammlung der Nationalbibliothek – ♿ Open Mondays 10am to 6pm, Tuesdays to Fridays 10am to 5pm; July and August, Mondays to Fridays 10am to 4pm. Closed 1 to 21 September. 40 ATS (No charge for admission on 26 October). ☎ 01/53 41 03 23

Parlament – Guided tours (45 minutes): end of June to mid September, Mondays to Fridays at 9am, 10am, 11am, 1pm, 2pm and 3pm; mid September to the end of June, Mondays to Thursdays at 11am and 3pm, Fridays at 11am, 1pm, 2pm and 3pm. Closed at Easter, 1 May, 24 December to 6 January and when Parliament is sitting. 40 ATS. ☎ 01/4 01 10 25 79

Pasqualatihaus – Open Tuesdays to Sundays 9am to 12.15pm and 1pm to 4.30pm. Closed 1 January, 1 May and 25 December. 25 ATS (No charge for admission on Friday mornings). ☎ 01/5 35 89 05

Pathologisch-Anatomisches Bundesmuseum – Open Wednesdays 3pm to 6pm, Thursdays 8am to 11am and every first Saturday in the month 10am to 1pm. Closed on public holidays and in August. No charge for admission. ☎ 01/4 06 86 72

Peterskirche – Open daily 8am to 6pm. No charge for admission.

Piaristenkirche Basilika Maria Treu – The church may be viewed only by appointment at the presbytery. ☎ 01/40 50 42 50

Planetarium – Open Tuesdays, Wednesdays and Thursdays at 9am, 10am and 11am, Sundays at 3pm and 5pm. 50 ATS. Closed August to mid September. ☎ 01/7 29 54 94

Parliament building

Postsparkasse – ♿ The counters room is open Mondays to Fridays 8am to 3pm (Thursdays to 5.30pm). Guided tours only by appointment. Closed on all public holidays. 30 ATS. ☎ 01/5 14 00 23 43

Prater-Museum – Open Tuesdays to Fridays 9am to 12.15pm and 1pm to 4.30pm, Saturdays, Sundays and public holidays 2pm to 6.30pm. 25 ATS. ☎ 01/7 29 76 83

Puppen- & Spielzeug-Museum – Open Tuesdays to Sundays 10am to 6pm. 60 ATS.

R

Riesenrad (Giant Ferris Wheel) – ♿ Open January, February, November and December 10am to 6pm; March, April and October 10am to 10pm; May to September 9am to midnight. Closed mid January to mid February, 24 December. 55 ATS. ☎ 01/7 29 54 30

Römische Baureste – Open weekends and public holidays 11am to 1pm.

Römische Ruinen – Open daily except Mondays 9am to 12.15pm and 1pm to 4.30pm. ☎ 01/5 35 56 06

Ruprechtskirche – ♿ Open Mondays to Fridays 10am to 1pm and 4pm to 6pm. Donations requested. ☎ 01/5 35 60 03

S

Sammlung alter Musikinstrumente – Same opening times as for the Hofjagd- und Rüstkammer. 30 ATS. ☎ 01/52 52 44 71

Sammlung Religiöse Volkskunst – ♿ Open Wednesdays 9am to 4pm, Sundays 9am to 1pm. 25 ATS. ☎ 01/4 06 89 05

Schatzkammer – Open daily except Tuesdays 10am to 6pm. Closed 1 January, 1 May, 1 November and 25 December and mid January to the end of January. 80 ATS (No charge for admission on International Museum Day, 26 October, 24 December). ☎ 01/5 33 79 31

Schatzkammer des Deutschen Ordens – Open May to October, Thurdays and Sundays 10am to noon, Wednesdays 3pm to 5pm, Fridays and Saturdays 10am to noon and 3pm to 5pm; November to April, Thursdays 10am to noon, Wednesdays and Fridays 3pm to 5pm, Saturdays 10am to noon and 3pm to 5pm. Closed on all public holidays. 50 ATS. ☎ 01/5 12 10 65

Schloß Schönbrunn

Wagenburg – ♿ Open 1 January to 23 March, November to December, Tuesdays to Sundays 10am to 4pm; end of March to October, daily 9am to 6pm. Closed 1 January, 1 and 2 November, 24 and 25 December. 50 ATS (No charge for admission on International Museum Day and 26 October). ☎ 01/8 77 32 44

Besichtigung der Appartements – ♿ Open April to October 8.30am to 5pm, November to March 8.30am to 4.30pm. 90 ATS (Imperial Tour), 120 ATS (Grand Tour), 145 ATS (guided Grand Tour). ☎ 01/81 11 32 39

Schloßpark – ♿ Open all year from 6am till nightfall. No charge for admission. ☎ 01/8 77 50 87

Palmenhaus – Open May to September 9.30am to 5.30pm, October to April 9.30am to 4.30pm. 40 ATS. ☎ 01/87 75 08 74 06

Tiergarten – ♿ Open January, November and December 9am to 4.30pm; February 9am to 5pm; March and October 9am to 5.30pm; April 9am to 6pm; May to September 9am to 6.30pm. 95 ATS. ☎ 01/87 79 29 40

Schmetterlingshaus – ♿ Open April to September 10am to 5pm, October to March 10am to 4pm. 70 ATS. ☎ 01/5 33 85 70

Gloriette – Open daily mid April to mid October 9am to 5pm. 20 ATS. ☎ 01/81 11 32 39

Schubert-Sterbewohnung – Open Tuesdays to Sundays 1.30pm to 4.30pm. Closed 1 January, 1 May and 25 December. 25 ATS. ☎ 01/5 81 67 30

Secessionsgebäude – ♿ Open Tuesdays to Saturdays 10am to 6pm, Sundays 10am to 4pm. Closed 25 December. 60 ATS. ☎ 01/5 87 53 07

Sigmund-Freud-Museum – Open daily July to September 9am to 6pm, October to June 9am to 4pm. 60 ATS. ☎ 01/3 19 15 96

Spanische Reitschule – Summer break in July and August. Vorführungen (parades): in March on Sundays (10.45am); April to June on Sundays (10.45am) and Wednesdays (7pm). Tickets should be ordered as early as possible in writing from the Spanische Reitschule (Hofburg, Michaelerplatz 1, A – 1010 Wien), the ticket agencies or Reisebüros (send no money). Tickets for the morning training sessions (10am to noon except Mondays) can be obtained on the same day at the entrance, Josefsplatz Tor 2. Parades: 200-900 ATS, training session: 100 ATS. ☎ 01/5 33 90 31

Staatsoper – ♿ Guided tours (40 minutes): July and August at 11am, 1pm, 2pm and 3pm, November to April at 2pm and 3pm; May to June, September and October at 1pm, 2pm and 3pm. 60 ATS. Closed 1 January and during rehearsals, telephone first ☎ 01/5 14 44 26 13

Stephansdom – ♿ Open all year round, Mondays to Saturdays 6am to 10pm, Sundays 7am to 10pm. 40 ATS. ☎ 01/5 15 52 37 67

Towers (Aufstieg zu den Türmen) – It is possible to climb the high tower on the southern side of the cathedral: 9am to 5.30pm. 30 ATS. North tower (express lift to the "Pummerin" great bell): April to October 9am to 6pm (July and August to 6.30pm), November to March 8.30am to 5pm. 40 ATS. ☎ 01/5 15 52 37 67

Catacombs – Guided tours (30 minutes): Mondays to Saturdays every half hour from 10am to 11.30am and 1.30pm to 4.30pm; Sundays every half hour from 1.30pm to 4.30pm. 40 ATS. ☎ 01/5 15 52 37 67

Straußhaus – Open Tuesdays to Sundays 9am to 12.15pm and 1pm to 4.30pm. Closed 1 January, 1 May, 25 December. 25 ATS. ☎ 01/2 14 01 21

King of Rome's cradle, Schatzkammer

Kunsthistorisches Museum

U

Uhrenmuseum der Stadt Wien – Open Tuesdays to Sundays 9am to 4.30pm. Closed 1 January, 1 May, 25 December. 50 ATS. ☎ 01/5 33 22 65

Ulrichskirche – &♿ Open Mondays to Fridays 9am to 11.30am and 3pm to 5pm. 40 ATS. ☎ 01/5 23 12 46

UNO-City – Guided tours(1 hour)Mondays to Fridays 11am and 2pm. 50 ATS. ☎ 01/2 60 60 33 28

Urania-Sternwarte – Guided tours in clear weather, Wednesdays, Fridays and Saturdays at 8pm (9pm summer time). Closed August to mid September. 25 ATS. ☎ 01/7 12 61 91 15

V – W – Z

Virgilkapelle – Open Tuesdays to Sundays 1pm to 4.30pm. ☎ 01/5 13 58 42

Votivkirche – &♿ Open Tuesdays to Saturdays 9am to 1pm and 4pm to 6.30pm, Sundays 9am to 1pm. ☎ 01/4 06 11 92

Wagnerhaus – Guided tours (30 minutes): by appointment. ☎ 01/5 23 22 33

Wagner-Villa – Open Mondays to Fridays 10am to 4pm. 140 ATS.

Weinbaumuseum – Open Saturdays 3.30pm to 6pm, Sundays 10am to noon. Closed July and August, all public holidays. Donations requested. ☎ 01/3 68 65 46

Wiener Straßenbahnmuseum – &♿ Open May to the beginning of October, Saturdays, Sundays and public holidays 9am to 4pm. 20 ATS. ☎ 01/7 90 94 49 00

Wotrubakirche – Open Thursdays and Fridays 2pm to 4pm, Saturdays 2pm to 8pm, Sundays and public holidays 9am to 5pm. Contact the Kratochwil family ☎ 01/8 88 50 03

Zentralfriedhof – &♿ Open November to February 8am to 5pm; March, April, September and October 7am to 6pm; May to August 7am to 7pm. No charge for admission. ☎ 01/7 60 41

Fotostudio Otto/Museen der Stadt Wien

Uhrenmuseum: astronomical clocks

In the Vienna area

BADEN

Beethoven-Gedenkstätte – Open Tuesdays to Fridays 4pm to 6pm, Saturdays, Sundays and public holidays 9am to 11am and 4pm to 6pm. Closed 1 January, 24 and 31 December. 20 ATS. ☎ 0 22 52/86 80 02 30

EISENSTADT

Österreichisches Jüdisches Museum – Open May to October, Tuesdays to Sundays 10am to 5pm. 50 ATS (permanent exhibition and synagogue). ☎ 0 26 82/6 51 45

Burgenländisches Landesmuseum – Open Tuesdays to Sundays 9am to noon and 1pm to 5pm. Closed 1 November, 25 December to 6 January. 30 ATS. ☎ 0 26 82/6 26 52

P. Koller/BILDAGENTUR BUENOS DIAS

Baden: Ladies' baths

Kalvarienberg und Bergkirche – Open Palm Sunday to the end of October 9am to noon and 1pm to 5pm. 30 ATS. ☎ 0 26 82/6 26 38

Schloß Esterházy – Open daily, April to mid November 9am to 5pm; mid November to March, Mondays to Fridays 9am to 5pm. Closed on all public holidays. 50 ATS. ☎ 0 26 82/6 33 84 16 Haydn-Saal: same opening times. 20 ATS. ☎ 0 26 82/6 33 84 15

Stift HEILIGENKREUZ

Abbey – Guided tours (45 minutes), Mondays to Saturdays at 10am, 11am, 2pm, 3pm and 4pm, Sundays at 11am, 2pm, 3pm and 4pm. Closed on Good Friday and 24 December. 65 ATS. ☎ 0 22 58/87 03

KLOSTERNEUBURG

Stift Klosterneuburg – Guided tours (1 hour): Mondays to Saturdays 9am to 4.30pm, Sundays 11am to 4.30pm. Closed 25 and 26 December. 60 ATS. ☎ 0 22 43/41 12 12

Stiftsmuseum – Open: May to 15 November, Tuesdays to Sundays 10am to 5pm. Closed 16 November to April. 50 ATS. ☎ 0 22 43/41 11 54

LAXENBURG

Park – Open 10am to 6pm. 16 ATS.

MAYERLING

Kronprinz-Gedenkstätte – Guided tours (20 minutes), Mondays to Saturdays 9am to 12.30pm and 1.30pm to 6pm in the summer (to 5pm in the winter), Sundays and public holidays 10am to 12.30pm and 1.30pm to 6pm. 20 ATS. ☎ 0 22 58/22 75

NEUSIEDLER SEE

Neusiedl am See: Pannonisches Heimatmuseum – Guided tours (45 minutes), May to October, Tuesdays to Saturdays 2.30pm to 6.30pm, Sundays and public holidays 10am to noon and 2.30pm to 6.30pm. Donations requested. ☎ 0 21 67/81 73

PERCHTOLDSDORF

Türkenmuseum – Open from Palm Sunday to the beginning of November, Saturdays, Sundays and public holidays 10am to 5pm. 25 ATS. ☎ 01/86 68 34 00

PETRONELL-CARNUNTUM

Archäologischer Park Carnuntum – Excavations and information centre, Palm Sunday to the beginning of November, Mondays to Fridays 9am to 5pm, Saturdays, Sundays and public holidays 9am to 6pm. 48 ATS. ☎ 0 21 63/3 37 70

Archäologisches Museum Carnuntinum – Open 16 January to 14 December, Tuesdays to Sundays 10am to 5pm. 60 ATS. ☎ 0 21 63/3 37 70

Schloßhof – Open Easter to 1 November, Tuesdays to Sundays 10am to 5pm daily. 70 ATS. ☎ 0 22 85/65 80

ROHRAU

Harrach'sche Gemäldegalerie – Open Easter to 1 November, daily except Mondays 10am to 5pm. 60 ATS. ☎ 0 21 64/22 53

Geburtshaus Joseph Haydns – Open daily except Mondays 10am to 4pm. Closed 1 January, 24, 25, 26 and 31 December. 20 ATS. (No charge for admission on 26 October). ☎ 0 21 64/22 68

SOPRON

Environs

Raiding: Liszts Geburtshaus – Open from Easter to the end of October, Tuesdays to Sundays 9am to noon and 1pm to 5pm. 20 ATS. ☎ 0 26 19/72 20

WIENER NEUSTADT

St. Georgskathedrale – Guided tours (20 minutes), daily 8.30am to 5pm. No charge for admission. ☎ 0 26 22/3 81 20 66

WIENERWALD

Naturpark Sparbach – ♿ Open April to September 9am to 6pm; October 9am to 5pm; November to March, Saturdays and Sundays only 10am to 3pm. May be closed during wet or blustery weather. 20 ATS. ☎ 0 22 37/76 25

Hinterbrühl: Seegrotte – Guided tours (45 minutes), April to the end of October 9am to noon and 1pm to 5pm; November to March, Mondays to Fridays 9am to noon and 1pm to 3pm (Saturdays, Sundays and public holidays to 3.30pm). 55 ATS. ☎ 0 22 36/2 63 64

Index

MANUFACTURE FRANÇAISE DES PNEUMATIQUES MICHELIN

Société en commandite par actions au capital de 2 000 000 000 de francs

Place des Carmes-Déchaux – 63 Clermont-Ferrand (France)

R.C.S. Clermont-Fd B 855 200 507

© Michelin et Cie, Propriétaires-Éditeurs 1997

Dépôt légal novembre 1997 – ISBN 2-06-150901-0 – ISSN 0763-1383

Printed in the EU 11-99/2

Composition : NORD COMPO, Villeneuve-d'Ascq

Impression et brochage : AUBIN Imprimeur, Ligugé

Illustration de la couverture par Patricia HAUBERT

Michelin
Green Guide
Collection

France

- *Alsace, Lorraine, Champagne*
- *Atlantic Coast*
- *Auvergne, Rhône Valley*
- *Brittany*
- *Burgundy, Jura*
- *Châteaux of the Loire*
- *Dordogne, Berry, Limousin*
- *French Alps*
- *French Riviera*
- *Normandy*
- *Northern France and the Paris Region*
- *Paris*
- *Provence*
- *Pyrenees, Languedoc, Tarn Gorges*

World

- *Austria*
- *Belgium, Luxembourg*
- *Berlin*
- *Brussels*
- *California*
- *Canada*
- *Chicago*
- *Europe*
- *Florida*
- *France*
- *Germany*
- *Great Britain*
- *Greece*
- *Ireland*
- *Italy*
- *London*
- *Mexico, Guatemala, Belize*
- *Netherlands*
- *New England*
- *New York, New Jersey, Pennsylvania*
- *New York City*
- *Portugal*
- *Quebec*
- *Rome*
- *San Francisco*
- *Scandinavia, Finland*
- *Scotland*
- *Sicily*
- *Spain*
- *Switzerland*
- *Tuscany*
- *Venice*
- *Vienna*
- *Wales*
- *Washington DC*
- *The West Country of England*

MICHELIN